SNO-ISLE REGIONAL LIBRARY

OCT   2003

D1083282

GOING LONG

THE WILD 10-YEAR SAGA OF THE RENEGADE
AMERICAN FOOTBALL LEAGUE
IN THE WORDS OF THOSE WHO LIVED IT

JEFF MILLER

Contemporary Books

Chicago   New York   San Francisco   Lisbon   London   Madrid   Mexico City
Milan   New Delhi   San Juan   Seoul   Singapore   Sydney   Toronto

The *McGraw·Hill* Companies

Library of Congress Cataloging-in-Publication Data

Miller, Jeff, 1955–
    Going long : the wild ten-year saga of the renegade American Football League in the
words of those who lived it / Jeff Miller.
        p.   cm.
    Includes bibliographical references and index.
    ISBN 0-07-141849-0
    1. American Football League—History.   I. Title.

    GV955.5.A45M55   2003
    796.323′64′0973—dc21   2003043980

Copyright © 2003 by Jeff Miller. All rights reserved. Printed in the United States of America. Except as permitted under the United States Copyright Act of 1976, no part of this publication may be reproduced or distributed in any form or by any means, or stored in a database or retrieval system, without the prior written permission of the publisher.

1 2 3 4 5 6 7 8 9 0   AGM/AGM   2 1 0 9 8 7 6 5 4 3

ISBN 0-07-141849-0

McGraw-Hill books are available at special quantity discounts to use as premiums and sales promotions, or for use in corporate training programs. For more information, please write to the Director of Special Sales, Professional Publishing, McGraw-Hill, Two Penn Plaza, New York, NY 10121-2298. Or contact your local bookstore.

This book is printed on acid-free paper.

To the vision of Lamar Hunt

Also by Jeff Miller

Down to the Wire: Nineteen Sixty-Seven—The Greatest Pennant Race Ever
Sunshine Shootouts: The Florida–Florida State–Miami Rivalry

CONTENTS

INTRODUCTION

There are many individuals who are given well-deserved credit for the development of the American Football League from its rickety beginnings to, arguably, the greatest success story in American sports, from teams that gave away tickets and hung their uniforms on nails in makeshift locker rooms to a force that gained equal footing with the established National Football League in less than a decade.

There is Lamar Hunt, who as a young Texas millionaire provided the league with its first breath. There is Joe Foss, the AFL's first commissioner, who lent legitimacy in the early going through his All-American image. There is Sonny Werblin, the show-biz whiz who saved the league's New York franchise from near-certain disaster. There is Joe Namath, the brash stoop-shouldered quarterback from Alabama whose $427,000 contract with Werblin's Jets shook all of professional sports to its roots. There is Al Davis, the coaching prodigy whose 60-day term as commissioner featured a declaration of all-out war with the NFL and the signing of top NFL players who worked hand in hand—or in complete cross purposes, depending on whom you believe—with the closed-doors efforts of Hunt and company to merge with the NFL.

All worthy figures. The AFL would not have been the same without them. And any significant change in the AFL would surely have changed the course of pro football's growth and the establishment of the Super Bowl. Hats off to all of them and many more inside the game.

But I like to commend the efforts of people like Archie Diemer.

Who?

The name isn't familiar like that of Billy Cannon or Hank Stram or Jack Kemp. But Archie Diemer was the reason that the AFL succeeded despite all those empty seats at the Los Angeles Coliseum and all those New York Titans paychecks that bounced. Archie Diemer, you see, is credited with being the first season-ticket holder ever for the Buffalo Bills. While he never rivaled the likes of Cookie Gilchrist or Jack Kemp or O. J. Simpson among Buffalo fans, Archie Diemer became something of a local celebrity simply by being first in line when Bills tickets went on sale in downtown Buffalo in 1960. "I don't drink. I don't smoke. I don't celebrate. I like football," he told the *Buffalo News* years later.

Archie Diemer was still a season-ticket holder in 2001—seven seats by then, all on the 50-yard line—when he died at age 81 following a lengthy illness, only days before the Bills' regular-season opener. His wife of 54 years reported that he had attended two preseason games that year, in a wheelchair.

Each one of the eight original AFL teams had some Archie Diemers, people who were willing to fork over funds for an unknown product, to take a chance on the infant professional football league. In Los Angeles, the dream lasted only one year. In Dallas, the hometown of the league founder, it was over after only three seasons—disappearing in the shadow of an AFL championship.

But men like Hunt and Foss and Werblin and Bud Adams in Houston and Ralph Wilson in Buffalo and Barron Hilton in California and Bob Howsam in Denver wouldn't let the American Football League wither and die. Yes, the league wobbled and skittered and shook with each of its early steps. But top college players followed Cannon and kept coming, owners and cities provided better facilities, and a breakthrough, lucrative television contract with NBC allowed the AFL to look the NFL squarely in the eye.

And along the way, there was Houston's Hogan Wharton thinking that he had gone blind . . . because Denver's Bud McFadin had forearmed him in the head so hard that he was looking out his helmet's earhole. There was Al Davis spending his first day as AFL commissioner breaking up a brawl involving one of his owners. There was Joe Namath spending a week at the All-Star Game with his roommate, actress Mamie Van Doren. There was coach Lou Saban getting so mad that he would cut a player . . . *during* a game!

Those are the stories that are told here, primarily in the words of those who lived them or those who witnessed them. From the most well-heeled businessmen (that would include Hunt, though his shoes often featured a breeze through his soles) to those like Joanne Parker, hired as the Boston Patriots' first secretary straight out of Katherine Gibbs School. The recall might not be precise after so many years, but the more than 170 individuals interviewed for this book provide an inside glimpse at a fascinating story of beating the odds.

The interview transcriptions found in this book were all obtained in personal interviews over a period of more than two years. The pursuit of these stories provided a textbook example of a journey being more enjoyable than simply reaching a destination.

There was the meeting with Hank Stram in the football room of his spacious home north of New Orleans, a session interrupted when his wife, Phyllis, insisted on serving bowls of peach cobbler.

There was traversing the back roads of West Texas in search of Sammy Baugh's home of more than 50 years—no real road signs to go by or any street addresses to check. Make a left at the gas station, go about four miles, and turn right at the double mailbox.

There was spending an afternoon at the Louisiana Boys Home in Monroe, where Johnny Robinson does his best to provide a moral foundation to another generation.

There was watching Joe Namath demonstrate proper handoff techniques to boys who never saw him play but whose parents gladly signed them up for the Joe Namath–John Dockery Football Camp in the quiet town of Dudley, Massachusetts. As practice ended, many of those parents tentatively emerged from the cars, toting a cap or a jersey or a ball in almost covert fashion in hopes that Joe would grace them with his signature.

There was seeing the smiles on the faces of Buffalo Bills players who hadn't taken a snap in 30 or more years as they attended a reunion weekend arranged by Ralph Wilson. They only rarely had to resort to peering at a nametag to identify a former teammate from so long ago.

There was hearing the humorous wails from a similar group of Denver Broncos alumni when talking about the bizarre and embarrassing uniform socks with vertical stripes that now are collectors' items.

There was sensing the pride in Lamar Hunt as he described his personal attention given to the design and construction of a monument to his 1970 Super Bowl champion Kansas City Chiefs, the last AFL winners.

There was recognizing the same feeling when Ernie Warlick acknowledged that he has saved in his suburban Buffalo home the tablet on which he scribbled down the statement that he was chosen to write and deliver after AFL All-Stars elected to boycott the January 1965 game in New Orleans because of discriminatory actions directed toward the black players.

There was accompanying Bake Turner, the favorite son of Alpine, Texas, as he patiently described the Jets' startling Super Bowl III win yet again while making an appearance at the grand opening of the town's new U-Haul dealership.

I thank all of them and so many others for making themselves and their memories available. And I also thank a select group without whose assistance this project wouldn't have made it into print: my agent, Jim Donovan, and my editor, Mark Weinstein; and the entire Miller family—wife, Frances; daughter, Kim; and sons, Jason, Kevin, and Joseph—who all helped in some fashion and now know more about Frank Youell Field, Earl Morrall's flea flicker, and Hank Stram's 65 toss power trap than any of them would want to admit. And thanks also to helpers Chris Miller (my nephew), John Chou, Daniel Rowland, Joe Draut of the Houston Public Library, veteran Denver Broncos publicist Jim Saccomano, Buffalo Bills publicist Scott Berchtold, the aforementioned John Dockery, and Tom Gillman, son of legendary coach Sid Gillman.

VOICES OF THE AFL

ED ABRAMOSKI Bills trainer

BUD ADAMS Oilers owner

DAVE ANDERSON *New York Times* columnist

DONNY ANDERSON Packers 1966–69

HOUSTON ANTWINE Patriots 1961–69

JOE AUER Bills 1964–65, Dolphins 1966–67

SAM BAUGH Titans coach, Oilers coach

BOBBY BELL Chiefs 1963–69

AL BEMILLER Bills 1961–69

DENNIS BIODROWSKI Chiefs 1963–67

FURMAN BISHER *Atlanta Journal-Constitution* columnist

MIKE BITE Birmingham attorney

SAM BLAIR *Dallas Morning News* columnist

GIL BRANDT Cowboys vice president

MARLIN BRISCOE Broncos 1968, Bills 1969

TOMMY BROOKER Texans 1962, Chiefs 1963–66

CHRIS BURFORD Texans 1960–62, Chiefs 1963–67

CHUCK BURR Bills management, Dolphins management

BUTCH BYRD Bills 1964–69

GINO CAPPELLETTI Patriots 1960–69

DICK CLINE NBC Sports employee

JOE COLLIER Patriots assistant, Bills assistant, Bills coach, Broncos assistant

BRUCE COSLET Bengals 1969

DAVE COSTA Raiders 1963–65, Bills 1966, Broncos 1967–69

PAUL COSTA Bills 1965–69

LARRY CSONKA Dolphins 1968–69

BILL CURRY Packers 1965–66, Colts 1967–69

BOB DAILEY CBS Sports producer

ELDON DANENHAUER Broncos 1960–65

BEN DAVIDSON Raiders 1964–69

COTTON DAVIDSON Texans 1960–62, Raiders 1963–68

LEN DAWSON Texans 1962, Chiefs 1963–69

BUDDY DILIBERTO *New Orleans Times-Picayune* sportswriter

MIKE DITKA Bears 1961–66, Eagles 1967–68, Cowboys 1969

DAVE DIXON New Orleans businessman

JOHN DOCKERY Jets 1968–69

DALE DODRILL Broncos assistant

ELBERT DUBENION Bills 1960–68

LOU DUVA boxing promoter

LARRY EISENHAUER Patriots 1961–69

BOOKER EDGERSON Bills 1962–69

JOHN ELLIOTT Jets 1967–69

JACK FAULKNER Chargers assistant, Broncos coach

MILLER FARR Broncos 1965, Chargers 1965–66, Oilers 1967–69

LARRY FELSER *Buffalo News* columnist

Ric Flair professional wrestler

Tom Flores Raiders 1960–66, Bills 1967–69, Chiefs 1969

Joe Foss AFL commissioner, 1960–66

John Free Jets traveling secretary

Roman Gabriel Rams 1962–69

Larry Garron Patriots 1960–68

Sid Gillman Chargers coach

Bob Gladieux Patriots 1969

Pete Gogolak Bills 1964–65

Goose Gonsoulin Broncos 1960–66

Curt Gowdy ABC Sports announcer, NBC Sports announcer

Larry Grantham Titans 1960–62, Jets 1963–69

Tom Gray Bengals equipment manager

Dave Grayson Texans 1961–62, Chiefs 1963, Raiders 1964–69

Jack Grinold Patriots publicist

Bob Griese Dolphins 1967–69

Bill Grigsby Chiefs announcer

John Hadl Chargers 1962–69

Bob Halford Texans publicist, Chiefs publicist, Raiders publicist

Bill Hampton Jets trainer

Merle Harmon Chiefs announcer, Jets announcer

Sid Hartman *Minneapolis Star and Tribune* columnist

James Harris Bills 1969

Abner Haynes Texans 1960–62, Chiefs 1963, Broncos 1965–66, Dolphins 1967, Jets 1967

SHERRILL HEADRICK Texans 1960–62, Chiefs 1963–67, Bengals 1968

AL HEIM Bengals publicist

CHARLIE HENNIGAN Oilers 1960–66

DAVE HERMAN Jets 1964–69

MICKEY HERSKOWITZ *Houston Post* columnist, AFL staff

WINSTON HILL Jets 1963–69

BARRON HILTON Chargers owner

MIKE HOLOVAK Patriots assistant, Patriots coach

E. J. HOLUB Texans 1961–62, Chiefs 1963–69

BOB HOWSAM Broncos owner

JIM HUDSON Jets 1965–69

LAMAR HUNT AFL founder, Texans owner, Chiefs owner

JERRY IZENBERG *Newark Star-Ledger* columnist

FRANK JACKSON Texans 1961–62, Chiefs 1963–65, Dolphins 1966–67

AL JAMISON Oilers 1960–62

BILLY JOE Broncos 1963–64, Bills 1965, Dolphins 1966, Jets 1967–69

CURLEY JOHNSON Texans 1960, Titans 1961–62, Jets 1963–68

DARYL JOHNSON Patriots 1969

TOM KEATING Bills 1964–65, Raiders 1966–69

JACK KEMP Chargers 1960–62, Bills 1962–69

JIM KIICK Dolphins 1968–69

AL KING Broncos publicist

LARRY KING Dolphins announcer

CHUCK KNOX Jets assistant

DAVE KOCOUREK Chargers 1960–65, Dolphins 1966, Raiders 1967–68

ERNIE LADD Chargers 1961–65, Oilers 1966–67, Chiefs 1967–68

PETE LAMMONS Jets 1966–69

DARYLE LAMONICA Bills 1963–66, Raiders 1967–69

JACKY LEE Oilers 1960–63, Broncos 1964–65, Oilers 1966–67, Chiefs 1967–69

PAUL LEVY Yale Bowl volunteer

BOB LILLY Cowboys 1961–69

KEITH LINCOLN Chargers 1961–66, Bills 1967–68, Chargers 1968

FLOYD LITTLE Broncos 1967–69

AL LoCASALE Chargers scout, Bengals scout, Raiders management

JERRY MAGEE *San Diego Union-Tribune* sportswriter

DON MANOUKIAN Raiders 1960

WELLINGTON MARA Giants owner

BILL MATHIS Titans 1960–62, Jets 1963–69

DON MAYNARD Titans 1960–62, Jets 1963–69

WAHOO McDANIEL Oilers 1960, Broncos 1961–63, Jets 1964–65, Dolphins 1966–68

RON McDOLE Oilers 1962, Bills 1963–69

WILL McDONOUGH *Boston Globe* columnist

BUD McFADIN Broncos 1960–63, Oilers 1964–65

WALT MICHAELS Raiders assistant, Jets assistant

RED MILLER Patriots assistant, Broncos assistant

VAN MILLER Bills announcer

GENE MINGO Broncos 1960–64, Raiders 1964–65, Dolphins 1966–67

RON MIX Chargers 1960–69

JOE NAMATH Jets 1965–69

BILLY NEIGHBORS Patriots 1962–65, Dolphins 1966–69

LeROY NEIMAN Jets artist in residence

JIM NORTON Oilers 1960–68

BOB OATES *Los Angeles Times* sportswriter

JIM OTTO Raiders 1960–69

BABE PARILLI Raiders 1960, Patriots 1961–67, Jets 1968–69

JOANNE PARKER Patriots staff, Raiders staff, AFL staff, Broncos staff

VAL PINCHBECK AFL staff, Broncos staff

EDWIN POPE *Miami Herald* columnist

FRANK RAMOS Jets staff

JOHN RAUCH Raiders assistant, Raiders coach, Bills coach

JACK READER AFL game official

JOHNNY ROBINSON Texans 1960–62, Chiefs 1963–69

PAUL ROBINSON Bengals 1968–69

PAUL ROCHESTER Texans 1960–62, Chiefs 1963, Jets 1964–69

LOU SABAN Patriots coach, Bills coach, Broncos coach

GEORGE SAUER JR. Jets 1965–69

GALE SAYERS Bears 1965–69

TEX SCHRAMM Cowboys general manager

HARRY SCHUH Raiders 1965–69

BILLY SHAW Bills 1961–69

BLACKIE SHERROD *Dallas Times Herald* columnist

BUBBA SMITH Colts 1967–69

MATT SNELL Jets 1964–69

BART STARR Packers 1960–69

ROGER STAUBACH Cowboys 1969

JAN STENERUD Chiefs 1967–69

D. L. STEWART *Dayton Daily News* sportswriter

JOHN STOFA Dolphins 1966–67, Bengals 1968, Dolphins 1969

HANK STRAM Texans coach, Chiefs coach

MIKE STRATTON Bills 1962–69

JERRY STURM Broncos 1961–66

PAT SUMMERALL CBS Sports announcer

MIKE TALIAFERRO Jets 1964–67, Patriots 1968–69

BOB TALAMINI Oilers 1960–67, Jets 1968

LIONEL TAYLOR Broncos 1960–66, Houston 1967–68

OTIS TAYLOR Chiefs 1965–69

FRANK THOMAS JR. Birmingham businessman

JIM TRECKER Jets staff

FRANK TRIPUCKA Broncos 1960–63

DON TRULL Oilers 1964–67, Patriots 1967, Oilers 1968–69

BOB TRUMPY Bengals 1968–69

BAKE TURNER Jets 1963–69

HOWARD TWILLEY Dolphins 1966–69

LARRY VARNELL Denver businessman

TONY VETERI AFL game official

BILL WALSH Raiders assistant, Bengals assistant

AL WARD AFL staff

ERNIE WARLICK Bills 1962–65

Don Weiss NFL management

Hogan Wharton Oilers 1960–63

Fred Williamson Raiders 1961–63, Chiefs 1965–67

George Wilson Jr. Dolphins 1966

Ralph Wilson Bills owner

Ron Wolf Raiders management, AFL management

Sam Wyche Bengals 1968–69

Tom Yewcic Patriots 1961–66

1

The Beginning: Good Luck

This all could have been avoided, or at least delayed. The garish commissioner's party. Diana Ross rising out of a stage at midfield to join hundreds of brightly costumed singers and dancers. Multimillion-dollar commercials that have almost upstaged the main event itself. Everything associated with the Super Bowl's ascension to its status as American sports' contribution to the national calendar wouldn't have happened when it did were it not for Violet Wolfner.

Violet was the widow of Charles Bidwill, who had bought the National Football League's Chicago Cardinals during the 1930s. (She later married Walter Wolfner.) The club struggled through most of the 1950s, played in the shadow of the crosstown Bears, and often played before home crowds of fewer than 20,000. By the late '50s, it appeared inevitable that the Cardinals would need to find a new home, whether under the existing ownership or with one of the many outside entities interested in purchasing the team.

Two of the primary suitors for the Wolfners' Cardinals came from deep in the heart of Texas, the nation's largest state at the time but virtually untouched in terms of professional sports. The NFL ventured there briefly with a team called the Dallas Texans in 1952, but the local response was almost nonexistent, and the team was relocated to Pennsylvania before the close of the season. But it was to the same Dallas that billionaire businessman Lamar Hunt—at 26, younger than many of the men playing pro football—sought to bring a franchise to play in the Cotton Bowl. And down close to Texas' Gulf Coast, a transplanted Oklahoman named K. S. Adams Jr.—he went by the nickname "Bud"—considered his adopted hometown of Houston a gusher for the pro game.

High-level NFL officials frequently stated that the league wasn't interested in adding to its 12-member fraternity. So as the Cardinals auditioned potential new homes by scheduling regular-season home games in Buffalo and

Minneapolis, Hunt and Adams began their separate quests to complete what seemed to them like the most obvious of business opportunities—provide the franchise new roots in the warm Texas sun, allowing it to thrive for years to come. Likewise, other individuals and groups from coast to coast dreamed of establishing their own big-league pro football franchises.

BUD ADAMS: In the spring of 1958, I went out to Los Angeles to talk with Ed Pauley, who owned a quarter interest in the Rams. He told me the NFL was not going to expand. "Some of those guys, that's their livelihood. They don't have an oil company like you do. They need all the revenues they can get on the front end and not be dividing it up." I knew him well enough that he'd be telling me the straight poker on the thing. And he said, "I want you to meet a fella who can talk to you about the NFL in a lot more detail. He's our general manager, was our P.R. guy." The guy couldn't have been nicer—Pete Rozelle.

LARRY FELSER: The Cardinals played four games in Buffalo in the summer of '58, three exhibitions and the opening regular-season game against the New York Giants team that went on to play Baltimore for the championship, the first nationally televised professional football game. I covered all the games for the *Buffalo Courier Express*. That opener drew 22,000 fans. I went to Mr. Wolfner after the game and asked him his reaction to the crowd. He was disappointed. And I went to Wellington Mara, the owner of the Giants, and told him that Mr. Wolfner was disappointed in the crowd. He chortled and said, "It's about 4,000 more than we would have gotten in Chicago."

LAMAR HUNT: My first thought in getting a pro football team was to go to the National Football League and inquire about an expansion team for Dallas. I went to the commissioner, Bert Bell, late in 1958. He said the league really wasn't interested in expansion, that they had in particular a problem with two teams in Chicago at that time. There was a strong feeling that they needed to resolve that problem. I could never get the Wolfners to the point where they said they'd be willing to move the team. During the course of my conversations with them over several months, they had mentioned a number of people who had also tried to buy the Cardinals and move them to their city.

TEX SCHRAMM: I sat in a courtroom when Lamar brought his suit against the NFL in '61 or '62, and I heard his testimony. He testified that when he met with Bert Bell, he had already determined he was starting a new league and he was starting to get information that would be helpful in starting a new league, in operating teams. He made a list of questions that he carried with him. After they got so far through an interview, he'd go to the bathroom and read the list and see what points he hadn't covered.

LAMAR HUNT: I remember going over notes to myself. I tend to make notes to myself before a meeting of things I wanted to make sure to mention, questions I wanted to ask. I don't know why that came up during the trial. I was disappointed that we lost, disappointed and surprised. We got legal advice, that this would be a smart and intelligent thing to do. I was very young and naive, so it was a new experience for me.

In January of '59, I was flying back from what was the last meeting with the Wolfners in Florida. And the thought just occurred to me. I've heard about all of these people that want to buy the Cardinals and move them, to Houston or Denver or Minneapolis. Why wouldn't it be possible to form a second league? Later, I kiddingly said it was like the lightbulb coming on over your head. I can remember sitting in that airplane when it dawned on me that that was maybe a better alternative. It was a one-man thing for a while, until I called Bud Adams in Houston. He was the first person I contacted because I felt it was important to have a Dallas-Houston rivalry.

BUD ADAMS: I didn't know Lamar. I knew his brother, Bunker Hunt, who was two years behind me at Culver Military Academy. Bunker didn't play any sports, but he was a good sports fan. Back then, when a guy's in a military uniform, you don't know if he has five cents or five dollars or five million dollars. Bunker called me up, I want to say in March of '59, about Lamar wanting to talk to me. Lamar flew down to Houston the next day, and we had dinner at a steakhouse that I owned, the Charcoal Inn. Lamar was somewhat shy back then. We talked about everything, but I couldn't figure out what he wanted. I drove him back to the airport, and we were about two blocks away when he said, "I know you tried to buy the Cardinals. I did, too. . . . Would you be interested in starting a new league up?" I said, "Yeah, I would." About then, we pulled up. He was getting out of the car and said, "Well, I'll get back in touch with you."

LAMAR HUNT: Houston, Denver, Minneapolis, and Seattle—those are the first four people I went to contact. Barron Hilton in Los Angeles and Harry Wismer in New York came from other inquiries. Willard Rhodes from Seattle was definitely willing to do it if they could find a place to play but was turned down by Husky Stadium, by the University of Washington. So they could not proceed forward.

BOB HOWSAM: After World War II, I came back home to Denver and ended up being secretary of baseball's Western League, which was just being formed there. Three prominent Denver people got the franchise, but they thought you'd open up the gates and everybody'd run into the games. So they wanted to sell soon after. I talked my dad and brother into going in with me, and we bought controlling interest in the Denver Bears. They were playing in a splinter haven of a park, so we went out and sold bonds to private people so we could build a new stadium. We bought what was actually a dump, but it was close to the city, and built Bears Stadium.

We drew really well. I think in '49 that we drew more fans in Class A ball than the St. Louis Browns or the Philadelphia Phillies or A's. In 1955, we went Triple A. Then Branch Rickey tried to start the Continental League, and I was busy trying to promote that. The American and National Leagues stopped the Continental League by adding clubs, but during that period, Lamar Hunt gave me a call and asked if I thought Dallas could get a major league baseball club. Soon after, he asked to come to Denver and meet me at the Brown Palace. He asked if we had any interest in a new football league, that he had already talked to Bud Adams and he was on his way to talk to people in Minneapolis. We had been hoping among ourselves that, down the road, we might be able to get an NFL team but never really talked about it. Not only was football a sport that we enjoyed, we frankly wanted more games and more activity in our stadium. So we got some outside investors, but my family had control. I was the largest stockholder. I had over one-third of the whole club. I always talked to the family about decisions, we were a close family, but basically it was my opinion [that counted].

The prospective Minneapolis ownership group was centered around three prominent Twin Cities business figures—Max Winter, E. William Boyer, and H. P. Skoglund. The area's only big-league sports team was basketball's Minneapolis Lakers, but the construction of Metropolitan Stadium in suburban Bloomington made it attractive for both pro football and major league baseball. Winter, a sports promoter who had managed boxers, was the leader of the group. Having discussed the AFL plan with that group, Hunt moved on to what likely was the toughest challenge in giving this idea life.

LAMAR HUNT: A major league without New York and Los Angeles was not really a major league, so I made inquiries as to who might be a logical person in each of those cities. The person that I went to in New York was a fellow named Bill Shea, an attorney who Shea Stadium would be named after, who was involved in the Continental League there. I had dinner with him one night, and he recommended Harry Wismer. Harry was already in pro football, owning interest in the Detroit Lions and the Washington Redskins. Then I had a friend in Los Angeles by the name of Gene Mako, a great international tennis player, Don Budge's doubles partner when Budge was on top of the tennis world. Gene was a tremendous pro football fan, and, in about two weeks' time, he told me, "I think I've got the perfect guy for you." He recommended Barron Hilton.

BARRON HILTON: I was running Carte Blanche, a credit card company that I started. It was arranged for Lamar to meet with me at my office on Sunset Boulevard. Lamar told me he was going to start this league, gave me a little history about how he and Bud Adams had tried to get in the NFL, and he wanted to know if I would be interested in the new league's Los Angeles franchise. I said, "Let me think it over, and I'll let you know." It didn't take me very long, perhaps the next day or so. I told him I'd be happy to do that.

Owning the New York franchise would present a particularly difficult mission. Who would want to take on the challenge of going up against the NFL's powerful Giants and their glamorous stars like Frank Gifford and Sam Huff? Harry Wismer, then a colorful and popular football broadcaster in addition to being a stockholder for both the Lions and Redskins, was eager to become one of the big cigars in sports. He liked big names and bright lights. He greeted most strangers with a hearty "Congratulations!"—he explained it as meaning that every person had probably accomplished something in his life and deserved such a salute. Skeptics wondered if Harry considered it the person's honor to have encountered him.

JERRY IZENBERG: Harry would invent things. He would see things. When he was a broadcaster, he would say, "Here we are at Notre Dame Stadium. . . . Oh, look, General MacArthur is here! Hello, 'Dugout Doug!'" General MacArthur wasn't in the park. He wasn't in the country! [Harry] would just reel off names that were his "personal friends." That was his whole thing. He was a trophy collector in terms of friendships with people.

But just as the AFL efforts were beginning to come together, there came a curious invitation from Chicago. George Halas, the founder and longtime coach of the Bears, summoned Hunt and Adams to the office of his sporting goods store. If the undisclosed intent was to discuss future NFL entry, this swam against the current that the league was displaying to the public. Hunt decided to bring along Howsam from Denver.

BUD ADAMS: We went up and met with George Halas in August 1959 on a somewhat stealth-type flight that no one else knew about. I picked up Lamar on my way from Houston. We had to decide if we were going forward with the new league. Halas kind of indicated he didn't think the NFL was going to expand. He was very nice but very discouraging about a new league. He said, "The All-American league [a challenger to the NFL in the late 1940s that folded after four seasons] had some wealthy guys, but they lost a lot of money and we lost a lot of money. That's going to be the same story, second verse. Why don't you wait 'til we expand, do it in an orderly fashion, and we'll get you in." I wasn't believing too much of it.

BOB HOWSAM: Halas said, "Lamar, I'll give you the Dallas franchise in the NFL. Bud, I'll give you the Houston franchise. But I don't want to do anything with Denver." I never did know why he didn't like Denver. Maybe he thought it was too small. He told me, "I'll help you buy into any NFL club you want." And I said, "I don't want to buy into a ballclub. We would like to have a franchise in Denver." It was left that way. We went back to the Sherman Hotel and talked it over. After a long discussion, Lamar and Bud both said, "We're going to stick with you, and you can have the Denver franchise in the American Football League."

LAMAR HUNT: We had made a commitment to our partners. We had signed association papers. Each team had put up $25,000 to the league treasury. It would be very bad faith on our part not to go forward.

BOB HOWSAM: Here were two men who were offered successful franchises immediately, yet they were willing to stay together as a new league. I've always had such great respect for Lamar and Bud for doing that.

LAMAR HUNT: In August 1959, the Bears and Pittsburgh Steelers were having a preseason game in Houston, actually promoted by Bud Adams, by then announced as an AFL owner. Mr. Halas and Art Rooney, the Steelers' owner, had a press conference in Houston and, independent of the league, announced they were going to recommend that the NFL expand to Dallas and Houston. Well, this was three or four weeks after our first announcement, and up until then there had been great euphoria about this new league. This created a great deal of uncertainty. This was the first cannon shot in what turned out to be the pro football war.

Behind the scenes, the NFL was trying to see if they could get Rice Stadium in Houston for a team and also the Cotton Bowl in Dallas. They were turned down at Rice. Bud Adams was going to take a high school stadium and expand it because Rice would not rent the stadium to a professional football team. Then the NFL said their recommendation was to go to Dallas and Minneapolis. Once there was an NFL team announced for Dallas, everybody was kind of horrified. The city fathers knew they needed to keep their commitment to us on the Cotton Bowl. At the same time, they didn't want to turn down the Murchisons, the Cowboys' owners, who were a very prominent family. And everybody would have felt that the NFL was the better choice.

TEX SCHRAMM: I was working for CBS in the summer of 1959, after working for the Los Angeles Rams. There had been a lot of talk about an NFL franchise for Dallas. I had a friend who had just moved to New York from Dallas, and he called Clint Murchison. I had an interview and, right after that, Clint called back and said, "Are you willing to make a commitment?" I said, "Yes, I am." It was fine with CBS as long as I stayed through the 1960 Winter Olympics, which I happened to be doing. So from that point on—June or July of 1959—I was working for the Cowboys.

All Clint Murchison wanted was a team in Dallas. And he didn't have the nature that some of the owners have, that it had to be his team. He said to Lamar, "You know, you want the team? Fine. You can have the team. Or you can join us and run it or you can do whatever you want, virtually an open door." Lamar turned that down because he already had his own plan.

On August 14, 1959, the fledgling American Football League was unveiled at a news conference in Chicago. Plans called for at least six teams—in New York, Los Angeles, Houston, Dallas, Denver, and Minneapolis—with the intent to begin play in the fall of 1960. The idea wasn't all that revolutionary. A similar venture took place right after World War II, called the All-American Football Conference (AAFC). It drew large crowds in some cities but lasted only four seasons before three of its more successful clubs—the four-time champion Cleveland Browns, the Baltimore Colts, and the San Francisco 49ers—were absorbed into the NFL beginning in 1950.

LAMAR HUNT: My original thought was that we would be better off to go with six good, strong teams the first year. The National Football League had only 12 teams. The National Hockey League had only six teams, and they were a very well-respected league. Once we announced the six teams at the first organizational meeting in Chicago in August of '59, there was so much public interest, people were just coming out of the woodwork. Within days of the announcement, Ralph Wilson got in touch with me. He was a minority interest holder in the Lions, and he said he would like to have a team in Miami.

Ralph Wilson was an insurance and trucking magnate in Detroit and a regular at Lions games at Briggs Stadium. His interest in the business side of pro football increased dramatically when the NFL built a much higher national profile in the late '50s thanks to increased television exposure.

RALPH WILSON: I had a couple of racehorses in Saratoga, New York, and was up there in 1959. I read in the *New York Times* that a young fellow from Dallas was starting a new football league. The paper named the prospective sites where the franchises would be. One of them, of course, was Dallas. And there was Barron Hilton in Los Angeles and Bud Adams in Houston. It mentioned Miami as a possible site. I had a winter home there and thought it would be nice if I could get that franchise. I phoned Lamar Hunt and introduced myself. He said, "We've got about three applications for the Miami franchise. So if you're interested, you'd better get down and see me very quick." I called up a friend, and we flew to Dallas the next day. We went into Lamar's office, which, although he's one of the world's richest men, was about the size of a telephone booth. He allocated me the franchise, and then I went down to Miami. I had to have a place to play, and they had only one—the Orange Bowl. Now, Miami had a bad experience in the All-American Conference. I think the team went broke in the second-to-last game, in the third quarter. And they didn't want to talk about granting a lease to a team in another new league. Basically, they said they'd wait a few years for the National Football League.

I was home in Detroit when Lamar called and said, "We need another team. You can have your choice of five cities. He named Buffalo, St. Louis,

Cincinnati, Louisville, and Atlanta. I said, "I don't know anyone in any of those cities." He said, "Just think about it." Well, I talked to Eddie Hayes, the sports editor of the *Detroit Times*, and Nick Kerbawy, the general manager of the Detroit Lions. I asked each of them, "If you were darn foolish enough to go into a new league, which one of these cities would you take?" And both of them said Buffalo. I told Eddie that I really wasn't interested, and he said, "Let me call a friend of mine who is the editor of the *Buffalo News*. His name is Paul Neville, and I'd like to arrange a lunch and go over and see him." I did so reluctantly, flew over there and had lunch with Paul Neville. He gave me the sales talk and took me out to old War Memorial Stadium in downtown Buffalo. It was built back in the late '30s and was affectionately referred to as the "Rockpile." Seated about 35,000. I looked at it and said, "What the heck? It's big enough. It's a new league. I don't know whether this league's going to last." I said to Paul, "If I put a franchise in Buffalo and give it a three-year trial, will your paper support me?" He said, "Oh, definitely!" I kiddingly always say that's the last time the paper supported me.

Buffalo officially came on board in October 1959, and the team adopted the nickname of the city's old team in the All-American Football Conference, the Bills. The AFL hierarchy then headed to Minneapolis in late November 1959 intent on accomplishing three things. First, there was the matter of adding the eighth and final charter member to play beginning in 1960. The competition for that club had come down to interests in Boston and Philadelphia before the Philadelphia group, led by the Carpenter family, which owned baseball's Phillies, stepped aside. That meant Boston would enjoy its first pro football since the demise of the NFL Boston Yanks in the late 1940s.

The franchise was granted to a group led by Billy Sullivan, a Boston College grad who once worked for the old Boston Braves baseball club and was the president of Metropolitan Coal and Oil Company. Sullivan was the front man for nine other men who owned equal parts of the new team, which was nicknamed the Patriots. Most well known among the rest of the group was former Red Sox outfielder Dom DiMaggio, president of American Latex Fibre Corporation.

LAMAR HUNT: How Boston came about, by this time, Frank Leahy had been named general manager of the Los Angeles Chargers. He called and said that he had an inquiry from a close friend named Billy Sullivan, who had put together a group in Boston. Of course, Boston is one of the top markets in the country. So I got on the phone with Bill Sullivan, had numerous phone conversations with him, talked to him for hours on the telephone. He was actually accepted in the league not ever having met him.

The AFL also earmarked time at its Minneapolis meeting to name Joe Foss, a World War II hero and former governor of South Dakota, as commissioner. It would be fitting that his appointment become official in Minneapolis because it was the local ownership group that had spearheaded his hiring. The search for a commissioner focused on people familiar with the game, mostly coaches and administrators on the college level. The owners conducted some preliminary interviews, including one with Fritz Crisler from the University of Michigan.

BOB HOWSAM: We decided to ask Bert Bell, the commissioner of the NFL, if he'd be our commissioner, too. I was chosen to fly to his home in Atlantic City. He felt very flattered but said he couldn't. As we were about to end the meeting, I said, "If you were forming a league, what would you think was the most important thing to do?" And he said, "Pool the TV money. We don't have that in the National Football League, but I'm working on it. That is a very important thing." I went back and talked to Lamar. We worked it out so that Harry Wismer made the motion to pool all TV money because he had the big city. That, frankly, started it out to be really a professional league.

HANK STRAM: The first time I went out to eat with Lamar Hunt, the first thing he asked me was, "We're looking for a commissioner. Since you were in the Big 10 at Purdue, what would you think about Fritz Crisler from Michigan?" I said, "Very frankly, I don't think it would be a good idea. He's a great coach, a great man, great athletic director. But he's a college guy. He's not interested in pro football." Lamar asked, "Well, who would be?" "I'm prejudiced, but Stu Holcombe, my coach at Purdue, would be terrific." So he pursued that. Stu was the athletic director at Northwestern at the time.

Weeks of discussions yielded no clear-cut candidate when league officials convened for a meeting in Los Angeles. That's when Joe Foss—former flying ace, former politician, and a successful businessman—was innocently invited to drop in on an AFL gathering that happened to be in the hotel in which he was staying on other business. His name recognition immediately appealed to the AFL officials, and the Minneapolis ownership group lobbied hard for its neighbor as a suitable first commissioner despite his void of experience in the football world.

JOE FOSS: They interviewed me in Los Angeles, and Tom Eddy of the Chargers came out with a statement: "The American Football League is only certain of one thing. That's that Joe Foss will not be commissioner." I guess I made him mad. They asked me if I ever coached. I said, "Yeah, I coached. I coached where it was life and death."

HANK STRAM: Lamar Hunt is very retiring, kind of quiet. They had gone far enough to where they were about to make their decision. I went over to Stu's house, right off Lake Michigan. Stu said, "Is there anything that I should know?" "Well, Lamar doesn't talk very much. So if you have any questions, don't be reluctant to ask." They met in his house and visited. And the telephone rang. It was Billy Sullivan from Boston. Billy and Lamar had previously agreed: "I'll interview Joe Foss in Boston, and you visit with Stu Holcombe at Northwestern." Lamar got on the phone, and Billy Sullivan said, "Joe Foss just agreed to a contract." "OK. Great. Good." Hung up the phone. That was it. Stu didn't know what the hell happened.

And the important first college player draft was scheduled to take place in Minneapolis starting Monday, November 23, the day after the owners would attend one of those nomadic Chicago Cardinals "home" games, against the New York Giants at Metropolitan Stadium. That would be the Cardinals' second "home" appearance in Minnesota during the 1959 season. A date against the Philadelphia Eagles in October attracted 20,112, not much different from the standard home crowds that the Cardinals drew that season to Soldier Field.

But the most dramatic event to date in the AFL's brief history wasn't penciled into the agenda—the sudden loss of the very Minneapolis ownership group that was hosting the session.

SID HARTMAN: All the Minneapolis owners—H. P. Skoglund, Max Winter, William Boyer—were good friends of mine. I had been kind of their contact guy with Halas. He later said if someone was driving you as crazy as I drove him, you'd give him a franchise just to get him off your back. The Green Bay games were televised in Minneapolis all the time, and there were a lot of NFL fans. They had one meeting that lasted until about 3:00 in the morning, and they decided to withdraw their application and try to get a team in the National Football League.

BARRON HILTON: I called Max the night before and said, "There's a rumor going around that you're going into the National Football League." He said, "Oh, no. I'm with you guys 100 percent." And the next day, he defected. I think the understanding he had with Halas was that he had to lead us down that rosy path. Halas's strategy was that he wanted to show the college players that the new league was already falling apart.

As the owners hastily met that night, an early edition of the Monday morning *Minneapolis Tribune* made its way into the meeting. It contained the headline, "Twin Cities May Get National Grid Team." In the story, sports editor Charles Johnson reported that he had received a telegram the previous Friday from Halas and Cardinals owner Walter Wolfner. Then the following Sunday, the morning of the Cardinals-Giants game in Bloomington, Halas wired the Minneapolis AFL ownership triumvirate. Johnson said he was authorized by Halas to make these events public after the game. He announced that the NFL initially wanted to award teams to Dallas and Houston starting play in 1960 but had to revise that plan because of the lack of an NFL-quality stadium in Houston. Plan B, as it turned out, was to proceed with plans to have Dallas begin play in 1960 and award the second expansion team to Minnesota with a starting date of 1961.

LAMAR HUNT: At our draft meeting, the bombshell hit. The NFL offered a team to our group, and our group felt they could not go forward with us. They were very embarrassed. We were at a dinner. They were very sheepish.

An emergency meeting lasted well into the wee hours of Monday morning. Max Winter departed around 2:00 A.M. and made the following statement to the press: "I have withdrawn from the Minneapolis–St. Paul football picture as far as the American League is concerned." That left Skoglund as the only member of the Minneapolis group in the meeting for the rest of the session. Afterward, Hunt told reporters that Minneapolis was still in the AFL. The owners went ahead with their college draft.

LAMAR HUNT: We had our draft and we were ill prepared. We had only three general managers, with the Chargers, the Texans, and the Broncos. We appointed them as a committee to conduct the draft. They graded the eight best players by position. They put their names on a piece of paper and put them in a hat. Each team pulled one out so that, for instance, each team had a quarterback.

We also felt it was important for each team to draft one highly publicized player. So each team got a special pick. We drafted Don Meredith, who was an outstanding quarterback in Dallas at SMU. The New York Titans drafted George Izo, Notre Dame's quarterback. Houston got Billy Cannon, the Heisman Trophy winner from LSU. We were ill prepared not only to draft these players but also to go out and sign them. We didn't have any employees. I was naive enough to think that we couldn't have conversations with Meredith, although I knew him personally from SMU, until after his last college game. That was against TCU in late November. We woke up on the Sunday morning after his last college game, and there was a story in the paper that Clint Murchison of the Cowboys had signed Don Meredith.

TEX SCHRAMM: We didn't have a franchise. We signed Don Meredith through a personal-services contract. We signed Don Perkins through a personal-services contract.

LAMAR HUNT: The NFL had allowed Murchison to do this because it realized it couldn't let Meredith go to the other league in the city where he had played college football. He would be a big attraction.

GIL BRANDT: The feeling was, to win the battle of Dallas you had to win the battle of Meredith. That was a coup to get him signed. But I think people found out that, as great a player as Meredith was, if your team won, people came. If you didn't win, it didn't make any difference if you had Meredith or Jones or Smith at quarterback.

The hiring of Foss was formally announced a week after the tumultuous Minneapolis summit. He stood as a popular, well-known figure despite being a neophyte in the business of professional sports. There was no honeymoon, given the gaping hole in the side of the AFL ship blasted open by the departing ownership group.

SAM BLAIR: Joe Foss gave them some unusual name recognition. George Halas had been the big wheel of opposition to the AFL, and at the press conference to introduce Foss, Bud Shrake of the *Dallas Times Herald* asked the highly decorated Foss, "What would you do if you saw George Halas flying a Japanese Zero?"

JOE FOSS: Everybody covering that introductory news conference laughed and laughed. They announced I was commissioner, and the reporters said, "You don't even have a football yet." Well, I did, so I brought it up. They said, "You have no stadiums, no coaches, no players." And they just started to throw us right down a hole. But we had a lot of confidence in what we were going to do.

Having scrapped and clawed at each other over franchise sites, it came time for the leagues to confront each other over the actual product—players. The AFL wasn't prepared to try to raid the NFL for current talent, so the highest priority was to cut it off at the pass—incoming college talent. And in the fall of 1959, no college player was more highly coveted than LSU's Billy Cannon. He would win the Heisman Trophy and practically bronze himself with a Halloween night punt return of 89 yards that provided the only touchdown in allowing the defending national champion Bengal Tigers to claim their 19th consecutive victory, 7–3, over the hated Ole Miss Rebels.

In the AFL draft that began in Minneapolis and dragged out for more than a week, Cannon's draft rights were scooped up by the nearest franchise, Houston. The time and location of the NFL draft of that year are difficult facts to verify. The team that came away with Cannon's rights was the Los Angeles Rams, led by their young general manager, Pete Rozelle.

BUD ADAMS: Billy met Pete Rozelle at the All-American Team presentation in New York, and they went down to Philadelphia, to Bert Bell's office, and signed him before LSU played in the Sugar Bowl. I didn't know all that. I couldn't get him on the phone.

CHRIS BURFORD: I was in Billy's room at the Waldorf Astoria when we were up in New York for the All-American Team. I was sitting on the bed when the Rams called. They said, "What do you want?" He said, "I want a ton. Twenty thousand." And they agreed.

TEX SCHRAMM: We had some people up at the All-American deal, and we got to talking to Billy Cannon. He indicated he would be interested in playing for the Cowboys. So I got Gil Brandt and said, "Go in there and sign him." As always, word got out and it got to Pete Rozelle, a very good friend of mine whom I worked with for the Rams, who had drafted Cannon. He said, "I understand that you signed Billy Cannon." And I said, "Yeah, that's right." He said, "Let me tell you, *we* signed Billy Cannon. We have a real good job for him because you won't have a football job because you won't get a franchise."

BUD ADAMS: There was a guy in Baton Rouge named Alvin Roy who had started players on weight training, like Jim Taylor who was with the Packers, and I thought he might know where Billy was. So, just as a wild shot, I thought I'd call up this Alvin Roy. He said, "Oh, yeah. Billy's been getting these awards here and there, been going to dinners." I said, "Let me tell you something, Alvin. Just tell Billy it doesn't matter if he signed with the Rams because he shouldn't have done that. He still has the Sugar Bowl to play. We'll sign him right after the game's over with. Tell him that whatever he signed for, I'll double it." Alvin said, "Say that again." "You tell him that, and here's my phone number. Tell him to call me collect." I told my wife, "Honey, I'll bet we're going to get a call from Baton Rouge, Louisiana, in less than 30 minutes."

Sure enough, about 28 minutes later, he called me. It turned out Alvin had a little trouble finding Billy. He said, "This is Billy Cannon. I've been wanting to talk to you." I said, "Did Alvin tell you what I told him?" "Sure did." "Well, I'm going to ask you a question. You have to tell me the truth. Did you sign or didn't you sign? It won't make any difference. We can still do business together." He said, "Yeah, I signed." And he told me he signed in Bert Bell's office. I said, "Just keep it under your hat, but I'll make you the offer that I told Alvin Roy I would. What did you sign for?" He said, "I signed for a $10,000 bonus. You're going to give me $20,000?" I said, "I'm going to give you a $20,000 bonus." Then he told me he signed three one-year contracts, each for $15,000. "Billy, I'm going to make them each 30, 30, 30, and I'm going to put 'em all on one contract." I got Adrian Burk—an All-American at Baylor, played for the Eagles, a lawyer in Houston—to sign him under the goal posts after the Sugar Bowl.

I brought Billy over to Houston ahead of time 'cause he said, "How do I know you're going to do all this? I'd like to see something first." I picked him up at the airport and went by my office. I said, "You don't have to take the contract to a lawyer. It says right here, bonus money $20,000." He said, "That's fine." Then we came by my house in my wife Nancy's car, a white four-door Cadillac. He said, "My dad works for Humble Oil, been in refinery work all these years. If I could go back home and say, 'Dad, this car's for you,' no telling what he'd do." I said, "Wait a minute, Billy. My God. My wife . . . I don't know what she'd do to me." Billy said, "Well, you can go out and buy her another one." I said, "Don't say anything about it. You've got the keys. When you're ready to head on back, just go out and get in the car and drive off." Nancy had gone off someplace in the house. When he left, I told her, "Billy's gone on and heading back home." She said, "Did he go by cab?" I said, "No, he's driving back." She said, "How's he driving back?" I said, "In your car." Then it hit the fan.

Cannon was one of three prized prospects who signed contracts with both leagues—coincidentally, all playing for Southeastern Conference schools. One of Cannon's LSU teammates, a talented two-way back named Johnny Robinson, provided his signature for both the Detroit Lions and the Dallas Texans. And back Charlie Flowers of Ole Miss doubled his pleasure with the Giants and the L.A. Chargers.

JOHNNY ROBINSON: I was the third number one draft pick of Detroit, ended up signing with them for a $2,500 bonus and a three-year contract for $10,000, $11,000, and $12,000. It was illegal to sign while still a college player but commonly done from what I understood. I signed with a guy named Anderson. He was the only guy I'd ever seen from the team. He flew down to Baton Rouge, called me up to a motel room, offered me a contract, and I took it.

LAMAR HUNT: In December, it came to our attention that some key players had already signed with the NFL—Billy Cannon, Johnny Robinson, Charlie Flowers—before their college eligibility was up. All three of them were playing in the Sugar Bowl game, LSU and Mississippi, so we devised a plan to get an acceptance from them and sign them on the field immediately after the game. This would not only be embarrassing to the NFL but they would not be able to defend their position. Each of the players sent notice a day or two before the game renouncing their previous commitments.

JOHNNY ROBINSON: Lamar contacted me after they got organized. I came to Dallas and decided that, for a Southern boy, Detroit was pretty far away.

I liked Dallas. It was a young town, seemed to be a great place to play. When Lamar came down to Baton Rouge, I ended up talking to an attorney who was a friend of mine and I signed with Lamar for the same figures. It was not choosing the AFL over the NFL. It was choosing to go to Dallas for the same amount of money. And I signed under the goal post of the Sugar Bowl.

The pro football fates of Cannon, Robinson, and Flowers rested in separate court cases. In the meantime, the fledging league still had to determine where to locate its orphaned Minneapolis franchise. Official notice of the defection came at the NFL's winter meeting in Miami in January 1960, when the league formally announced that the Dallas Rangers (yes, Rangers; the team actually changed its nickname to the Cowboys in March 1960 to snuff out building confusion with the Dallas–Fort Worth Rangers minor league baseball team) would join the league that fall, followed by the Minnesota Vikings in 1961.

LAMAR HUNT: We had hired a commissioner, Joe Foss, who had been recommended by the Minneapolis group. The first thing that Joe Foss did as commissioner was to recommend that we let Minneapolis out.

JOE FOSS: Anytime there's a better deal, most folks drift that way. As far as they were concerned—and everybody else, for that matter—it was a better deal to go into an established outfit than play marbles with someone who was just getting started. So I couldn't blame 'em. They were smart businessmen.

LAMAR HUNT: The NFL couldn't do anything until their annual meeting in January. There was still a great deal of confusion. You had people like the Redskins' owner, George Preston Marshall, who said he was opposed to expansion, that he wouldn't vote for it, and it took a unanimous vote. So there was a lot of uncertainty toward whether the NFL would actually expand. Our people in Minneapolis—basically Winter, Boyer, and Skoglund—said they could not proceed, that they couldn't fight city hall, that the public sentiment was strongly for them to take the NFL team. And we voted, not without controversy, to let them withdraw and actually refunded their $25,000.

AL WARD: About a year later, when money got tight, Billy Sullivan of the Patriots made a motion to try to get that $25,000 back. They were losing so much money that $3,000 for each team became important.

LAMAR HUNT: We had interest from people coming into the league. There were a lot of inquiries, conversations with people in Louisville, Atlanta, New Orleans. Nobody had stadiums. Barron Hilton of the Chargers was very anxious to have an opponent on the West Coast, and he felt very strongly that we should put a team in the Bay Area.

With league bylaws requiring a unanimous vote for establishment of a new team, the vote to pick a team from between two finalists—Atlanta and Oakland—began at the Dallas Statler Hilton. Three votes were taken the first day, starting with Atlanta leading 4–3, then 5–2, then 6–1, with only a proxy for Los Angeles' Barron Hilton preventing the club from being awarded. Realizing the gravity of the Oakland plight, Hilton cut short his business at home and traveled to Dallas to lobby for the Oakland group in person.

BARRON HILTON: I said to the other owners: "All of you have a rivalry except me. I'm sitting out here on the West Coast." They said, "All right. If you can put a team together, that would be all right with us." I flew up to our airport property in San Francisco. I think I brought Frank Leahy with me. I recall we had a meeting over in Oakland in one of the hotels. I should know the name of it, being in the hotel business. We convinced a group up there to take on the franchise. Chet Soda was the name of the original individual.

Hilton's emotional plea worked, with Oakland—its ownership group led by Soda, Wayne Valley, and Ed McGah—suddenly becoming the front-runner and earning all seven votes to gain admission. The city was in although it didn't have a suitable place to play. But city officials from neighboring San Francisco passed along word during the two-day vote that the club would be allowed to play temporarily on the west side of the bay, a humbling last resort for a city seeking to establish its own identity but, frankly, the only way that it could land the AFL team.

In June, the AFL scored a three-player sweep in its legal fight for the rights to Cannon, Robinson, and Flowers. The Cannon case, involving the reigning Heisman winner, attracted the most attention. Judge William J. Lindberg established that Cannon had signed prematurely with both teams but ruled the first contract that Cannon signed, with the Rams, invalid on the basis that only one of the three one-year contracts had been approved by commissioner

Bert Bell. Judge Lindberg also said Cannon had not been provided adequate legal advice before signing. "Not withstanding his prowess and agility on the gridiron, he is not an astute businessman. He is exceptionally naive for a college senior and a provincial lad untutored and unwise in the ways of the business world," the judge ruled.

The Flowers trial featured the most action. Giants coach Jim Lee Howell was called as a witness and had to be restrained by two U.S. marshals. The judge told him, "You will conduct yourself as a gentleman as long as you are in this court. Put your feet on the ground and restrain yourself." Flowers told the judge he was surprised that Giants owner Wellington Mara asked him to sign a contract at the All-American dinner in New York. Mara described the concealed contract as "harmless deception."

BUD ADAMS: The son of Ed Pauley, the Rams' general manager, was playing golf with Barron Hilton two days before the final decision in the [Cannon] case. He told Barron, "I don't know what Adams is thinking. He can't win this case. We signed him first." We tried to get a venue change and couldn't. So we at least got to bring in another judge, from the state of Washington, who played football. He said, "I'm going to award Cannon to Houston on the fact that, when he signed with the Rams, he didn't have the opportunity to talk to Mr. Adams. So he would have lost all that ability to earn additional money."

CHRIS BURFORD: They said at the trial, "This is just a young guy that didn't have much business experience." Baloney. Billy and Johnny Robinson had a section of tickets in that stadium in Baton Rouge. They knew more business than we all came across.

There was one other event worth noting in the notable off-season of 1959–60. On March 13, 1960, the ownership of the Chicago Cardinals was officially granted permission by its NFL brethren to relocate to St. Louis.

2

Sign In, Please

While pursuing college players and steering clear of veterans under contract to the NFL, the AFL began to seek players through another avenue—those unwanted by NFL clubs for whatever reason. And with only 13 NFL teams in operation, counting the new Cowboys, that left a lot of worthy players to consider.

DON MAYNARD: I went to the New York Giants as a rookie in 1958 from Texas Western, in El Paso. I didn't even know where New York was. There were about three rookies that they kept. I was fortunate there was a place for a punt returner and kickoff guy, and I was a backup halfback behind Frank Gifford and a receiver some behind Kyle Rote. In '59, they brought in Allie Sherman as an assistant coach. He just didn't like me. One thing led to another and we had a couple of words one day in workout, Sherman jumping on me. Probably the first time I'd ever talked back to a coach. He told me to quit that long stridin' and get to runnin'. I said, "I cover more ground in one stride than anybody you've got out here does in three." He just exploded and sent me to the other end of the field to stand by the goal post. Two or three days later, I was cut and went to Canada, got on with Hamilton. In 1960, I saw Sammy Baugh signed to coach the New York Titans. I'd played against his Hardin-Simmons teams three years, and he took me to the Blue-Gray game. When I called the Titans, Sam said, "Oh, yeah, man. I'd love to have you." So I wound up being the first Titan signed.

LARRY GRANTHAM: Don was four or five years ahead of his time. He wore long sideburns. He always wore blue jeans, boots, like he does now. And he had a belt—in the back, they cut the number 13 and it had "SHINE" on it. That was his nickname.

JACK KEMP: I was with the Giants in the '58 season. Don Maynard and I were both on the taxi squad, both got activated the same week. In '59, they kind of farmed me out to Calgary in the Canadian League to get some experience. That was Vince Lombardi's idea, and then he went to the Packers. I got cut from Calgary because, in those days, they could keep only one American quarterback, and they had Joe Kapp from Cal. I came back and went on the taxi squad of the 49ers, got activated when Y. A. Tittle got hurt. Commissioner Bert Bell then got a call from Paul Brown of the Browns right before we played them, saying it was illegal for me to play in Canada and the NFL in the same year. It was an obscure contractual problem that really disturbed me. If I knew then what I know now, I would have sued, because I didn't even get a chance to play in Canada. I don't think I played more than a quarter. But things worked out for the best. I was ready to sign a 49er contract for 1960 when I got a call from Don Klosterman on behalf of Frank Leahy and Sid Gillman, asking if I would fly to L.A. and talk to the Chargers. I'm from L.A. I think I got a guaranteed contract for two years at the magnificent free-market sum of $11,500. Which, in 1959, was a lot of money.

TOM FLORES: I had tried in Canada, had come home, had surgery on my throwing arm, and tried again with the Redskins and didn't make it. By the end of the week with them, I couldn't even lift my arm. So I went back to school and started working on my master's in education. I got a call from Eddie Erdelatz, the Raiders' coach, who asked if I was interested in trying out. I had nothing to lose. All of a sudden, the juices started flowing; I got excited again and made it. It was a bunch of guys, some who had never played pro ball, some who had but who were at the end of their careers. We were all there for the fun of it. We had no idea where it was going to go.

FRANK TRIPUCKA: I had played four years in the NFL and eight years in Canada by 1959. I had four kids at the time and didn't want to stay up there. I told them in Saskatchewan, "I'm going back to New Jersey." I went home and got a call from Dean Griffing, who was general manager in Saskatchewan when I first went there. He was offered the Denver GM job and said, "Come on out to Denver." I said, "Nah. I've had it. I've been around too long." He said, "Come on out and at least help us coach in training camp." So I went up to Golden, Colorado School of Mines. I was going to go up there for five or six weeks and come home. They had Tom Dublinski, backup of Bobby Layne at Detroit, and George Herring, who was the starting quarterback in Vancouver. We were playing an intrasquad game in Golden, the first experience that Colorado people would have of pro football. They went through the first half, and neither Dublinski nor Herring completed a pass. So Frank Filchock, the head coach, said to me, "These people paid five bucks a head. You'd better get dressed and give 'em their money's worth." I completed a couple of passes. Four years later, I was still there.

DALE DODRILL: There was a defensive lineman named Bud McFadin whom I knew from playing in the College All-Star Game in 1952. He went to the Rams, quit in '56 because of some sort of injury that wasn't associated with football, and went to live in Houston.

FRANK TRIPUCKA: Bud McFadin had shot himself in the stomach in an accident when he was with the Los Angeles Rams and retired after the 1956 season. We went to play an exhibition game in Houston, and Bud stopped in to practice to visit Jimmy Cason, our defensive backfield coach, who was a teammate of his with the Rams.

BUD McFADIN: I was about 30 pounds overweight and working in Houston. We ran a country club. Our business wasn't that great. Somehow or another, they talked me into going back. Hell, I almost died in the first six or eight weeks. I had that gunshot wound, didn't know exactly how that was going to turn out. I played a game the next weekend. I was so damn sore. I couldn't get out of bed. Liked to died. I stayed in the bathtub as much as I could to get over all that soreness. It took me a while to get back in shape.

Some players didn't have even a hint of an NFL résumé. Some of them couldn't even boast of playing for a major college. Or college ball at all!

ELBERT DUBENION: I played only one year in high school, my junior year. My problem was, I was from the South—Griffin, Georgia—but didn't go to high school until I came north to Ohio. In high school, they thought I was a new teacher. I was too old my senior year to play. I went from there into the army and played some football at training camp and in Germany. And I ran track in the service and went from a 10.5 100-yard dash to a 9.7. I got fed in the service, went from 162 pounds to 215 during basic training. I didn't know what three squares a day was until I got into the service. In 1955, my service coach told the coach at the University of Minnesota, Murray War-math, about me. But I didn't qualify and would have had to go to junior college. I went back home to Columbus, Ohio, and went to work in a steel mill. It just so happened that my quarterback in Germany played one year at Bluffton College in Ohio. He told them about me, and they contacted me. I had no intention of going there, but then after working two jobs—with the city sanitation department from 7:00 to 1:00 and Buckeye Steel Casting from 4:00 to 12:30 in the morning, I decided to go up there and visit. I enrolled that fall, played halfback, and was one of the heaviest players at 180. My left guard was about five-eight, 155.

Back then, scouts didn't check the age factor too close. I was 26 when I came out after '58. I was drafted by the Browns and was chosen to go to the College All-Star Game in Chicago to play the Colts. Otto Graham coached that team and would line us up to run. Lou Saban, who was one of the coaches, would pick me. Otto Graham picked Willmer Fowler, who was the Big 10 sprint champion. I beat him by 10 yards. I didn't know he was the Big 10 champion in the 100 and 220. Had I known, I would have folded up. But I got hurt before they played Baltimore and missed the '59 season. It was a good thing I got hurt—I never saw so many big guys. After I recovered, the Browns wanted me to go to Canada and play defense. I didn't care for that, so I came back and sat out the season. In 1960, Dick Gallagher, who had scouted me for the Browns, went to Buffalo as general manager. I was one of the first guys he signed. I knew I couldn't play for the Browns.

SHERRILL HEADRICK: In 1959, my grade points at TCU were not good enough to stay, so I decided to play in Canada. But I didn't want to be that far from home. I kind of like to stay close to the house, Texas. So I came back and worked in the oil fields. I worked for Joe Don Looney Sr., and he owned just a little piece of the Dallas Texans. The Cowboys actually scouted me and sent me a contract for $500 less than I wanted. I wanted $500 to put in my pocket right then to get out of the oil fields. I called Looney because I thought there was just one Dallas team, the Cowboys. He said, "Well, Sher-rill, there haven't been any contracts sent out . . . 'by the Texans' . . . but I'll guarantee you, you'll have a contract there tomorrow and the $500." I broke my jaw before we went out to training camp in New Mexico, and I weighed only 185 pounds. I think I told them I was in a little bit of a car accident, but

I think I was in a *bar* accident—a drunk hit me with a beer bottle. I got hurt the first day, so I was able to eat and get my weight back to 200. I was scared to death about making the team, but I didn't want to go back to the oil fields.

GINO CAPPELLETTI: I was not drafted out of college in Minnesota. I was not called as a free agent. I went up and played for a year in a semipro league in Canada called the Ontario Rugby Football Union. I got a tryout playing quarterback the following year with Detroit, which was only about 50 miles away. I was there about 10 days, and they let me go. I went back to Minneapolis, tended bar at my brother's place. The bar had a team that played Minneapolis Park Board touch football, so I played there. Then I got a call from the Patriots.

GENE MINGO: I was born and raised in Akron, Ohio. I played two years of high school football but dropped out of high school at the beginning of my junior year. I didn't enjoy school. My mother had been sick for about five years, and my dad said, "Since you don't like going to school and you seem to keep getting into mischief, why don't you stay home and take care of your mother." I did that for three years. Then when she passed, I promised her that I would go back to school and I went back. And during those days, a lot of Southern whites came up to Akron and became schoolteachers. I just got tired of asking teachers for help when I saw them go to the white kids and make sure they got what was on the board. I was three years older than all the kids in that grade. When I asked for some help, all the heads would turn and look at Gene. Because Gene was older, he was supposed to know. And I was embarrassed. I just said the hell with this white man's learning. And, in 1956, I joined the navy.

I played service ball. I was actually throwing a loaf of bread around in the mess hall and the head cook got mad and said, "If you think you can play football, we'll send you over to Little Creek Amphib. Base." I went over to Little Creek, Virginia, a sub base, and made the team. Made all-service. My introduction into pro football was when I played against Fort Dix, New Jersey. They had Rosey Grier, who played tackle for the New York Giants, and Sherman Plunkett and "Big Daddy" Lipscomb. Weeb Ewbank came down to Oceania Naval Air Station and saw my chief when I was special service. He said, "We sure would like to have Gene join the Baltimore Colts." They offered me a contract, around $9,000. When I got to Baltimore, they said they couldn't pay me what Weeb had offered. I guess when he got back, they told him, "This guy has no college. You can't give him that kind of money." Anyway, they offered me $5,000. I said, "Well, the heck with that. I can go home and work in the factories and make almost that much. And I don't have to worry about being banged up."

There was an army guy out of Fort Kit Carson, Colorado, and the Broncos signed him to a contract. So after getting out of the navy in 1959, I wrote the Broncos a letter. I took it to my sister because my spelling wasn't that good. Dean Griffing, the general manager, had heard of me playing service ball and sent me a contract for $6,500. And I was a Bronco. I tell people there have been miracles in my life. I came to the Broncos to be a running back and a defensive back. A week before our last exhibition game, Frank Filchock was trying to find our kicker. Bill Miller, who was in the navy with me, hollered out, "Mingo can kick!" I kicked in the service, but when I tried extra points in high school, I was lucky if I kicked one out of ten through the goal posts. They pushed me out 'cause I tried to hide. And Filchock said, "If you think you can kick, come on down here." I didn't even have a kicking shoe on. The first one, I kicked through the uprights. It was just an extra point. And that was the start of my pro football career, as a field-goal kicker and also a halfback. I played seven positions for the Broncos.

The AFL sought to establish an identity distinct from the NFL by adopting college football's two-point conversion and by putting last names on the backs of player jerseys.

With the beginning of the season only a few months away, each club began the arduous task of sifting through talent—not always an appropriate description—through open tryout camps and the subsequent formal training camps. Players of all shapes and sizes sought out the nearest opportunity to gain entry into pro football.

JACK FAULKNER: All the bartenders in L.A. and anybody that had ever played thought they had a chance. We had, I don't know how many, 300 guys running around there at these open tryouts. Ran 'em through some drills. It took all day to do that. We planted a couple of guys. I forget the kid's name. Wide receiver, a fast guy. His dad was a big-time actor. We had a couple guys that we were already going to sign, but they came through there.

GOOSE GONSOULIN: I went up to Denver, and there were already 120 guys that had come through camp. And then there were 90 of us coming in, the second wave. We stayed in a huge gym, an auditorium. It was bed after bed, side by side, bunk beds. Guys waking up all during the night. You couldn't sleep. There were just a couple of restrooms for all these guys.

DALE DODRILL: I remember things a little different than what the players probably say. They said their living conditions weren't too good, and anything they told you is probably correct. To me, it wasn't that important a deal. When I played for Pittsburgh in the early '50s, our locker room was a pallet on dirt floors with a couple of nails in the wall. I never thought the Bronco players' conditions were that bad, but, yes, they were paying a price for being part of something that was just starting up.

AL JAMISON: I was in the first trainload that got to Oilers camp in Houston, and everyone in that first wave was expecting to be cut. There were about 342 guys that came through the camp looking for 33 jobs. Don't get close to your roommate. It wasn't likely you were going to see him after a week. I got to Houston July 5. The night before, I was watching a fireworks display in northern Ohio with a jacket on. I got to Dallas and got off that Braniff plane, and I thought the engines were still on. Then we got to Houston, and it rained for 28 days out of 30 days. It was stinking, wet, and hot with maggots on the ground.

HOGAN WHARTON: I'm from down in the Houston area, raised in Orange, Texas. After spending a year in Baltimore freezing my Goddamn feet off, hell, why wouldn't I want to go back when they were starting a new league in Houston? If I got my ass fired, I'd be home. I got heat stroke. They packed me in ice, but that wasn't any worse than what happened to a lot of other guys. Hell, they gave me the day off. But under our coach, Lou Rymkus, I didn't want them to tell the coach. He might run your ass off.

COTTON DAVIDSON: That first Texans training camp in Roswell, New Mexico, was quite an ordeal. Training camp is bad when it's as good as it gets. They had a contract with the school, New Mexico Military, to feed us. And they fed us like a military school. It was the worst food in the world. We had to go show up. So we'd go through the dining room and out the back end. There was a Dairy Queen across the road. That's where we wound up eating.

The first year, Lamar and Bunker Hunt would get over on a field away from where we were working out, and they'd kick and throw. And after practice, we'd have a kicking contest with Lamar. It amazed me.

HANK STRAM: There was a lot of talk about, "Ah, the league's not going to last. It's going to fold." So in our first meeting, I said, "Take out your pads, and get a pencil and write down what I'm going to tell you. There's a lot of speculation about what's going to happen with this league. I don't know how long it's going to last, but when it's all over with, we are going to be the winningest team in the history of the American Football League. Write it down, and remember that. That's what we're all about." So they all wrote it down.

Rookie decisions on whether to cast a lot with the established NFL or take a chance with the new kids were as different as the players themselves.

CHRIS BURFORD: The big consideration was whether the AFL would even play. I was drafted by the Cleveland Browns and the Dallas Texans. I had some pretty good counsel that indicated the Browns would offer like $8,500 and a $500 bonus. That might not sound like much, but there were All-Pros that were getting $6,000 and $7,000 then. I was living in Stanford's track house, where they store track equipment. That's where I first met Lamar Hunt and Don Rossi, the Texans' general manager. They showed up in what was probably a 1938 or '39 Chevrolet that they borrowed from some friend of Rossi's. The week before, I had a meeting with the Browns' people and told them I was going to see Lamar and Rossi. The Browns said, "We want you to either sign with us now or not sign." I said, "I really can't do that 'cause on Sunday I promised I was going to meet with Lamar Hunt and Don Rossi." The Browns came out in the *San Francisco Chronicle* the day before Rossi and Lamar got there and said, "Browns Withdraw Offer to Burford." I talked with Lamar and Rossi a while, and they said, "What's it going to take to sign you?" And I said, "12,000." Then I said, "and a $2,000 advance." Not a bonus, an advance.

RON MIX: Since it was a start-up league, the league as a whole was more interested in signing top-tier players for the league identity even if it meant that your club may not get that player. The club that had your draft rights would cooperate. Coming out of Southern Cal, I had been the number one draft choice of the Baltimore Colts and had been a draft choice for Boston. Don Klosterman of the Los Angeles Chargers asked me what I was going to be doing. I said, "If I have to go back East, I'm definitely going to the Colts." He said, "What if the Chargers can get your rights? Would you be interested in joining the league?" I said I would, and the next thing I knew the Chargers had my rights. The Colts' initial offer was a $1,000 bonus and a $7,500 salary. The Chargers offered a two-year guaranteed contract at $12,000 each year plus a $5,000 bonus. I told Don Keller of the Colts that I would prefer to play in the NFL if they would give me a $2,000 bonus and a $10,000 contract. He said, "Ron, that would totally disrupt our salary structure. That is more money than most of the veterans are making. To tell you the truth, we think this league is going to fold after one year. Then we'll get you with a year's experience, and it'll all work out."

There's another funny story about all this. My dad came over from Russia by himself at age 13. The family name was a Russian-Jewish name—Rubinewicz. He went to work on a farm in Georgia. He took the name of the family that owned the farm—Mix. Several years later, I was told that Carroll Rosenbloom, the owner of the Colts then, remarked, "My God. If I'd have known Mix was Jewish, I'd have signed him." They had a big Jewish population. If my father hadn't taken that family's name, I'd have been a Baltimore Colt.

JIM OTTO: I graduated from the University of Miami in the spring of '60. I didn't get drafted by the NFL. One morning in the student union, someone said that I'd been drafted by the American Football League's Minnesota franchise. "Oh, wow!" I said. Our coaches had told me they'd get me a tryout with somebody in the NFL, which they never did. So the only choice I had was the American Football League. When Minnesota dropped the franchise, the rest of the teams picked up their draft picks. I signed with the Houston Oilers. And when Oakland took over the franchise, the rest of the teams gave back only what they wanted to give back. About a week after I signed, I was property of the Raiders.

LARRY GARRON: Chicago, Cleveland, Philadelphia, and Green Bay had sent me letters. We had just won the conference championship at Western Illinois for the second time, and then Lou Saban left us to sign with the Patriots. I was from Chicago and, when I was home, would work out with George Blanda. It would have been good to play for Chicago because I knew all the guys. I talked with Vince Lombardi. He sent down an IQ test. He said, "We're not ready for a black quarterback, but you can play defensive back." I signed with Lou in Boston and became a running back.

The Denver Broncos' camp was as humble as any, set up just west of the city at Colorado School of Mines. But what would set apart this team from the other struggling AFL operations wasn't so much the quality of the players in the uniforms as it was the uniforms themselves. They had to be seen to be believed.

BOB HOWSAM: Dean Griffing, our general manager, said, "I can get all-but-new uniforms." Then he asked me about the socks. I said, "We want good equipment for our people."

FRANK TRIPUCKA: We had the lousiest-looking uniforms—yellow shirts and brown pants with vertical-striped socks, bought from some All-Star game that went broke. They didn't fit. I used to cut the armpits of them so I could raise my arm to pass. And those socks!

GOOSE GONSOULIN: Those ugly striped socks made you look like you were a spike in the ground.

ELDON DANENHAUER: They were probably *the* cheapest, ugliest uniforms that you could imagine. The thing that made it so cheap, there wasn't any stretch material at all. Some players' calves were so big, they couldn't get the socks on. I had to sweat to get mine on. We had a fullback named Dave Rolle out of Oklahoma, had great big calves. He had to actually cut the back of [the socks] just to get 'em on. Then he had to tape 'em vertically to match the stripe on the sock.

DALE DODRILL: To me, the striped socks . . . if you had that kind of publicity thing going for you today, they'd blow it out of proportion. Back then, they ridiculed it. We were in Plainfield, New Jersey, between games on the East Coast early that first season when one of the players went to Frank Filchock and said, "We need a meeting. The players are going to revolt. They've had so much ridicule with these socks, they won't play again." Two hours later, Filchock sort of read 'em the riot act. Any of them that wanted to leave could, right then. Their feeling against the socks wasn't so great that they would walk out. None of 'em got up and left.

AL WARD: In league meetings, they would talk to Bob Howsam about the socks. The owners would get on him, and he wouldn't change the socks. I would take the owners out to meet the press. The first thing they asked Howsam was, "How 'bout those stupid socks?" And his answer was—this was the guy who later became the genius behind the Cincinnati Reds in the 1970s—"See? You wouldn't have asked about those if they weren't interesting. We're not gonna take 'em off."

BOB HOWSAM: I said, "At least they'll have people talking, so go ahead." And, you know what people remember about the Denver Broncos football team that first year? The socks. They're still talking about them.

3

The Curtain Rises

The AFL's first season began in Boston only by happenstance, only by what the league couldn't do in its infancy. Games were scheduled for the opening weekend in Boston, Los Angeles, Oakland, and New York. The Patriots chose to play all of their home games that season on Friday nights to avoid competing with college and NFL games, so their September 9 date with the Denver Broncos—funny socks and all—became by default the first AFL game. The Los Angeles Chargers opened at home at the Coliseum the next night against the Dallas Texans. The only games scheduled for the traditional Sunday afternoon kickoff were Buffalo at New York and Houston at Oakland.

JOANNE PARKER: I joined the Patriots in 1960 as one of the secretaries after graduating from the Katherine Gibbs School in Boston. I had actually been accepted to go work for the CIA, but I always wanted to be in sports. The general manager, Ed McKeever, asked me to come in and interview. I really didn't think I was going to get the job because one of the questions was to identify where all the 11 offensive positions were. I didn't know which ones were the guards and tackles. The office was right in Boston, 522 Commonwealth Avenue. Our total square footage was 500 square feet. When I started, there was one other girl who was working for Ed McKeever. I was basically working for everybody else. All the coaches. Two P.R. people. The ticket manager. We had 10 owners, and Billy Sullivan was elected president. Dom DiMaggio and all of them were in and out of that office. Dean Boylan was president of Boston Sand and Gravel. Billy Sullivan's uncle, Joe Sullivan, was in the printing business. Dean Marr Sr. was in the scaffolding business.

Billy was a wonderful man. I thoroughly enjoyed working for him. He lived west of Boston in Wellesley and was also president of Metropolitan Oil and Gas in downtown Boston. When he drove from Wellesley, he came right by the Patriots' office. He'd often come in and say, "I've got a lot of dictation I need to give to you. You've got to get in the car." And he'd dictate. Back then, there were no Dictaphones. Of course, I knew shorthand. He would dictate all the way down. I would sometimes spend two hours in his office, then I would take the subway up to Kenmore Square, a half block from our office, and transcribe all the letters in addition to typing public relations releases and contracts for players. As we would get into the summer and our season-ticket sales, the ticket manager and I—after regular business hours— would go up to Boston University field house and manually chart our season-ticket holders on huge poster boards. We did that two, three, maybe four nights a week. But I loved it.

LOU SABAN: We had played the Broncos in a preseason game and did a pretty good job on them, 43–6. Then we played our last preseason game at home against the Oakland Raiders. It was a bloodbath. The coach was a fellow from Navy, Eddie Erdelatz. I told him, "We've got to stop this mess! We're not going to have enough players to start the season!"

WILL McDONOUGH: The Patriots were established as a pretty good favorite over the Broncos coming up to that opening game. Now, the Broncos stayed at the old Kenmore, where you could take a streetcar right inside Braves Field. They practiced at about 5:00 the day before the game. And when they got through, the Patriots came out on the field. Frank Filchock, the coach of the Broncos, was one of the last guys out of the locker room. The field was lower than the street, so you walked up at an angle to get out to Commonwealth Avenue. The lights were on. The Patriots were on the field practicing, and the gate was open. So Filchock walked in and stood up in the back. Normally, the practice the day before the game is nothing. But Lou Saban, very nervous guy, very hyper, decided he was going to have a full practice. They didn't hit anybody, but they ran every offensive play they were going to run, every defensive play. Filchock stood up there and watched all this stuff and went back and had a team meeting.

That morning's *Boston Globe* featured a story about the upcoming game by Clif Keane, who asked, "Is top professional football here for the third and last time or for a third and lasting time?" The Patriots spent $325,000 renovating the park. Before kickoff, Broncos quarterback Frank Tripucka complimented Boston owner Billy Sullivan on the condition of the field: "I haven't seen grass like this since I left Canada." And with good reason. The grass had been imported from Canada.

A crowd announced at 21,597 occupied the old ballpark, which could seat about 24,000. The Patriots won the toss and kicked off, which made Boston kicker Tony Discenzo the man who actually began AFL play. As if predestined to establish the AFL's reputation for razzle-dazzle play, the Broncos' Bob McNamara handed off to Al Carmichael on a reverse. Gino Cappelletti accounted for the league's first points on a 34-yard field goal. Playing for the high-strung Saban, Cappelletti set up for the kick wondering whether a miss would result in immediate benching and a postgame pink slip. Denver's Carmichael scored the first AFL touchdown, transforming what initially looked like a harmless pass out in the flat into a 59-yard score. Denver's Gene Mingo, playing in the backfield only because of a first-quarter injury to McNamara, displayed his prowess as a runner to lead the Broncos to what proved to be the winning scoring drive. Tripucka, the retread from Canada, completed 10 of 15 passes for 190 yards, 120 of those to Carmichael. Because of the Patriots' unwillingness to buck college football that Saturday and a New York Giants local telecast on Sunday, the Denver Broncos were the first undefeated team in AFL history, thanks to a 13–10 triumph.

Next on tap for the infant league was the first game for the founder's own franchise, the Dallas Texans, with a Saturday night date in the league's largest facility against the Los Angeles Chargers.

BOB HALFORD: We had the first telecast of an American League game. The AFL had a contract with ABC, but that was for Sunday games. Our game was a Saturday game at the Coliseum, and Lamar spent $10,000—which was a whole lot of money at that time—to broadcast our game with the Chargers back to Dallas. Charlie Jones was the announcer, and a guy named Fred Benes who played for SMU was the color man. The producer was Roone Arledge. We went up against the Miss America contest, which meant nobody watched. But enough people watched to tell Fred Benes how bad he was.

HANK STRAM: We were beating the hell out of the Chargers at halftime. I was going back to the locker room, and Lamar was coming down from the press box. I thought he'd be tickled to death that we were winning. He said, "Oh, man. This is going to hurt the league. It's going to hurt this franchise." I said, "Lamar, are you kidding me? Don't worry about all that other stuff. Let's worry about winning the game." The Chargers came back, and we lost, 21–20.

And so, following a weekend in which an owner was concerned that his team would look too good, the AFL began its quest to establish a foothold in the American sports consciousness. From the largest markets where the NFL had long been established like New York and Los Angeles to locales that weren't recognized as major league towns like Buffalo, Denver, and Oakland, the league settled in for what could at best be a long, bumpy ride toward respectability.

VAN MILLER: The Bills' first regular-season game was against the Titans at the Polo Grounds. My broadcast vantage point was in the baseball press box behind the goal post in the end zone. I could see out to about the 20-yard line. Beyond that, I didn't have a clue. I watched the chain gang on the sidelines and could see how far the guy with the down marker moved up from the start of the play. The Bills lost, 27–2, and I think every point was scored at the far end of the field. The next year, they put us up around midfield, but it was in the baseball scoreboard where they used to have handheld numbers. We looked through the holes.

LARRY GRANTHAM: The Polo Grounds was impressive to a kid like me from the South. I'd seen Willie Mays play there, that famous catch over his head in deep center. But it really wasn't a good place to play football by the time we got there. There were rats in the locker room. What made it worse was Harry Wismer would announce 19,800 over the PA system. We'd look up in the stands, and our wives were sitting with their own personal hot dog vendors.

FRANK TRIPUCKA: You went to take a shower at the Polo Grounds, and the damn water would overflow all over the locker room. Most of the league was a ragtag operation. We played at Bears Stadium but couldn't get in there until the baseball season was over. The first three games we would play on the road against the Titans, Boston, and Buffalo. That way they saved money instead of flying back to Denver.

It was on the Broncos' first cozy East Coast stay-over that they practically stumbled upon a player who would become one of their mainstays for years to come. The club was working out at its home away from home in Plainfield, New Jersey, when a recent camp cut of the Chicago Bears caught up with them.

LIONEL TAYLOR: I was a free agent coming out of a small school, New Mexico Highlands. My college coach got me a tryout with the Bears, as a linebacker and defensive back, and they found out very quickly that I didn't play defense. I got released just before exhibition season and went out to California to play semipro ball in a league with Jack Kemp and Tom Flores. I played for the Bakersfield Spoilers. You had to have another job or you'd starve to death, so I worked construction. After each ballgame, I would take the write-ups and mail them to George Halas. I would never put my name on them. I'd write, "Look at the mistake you made. Here's a guy you let go." One time, I'd print sideways, another time a different way. George Halas called me about coming back, and I said, "Only if I can play wide receiver." I played 10 games for the Bears as a starter. Well, I was on the kickoff and kickoff-return teams, so I jokingly call myself a starter. They were going to do the same thing with me in 1960, and George Halas said, "Why don't you go home and visit." I figured I'd take a look at the new league, make a name for myself, come back to the National Football League. Dean Griffing, the general manager of the Broncos, was running the Tucson Rattlers when I played semipro ball and asked me to come try out with the Broncos while they were in New Jersey on their first road trip.

FRANK TRIPUCKA: Here was this guy at practice grabbing the ball with one hand. They stopped practice, and somebody said to him, "Can you do that all the time?" "Oh, yeah. No problem."

LIONEL TAYLOR: I signed an hour or two before the game because I was arguing over money. Frank and I didn't even know each other's names. In the huddle, I told him I could run a down-and-in pattern, and he didn't say anything. The next series, he said, "Hey, you. Can you run the post pattern?" And he hit me for a touchdown.

FRANK TRIPUCKA: I had to draw the plays on the dirt in the Polo Grounds to show him where to go.

LIONEL TAYLOR: And after the game, we got our per diem money. It was two dollars. Two one-dollar bills, for New York. I couldn't believe it. I still had some money from the Bears, so I was loaded.

Two teams appeared to have done the best job of collecting talent, the Houston Oilers in the East and the Los Angeles Chargers in the West. The Oilers, if nothing else, began the season boasting two of the most recognizable names on AFL rosters. There was Cannon, the immediately golden boy of the league coming off his Heisman-winning season at LSU. And the Houston quarterback was George Blanda, a veteran of NFL wars who was returning to football following a year's retirement.

BUD ADAMS: John Breen, our general manager, was responsible for signing George Blanda. John was from Chicago, and he knew that Blanda was working for a trucking line up there. Halas had cut him because he had Ed Brown at quarterback, but he didn't want Blanda playing against him. He was paying him $9,000 out of the Bears' pocket on top of the salary where he was, so he was paying him about $16,000. John said, "This guy can do the job. If Halas didn't have Brown in there, he'd have Blanda." We talked to Blanda about coming in and signed him for $18,000 'cause he wanted to get back into football. So we had the quarterback and were getting the running back, Billy Cannon.

JIM NORTON: George was brilliant at signal calling, audibling, one of the best passers of all time. The only thing was, he wasn't going to run out of the pocket. But as far as pure pocket passers, I don't know of anyone who was better. And God help you if you didn't block for him. You never heard the end of it, and he'd do it right on the field. Scream at you. Throw the ball at you. If you didn't run a pattern right or if a receiver didn't block for him, he didn't throw to the receiver anymore.

BUD ADAMS: Cannon was kind of a strange guy, kind of a Dr. Jekyll and Mr. Hyde. I really thought he was just a jock. Then my wife's dentist came home one time from the dental board at the University of Tennessee and told my wife, "Tell Bud he'll be pleased to know one of the top two students that graduated from the Tennessee dental school was Billy Cannon." He was going up there and going to school on the quarter system, never said anything about it. Set up a dental practice and was actually an oral surgeon.

JIM NORTON: Cannon was a smart-ass, just arrogant. But in our ways, we were all like that. He was a great athlete. I don't think he ever ran to his potential. They had guys like Dave Smith who did a better job than Cannon. He just didn't give the effort. But coming out of the backfield on a pass coming down the middle of the field, I've never seen anybody with that kind of explosive speed. I came to camp with the Oilers after getting cut by Detroit. I went back to a little town where my wife's folks lived called Kettle Falls, Washington. Dallas owned my AFL rights but only wanted to bring me in for a tryout for a day, and I wasn't going to do that. I got them to give me my release, and I started calling around. Got the Oilers' answering machine. It was Mary Kay Ashmore. John Breen called me back, and I had two practices to make the team. I had the flu, and I could barely get through. They had Billy Cannon, and I thought, "Lou Rymkus is from the old school. He's gotta hate Cannon because he's making more money than he is. I'm gonna bust the hell out of Cannon." We were in a semiscrimmage, and they tossed the ball out to Cannon. I came up and forearmed him. Now, I'd only been there since the morning. Cannon came back, threw the ball at me, and said, "What the hell are you doing? Who are you?" "I'm here to play ball with this team!" Everybody was standing around. I figured that would make an impression. I was throwing up after practice, the last one in the cafeteria line. Rymkus came over—I thought he was going to cut me—and said, "Jim, you look like shit. Go back to the training room and get well. I want you to get over that stuff. I think you can play for our football team."

CHARLIE HENNIGAN: During training camp, when there were about 200 people out there and the team was going to keep only 33, George and Billy Cannon used to say, "Oh, Lord. Just let this team fold where we can go get our money and go home." Their approach was a lot different from mine. I just wanted to make the team. I had been out of school in northwestern Louisiana for a couple of years, gone to play in Canada, been cut, and taught biology in Jonesboro, Louisiana. I wanted to play ball so bad that I almost didn't make it because I couldn't catch the ball. The middle of the first season, we went out to play the Chargers and a guy I knew named John Carson, who played for the Redskins before tearing up an Achilles tendon, came to see me at the Hilton. He said, "Hoss, you've forgotten how to believe." He gave me the book *The Power of Positive Thinking* and a football and said, "Now, read this book. You could catch when you came to this team, so you can still catch." The next year, I had a year that no pro receiver had ever had before. I was the first player to gain more than 1,500 yards in a season—did that in 12 games—and gained 1,746 yards in the full season. I did it not because I was that good but because I had the mental frame of mind.

At the helm of the Oilers was Lou Rymkus, with 17 years' experience in pro ball as a player and coach. His pedigree was discipline and conditioning, first molded as an All-American at Notre Dame in the early 1940s and further honed as part of Paul Brown's amazing run of Cleveland champions in both the All-American Conference and the NFL.

HOGAN WHARTON: He was a killer, but he was a player's coach. He'd kill you, but if you got in a jam he'd come get you. But you knew you were going to die for it. He was one of the first guys to tell me, "You don't have to like the son of a bitch to work with him." He never let personalities get in the way. I always liked Lou for that.

BUD ADAMS: Actually, the first coach I went for was Tom Landry when he was still an assistant coach with the New York Giants. I went up and met him at a hotel. He was so nervous, kind of a shy guy anyway. He said, "I can't be seen with you." I said, "Well, you can come up to my room." I was also talking to some players on that trip, and one of them knocked at the door when I was talking to Landry. He said, "Oh, what do you want me to do?" I said, "Well, get in the closet, and I'll get rid of him." I thought I was going to get him. His wife was from Dallas, and her dad had an insurance company. I think his wife wanted to live in Dallas, and there was the opportunity when Clint Murchison talked to him about being coach of the Cowboys.

In Los Angeles, the Chargers went for a veteran with NFL head coaching experience—and landed one who also owned a lay of the land. Sid Gillman was recently relieved of the head coaching duties of the L.A. Rams following five seasons. His first Rams club played for the NFL championship, but he could produce only one more winning record before being shown the exit.

BOB OATES: I was at the office one day when Barron Hilton called up and wondered if I had any recommendations for a coach. I told him, "Sid Gillman is as good a coach as you could have, at least to start out with." And he went along with that.

SID GILLMAN: I thought maybe I'd sell stocks back in New York. Frank Leahy was looking for a coach for the Chargers, and he figured I wouldn't be too shabby. I met Barron upstairs at the Hilton Hotel. He didn't know anything about football. That's the type of owner you want to have.

BARRON HILTON: I had an understanding with Sid Gillman. He wasn't going to tell me how to run the hotel business, and I wasn't going to tell him how to run the football club. And that arrangement worked out just fine. He was really a professor when it came to football.

SID GILLMAN: Coaching had always been my number one interest. And anytime I could grab onto a film and learn something, I'd grab it. My folks owned theaters in Minneapolis. In those days, there were all the newsreels. I was working at the theater and thought it was a great idea to pull those shots out. The best shots came out of football newsreels. So I thought of the idea of grabbing onto the football films. The girls that used to rewind them would cut 'em out and make sure I got 'em, which was totally illegal. On our honeymoon, I stopped at a pawnshop and bought a 35-millimeter projector for, I think, $15.

Gillman loaded his projector and built an offense around the running of Oregon State's Paul Lowe and the passing of a reclamation project cut by the

NFL, Jack Kemp. He led Los Angeles to eight wins in its final nine games, including two performances of more than 50 points.

JACK KEMP: Sid was a bona fide Hall of Fame coach even in 1960. Look at the coaching staff he had: Chuck Noll, Jack Faulkner, Al Davis, and Joe Madro. Sid was a genius at organizing a team and a game plan. One night at camp at the University of California–San Diego, I was hustling to meet my wife and our youngest son, Jeff, to go home for a Saturday night. I walked by his apartment and Sid whistled at me from in the shower: "Kemp, is that you?" He ran out with a towel around him and said, "I just thought of a great idea." He drew a play, and darned if it worked.

Al Davis was a brilliant end coach. He turned out to be a brilliant offensive coach as well. Al taught our ends how to run the best comeback patterns in pro football. I could have completed those in the dark, in my sleep. We lived off those. They weren't invented by Al Davis, but he perfected the passing game. And not many coaches in those days were throwing from their own zone as heavily as we did.

RON MIX: Sid was really a very interesting guy to play for. I don't think there's any argument about him being the father of the passing game. Lately, they talk about Don Coryell, about Bill Walsh, but it started with Sid. He also, at a time when many teams in the AFL were pinching pennies, saw to it with Barron Hilton that everything about the Chargers was first class. From training camp to the food we ate, method of travel, uniforms, hotels we stayed at. And he demanded punctuality. You paid attention in meetings, and he demanded that you worked hard. He probably intimidated everybody. Things were a little different then. The players were brought up in an era in which you accorded coaches full respect. Whether it was accurate or not, people were concerned about keeping jobs, no matter how good they were. It was kind of a nice life, and you wanted to maintain it, so you wanted to keep your boss happy.

DAVE KOCOUREK: One time Sid was sitting on the couch in his office when I came in. He kind of started talking to me and started to relax a little on the couch. He talked a little bit more and relaxed a little more. Two minutes later, he was snoring. So I just left. I wrote him a note: "Nice talking to you." I never thought of it as a snub. I just thought he was working too hard.

AL LOCASALE: In 1959, Al Davis and I were on the staff of the University of Southern California. Al was the defense. I was the administrative assistant to the head coach. We knew Sid Gillman because he was the coach of the Rams and we shared the stadium with them. Al was named to the coaching staff, recommended me, and I became assistant director of player personnel, assistant to Don Klosterman. As a coaching staff, there would be some marvelous arguments because they were all intelligent football people. They all had great ability to work for the common goal, which in those days was twofold. You had to win, but you had to help establish the product.

I've never seen anyone who spent that many hours with game film and loved it as Sid did. In the off-season, Sid would be up in our offices, which early on were in a hotel. He might be down to his underwear, sitting there with his pipe, looking at film. Every once in a while at 11:00, 12:00 at night, he'd start to go down to one of the restaurant kitchens. And he'd realize, "Whoops. I'd better put some clothes on." If Sid saw new ideas, he would almost bang his head against the wall and say, "How could I not have realized this for the last 15 years?" He was not locked to his way as the only way. He and Al were like sponges, absorbing football.

DAVE KOCOUREK: Al Davis was end coach with the Chargers, a very instrumental part of my career. He was so exacting. "Put your foot here. You're three inches too far this way. You've got to do it this way." He taught me a lot of discipline.

GOOSE GONSOULIN: We were playing the Chargers on the road, and I intercepted a pass or two. Afterward in the dressing room, this guy walked up to me and said, "Good game." He had a little notepad in his hand. And he said, "Tell you what, what's the hardest play for you to cover?" And he handed me a piece of chalk. So I went over to a blackboard, and I thought, "God, this is weird." So I drew an easy play for me to cover, turned around, and said, "It's this option play right here because this happens, this happens." He said, "Oh. OK. Good." And he was writing on his little pad. I thought he was a sportswriter. So Dean Griffing, our general manager, came over and said, "Al, get your ass out of the room." It was Al Davis.

The AFL's first championship game, played on New Year's Day 1961, afforded a glamour matchup of Gillman's glitzy offense and Houston's determined defense, meeting at the renovated high school field in Houston called Jeppensen Stadium. If commissioner Joe Foss ordered a seesaw battle to maintain interest throughout, the teams complied. They traded the lead back and forth, neither building a margin of greater than a touchdown. The Oilers led 17–16 in the fourth quarter when Blanda and Cannon hooked up on an 88-yard touchdown pass that put the game away, to the delight of most of the 32,183 in attendance. It was Houston that dominated the aerial assault, Blanda passing for 301 yards while Kemp's 21-for-41 performance was good for 171 yards.

JIM NORTON: Lou Rymkus had been an assistant with the Rams, and he hated Gillman. That was his motivation. Anytime we played the Chargers, it was called "Charger Week." And all he would talk about was killing Gillman. Everybody would say, "Is this guy for real? Does he really hate Gillman, or is this a show?"

Known to only a few at the time, even as the Oilers were posing for celebration pictures and the Chargers were begrudgingly accepting polite praise for a successful season, the AFL was about to raise its first white flag, the first crack in the ship's bow. After only a single season, one owner came to the sobering conclusion that his team could not continue to operate even one more year under the same conditions.

BARRON HILTON: Toward the end of the first season, I made the decision that we'd have to move out of the Coliseum, out of Los Angeles. We were having a problem in having sufficient crowds to be able to cover our costs to some degree.

AL LoCASALE: It was tough selling football in the L.A. market. The *Los Angeles Times* had a very strong relationship with the Rams. They sponsored the Rams Charity Game. The *Herald-Examiner*, the competition, which was considerably smaller, got involved in sponsoring a charity game involving the Chargers. You were sitting there with that huge stadium, 100,000, and you draw 300,000 for the season. As Sid once said, it looked like they ought to take the players and, instead of introducing them as they run onto the field, send them up in the stand and shake hands with the fans. You had the other team in the other league, with NFL commissioner Pete Rozelle—that was his home base. They were very, very entrenched. We were very much the "other" league. We were flying to Houston for the first championship game, and the plane stopped in San Diego to pick up some of the San Diego press. That's the first time I had a feeling that we were going to end up in San Diego. I couldn't figure out any other reason why we were doing that.

Bob Oates: If the Chargers had stayed in Los Angeles, they would have probably done at least as well as the Rams. Back in the late '40s, there was an All-American Conference team in L.A. called the Dons. They got more public acceptance every year. The last year they were in Los Angeles, the year they folded, they were conspicuously more popular than the Rams. The difference with the AFL in Los Angeles was the National League was better everywhere else, but it wasn't really better in L.A. To this day, Los Angeles seems to be the least interested in the NFL of all the big towns.

Barron Hilton: Jack Murphy, the sports editor in San Diego, went when we played Houston for the championship. At that time, I think Anaheim perhaps wanted us to consider that location, but I didn't think about Anaheim as a viable city to go then. I thought San Diego would be the best place for us to go, and I don't have any regrets to this day. They gave us a home when we needed one.

Jerry Magee: I was covering pro football at the *San Diego Union* at the time. Balboa Stadium was built as a WPA project and had just one level. In order to assure that the Chargers would come, the city voted to put on a second deck. The Chargers were an instant hit from the beginning. They came into a town that had kind of been in the doldrums following World War II. The town was looking for a catalyst, something to rally the folks. The Chargers were fun to watch. They could strike. They had good players and good schemes. I think they won their first 12 games in 1961. That'll help.

And, surprisingly, the waters had become much more muddied for the champion Oilers, almost from the moment that they vacated Jeppesen Stadium's champagne-stained home locker room. It seemed to begin with a simple, almost overlooked aspect of a title team—the championship ring.

Jim Norton: Because the television money wasn't much, the check for winning the championship was like $1,500, not much. Bud Adams said if we won the championship, he would double our game salary and give us championship rings. So Lou got up in front of the team before the game and said, "Now, Mr. Adams has promised this . . ." And I'm sure he did, or Lou wouldn't have said that. Lou was just as solid as a rock. And he was excited about that. After about two months, I thought, "What about those rings and that extra check?" Well, it never came. Lou apparently finally confronted Adams on that. Lou told me later that he said, "You get me up, make a fool out of myself, promise something like that, and don't follow through on it." And Bud just said, "I'm just not going to get 'em." Just flat out said he wasn't going to do it.

BUD ADAMS: I decided that the next year, the team would have training camp in Hawaii, a nice reward for winning the championship. And [we] set up two games out there, against Oakland and San Diego. It wasn't the best decision to make. I forgot about all those girls on the beaches.

JIM NORTON: So Lou getting into a hassle with Bud over those rings and checks was the first round. The second round was going to Hawaii. Lou said, "Bud, this is the worst thing we can do."

The arrangement called for the Oilers to stop in San Diego for an exhibition game, then head to Honolulu for two weeks, playing host to the Raiders and the Chargers. It quickly turned into paradise lost. Adams didn't do himself any favors with the rest of the team by checking in at the surfside Hawaiian Village Hotel while the rest of the club's players and staff were nestled in at the Hickam Field bachelor officers' quarters. Almost from the start, episodes occurred that made the camp more like a Chevy Chase "vacation" movie. There was the curious case of the four players who hitchhiked back from downtown Honolulu one night and were picked up by two sailors. The driver, having apparently imbibed more than he should have, passed out at the wheel. The car jumped a curb on a curve and came to rest about 50 feet from the road in a 15-foot-deep tidewater canal. Though none of the four players would survive cut-down day during camp, they displayed a degree of desperate resourcefulness to escape the vehicle as water rose all around it.

AL JAMISON: The trip was a fiasco. Everybody was playing and partying and just raising hell. As soon as the coaches made bed check, the coaches would go out one door and the players would go out the other. That was my first year as captain, and I never broke training. So I called a meeting and said, "Look, you guys are fucking with my paycheck. I'm going to do two things. The next guy that breaks curfew, I'm gonna whup your ass. And I'm gonna turn you in to Lou." Billy Cannon said, "OK, I won't go out after curfew if you'll wear this badge." So for the rest of the week, I wore a badge that said, "I'm a prick."

The team arrived in the islands already smarting from a 27–14 loss to the Chargers in the first AFL game played at San Diego's Balboa Stadium, which was being hastily renovated and expanded for the coming season. All must have been forgiven, though, when Houston's first Hawaiian date produced a 35–17 victory over Oakland, because Rymkus elected to give the players the next two days off. Just what they needed—more free time. At least part of the scorecard from the bonus rest and relaxation consisted of one player over-turning a motorcycle; one player suffering a sprained ankle as a result of a second-floor leap from a hotel room to escape the inhabitant's less-than-understanding husband; and trainer Bobby Brown's noticing a player one morning trying to make what must have been a grievously tardy phone call to his wife—through a coat hanger. Rymkus tried to get in the spirit of things by charging drinks at the Hawaiian Village for fans and friends—to a tab that he signed in the name of general manager Don Suman. It was soon determined that Suman wasn't the source of the signature because his name was misspelled.

When the Chargers came west for their second meeting with the Oilers in two weeks, they brought some new friends. Since the clubs' meeting in San Diego, three rookies joined the Chargers after playing in the College All-Star Game against the NFL champion Philadelphia Eagles—defensive linemen Ernie Ladd and Earl Faison and running back Keith Lincoln. The new-look Chargers wasted little time continuing to deliver misery to the Oilers. Their lead at the half was 39–0.

AL JAMISON: We were going in the dressing room at halftime. Hogan Wharton turned around to me, not seeing Lou, and said, "Close the door. The Chargers can't get us in here."

The Oilers managed to make the final score look respectable, losing 42–28. But just when it appeared this holiday-turned-horror couldn't get any worse,

Adams announced to reporters his intention to take his team on an even longer trip for camp in 1962—to Madrid, Spain. Rymkus offered a terse comment, calling the Hawaii sojourn a three-ring circus and lodging his early vote against such a European excursion.

The soap opera was really just beginning for the '61 Oilers. They opened at home against the Raiders and rewarded all of about 16,000 fans with a resounding 55–0 victory. But Houston lost its next three games, beginning with a 34–24 loss at San Diego in the teams' third meeting in less than two months. But the next two losses, including at home to a marginal Buffalo team, incredibly resulted in the league's defending champion coach fighting for his job.

MICKEY HERSKOWITZ: They were going to Boston, and the headlines in all the Houston papers said, "Rymkus Out if Oilers Don't Win." I guess that was pretty much the line out of the front office. For the game, Rymkus benched George Blanda and Billy Cannon and three or four of his starters. Rymkus, a Notre Dame guy under Frank Leahy, was always of the mind that some sort of psychological stroke like that could turn a team around. All it did, of course, was piss those guys off. Jacky Lee stepped in at quarterback and had a great game, broke the AFL record for yards in a game with over 400. Blanda was on the bench the whole game. They did put in Cannon and some of the others. With five seconds to play, they needed a 24-yard field goal to tie the game. It was kind of a nasty night in Boston. Conditions were wet and slippery. It wasn't going to be an easy kick, so they sent in Blanda. In the huddle, Billy Cannon whispered to him, "Miss it." They wanted Rymkus's ass out of there. And Blanda said to me years later that it crossed his mind. But he said going back to junior high school, he had never missed a kick when a game was on the line. He made the kick, and they ended up tying. The tie wasn't good enough. Adams fired Lou anyway.

BUD ADAMS: I went in after the game and said, "I'm gonna make a change." And I said I was going bring back Wally Lemm as head coach. Lou was getting outcoached. He was kind of a gung ho . . . hell, he'd tell 'em in so many words. He used the four-letter word quite a bit. The teams we were playing hadn't changed that much, either. Actually, we made some additions that second year. And I thought Wally Lemm was an excellent defensive coach.

He didn't have a whole lot to say about it because Lou was trying to run the thing his way.

The AFL scorecard less than two months into the second season: the defending champions' coach didn't get a ring, but he did get a pink slip. The runners-up still had the same coach, just not the same address. Rymkus's replacement, Wally Lemm, served as an assistant on the original Oilers coaching staff but then quit to return to private business back home in Illinois.

And Rymkus wasn't even the first coach fired that season. That inglorious distinction went to another Lou, the Boston Patriots' Lou Saban. He didn't win any supporters among the club's numerous owners in 1960 by guiding the club to a last-place finish in the Eastern Division at 5–9. With a 2–3 record five weeks into the following season, Lou Saban was about to lose his first pro coaching job . . . but certainly not his last.

LOU SABAN: The good Lord takes care of people who get wounded once in a while.

Saban decided while attending high school that coaching was a noble profession. Ironically, a man who would earn professional notoriety through his excessive mobility was drawn to the field by the stability displayed by his own high school coach, who declined to pursue promotions and said, "This is where I belong." And Saban learned early—at his first coaching stop, at Case Tech in Cleveland following a playing career with the AAFC Browns—that there often was wisdom in staying one step ahead of an unpredictable employer.

LOU SABAN: My job was to teach and accept what I had and make them better than what they were. After the third year, the president of Case Tech walked into my office about March and said, "What would you do if we dropped football?" I was stunned, said, "I'd have to get out of here, get myself another job." "Well, just what I expected from a football coach!" From there, I wanted to come back and bounced around quite a bit.

I then happened to take over a terrible program, Northwestern, that, like a lot of young fellas, I thought I could get turned around. One day, a guy that I knew from Cleveland came out to practice looking for a job. I'd known

George Steinbrenner from 1948, when he wanted to help out in an Olympics-type thing we had there. I put him in charge of track, and his people won all the medals and the ribbons. I asked him, "Where did you get these fellas?" He looked at me and said, "Never mind! We won, didn't we?" I figured he could do a good job of recruiting, could also do a good job of raising money, and he was the receivers coach. One time, George said to me, "You know, I'm going to own the New York Yankees." And I told him, "George, do you have a problem?"

I had a five-year handshake deal there. That handshake didn't last but four or five weeks before everything became turmoil. They hired Stu Hol-combe, and we played him in our last game. Our staff was to meet him at the Orrington Hotel in Evanston. He was about 30 minutes late. Walked in and said, "I'm sorry I'm late. I got hung up on a couple of details. But I just wanted to tell you, you're fired." Some of my coaching staff wasn't hired until August or September and hadn't yet unpacked. Well, about the same time George bought the Yankees, Stu Holcombe went with the Chicago White Sox. There was a vote on what the White Sox were going to do with their television deal. They got to George, and he said, "Do you remember who was the coach at Northwestern you replaced?" He said, "Lou Saban." "Did you know anybody on the staff?" Stu said, "No, I don't recall." George said, "You fired us that day. I was one of the members of that staff, and I vote no!"

While Saban wasn't concerned for his job a game under .500 in early October, he was bewildered and troubled that his offensive assistant, Mike Holovak, didn't report to practice on the rainy Tuesday after Boston's 38–27 loss to the undefeated Chargers.

LOU SABAN: I was quite concerned that Mike didn't show up for practice. He was also our personnel man. Finally, about 5:00, just as we were finishing our kicking game, out came Billy Sullivan. I said, "I knew there was something wrong. You got yourself a new coach. Is that what you did?" He said, "Yes, that's what we did." I said, "OK. Fine. Make sure I get the rest of my contract taken care of, and I'm outta here in three minutes." He said, "Don't you want to talk?" I said, "No. Mike Holovak got the job? This is the man I picked up off the deck to come along with us." I didn't even change. I was soaking wet. I told my staff, "Let's go home." We were driving just one car, the four of us. As I drove back to Lexington, not a word was said by the staff. I said, "Guys, good luck to you. Hope you finish out the season. You now have a good football team."

Mike Holovak's Patriots came out and settled for a last-minute tie with Houston, 31–31, in Lou Rymkus's final game before being yanked by Bud Adams. From that point through the rest of the season, each team was practically unbeatable. Boston went 7–1–1 under Holovak, losing only at Houston. Once Wally Lemm took over with the Oilers, the Eastern champs reeled off nine consecutive victories. The result was Houston's winning another division title, one game ahead of Boston in the final standings.

HOGAN WHARTON: I thought Wally Lemm was the best coach we ever had, and that covers some ground as far as good coaches. He had been on our staff the year before. Mac Speedie and Fred Wallner left the staff when Lou was fired to show an allegiance to him. We finished the '61 season with three coaches—Wally, Walt Schlinkman, and Joe Spencer. Wally handled the defense. Joe handled the defensive and offensive lines. Schlinkman handled the offense and the backfield. And I don't know if I ever worked for a better staff. Those three guys worked their asses off, and they had us prepared for every game.

JOE COLLIER: I don't want to knock Mike Holovak's accomplishment, but I think the same thing would have happened if they hadn't fired Lou Saban. Sometimes, it takes time. We would have had a good season.

MIKE HOLOVAK: There was only one way we could go. That was up. We had our share of luck.

The Oilers' run to the Eastern title included another meeting with the Chargers, at Jeppensen Stadium in early December, in which the visitors brought an 11–0 record to Houston. The Oilers, having lost to the Chargers three times to date that year in exhibition and regular-season play, picked a good time to make a statement. They dominated the Chargers 33–13 before a record home gathering of 37,854. They were prepared for another meeting in San Diego in a few weeks to decide another AFL crown . . . if they could just survive the season on and off the field.

HOGAN WHARTON: We were staying in San Diego getting ready to go to Hawaii, and we had a few beers after the game. We had a guy with us named Jack Davis who had wrestled professionally. He and I and Willard Dewveall got to horsing around. Some people at the hotel thought we were really fighting, called the police, and they sent two squad cars. We kept having a little fun, and they finally got us in the room. Then we started it over again right in front of 'em. They didn't try to break us up. They called the police again. They wound up with about 15 or 20 squad cars. Rymkus sure was hot when he got us the next day. Of course, we'd gotten beat by San Diego and he'd already taken on a load and passed out. I think what really did it was I fake punched Davis and he fell in the swimming pool with a suit and tie on. He did like a dead man's float. Dewveall said, "Well, why don't you go get him out of there." I said, "Oh, hell. Let him die."

AL JAMISON: One time we were flying over the Gulf of Mexico in those old DC6s and had to dump fuel. I told the pilot to make an announcement directed at our equipment manager, George Greene: "We've got to lighten our load. . . . Would George P. Greene please report to the center entrance door?" He didn't think that was funny at all. And we used to carpool to the airport, me and Bob Talamini and Hogan Wharton and one of the assistant coaches, Joe Spencer. Well, I signed for $8,500. I had this VW bug. We were severely overloaded. Because it was my car, I got to put my suitcase in the front bonnet. The guys in the back would have to put theirs in their laps. And the guy sitting up front on the passenger side would have to hold his out the window.

CHARLIE HENNIGAN: One time we played the Texans, and some state representative's wife spent the night going from room to room. The next day, it rained, the wind was blowing in our faces, and the Texans just killed us. Our coach, Lou Rymkus, was an old Cleveland Brown and a Notre Damer. He believed you paid the price, and you won. He found out about what happened the night before. So the day after the game, we were practicing in the old Houston Buffaloes baseball stadium. He called us all together in the stands and said, "If you lay together, you play together."

HOGAN WHARTON: There was a game where some asshole, Mel Branch of Dallas, knocked my nose off. Tore it away from my upper lip. The tight end and the tackle were double-teaming him. He spun out, and I was pulling, trying to clear the way. As he was rolling out of the block, he brought his elbow around and hit just right into the point of it. It was the only time I ever saw Blanda hesitate in the huddle. He looked up, and he looked at me again and said, "Shit!" We didn't have anymore guards. They were all hurt. I ran over to the sideline like I was going to leave. The trainer said, "Get your ass back out there. We don't have anymore."

The second championship game brought together two of football's most feared offensive attacks and produced only one scoring play in the first half. Turnovers, there were plenty of: fumble by San Diego, interception by San Diego, interception by Houston, fumble by San Diego, ball turned over by Houston on a botched fake field goal, interception by San Diego. But a play that was neither touchdown nor turnover proved to be the half's most memorable—except for one of the key participants.

JIM NORTON: Jack Kemp was one of the best running quarterbacks, and I noticed that he usually ran to the sidelines. We were laying back on a pass play in the second quarter, and he took off to the sideline. A defensive back hates that. I thought, "I'm just gonna hit this son of a bitch right at the vortex with everything I've got. I'm gonna tear his damn head off." I didn't think he was going to cut back because he never did, so I ran right at him. And he kind of turned up, trying to get an extra yard. I started running at him from about 15 yards away and hit him head-on, face-to-face. He broke a finger on his left hand, and I jammed my neck. I was really knocked. When the team went in at halftime, I was sitting on the bench. They were trying to figure out where I was. I finally walked in, and Bobby Brown, the trainer, said, "Where the hell have you been?" "Out on the field!" I had to go back in when Freddie Glick, my replacement, got hurt. And I was still punting. But it's like a dream when you're half unconscious like that. It seemed like I was floating.

Norton's hit on Kemp and Paul Maguire's subsequent shank punt set up a 46-yard field goal from Blanda. The Oilers extended their lead to 10–0 early in the third quarter when Blanda, flushed from the pocket, found Cannon on a 35-yard touchdown on which Cannon escaped from the grasp of San Diego's

Bud Whitehead around the San Diego 17-yard line. Early in the fourth quarter, the Chargers converted Charlie McNeil's interception deep in Houston territory into their first score, a 12-yard field goal by George Blair. The AFL's top rivals, barely separated by more than a touchdown throughout the league's first championship game, were in the same position throughout most of the title rematch.

JIM NORTON: With about a minute left, the Chargers were going to send Dave Kocourek down on an angle pattern to try to get the touchdown. He ran that, and I obviously got too close to him, which I normally wouldn't if I had my senses. I grabbed him, and he was towing me. He hit my arm and was screaming at the referee. The ball went over his head. They threw the flag. On the next play, Julian Spence intercepted the ball. That was the end of the game.

George Blanda, whose pro career began in 1949, capped a year in which he was unanimously named the AFL's player of the year by accounting for all 10 points scored by the Oilers in the championship game. He had thrown 3,330 yards and would have led the league in scoring were it not for the eight touchdown catches made by Boston receiver-kicker Gino Cappelletti. All that from a 34-year-old who had retired from football two years earlier.

MICKEY HERSKOWITZ: I think pride brought him back to football. Blanda quit the Bears because he just couldn't catch a break from Halas. They always had great quarterbacks there—Luckman and Lujack. He had a good job with a trucking company, but trucking isn't a very exciting business—driving, parking, or anything. He wanted the chance to prove Halas wrong.

AL JAMISON: George Blanda probably was the single most important factor in our winning those two championships. But he was very irascible. We don't exchange Christmas cards.

HOGAN WHARTON: It was all business with George. This guy was a coach on the field. Hell, he knew his assignment and your assignment and everybody else's assignment. He knew when somebody fucked up . . . and would tell you. "We're not out here fartin' around. You're supposed to do *this* on this formation, and you didn't do it. Get your head in the game." It never was where you wanted to quit on him. It was constructive criticism but still pretty stern. You knew you Goddamn didn't want to do it again.

BOB TALAMINI: We needed people who would kind of dress us down every once in a while, but sometimes George would go to the extreme. His whole shtick was, if he got tackled, he would stop practice and say, "OK, whose man was that?" Then curse the offensive lineman into going to confession. That got kind of old. Those guys were getting paid to knock him down, and you're getting paid not to let them knock him down. It's not always going to be a perfect play.

MICKEY HERSKOWITZ: George was definitely the leader of the team. He was a terrific personality. He had charisma. He was dynamic and forceful, but I don't think people saw a lot of that in Houston. He could rally players. One game, the Oilers were behind at home and he threw three touchdown passes to win the game. When he went in [at halftime], the fans booed, and at the end of the game they gave him a standing ovation. After the game, I waited until everybody cleared away from his locker, and then I went up to him. I didn't want to say "Congratulations" or anything corny. I just stood there smiling, happy for him, and then said, "Well, old man?" In the British sense. And Blanda looked up and said to me without a blink, "If you want to talk to me, knock off the 'old man' shit." The age issue had really gotten under his skin, and I didn't mean it that way.

JACKY LEE: George and I were roommates for three years. He was a chain smoker. He'd light one cigarette after another. We'd stay up to 11:30, 12:00, 1:00. He'd just tell me one joke after another. You could name a subject, and he could come up with eight or ten jokes. I think we liked each other. I liked him. I think he always kind of looked at me as the guy who was trying to take his job. His security wasn't all that good. There were factions on the team that supported him, some that supported me. I think he felt he had a bigger constituency. As it turned out, he ended up playing another 10 years after that.

4

Quarterback Reclamations

The date of Tuesday, September 25, 1962, isn't commonly recalled as one of the significant mileposts in AFL annals. Of course, no games were played that day. No multimillion-dollar contract was signed that day. No one decided that day to move a team to a better market. But a move was made that day that would ultimately turn around a team. And it began, simply enough, with a routine inspection of the AFL waiver wire.

JERRY MAGEE: The Chargers were playing the New York Titans, second game of the season. Jack Kemp was following through on a pass, and his hand struck the helmet of a defender. He severely damaged a finger. It was grotesque.

JACK KEMP: I severely dislocated the middle finger on my passing hand. There was some doubt whether I could ever throw a football again. The pressure from throwing a football comes heavily from that finger. I threw very, very hard and could throw far. I tried to gut it out and played the whole game with a finger that kept dislocating, flopping around. John Hadl, a promising rookie, was behind me, and I didn't want to give up my position very easily.

JOHN HADL: I was rooming with Jack Kemp. I first walked in our room, and he was lying on the bed reading a book on Barry Goldwater. He was working for him, actually. That was my initiation to pro football.

JACK KEMP: I put my hand on a football, and they put a cast over my finger. My finger fused in the shape of the football. I could not hold a football, much less throw one, for about eight weeks.

LARRY FELSER: There was no such thing as injured waivers then. If you had an injured player, you couldn't bring another player on your roster without dropping somebody.

AL LoCASALE: There was a gentlemen's agreement, an understanding among the coaches: if you're in an emergency situation and you've got to waive a guy on the weekend and you don't have a spot, nobody's going to claim him. You don't have to worry about recalling him. Then you cut somebody to make room, and you recall him. Jack said early in the week that he'd be OK. Turned out at the end of the week he couldn't handle the ball. So it was something we had to do over the weekend to make room for another quarterback.

The rookie Hadl started in Kemp's place and suffered rib damage as the Chargers were drilled by their old pals, the Oilers, 42–17. San Diego was prepared to turn to veteran Dick Wood awaiting the return of Hadl in the short term and Kemp in the long term, until . . .

LARRY FELSER: Lou Saban, coach of the Bills, got tipped because Jack Horrigan, who had covered the Bills for the *Buffalo News*, had been hired by commissioner Joe Foss as the P.R. guy for the league. Saban claimed Kemp off waivers for $100.

AL LoCASALE: Somebody said to Sid Gillman, "We ain't got no gentleman here."

JACK KEMP: I don't know if it was a gentlemen's agreement, but it was done enough so that they probably thought de facto there was an agreement. But three or four teams picked me up. Jack Faulkner in Denver, who had been with us, was interested. Al Davis told me it was perceived to be a mistake. I was quite disappointed originally because I loved San Diego, I had a beautiful home out in Point Loma, and I was the quarterback of the Chargers. I rested in the knowledge that the Raiders had tried to get me for Jim Otto and a draft choice and the Chargers turned that down. So, why would they have wanted to let me go for $100? Joe Foss told people that Buffalo asked first. He later told me that he just decided by fiat that he was going to send me to the Bills because they didn't have a quarterback and he wanted to balance out the league.

The Chargers staggered through eight losses in their remaining nine games after handing the starting position to young Hadl. The 4–10 finish would be the franchise's only losing season in AFL play. The door was opened for someone else to march off with the Western Division championship. Ironically, a fellow NFL castoff quarterback like Kemp took center stage in the Dallas Texans' ascension in the West. Len Dawson, who accomplished little in five seasons with Pittsburgh and Cleveland, was brought to the Texans primarily because Dallas coach Hank Stram had recruited him to play at Purdue in the mid-1950s.

HANK STRAM: I visited Lenny when he was with the Browns and was down in the dumps. I said, "How would you like to play for our football team?" He said, "Oh, I'd love to play, Coach." I said, "Tell Paul Brown that you'd like to be put on waivers. Then you'll become a free agent; we'll pick you up and bring you to Dallas." Paul called me and said, "I put Lenny Dawson on waivers today. I guarantee you nobody will pick him up." That's the kind of clout he had. And he added, "We're good friends, Coach. I want to make sure that you understand Lenny isn't the same Lenny that you had in college. His arm is not as strong. He's not a real student of the game. He doesn't have a good attitude." All those things were the opposite of what Lenny was really like.

FRANK JACKSON: Owners and coaches get a mind-set and stereotype players. Len had gotten a stereotype as a backup quarterback and having a soft arm. Hank, to his credit, had a better eye for talent than anyone I've ever seen. We had Cotton Davidson, who could throw a ball through a wall. Len came along and threw . . . not fluffy passes but firm passes. Pinpoint accuracy was his forte. He knew how to lead you away from trouble. Lenny came into camp and looked like a fugitive from a penal colony, like he was starved. Little ol' legs and arms. We thought he'd be broken in two on the first hit. He went out, and he could take a hit. He could scramble, could run. He came in and just took the job. Cotton went bye-bye.

With Dawson getting comfortable with Stram's offense and Hadl struggling with Gillman's, the balance of power in the AFL West shifted to Dallas. The Texans were unchallenged as they won the division title by four games over the surprising Broncos at 7–7. In the East, "Old Man" Blanda and the Oilers again edged Boston at the wire, clinching the title in the season's final weekend.

5

Kicking to the Clock

The AFL's first two owners, the men who hoped to form a rootin' tootin' Texas rivalry, saw that come to fruition in the third season of the young league. The two-time champion Oilers made it three Eastern Division titles under three coaches following an unusual "swap" at the top. Wally Lemm, undefeated upon his return to Houston taking over following the sacking of Lou Rymkus, skipped out on Bud Adams to coach the NFL's St. Louis Cardinals, closer to his Illinois home. So the Oilers promptly went out and hired the man whom Lemm replaced with the Cards, Pop Ivy. Houston outlasted Boston to win the division despite an offense in which quarterback George Blanda threw a whopping 42 interceptions.

The quarterback position was at the core of Dallas' rise to the top of the West. The Texans turned the offense over to Len Dawson, a quiet, calm presence who had floundered in five seasons with Pittsburgh and Cleveland in the NFL. At the same time, the two-time champion Chargers lost their starting quarterback Jack Kemp, first to a hand injury and then to the Buffalo Bills in a bizarre waiver transaction that San Diego had intended as a short-term technicality for stashing an injured player to free up a roster spot for one weekend.

LEN DAWSON: I had spent five years in the NFL with the Steelers and Browns and had started two games. Had never started and finished a game. Never played two games in a row. Hank Stram had recruited me out of high school to attend Purdue University, where he was then an assistant coach. When Hank became coach of the Dallas Texans, he told me to give him a call if I ever got free from the Browns. With Cleveland, the offense was Jim Brown, along with Bobby Mitchell. They had just made a quarterback trade, sent Milt Plum to Detroit for Jim Ninowski. I figured I wasn't going to get a shot. I asked for my release and surprisingly got it. And I signed on with the Texans.

Houston was favored by almost a touchdown when the division winners met at Jeppensen Stadium beneath an ominous cloud cover. The Texans' offense during the season featured one wide receiver, Chris Burford, and his 12 touchdown catches. But Burford was hurt late in the season, and Hank Stram decided to move versatile running back Abner Haynes out to flanker and bring veteran Jack Spikes off the bench to join rookie Curtis McClinton, the man who replaced Spikes, to spell Haynes as the second running back.

CHRIS BURFORD: During the season, we didn't have another wideout to complement, so we went to a double tight end and I played wideout on both sides. I was having a great year, had 12 touchdowns in the first nine games, which is still the team record for a season, when I got a real severe knee injury in the 10th game against the Raiders in the Cotton Bowl. I had my cleat in, and Freddie Williamson hit me from behind. In that game, they didn't have a wideout so they put Abner at wideout quite a bit. I was in a full leg cast and was on the sidelines the whole game.

The visitors stunned the Houston crowd by racing to a 17–0 lead at the half with Stram's makeshift offense working like a charm. Spikes rambled 33 yards to set up the first touchdown for a 10–0 lead. The next touchdown drive needed to cover only 29 yards following the second interception of Blanda. After Dallas' second touchdown, a two-yard run by Haynes, the Oilers appeared to be using the half's final minutes to get on the board and back in the game. Houston stood with first-and-goal at the Texans' 5-yard line and tried to hit running back Charley Tolar over the middle in a crowd for the score but instead found Dallas linebacker E. J. Holub, who returned the ball to midfield and out of harm's way for the visitors.

E. J. HOLUB: They were fixin' to score going into the halftime. I intercepted the pass, was running, and all I could see was daylight. I got tackled around the 50 when this big tackle came over and just touched me on the foot and I fell down. Otherwise, I could have scored.

Scoring became a problem for the Texans from then on. Everything that went Dallas' way in the first half suddenly clung to Houston. The Texans watched almost helplessly as the champion Oilers bowed their backs and slowly, steadily climbed back into the game. Blanda threw a 15-yard touchdown pass to Willard Dewveall in the third quarter. Blanda added a 31-yard field goal early in the fourth quarter, and the score was knotted with just under six minutes to play in the period when Tolar burrowed in from the 1. And the Oilers had a chance to grab the lead in the closing minutes when Blanda lined up for a 41-yard field-goal attempt. But Dallas got a tremendous rush from Sherrill Headrick and Dave Grayson, Headrick getting his hand on the ball and effectively sending the game into sudden-death overtime.

E. J. HOLUB: Before Abner and I went out for the coin toss for overtime, Hank said, "We want to take the wind, and we'll kick off to 'em."

HANK STRAM: I wanted to kick off because our defense was playing much better than our offense and I thought we could hold 'em and get the ball back in good field position.

Houston's captains, Al Jamison and Ed Husmann, were waiting at midfield when referee Red Bourne was ready to conduct the overtime coin toss. ABC's sideline reporter for the telecast, Jack Buck, was also there, mike in hand, to help bring the proceedings to the TV audience. Abner Haynes was the first Dallas captain to reach midfield, well before E. J. Holub.

Bourne explained that, beginning with the toss, it was as if a new game was beginning—except for the sudden-death aspect. If no one scored through 15 minutes, the teams would change ends. He noted that the Texans would again get to call the toss since they were the visiting team. He then directed his attention toward the Dallas captains and said, "You call it while the coin is in the air, and call it loudly, now." He flipped the coin: "Call it."

"Heads!" said Haynes, standing next to Buck and his microphone and in front of Holub. "Heads!" Bourne repeated. He looked down at the coin on the field and said, "Dallas won the toss. You have your choice, of course, receiving or kicking."

Haynes, leaning into Buck's microphone, said, "We will kick to the clock." The clock happened to be at the north end of the field, and a wind of about 14 miles per hour was coming from the north. "You're going to kick," Bourne said, making sure he understood Haynes's call correctly. "Yes," the Dallas captain said. "To the clock," Bourne said. "Right," Haynes said. The sound track to this exchange was a wail of disbelief coming from the stadium crowd. As

Haynes confirmed his call to Bourne, Holub hopped away from the confab abruptly and began to run back to the Texans' bench looking like a frontier scout with news that the Indians were riding toward camp. And Buck reported on the air back to Curt Gowdy in the TV booth: "Well, I'll tell you, Curt, around that Dallas bench they're going crazy. They don't know what's going on." And Gowdy followed, sounded stunned, "Kicking against the wind."

Another note of clarification: anything that Haynes said after "we will kick" was irrelevant. After winning a toss, a captain can pick one of three options—receive, kick, or defend a particular end of the field. At that point, the opposing captain receives the remaining option. Houston's captains, once Dallas had chosen to kick, naturally took the wind.

AL JAMISON: The first thing I did was grab Ed Husmann and say, "C'mon, Ed. We've got the game made." Red Bourne called me back and said, "You've got your choice of goals." We had the football and the goal.

E. J. HOLUB: They gave the sign, and I went to the sideline: "Holy shit! What's goin' on?"

CHRIS BURFORD: We really wanted to defend the clock side. Abner said, "We'll kick to the clock." Problem is, the first thing you say is your choice. Then the other team automatically has which way they want to defend. So we lost the ball and the wind.

HANK STRAM: The official never gave Abner all the choices. That's what screwed it all up. The normal procedure is to ask if you want to kick, receive, or defend the goal. But the official said, "What are you going to do, kick or receive?" Poor Abner's been taking the heat all these years, but that's really what took place.

ABNER HAYNES: I was thinking running game. The field was slanted. So when I said, "kick to the clock," I was simply pointing downhill. It was a stupid statement 'cause you're supposed to be checking the wind. I didn't want to give them the wind. That was my mistake.

CHRIS BURFORD: The tornado warnings were out. The conditions were terrible. Everybody was worried about the tornado coming. And we were kicking against the wind in overtime.

TOMMY BROOKER: It was a tremendous wind. Wasn't anything we could do about it once we made the choice. I quicked a squib kick, which was very difficult to handle. A low line drive and hooked it a little bit. It was going to penetrate the wind better. A normal kickoff, end over end, the ball would get up in the air and just hang there. We might have even overrun it.

The Texans kicked into the wind, with the Oilers beginning the initial overtime possession in excellent position at their 34-yard line. They punted, stopped Dallas, and opened their next series in even better shape, at their 45. But Blanda was intercepted by Johnny Robinson. Again, the Texans couldn't get anything going on offense and then forced Houston to begin at their 17. Blanda marched the Oilers out of trouble and down toward his own field-goal range before throwing his fifth interception, returned by Bill Hull to midfield.

CHARLIE HENNIGAN: We were moving downfield. George called a quick-out to me. The Texans had a six foot eight defensive end named Bill Hull. He dropped off the line and caught the ball that was intended for me. That guy caught the ball 13 feet in the air.

Time ran out in the fifth period and, more than 75 minutes after the initial kickoff and 25 degrees colder, a 19-yard Jack Spikes run around left end to the 19 put Dallas in position to attempt the winning field goal, from 25 yards by Tommy Brooker, early in the sixth period.

CHRIS BURFORD: It just so happened, going six quarters, the wind was in our favor at the end of the game. Blanda blew it. He forced an interception. Hell, they could have kicked a chipee field goal. Blanda just wanted to force the damn ball in there. That was kind of his history.

TOMMY BROOKER: It was very quiet in the huddle, sort of like you were in church. Lenny was cleaning one of my cleats. I was leaning on Curtis McClinton, our fullback, one of the rookies we had. He was hardly even taking a breath, but I could feel his eyes on me. I don't even know who cleaned off the other one. I lifted up my shoe, and somebody else got it. To me, it was just another play in the game 'cause I had been playing end. It wasn't like I came off the bench, a specialty guy. I told them not to worry. I think E. J. Holub was my snapper 'cause he got the ball back real fast. The objective is to kick in 1.3 or 1.4 seconds. Lenny held the ball. Everything looked like it went pretty smooth.

The kick, coming 77 minutes and 54 seconds into the game, prevented the Oilers from winning their third league title. There was cheering in some corners for that fact from those who feared that a Houston dynasty could do to the AFL what the Cleveland Browns' dominance did to the All-American Football Conference of the late '40s—namely, destroy interest across much of the league.

None of that was really important to the Texans and their fans. And maybe none of the Dallas players was more pleased with the victory than Abner Haynes, whose decision surprised those in the stands and on both sidelines at Jeppesen Stadium and was portrayed as near madness on the ABC telecast.

ABNER HAYNES: My mother and dad were in tears the way the TV guys had dogged me and how stupid I was. If the Oilers had taken the kick and scored, I'd have had to leave the country.

HOGAN WHARTON: Had the toss had a direct impact on the game, it might be worthy of some kind of comment. Abner was confused. Hell, I might have done the same thing.

TOMMY BROOKER: I let the wives of some of the married guys drive my Galaxy 500 down to Houston. Bobby Hunt, another rookie, from Auburn, and I left immediately after the game and drove to Alabama. We drove all night long. Had a little car trouble. The thermostat froze up. The girls driving down from Dallas to Houston didn't tell us that. Well, that light came on. We didn't know what to do about it. Seemed like the faster we drove, the pinker the light got. We made it to my hometown, Demopolis, in west Alabama. We went right through Demopolis and I dropped off Bobby Hunt with his brother. I went to see my folks, then went to Tuscaloosa to get a haircut. Still had no sleep. That's how lit up we were.

6

Two's a Crowd

Lamar Hunt and Clint Murchison each set out in early 1960 with noble intentions, to transform Dallas, Texas, into a hotbed for professional football. This time would be different from the half-baked effort undertaken by the NFL eight years earlier with a club that was practically dumped on the civic doorstep.

But pro football was again failing in Dallas because it was a commodity with too great a supply. Where there had been no pro ball only a year earlier, there were 13 combined regular-season home games for the NFL Cowboys and AFL Texans. Two teams might be workable in New York or Los Angeles. In Chicago, it wasn't exactly a thriving format, forcing the move of the Cardinals to St. Louis.

There were too many empty seats, too many giveaway tickets.

Something else had to give. Or else they might both collapse.

BLACKIE SHERROD: I had been exposed to the first attempt to put pro football in Dallas, in 1952 when I was at the *Fort Worth Press*. It was embarrassing. I also realized that Texas at the time was a high school and college football state. The only NFL exposure was the Chicago Bears games on TV. You would follow the Southwest Conference guys in the pros with a certain curiosity. And when they brought teams to Dallas for exhibition games, they looked to bring teams with Southwest Conference players that people were familiar with—Detroit, with Doak Walker and Bobby Layne.

TEX SCHRAMM: I made a deal with Dan Reeves, who was head of the Rams. I was very familiar with all the scouting stuff because I had been there. I said, "I'll give you $5,000 or whatever you want for the records on the players that are not drafted that I can sign as free agents." Of course, free agents today means a lot different than free agents in those days. So after the NFL drafted, they gave me the rest. At that point, I engaged Gil Brandt and several other people to go out and try to sign these players that we looked at and felt were worth signing. We signed a lot of people who didn't last too long.

GIL BRANDT: The first player I signed for the Cowboys was Jake Crout-hamel. I was elated. I couldn't wait to tell Tex. Of course, Tex's first question was, "How much did we pay?" In those days, you sent a contract through the mail to a guy for $4,500. If there was Canadian League interest, you might make it $5,500. I got into a bidding war with Frank Leahy, general manager of the L.A. Chargers. I won the contest—$8,500, no signing bonus.

BLACKIE SHERROD: Tex Schramm was a great organizer. When he first got to town, he asked Field Scovell, the main sports contact in town, "Who's the best guy in town to get things done? To get a tractor, get a truck, to charter a plane?" That was the pro way to go about it. The Texans hired a loner, Willie Walls, to head up their scouting. He used to write notes on the back of a matchbook. And a high school coach, Don Rossi, to be their general manager. The Texans hired a college assistant from Miami who had no pre-vious connection to pro football, Hank Stram, to be their head coach. The Cowboys hired Tom Landry, who, in essence, coached the New York Giants.

The Texans had a combination of older guys that, frankly, hadn't been able to make it, and young guys that they could sign. The Texans players were much friendlier. And there were never any complaints from them about the amount of space given them in the newspaper. You heard a lot from the Cowboys. It was a hard thing to try to balance, to be fair. We changed out the beat people assigned to each team after a year or two.

BOB HALFORD: It was a constant war in Dallas. It wasn't easy. We gave away a lot of tickets. I got the bright idea to give everybody in the backshop at the *Morning News* and the *Times-Herald* tickets. One morning, a guy that I knew who worked in the backshop at the *News* comes up and asks me if I want to buy a ticket.

Anyway, we did everything we could. We did a lot of promotions, and some of them were out of Lamar's fertile brain. Some of them were out of mine. Some of them were out of our announcer, Charlie Jones. We had Friend of the Barber Day, when everybody who came in in a white smock got an upper-deck seat. The Cowboys used the Rams plan—if you bought one ticket you could get five kids in. That was one that Schramm had brought from Los Angeles. We got Dr Pepper to work with us and had what we called the Dallas Texans Huddle. We sold what amounted to season tickets to a child, a kid, for a dollar. We tried everything.

LAMAR HUNT: We did every crazy thing we could think of—and a few more—because we knew we had to pull out all the stops. Not that we were any great shakes as salesmen. During the years that we were in Dallas the highest we ever got our season-ticket sale was 3,100. During that same time period, I believe the highest the Cowboys ever got to was 1,900. But they clearly had the advantage when a big-name team came to town. We probably outmarketed them, but at the end of the third year each team was drawing only an average of about 10,000 paid, and that counted every kind of cheap ticket you could think of.

We had thousands of those Huddle Club kids. And, if you can believe it, they got a T-shirt to go with it. There was so much inflation of attendance. The Cowboys announced that their ticket prices were going to be $3.90, which was the same price as the colleges in Texas. After that, we came out and announced that our tickets were going to be $4. The inference there was that we were a professional football team and we were 10 cents better than the Cowboys. That may not have seemed like a big deal, but we had the Cowboys in a corner. They were kind of put on the defensive.

TEX SCHRAMM: Their philosophy was very different from our philosophy. Theirs was promotion, if you want to call it that. Barbers that wear their jackets get in free. Giveaway tickets. I don't know why anybody bought any. Very heavy on tradeouts with grocery stores. "We will give you 10,000 tickets, and you can advertise and give those away with anybody that comes in the store." Ours was that the main thing we had to do was build our football team into one that could win and be successful on the football field. We had the only teams coming in to play that anybody had ever heard of. We had the National Football League coming in. Our job was to become competitive with those teams.

BLACKIE SHERROD: It split the town in half. Lamar Hunt had a contract with the Cotton Bowl, ironclad, the only professional team in town. The Cowboys started up, and Lamar had to relent. Some of the bigwigs in town had previous connections with the National Football League. Many of them were members of the Salesmanship Club, the local organization that promoted the NFL exhibition games at the Cotton Bowl. The Cowboys' supporters were the "in" crowd. The Texans' supporters were the rebels and young guys who, frankly, wanted to be associated with Lamar Hunt. Both teams had boosters clubs. The Texans' boosters all wore these red sport coats with an emblem on the front.

Two popular Texas college stars became the embodiment of the struggle between the Texans and the Cowboys. In the 1961 drafts, TCU defensive tackle Bob Lilly was picked in the first round by the Cowboys and in the second round by the Texans. E. J. Holub, a linebacker from Texas Tech, went in the first round to the Texans and the second round to the Cowboys.

BOB LILLY: I was probably really leaning toward signing with the Texans 'cause they had an earlier draft and they signed a bunch of my buddies. But I talked to Abe Martin, my coach at TCU. He said, "I don't know, Robert. The NFL's been around a long time. I think if the money was about the same, I believe I might go with the NFL." E.J. and I roomed together at the Shrine Game at Stanford. I mean, everybody was hounding all the guys out there. We had a hard time concentrating on learning our plays and practicing. We kind of ducked them as much as we could.

E. J. HOLUB: I was supposed to be the number one draft choice of the Rams. They gave me an ultimatum. They threw a bunch of money out there—I think it was $5,000—on the bed. I'd never seen $5,000 in my life. I called a coach that I dealt with who became my father-in-law, Jim Palmer, who told me, "Don't do it!" I told the Rams I wouldn't, and they said I was going to the Cleveland Browns. I told the Browns, "I'm not playing up north." So the NFL said, "OK, go to the Cowboys so we can fight against the AFL."

The Cowboys wanted me to sign right away. They had some guys out at the East-West Shrine Game. They were after us all the time. I told them, "Leave me alone. I want to play football. I'll talk to you after the game." Lamar was there, and he said, "OK. If you promise . . . we won't bother you anymore." I told him, "I will not sign anything or commit myself to anybody." He left me alone. The Cowboys kept badgering me. I just felt like Lamar was an honorable man, so I went with him.

BOB LILLY: I think E.J. and Jerry Mays, from SMU, both signed or had committed to the Texans before I committed. I met with Lamar Hunt a couple of times. He was very, very nice. I think the Texans offered me $11,000 and the Cowboys $12,000, and the signing bonus was about the same. It wasn't very much, but it bought a new car.

For a few years, I regretted signing with the Cowboys. I really spent more time my first couple of years socializing with the Texans players from the Southwest Conference than I did my own team. One of my TCU teammates, Jack Spikes, was on the Texans for a while. And Sherrill Headrick. There was a place over by SMU where we all used to go to eat pizza, drink beer, and visit. That's when I kind of wondered if I'd made an error. I did think a lot of Coach Landry, but we weren't doing very well and the Texans were.

BOB HALFORD: We knew both teams weren't going to exist in Dallas. And there was a good chance that the first team that got a good opportunity to go someplace else would take it. And we got it. I don't know if the Cowboys would have left or not. Maybe Murchison wouldn't have. But if we hadn't left, I don't think that Murchison would have kept ownership of the team because his money was getting short at that time. His pockets weren't as deep as Lamar's.

E. J. HOLUB: I thought the Texans would stay and the Cowboys would have to move. But I didn't know the financial aspects of it. While the Cowboys only played before 2,000 people there at the Cotton Bowl, they went and played before a full house when they played in Philadelphia, Detroit, and all those places. Then Uncle Sam stepped in and told Lamar, "You're losing a million dollars a year. If you don't start making some money on this thing, it's going to be a hobby and you're no longer going to be able to write it off."

LAMAR HUNT: It came about after three years of operation and lack of progress in establishing ourselves as a successful entity, specifically because we had two teams competing for the dollar. Neither team was succeeding. So I just made an evaluation. I had read a magazine article about the mayor of Kansas City. He was a very dynamic guy. He called me. A lot of people who follow sports knew that the two teams in Dallas were not drawing flies. So he called me, and one thing led to another. There was research done. Maybe two months went by. It seems to me that it was mid-February when the details were worked out.

TEX SCHRAMM: It was only a matter of time until it worked out the way it did. The product was going to be the thing that eventually determined the outcome. I was pleased when they moved. I don't know that I was particularly surprised, more like, "Jesus Christ, this is over." The bad thing about having two teams in one city is not the actual competition. It's the fact that it totally separates your city. I'm sure that both teams feel the same thing in New York, where they have the Giants and the Jets. When I was with the Rams, for several years there was a new league at that time, too. There was the Los Angeles Dons of the All-American Football Conference in the late '40s. I learned then of the problems in a two-team city. And the biggest example was at the newspapers. In Dallas, we had writers there that were Cowboys writers, and we had writers there that were Texans writers. And they weren't friendly.

LAMAR HUNT: I didn't ever look seriously at moving before that. The one that was at least in my mind was New Orleans. It was a good football city. In those days, air travel was much slower. We were looking for a place that was relatively close to Dallas. As an example, I would not have had any interest in going to Seattle because it would have been so far from my own home.

DAVE DIXON: I was in the real estate business when the AFL was starting and was part of a group that tried to get New Orleans in the league then, with Tulane Stadium. Lamar and I got to be pretty good friends. When he later was looking to move his team, he came down to New Orleans and we went to lunch with several key members of the Tulane board of administrators. The president of the board was a wonderful man named Joseph Merrick Jones. He said, "Mr. Dixon, if something is good for New Orleans, Tulane should be a part of it. When the time comes, I will support you."

I couldn't get Lamar to say—and he never really did tell me—that it was for him. He kept saying it was for an AFL franchise. He had come so far as to bring Jack Steadman with him and ask me if I would be GM of the team and have a little percentage of ownership. I had to tell the Tulane board. "He was talking about himself. To pass up a connection with this guy, who's obviously a very nice young man—this could be a dream for Tulane University and the City of New Orleans." There were a couple of old-timers on the board that were dreaming of Tulane making a comeback in college football and not interested in pro football. The board said, "You've got to get a commitment from him." I never could get him to say it. So we never did work it out for that reason. We could never quite get the Tulane board to agree.

FRANK JACKSON: Right after the championship game was over, I was notified that if I didn't hook on with a reserve unit that I was going to be drafted. That's four years in the army. So I got on with the 49th Armored Division in Dallas and was scheduled to go on active duty on January 3, 1963. I was on a train to Fort Polk, Louisiana. Missed the parade in Dallas. Missed them awarding rings. I was in basic training, with Pettis Norman and Mike Gaechter from the Cowboys. I got my championship ring in the mail, had to hide it the rest of the time there or it would get stolen. And when the announcement was made that the team was moving to Kansas City, I was out marching in a damn rainstorm. I was told by a platoon sergeant who heard it on the radio.

BOB HALFORD: It meant a lot to Lamar to have to leave his hometown, so much so that he wanted to name the Kansas City team the Texans. I think Lamar just threw it out one day, and it was thrown back at him.

The team's acclimation to the new town became a secondary issue before the Chiefs had played their first regular-season game. After drawing fewer than 10,000 fans to each of two home exhibition games, the Chiefs were closing the preseason against their former Texas brethren, the Houston Oilers, in Wichita, Kansas. A rookie return man out of Grambling, Stone Johnson, was intent on making a good impression in his efforts to secure a roster spot.

ABNER HAYNES: He was our quarterback at Lincoln High School in Dallas and on the track team. We were close partners. We walked up Malcolm X Boulevard every day, maybe 20 blocks, to get to Lincoln. There were fights, prostitutes, graveyards. You develop relationships in that walk. Stone hung around the Texans' practice field when I got there. He was going to join us at North Texas. We were getting the best brothers in the state. We were the only white school "open." And coach Eddie Robinson had someone drive to Lincoln, put Stone in the car, and took 'im to Grambling.

Johnson decided not to follow Haynes and attend North Texas State; instead he favored Grambling. While participating in both football and track, he qualified for the 1960 Summer Olympics in Rome. He set a world record in the 200 meters at the U.S. trials. He finished fifth but brought home a silver medal as part of the 4 × 100 relay team. In 1962, he was drafted by the Dallas Texans in the 14th round. He had not played much football, but the potential was worth taking a chance on.

Abner Haynes: You could see what Don Klosterman was thinking. If you got Stone the ball, the guy was murder. He was going to make the team. He was going to bring us the dimension that Bob Hayes brought to the Cowboys.

Hank Stram: Our oldest son, Henry, was never very much involved in athletics. He was always into music, played the piano. All the other kids—Stu and Dale—would come to camp and want to see the players. Hanky would go right to where the piano was on campus and play. But Hanky took a liking to Stone and Stone to him. Every time Hanky would come to practice, Stone would take him down to the city and buy him an ice-cream cone.

But Johnson's pro football career ended before it began, late in the first quarter of Kansas City's final exhibition game for 1963. While blocking for teammate Frank Jackson on a punt return, he fractured his fifth cervical vertebrae and suffered damage to his spinal cord. He was paralyzed from the chest down and hospitalized, and he died 10 days later.

Frank Jackson: I was just a few yards away when Stone Johnson speared Don Floyd and broke his neck. Stone was with us as a rookie, as a return guy. They were testing him on special teams. I took the kickoff. Whichever back didn't get the ball kept the defensive team's guys off you so you could catch the ball. You took the first person down, which was Floyd.

Bob Halford: Stone was reasonably tall and thin. He was trying to block, and his technique was wrong. His head was too low.

Frank Jackson: I looked just as Stone was spearing him with his head. Hell, Stone weighed about 165 pounds soaking wet. Floyd weighed about 260. He just crumbled. Then Stone was on the field, all stretched out.

Abner Haynes: He was lying on the field, saying, "They got me." Jim Tyrer, the big tackle, ran up and grabbed him by the arm and said, "C'mon,

Stone." And I think Fred Arbanas said, "No. No. Don't move him. He's hurt bad." Then everybody kind of realized that the way he was lying was so unusual.

MERLE HARMON: The night we were in the airport in Wichita, I found Abner sitting in the hallway sobbing uncontrollably.

CHRIS BURFORD: Stone was a good kid, just a fun kid. A good friend of Abner's. That had a tremendous effect on our whole team. Five or six of us went down to Dallas and were pallbearers for Stone. I was one of them, spent several days there with his family and friends. I don't think Abner was ever quite the same.

HANK STRAM: That game in Wichita was the only game Hanky went with me. When Stone got hurt, he cried like a baby. And when he died, Hank came over and grabbed me and hugged me and said, "Dad, I thought football was just a game. How could anybody get killed playing football, playing a game?" Oh, man, he was just out of it completely.

ABNER HAYNES: Coach Stram called me and told me, "Our boy went home to higher glory." He was very, very brave about it. He handled it very well. We just cried there together. That's all you could do.

CHRIS BURFORD: It's a real eye-opener when you have a teammate die. It's hard to stay focused. It's not just a "fun" game.

HANK STRAM: I spoke at the funeral, and Hank asked me to bring back something. I brought him a rose. To this day, he has it in a prayer book.

7

The "World Champion" Chargers

Following the embarrassment of the 1962 season, San Diego coach Sid Gillman was looking for a change of scenery in his efforts to return to the top of the Western Division. His most tangible move was to bring in a new quarterback to give young John Hadl time to mature behind a seasoned veteran. Enter 13-year pro Tobin Rote, who won an NFL championship with Detroit in 1957 and played the previous three seasons with Toronto. A less tangible extension of Gillman's desire for a makeover came in his choice of training sites.

JERRY MAGEE: The Chargers had trained at the University of San Diego the previous year. The team went 4–10 after winning two division titles, and Sid felt there were too many temptations. So he found this remote outpost to train. It was unbelievable. It's still there. I've gone back. It's no place you want to go on your vacation.

DAVE KOCOUREK: Rough Acres Ranch was a facility about 70 miles east of San Diego, in the foothills. It was built by a doctor who was rehabilitating alcoholics. It was going to be a dude ranch.

KEITH LINCOLN: If it wasn't the end of the world, you could see it from there. I mean, the middle of nowhere. Hotter than hell. There were a couple of old donkeys and some cattle. Sagebrush. There were some Quonset huts. There was no one around, so they literally put up some six-foot fencing and some tarp cover around it for the showers. No roof.

DAVE KOCOUREK: Have you ever taken a shower in a lightning storm with pipes and canvas?

JOHN HADL: It *was* up in the mountains, but those California mountains are a little dry. Every morning when they were watering the practice field, they'd have to shoo the rattlers off the field. I always kept a golf stick with me 'cause you'd come in to eat and they might be lying under the porch or somewhere where it's cool.

DAVE KOCOUREK: Ernie Ladd was a great Ping-Pong player. He would go over and pick up the ball in a tree well, and in the tree well was a snake. We killed about 20 rattlesnakes in the course of training camp.

KEITH LINCOLN: The fields—I swear to God, they mixed in sawdust or something. It wasn't fun, but everybody got in shape.

JERRY MAGEE: They couldn't keep a cook around for more than a couple of days. There wasn't a woman within miles. Guys would be walking around naked. Our "leave town" was Tecate, Mexico. Sid had two air-conditioned chambers in that place. That was the year Tobin Rote joined the Chargers and got hurt during the preseason. Sid's gesture to Tobin was to let him sleep in the other one.

The Chargers established themselves as the favorites in the West during the first half of the season by sweeping a pair of games from the transplanted division champions, the Kansas City Chiefs. Any thoughts that Denver could contend, building from a 7–7 finish the previous season, were blunted with a 2–4–1 start. And former Chargers assistant Al Davis got his Oakland Raiders off to an improved start—anything would have looked good after going 1–13—by winning three of seven games. All of San Diego's parts were meshing. Veteran quarterback Tobin Rote provided what Hadl couldn't in '62. The running game featured the league's best one-two punch in Paul Lowe and Keith Lincoln, who would have been the featured back on any other team. And second-year receiver Lance Alworth blossomed into one of the AFL's top pass catchers and one of the most entertaining players to watch.

Alworth's path to San Diego was almost as difficult to cover as one of his winding pass routes. The Chargers had selected the All-American out of Arkansas in the notorious secret draft in November 1961 that commissioner Joe Foss discovered after the fact and disallowed. Drafting Alworth in an actual formal draft might lead to legal questioning of whether San Diego should own his rights, so the club had to find a proxy club to pick him with the idea of subsequently trading him to the Chargers. Enter the Raiders, who agreed to go through the charade in exchange for a number of San Diego veterans. (The Oakland pseudoselection of Alworth, though, is strangely absent from the Raiders' list of picks from that draft.) And he was the eighth pick in the NFL draft, the first selection of San Francisco.

From that point, the Chargers assigned then-assistant Davis to the case. He wooed Alworth. He wooed Alworth's parents. At a coffee-shop rendezvous in Little Rock before the Razorbacks' Sugar Bowl meeting with Alabama, Davis made a presentation that has become football—and dining—lore. As young Alworth looked on breathless, Davis marked up the tablecloth as if it were a coaching chalkboard: "That X is where the flanker lines up. Lance, as soon as you sign with us, you're my X and nobody can take that position away from you." All that was required was for Alworth to "X" a San Diego contract, which he did only moments after the Sugar Bowl. His signing with the new league marked its most significant acquisition—the highest NFL draftee to flee the establishment—since the tug-of-war over Billy Cannon. (Three picks later in the NFL draft, Detroit lost one John Hadl to the same Chargers.) He was nicknamed "Bambi" by teammate Charlie Flowers, became a seven-time AFL All-Star, and became the first player who began his career in the AFL to be selected to the Pro Football Hall of Fame, in 1978.

KEITH LINCOLN: Lance was married coming out of high school in Mississippi. I think that's why he ended up going to Arkansas instead of Ole Miss, because Ole Miss wouldn't take married athletes. Such a good competitor. Tough guy. Hard worker. God dang it, he could play. He and I roomed together for seven or eight years. My second son is named after Lance, I thought so much of him.

JERRY MAGEE: He didn't do much as a rookie in '62, often had problems with his legs. But it was obvious there just weren't many guys walking around like him. He had huge muscular legs and a very thin waist. Very thin upper body. Kind of looked like a ballerina. But he was clearly an exceptional athlete. He had great speed and great leaping ability. It was as if he had eyes in the back of his head. Plus, he worked hard on his moves. I think when he first came into the league, he didn't think he needed them. I've never seen a guy who could balance better in the mud than he could.

AL LoCASALE: The player who most established our identity in the college football ranks was Lance Alworth. I would go recruiting, and people would say to me while I was asking them about their wide receivers: "Hey, this kid we have and the kid over at SMU are good. But, hey, they're not Alworth." That was the first time in my recollection that an AFL player was used as the standard of comparison at a position.

RON MIX: Lance Alworth is the finest receiver I've ever seen, and that includes today. The extent that we were in awe of him is best illustrated by an incident that happened when we were flying home from an eastern road swing. We hit some real bad weather, and the plane dropped 500 feet, 1,000 feet. I thought we were going to crash. Then I remembered that Lance was on the plane, and I immediately relaxed. I thought, "There's no way God would kill Lance."

JERRY MAGEE: Somebody asked me if Lance was better than Jerry Rice. You put them in a footrace, Lance would win easy. You put 'em in a jumping contest, I'm sure Lance would win, too. And nobody ever had any better hands than he did. Alworth would make one of those great catches, and a lot of people in the stands would leave. That's just what they came to see.

The Chargers' first of two meetings with Oakland actually provided a wake-up call against their former colleague Davis. It turned out to be a shoot-out, with a last-second Oakland touchdown trumping a 51-yard Lincoln touchdown run just minutes earlier. Davis's upstarts proved to be San Diego's only competition in the West. The Raiders stood two games behind the Chargers for much of the second half of the season and closed the gap by surprisingly winning the teams' rematch at Balboa Stadium in early December with two games to play. The Raiders just kept winning, finishing the campaign with an eight-game winning streak, but San Diego managed to remain a length ahead in the race. It took a dizzying 52–49 victory on the season's final Sunday over their old pals the Oilers for the Chargers to claim their third division title in four seasons.

San Diego had a week to sit back and await the winner of a special divisional playoff game between Boston and Buffalo, which tied for first in the

East with paltry 7–6–1 records. The game was played with temperatures in the mid-20s and the War Memorial Stadium field as hard as ice—when it could be located beneath the snow that fell throughout the game. The hosts won the toss but did little else right afterward. The Bills' first two possessions resulted in a fumbled kickoff and an interception. Boston built a 16–0 lead at halftime and held Cookie Gilchrist, one of the league's top rushing threats, to seven yards on eight carries in a 26–8 Boston upset.

GINO CAPPELLETTI: To be honest, I don't think we thought we were going to win that game. They had a blizzard there, not that that meant anything. But we could have clinched the division the last game, and we got slaughtered 35–3 by Kansas City. It's hard to get your confidence up for a playoff game getting whipped like that.

LARRY GARRON: Lou Saban asked me one time when I played for him at Western Illinois about running on a frozen field: "What are you going to do? You know the regular cleats aren't going to do you any good." Being a pitcher in baseball, I went out and got some baseball cleats, which were excellent. That's what I used in that game, and my traction was better. Guys couldn't figure out why I could stop and turn.

GINO CAPPELLETTI: Ron Burton went against doctors' advice and came back from a back injury to help us. He busted up on the first play from scrimmage for about 12 yards. Then we got going, and Babe started hitting Larry Garron on long passes. I caught a few. I kicked four field goals. We had to play in sneakers, so I had to run off on third down and take my sneaker off, put my kicking shoe on in case I had to kick a field goal. We beat 'em, and we beat 'em good.

LARRY GARRON: I talked to Lou after the game. He looked at my shoes and said, "Yeah." He was very complimentary: "Now you're on your own, you blankety-blank!"

So it was off to sunny San Diego for the Patriots, to face the Chargers. There was already an atmosphere of accomplishment around the Boston club as it headed to California to face a well-rested opponent. But for the Patriots, more excitement would occur back at the team hotel involving one of the team's most colorful players, defensive lineman Larry Eisenhauer.

LARRY EISENHAUER: Because I was a little bit wild, it was decided that my father would be my roommate at the Stardust Inn. We were all sitting around the pool one day. It was getting toward the end of the day. Shadows were getting long. It was getting a little cool. I suggested to my dad, "They've got another pool that's heated. It's private. I think you'll like it." This was the pool where they did the underwater ballet, the girls in skimpy swimsuits, which was located inside the bar.

So I took him up on the roof, and we dove in. We were swimming around there. Meanwhile, some of the players were sitting inside and they were going absolutely nuts. Naturally, I was mooning them. My father didn't.

TOM YEWCIC: Babe Parilli and I were eating right there. The mermaids would come down and swim. We're looking, and somebody's smiling through the glass. It's Larry Eisenhauer. He's waving at everybody. Next thing, Ronnie Hall's in there. The owners of the Stardust never complained, never said anything. Thought it was a little crazy.

LARRY EISENHAUER: Then somebody called the police. I had to get Dad out of there real quick. Over the years, the story has been adulterated to the point my father took his pants off or went in naked. My dad was a very modest man. I think he even read that story and went, "Oh, my God. How could they put something like that in there?"

The Patriots had other problems, aside from keeping Larry Eisenhauer fully clothed. Their "team friendliness" extended well beyond the heated pool in the Stardust bar. It went all the way, in fact, to their practice field in San Diego.

WILL McDONOUGH: Mike Holovak was like the nicest guy you could ever meet. One of his weaknesses was he believed everybody. Sid Gillman called up: "I've got it all set up for you. You're going to train at a navy base. They're going to have everybody ready to help you." Mike said, "Hey, this is great!" What he didn't think about is, the Chargers had several people dressed as navy guys watching practice all week long and knew what the hell we were doing.

JERRY MAGEE: Sid put in a great game plan, called it "feast or famine." He gave a title to his game plans, which many coaches do. He apparently figured it would go real big or it wouldn't. It went real big. He introduced some things that he hadn't used and I don't think very many teams had. He used motion. Sid wanted to occupy their linebackers.

Paul Lowe and Keith Lincoln were not ordinary backs. Paul Lowe was a beautiful back to watch. He had a tryout with the 49ers before he came to the Chargers, and the Chargers gave him a job in the mail room of one of the Hilton hotels before they actually got him on the field. He had been a champion high hurdler in high school. Before games, he had this custom: He kind of walked a hundred yards down the sidelines, and then he would kind of jog a hundred yards. Then he would sprint a hundred yards. I used to try to get to the stadium early just to watch him do it, he had such a beautiful gait. He and Lincoln had very diverse styles. Paul weighed about 176, got up to about 190, and Lincoln was stocky. Lincoln also was very fast, but he was more of a power runner. Sid used to say, "He kicks 'em aside."

KEITH LINCOLN: Sid listed me as the fullback and Paul as the halfback, but it was interchangeable. We ran a lot of the same plays. We tried to push each other. Paul sure didn't want me to get more yards than he got.

BABE PARILLI: We were a blitzing team. We weren't that good in the secondary, and we couldn't rush just four guys. So we always got to the passer, and we had a lot of interceptions. So we were blitzing Tobin Rote, my old teammate with the Packers. They were pitching out, and there was no one containing. They just took the old-fashioned pitch to Keith Lincoln and Paul Lowe, and they just killed us.

AL LoCASALE: We beat the hell out of the Patriots. It was 31–10 at the half. We had arranged for the Grambling band to come out, one of their first big appearances. Sid finished his halftime stuff early and said, "I want to watch the band."

The final margin was 51–10, making up as much as possible for the frustration of losing close championship games to the Oilers following the first two seasons. Keith Lincoln put together one of the great championship performances in pro football history—206 yards rushing, including a 67-yard touchdown run, and seven catches for 123 yards and another score. Paul Lowe complemented him with 94 yards rushing, including a 58-yard TD sprint that gave San Diego a two-touchdown lead in the first period after the Patriots scored what proved to be their lone touchdown of the afternoon. Lance Alworth was not shut out on big plays, a 48-yard touchdown catch among his credits. The 610 yards allowed by Boston still stand in the club record book.

John Hadl: It was a great feeling, winning and being part of a championship team. With Sid winning, everybody stayed in a good mood. If you lost, it was your ass 'til about Thursday. I was very lucky. I had Tobin for position help, and Sid was a great, great teacher. My first two years, I didn't have a day off. I was in there every Monday morning at 8:00 going with him. Which was great, 'cause I was learning fast and it really paid off.

Will McDonough: Here's something I *didn't* like about the game. On the second-to-last touchdown, which made the score 44–10, they had a two-point conversion. John Hadl rolled out and threw to somebody. They said the play was screwed up. I was standing on the field. The play wasn't screwed up.

Larry Eisenhauer: I can still see Keith Lincoln. Every time he touched the ball, he gained 20 yards. He ran for touchdowns. He caught passes for touchdowns. He even completed a pass. It was like we didn't even show up.

Will McDonough: Going to the locker room after the game, Tommy Addison, our linebacker and captain, looked at me and said, "I've never been on my knees so much in my life. I got knocked down on every Goddamn play."

Larry Garron: The Chargers' people knew everything that we were doing. The only way we were able to score was that Babe Parilli came back to the huddle and designed a play that they didn't know.

Gino Cappelletti: All that noise going around Boston after the win in Buffalo, all the excitement. We started to come down then a little bit during the middle of the week. We just couldn't get ourselves back up for that championship game.

Will McDonough: The Chargers were a great club, all kinds of players all over the field. Sid made a pronouncement after the game: "We are the greatest team in the world!" Flying home on the commercial flight the next day, I was sitting in the back with Bob Dee, one of the greatest guys you'd ever meet. The pilot came on and said, "We're going over Albany, New York; we're going to prepare for our approach for landing into Boston." Dee was sitting next to the window. He looked at me and said, "Gee, some jets are right off our wing, three of 'em. Massachusetts Air National Guard. I bet the governor sent them up here to shoot us down." Then he paused and said, "And I don't blame 'em."

AL LoCASALE: We put "world champions" on the ring and believed it. Billy Wade was the quarterback of the Bears, the NFL champs, and Sid said, "I coached Billy. There is no way a Billy Wade–led ballclub can score more than 14 points on us, and we can't be held under 14 by anybody. We have better talent than they do. We're the best football team."

LARRY FELSER: About Super Bowl VIII in the mid '70s, NFL Properties had Point Counterpoint in the program between the NFL and the AFL. The game I picked was, if in '63, the Bears had played San Diego. The Bears had no quarterback, not much of a running attack. They had outstanding defense coached by George Allen. But the Chargers had Lowe and Lincoln, Alworth, Ron Mix, Tobin Rote backed up by John Hadl. I mean, great offense. Tex Maule, who covered the NFL for *Sports Illustrated*, took the point that the Bears would have killed them.

MIKE DITKA: If the Chargers would have played us, they would have gone up against one of the best defenses that ever played in the league. They talk about the '85 Bears defense; the '63 defense was awfully good. The Chargers had a lot of firepower. It would have been a hell of a game.

KEITH LINCOLN: A person could put up a good argument that Sid Gillman is the father of the West Coast offense. His thing was to stretch the field. That was the big complaint about the AFL back then. The old-timers in the NFL said, "My God. Look what the scores are!" Well, everything that's been done has copied that. They changed the rules to make the offense better. They're throwing the Goddamn ball. They're doing everything that they were criticizing Sid for. Look at the assistant coaches he had who went on to become head coaches—Jack Faulkner, Al Davis, Chuck Noll. He coached other coaches how to coach.

8

Urban Renewal

Many a sports economist believes that a pro sports league is only as strong as its New York franchise. The AFL learned that the hard way.

Harry Wismer set up shop for the new Titans in, of all places, his Manhattan apartment. Saving the overhead only went so far. The club seemed to be only a step ahead of the repo man throughout its early seasons. The Titans played in the Polo Grounds, which the football Giants had fled from following the 1955 season and which had been vacant since the baseball Giants moved to San Francisco after the '57 season.

One visitor to Wismer's digs stumbled upon hundreds of game tickets strewn across his bed. Considering how many Titans tickets were simply given away during the team's early years, prospects for ticket theft might have been welcomed. And the owner didn't do himself any favors in promoting himself almost as much as he promoted the team.

SAMMY BAUGH: I was coaching at Hardin-Simmons [in Abilene, Texas] when I heard they were starting a new league. Harry Wismer called me. I told him I was pretty satisfied where I was. I could come home anytime I wanted within an hour and a half. I didn't like Wismer. Nobody liked him. He was one of those guys who walks into a restaurant and hollers at somebody all the way across the room: "Hey, baby!" You hated to go anywhere in public with him.

JERRY IZENBERG: In 1960, I was at the *New York Herald Tribune* and *Dell Pro Football Magazine* asked me to do a whole section on the AFL. I decided this league was going to be something to write about when I first went to see Harry. He had an apartment, and the address was on Park Avenue, but the building was on Lexington Avenue. I wandered around in the neighborhood for like two hours trying to find it. His apartment had been converted into the offices of the Titans. I walked in, and there was a tremendous battle going on between a Scandinavian maid and Ted Emery, the first publicity guy. To go to the mimeograph machine, you had to walk through the bathroom. And the maid was screaming at Ted: "I told you! You must open the window! It stinks in there! It stinks in my kitchen! This apartment stinks!" The coaching staff was sitting at the dining room table. All over the living room there must have been thousands of tickets, with no order forms, of course. That was the business office. And Wismer's private office was the bedroom. We sat down, and he said, "You may wonder why I have chosen the name Titans." I said, "Well, Harry, it never occurred to me until just now." He said, "Good. I'm glad you asked. Because, what's bigger than a giant? A titan!"

His idea of a joke was to call a sportswriter's house at 1:30 in the morning if the team played a night game and say, "Mrs. So-and-So, this is Trooper Johnson from the state police. I'm sorry to tell you your husband's been killed in a head-on crash."

SAMMY BAUGH: If we won the last four games the first year, we would win the division. Harry said if we beat those teams, he'd give everybody a bonus. We won the first three, and the last game was against the Chargers. We had a hell of a ballgame. They'd score. We'd score. They'd score. We'd score. Harry—well, he was sitting on the bench to start with—he'd walk down the sideline and get even with the ball. We thought, "OK, we've got him worried about that bonus." We laughed about it. Every time we'd score, the boys would say, "We've got him worried." It was a good game all the way, and we wound up losing 50–43.

LARRY GRANTHAM: Wismer and I got to be really good friends. I got out of school early and went up there around March, and he got me a job in the Hotel Manhattan sales department. He was always pretty well straight with me . . . except about the finances. He wasn't really straightforward with anybody about that. But he took a liking to me. Matter of fact, when he got ready to fire the coach, he wanted my recommendation. Here I was, a young kid from Mississippi; I didn't know anybody, so I recommended one of the assistants at Mississippi, Bruiser Kinard. Mr. Wismer and I were in his office, in his apartment, and called Bruiser in Oxford, Mississippi. Bruiser was getting ready for a bowl game so he couldn't talk to us until after the bowl game. He was a very ethical person. So that fell through.

When you're playing, even though you're playing in front of sparse crowds in a lot of cases, you really didn't have doubts about the league. The only time we had doubts was in our third year, when the paychecks starting bouncing. Bob Mischak, who played guard for us, was the offensive captain, and I was defensive captain. We kept talking to Wismer, trying to get our paychecks. I used to go to a bank up in the Bronx. When I brought my check in there, the vice president would start shaking his head. Then all the players got together and decided we weren't going to practice unless we got paid with paychecks that didn't bounce. So Wismer decided: "If they aren't going to play, I'm not going to let our coaches coach, either." So we didn't have any coaches, but we worked out on our own. We finally called Lamar Hunt, and he came in and took care of all our paychecks. We didn't even have workmen's compensation insurance. They wouldn't let us play in the state of New York without that. Lamar took care of all that. Somehow, he got us a plane, and we flew to Buffalo on Saturday. We were so happy to get paid, we beat the hell out of them.

CHUCK BURR: That game was the famous beer-can barrage. We were supposed to beat New York. Their quarterback, Lee Grosscup, who did not have a lot of success as a pro football player, made us look pretty bad. In the third quarter, we were pretty much out of it.

LARRY FELSER: It was a Friday night game. Lee Grosscup had been cut by some NFL team and arrived at noon. The Titans were staying at the Sheraton in downtown Buffalo, and the coach, Bulldog Turner, was having lunch with a couple other coaches in the dining room. Grosscup came in. Bulldog told him to sit down, gave him the game plan—what there was of it—on the linen tablecloth for the next two hours. I don't think Grosscup had even met with his teammates until he went into the dressing room.

They used to have midget auto racing at War Memorial Stadium, and there was a track around the field. They pulled it out when the Bills came, and there was just cinder. So when the beer cans came down and hit the cinders, it was absolutely eerie. First, it was just a "plink, plink." Then, all of a sudden, it was like a hailstorm. Somebody threw a full one from above the players' wives section and hit Mike Stratton's wife right square in the back. It could have been really awful. It was the world's worst game.

CHUCK BURR: The guy who ran the press box told me, "Well, there's good news and bad news. Obviously, a lot of beer was sold for this game. But we don't sell beer in cans at the stadium." They had all picked up their beer at adjoining saloons. The next day, the stadium superintendent estimated about 3,500 beer cans were on the field. Fortunately, with that track surrounding the field, very few cans got close to the benches.

AL WARD: Nobody was more fun than Harry Wismer. We used to have league meetings, a couple a year, in one lil' ol' room. We had eight owners and Joe Foss and assistant commissioner Milt Woodard, and sometimes we had an attorney there. Wismer wanted to move the league to action: "We gotta do this. We gotta do this." He'd go along with it even though it cost money. Then we'd break for lunch. Everybody'd leave for an hour and come back; he'd be back in two hours. And, by then, he wasn't funny anymore. He was mean, was used to those two-martini lunches, I guess. One time they couldn't standardize the film exchange. He was bored with this kind of stuff. They were going around the room, and they got to Wismer. He said, "Huh?" "We're talking about films." He said, "Sammy"—Sammy Baugh—"Sammy doesn't like films. He likes cowboy movies. So we don't care."

JOE FOSS: Harry didn't especially love me. Never voted for me to start with. He was always bragging about that, and I said, "I know that. You wanted some coach who lost a few games. I'm running this league the way I want to." Harry was one of those guys who, after he got a few snorts, got very belligerent. A few months before Harry had to file under Chapter 11, Sonny Werblin from MCA was giving me a birthday party up in the Remington Room at [the club] 21. Everybody was having a good time. Harry said something to Sonny. He called him a name, which I don't like to even repeat, called Sonny a kike. Ol' Sonny jumped up and was gonna whip him right there with all the fancy furniture and million-dollar paintings. So I jumped between the two of them. I had one in each hand, had 'em by their neckties. They threw a few punches at one another, but I got most of them. I just said, "Sit down!" They sat down and then started yelling across at each other. And I just said, "Quiet! This is my birthday, and I came here to spend a nice evening! This should be the end of this deal right now!" So, Sonny had to get in one more . . . he said, "Someday, I'm going to *own* your team!" Ol' Wismer came off the wall again, and that was the end of it.

BUD ADAMS: I always got along fine with Harry. I thought he was real friendly, a sales type, good for the league. We played at the Polo Grounds the last game in '62, and we went out to dinner the night before. He said he felt he couldn't continue playing. I gave him $10,000 in cash.

JOE FOSS: I was trying to sell the club and we had an owners meeting. They all thought, "If Wismer had to file, that was probably the end of the league." And I just laughed: "You're getting rid of trouble when Harry goes." We had one more meeting in December '62, and they said, "Commissioner, what's the latest? Do you have anybody interested?" I had been talking to Joan Payson, owner of the New York Mets, and her son-in-law, M. Donald Grant. He was all for it. Wismer somehow got wind of it and put out a blast about it in the paper. Mrs. Payson was a sensitive, lovely lady. She didn't want to get in something where somebody was trying to knock her. She sent word through Grant that they wanted no more to do with it. I had to pick up steps on trying to figure out who in tarnation would buy the club.

LAMAR HUNT: Frankly, when the Titans failed at the end of the '62 season, I felt we should move out of New York. I didn't feel it would succeed, which was very shortsighted. The team was playing in the Polo Grounds. And though Shea Stadium was under construction, I didn't think anyone would come in and buy that team.

JOE FOSS: There were three men in South Dakota who were interested in buying half of it. I figured it would be simpler to get somebody to go along with them. Then, all of them backed out. There was a guy in Ohio who might have been interested, but he ran for the woods. It was drawing close to the end of the year. I went home to South Dakota for Christmas. Then I remembered what Sonny Werblin said to Wismer at that party . . . "Someday, I'm going to own your team." I tried to call him, but he was down at his vacation home in New Jersey. And his secretary said he left word that he was not going to be bothered for a month. I said, "Well, I'm just telling you that you'll be looking for work if you don't let me know where I can find him." She finally came through and said this would probably cost her her job. I said, "No, he'll be so happy the way you handled things." I got a hold of him, and he said, "Talk to me at the end of the month." I said, "That's too late. I've got to get this thing sold. The owners are down my throat all the time." He said, "How about meeting me tomorrow at 12:00? We'll have lunch together."

So I flew all night and got there in time for lunch. Walked in, and Sonny said, "You look tired." I said, "Yeah, I haven't been to bed since I talked to you yesterday." We went over to his office and talked it over, and Sonny said he'd give me $1,350,000 for it. He got out his checkbook and started writing the check. Bob Schulman, his lawyer, said, "This is probably the dumbest business deal you've ever made." I could have shot him right there. Sonny just turned around, smiled, and said, "I've always said that lawyers are poor businessmen." And he signed: "David A. Werblin." Part of the deal was Sonny asked me not to let anyone know for three days. I told Harry the club was sold. Oh, he was mad: "It's sold! How much?" I told him. "Who bought it?" And he just started a guessing game. Harry got so mad, he filed Chapter 11. When it went to court, which was down in the Village, there was a communications strike in New York and there wasn't a single soul from the press, thank the Lord. He had five lawyers, and they were high-powered guys. It was colder than a well digger's day off, and the only people in the audience were the winos who came in to get warm. The judge ruled a month or so later, against Wismer, and put the team up for bids. There was only one bid, for a million dollars, and that was Sonny Werblin. Wismer was really nuts. He lost, by that action, $350,000 and the cost of the court.

He was known as Sonny "as in money" Werblin, a dynamic talent agent at MCA who counted Ed Sullivan, Jackie Gleason, and a budding TV presence named Johnny Carson among his clients. Less than a month after Werblin's purchase, the transformation of the New York franchise began to take shape. Of immediate notice, the nickname was changed from the Titans to the Jets, which just happened to rhyme with the baseball Mets. And for long-range impact, New York brought in Weeb Ewbank, architect of two Baltimore NFL championships in the late '50s, to build a winner on the field.

BAKE TURNER: I was with Weeb in Baltimore. The word going around was he was senile. When I was 21 years old, I didn't even know what senile meant. They had too many wide receivers there. Don Shula called me in and said Weeb was interested in having me up there in New York. As long as I could play somewhere. Weeb had a real good talent for choosing assistant coaches. He didn't do a whole lot of coaching, but he had some real good people, like Walt Michaels, Buddy Ryan, Clive Rush, Chuck Knox.

CURLEY JOHNSON: I was with Baltimore in '58 and '59, thought I was going to get activated, and was put on the taxi squad. I didn't feel good when the Jets hired Weeb. I told my wife, "I guess this'll be a short training camp." Of course, he and I became great friends, and I stayed another five years. As a matter of fact, Bake, Winston Hill, Mark Smolinski, Dee Mackey, myself— all were from Baltimore and were familiar with Weeb's system.

JOHN FREE: My father owned part of the Baltimore Colts and I was in charge of pregame, halftime, and postgame entertainment. When Weeb got the job with the Jets, he asked me to join him in New York. I was the third person hired. We didn't even have an office.

WINSTON HILL: I got cut twice, by Baltimore and the Jets. When I got cut from Baltimore, I called my father: "Daddy, I did everything they asked me to, and I didn't understand why they cut me." He said, "Son, come on home. You don't have anything to be ashamed of. Never forget who you are. When you finished high school, nobody expected you to make college ball." When Weeb cut me from the Jets, I called home and said, "Fine. I'm ready to come home. I did everything they asked." And he said, "You go tell Weeb to let you stay on the team. Whatever he'd pay the guys in preseason, I'll pay you. Whatever he wants to charge for room and board, I'll pay the club. And if you have not made the team by the time the season starts, I will send you a ticket to come home. Hang up the phone, and go tell him now." I did, and Weeb put me on the taxi team.

9

The 12th Man and Other Unbelievable Characters

Nothing exemplified the AFL's reputation as a league in which anything could happen better than a bizarre incident at the finish of the Boston Patriots' home game against the Dallas Texans on a chilly Friday night during the first week of November in 1961. It was a night during which fans couldn't be faulted for trying to get close to one another . . . real close to the players, if the opportunity presented itself.

HANK STRAM: There was a little high school coach I met when I was in Boston before. He said, "Coach, anything I can do to help you. I'm not a great fan of the Pats, but I watch 'em practice and I watch 'em play. Anytime you play them, if you like, I'd be glad to tell you what they're doing in practice." I said, "Well, if you think you can do that—without getting caught—that's fine." We were getting ready to play this game, and he called me: "Coach, they're working on a double-reverse play. The quarterback, Babe Parilli, gives it to the halfback. The halfback runs out to the right. The flanker comes back around on a reverse, and he throws the ball downfield to the receiver. So you'd better practice that. They've been working on it very, very hard." We not only practiced it, we put it in *our* offense.

It was right near the end of the game, and we were behind by seven points. So we called the play. Abner Haynes was the halfback, Johnny Robinson the other back. We rolled out to the right. We had Chris Burford wide open. They had a defensive end, Larry Eisenhauer, and he smelled a rat and reacted to it. He was chasing Cotton Davidson, our quarterback. Cotton was running for his life. And he threw the ball downfield to Burford. Burford got behind a defensive back, caught the ball, but the guy got to him quickly. Chris was trying to right himself so he could turn around and run for a touchdown. He ran backward, slipped and fell, and was tackled at about the 5.

GINO CAPPELLETTI: The clock had run out, but somebody had called time-out. The official clock was on the field. So the officials had to push all the fans back off the field. They were right on the back line and on the sidelines around the end zone.

CHRIS BURFORD: Then we called a slant. I could beat this kid I was play-ing against. We came up to the line and had to go back in the huddle 'cause the officials were clearing the field, making sure everybody got off.

LARRY EISENHAUER: They had time for one more play. Davidson probably could have run with the ball. He chose to throw.

CHRIS BURFORD: I was split left. I went ahead, made a move, and was headed for the post. I saw Cotton, and I saw the ball released. It was com-ing right at me. I figured I was going to score. Then the ball went fluttering up in the air. I didn't know what happened. There was pandemonium, peo-ple on the field. The game ended. The game was over.

COTTON DAVIDSON: We set it up to move the backs one way to get the mid-dle linebacker to flow, to hit Burford in that void. That's right where some fan came and stood. I was all excited, upset. I told Hank, "A guy came out on the field, tipped the ball!"

GINO CAPPELLETTI: He didn't bat it down, but he ran in front of Burford. This guy snuck out of the pack, ran into the secondary, and was waving his hands. Not really picking out anyone in particular. Sure enough, he got in front of Burford. The pass was overthrown, anyway.

HANK STRAM: All of our coaches were down on the field by then instead of up in the box. It was bad enough we lost. Now Cotton was telling me a guy knocked the ball down. I said, "Oh, is that right, Cotton?" I thought he must have gotten hit in the head or something. We got in the locker room, he was taking a shower, and he came over: "Coach, I'm telling you. I could see a guy in a jacket knocking that ball down." Then we were flying home. I was sit-ting in the first seat, Cotton was in the back. He came all the way up to me:

"Coach, can I talk to you a few minutes? . . . I'm telling you, the guy in the jacket knocked the ball down." When he finished, I told him to send up Wayne Rudy, our trainer. I said, "Wayne, you'd better go back there and talk to Cotton because something's wrong with him. He says a guy in a jacket knocked the ball down."

CHRIS BURFORD: The coaches didn't find out what really happened until they looked at the film the next day. Then they saw a guy in a raincoat who came out onto the field before the play started and got led off. Then, just before the play started, he came back out, set up like a linebacker, crouched down. The play started. I was going to the post. Cotton was throwing the ball, and the guy in the overcoat jumped up and knocked the damn thing down.

JACK GRINOLD: It was suspected that a linebacker from Boston College who was being taxied at the time by the name of Frank Robotti was the hero, or culprit. He had been a starting linebacker the year before.

GINO CAPPELLETTI: Hank Stram and all the Dallas people were disappointed that something like that could happen. But, with everybody trying to make the league go, you didn't want to come up with protests. So they just let it go.

JACK GRINOLD: With the end zone surrounded by people, almost like you would see in high school games, we had another bizarre incident. It was in the final minutes of a game against the Chargers. Their quarterback, Bob Laraba, retreated into the end zone to pass. He was being rushed and dropped the football. A small boy dashed into the end zone. Bob Dee, our fine defensive end, covered the boy instead of going for the ball. He took the brunt of more than a thousand pounds as player after player piled on. We got the boy, and they got the ball. Tommy Addison, the linebacker, was quoted as saying, "I've never seen anything like it. The kid could have been killed. Instead, all he got was a good squeezing."

When defenders in trench coats or little kids weren't wandering onto the field, the most entertaining site in Boston often was Larry Eisenhauer. And the action wasn't always confined to the game itself. The former Boston College defensive lineman often went by "Ike" and, more accurately, "Wild Man."

LARRY EISENHAUER: Playing football was a wonderful thing for me. It really helped me express myself. I used to hit anything that ever moved on the field, including my own teammates. They'd get pissed off at me all the time. I used to get so wound up before a game that I'd start warming up with them. I'd get in fistfights in the locker room over programs. I'd be reading, and somebody would take it and not give it back. So, the natural thing was to haul off and belt 'em.

HOUSTON ANTWINE: He was a really, really, really strong competitor. I drew strength from Larry. Motivation, to see his enthusiasm, how he went at the game. It motivated a lot of guys on that defensive unit. I loved him as a teammate.

LARRY EISENHAUER: A couple of years later, we had a rookie defensive end from Northern Michigan named Lenny St. Jean. They all said, "Lenny, you take Ike on. We don't want him to hit us." So it was like a procedure we had before every game. I came flying out of the locker room during the introductions, running into the goal post. Then I'd make a beeline for the bench thinking, "Lenny! Where's Lenny?" I'd smack Lenny, and he'd hit me.

One of the league's most unforgettable figures was never selected for an AFL All-Star Game, was never picked as the MVP of a championship game. But were trophies awarded for, say, gulping down motor oil on a bet or shooting arrows in a training camp dorm, then one Edward McDaniel—better known simply as "Wahoo," because of his Indian heritage—would be more suitably and formally recognized for his contributions to pro football during the 1960s.

Wahoo grew up in the wide-open spaces of West Texas, in Midland. The best thing about Midland is Odessa. In the hierarchy of the Oil Patch of the 1950s, the laborers lived in Odessa while the managers lived in Midland. Wahoo's coach in a Pony League state tournament happened to be a local oilman named George Bush.

McDaniel was good enough as a running back to command a scholarship offer from Bear Bryant, coaching then at Texas A&M. But Wahoo turned down the Bear to play for the best program of the '50s, Bud Wilkinson's Oklahoma Sooners. Upon arriving in Norman, Oklahoma, Wahoo soon discovered that the Sooners were awash in running backs. Undaunted, he turned himself into a linebacker and established a niche there. To keep in shape in the off-season, Wahoo liked to work out with the school's highly respected wrestling team.

Both the Cowboys and the Chargers drafted Wahoo in 1960. He signed with Dallas and spent the exhibition season there but was cut loose. He took another shot at L.A. but was unsuccessful. But, back in Texas, he convinced the Oilers that he could play offensive guard for them. He started 10 games and helped the Oilers win the first AFL title over the Chargers.

WAHOO McDANIEL: And then I told them I wanted to play linebacker, so they traded me to Denver.

He also learned another new position in 1960, one whose duties aren't plotted out with *X*s and *O*s.

WAHOO McDANIEL: A wrestling promoter from Louisville, Kentucky, named Jim Barnett called me. They wanted an Indian to wrestle, and he wanted to fly down to see me. They looked me over and liked me. I trained for about three months. Then the next year, when football was over, I went straight to wrestling. I had a headdress and moccasins, breechcloth. It was expensive. I went through 10 or 12 sets of feathers a year. They really take a beating.

GOOSE GONSOULIN: Ol' Wahoo came into camp with the Broncos with this bow and arrow. We would come in from working out, everybody would be up and down the halls, going to get a shower, cleaning up, going out. He took that bow and arrow and shot it right down the hallway. He could have killed some guys if they'd walked out. Then one night, he came into my room: "Let's go out and get something to eat. This damn food isn't worth a crap." So we went to this drive-in hamburger place. We pulled up. A bunch of guys pulled up alongside, and they started smarting off. So Wahoo said, "You guys don't know who I am, do you?" The guys said, "Hell, no. We don't care who you are." "Well, I'm Wahoo McDaniel." Again, they said they didn't care. So Wahoo said, "Why don't y'all come meet us down the road." So we drove out someplace. Then Wahoo got out of the car. I didn't realize this, but he had a gun. He fired it up in the air. Those guys dove in the car and took off.

Later, after he got into that rasslin', we all got on his back. "Wahoo, that's the phoniest crap. What the hell are you doing rasslin' in the off-season?" He said, "Hell, I make more money doing that than I do playing football."

WAHOO MCDANIEL: I broke an ankle once, had a lot of stitches and cuts. I had some trouble with my back. I went to the chiropractor a lot. I wrestled all the big names, wrestled against them or with them. The Funks. The Briscoes. Bruno Sammartino. Andre the Giant. Bill Watts. Gorilla Monsoon.

GOOSE GONSOULIN: One time the players had a party at one of our houses, and there was a trade show in town. Mickey Mantle, Billy Martin, Paul Hornung—stars from all over were in Denver. We invited them out to this house. Wahoo went outside, and we didn't see him for a while. What happened was, Bobby Layne arrived. He got a cab from Denver and invited the cabdriver to come in. Wahoo went out, got in the cab, started driving around, and got it stuck in a creek.

WAHOO MCDANIEL: It was out in the country. We were knocking down bushes and everything. Just ran it right off in the lake. Got up on top and swam out.

JERRY STURM: The chief and I would go hunting all the time. One time he brought a double-barrel shotgun, and it ended up having a hair trigger. Our dog got on a point. The birdie came flying by, got about 10 feet away from us. Wahoo shot with both barrels, knocked him backward. He hit the pheasant dead center. The only thing that was left was one drumstick. On the way back, he had the gun inside the truck, an old panel truck we used for hunting. My dog was in the back. We had to go over a little thing, sort of twisted the car. The dog got all nervous and jumped into the front seat, and her foot hit the trigger of Wahoo's gun. The safety didn't work. That gun went off inside that car. My ears were ringing for 20 minutes. The BBs went down and hit the frame and ricocheted up into the radiator. We were able to drive for about a mile. We were out on the Valley Highway hitchhiking with two guns, a dog, and a couple pheasants. But a guy did pick us up.

In 1964, Wahoo was traded to the New York Jets. What was never intended to be a major acquisition took on new life beginning with one memorable night at Shea Stadium.

JACK FAULKNER: I traded Wahoo to the Jets just because he needed a change. And he wanted to go to New York for wrestling. He was a tough guy, but he wasn't very big. He wasn't a real good football player. He didn't have great speed, but he gave you effort. His wrestling was the big thing he wanted.

DON MAYNARD: Wahoo was probably the only guy that I know of, to this day, who had his first name on the back of his jersey. He got in there, got to playing and doing pretty good.

FRANK RAMOS: When he first came, Sam Huff of the Giants was the big defensive player in town. One of the first things Wahoo said was, "This town isn't big enough for the two of us." It turned out he was right 'cause Sam Huff was traded to the Redskins. Then, during the opening game at Shea Stadium, he was making a lot of tackles in the first half. Our PA announcer came to me and said, "Is it all right if I say, 'Tackle by, guess who?' and see what the crowd responds?" He did that, and the crowd responded, "Wahoo!" Some people thought we made up some of those statistics. Actually, we got our tackling statistics from the coaches.

WAHOO MCDANIEL: New York was great. The people treated you really good there as an athlete. You'd go out to eat, and they'd cut the price of your meal in half. The only thing that was bad there was, you'd get off football about 4:00 and it was 20 miles back to our condo at the beach on Long Island. About 15 of us lived there. And the traffic—bumper to bumper. It was like you'd never get home.

CURLEY JOHNSON: We were coming home from one of the exhibition games, stopped and got some beer and headed back to New York, and got pulled over by the cops. I think Bill Mathis was driving. Course, the guy found out who we were so he was real nice. Let us go. Told us to be careful. Then he looked over and said, "What's that son of a bitch doing?" Wahoo was peeing over his police car. We thought, "Goddamn, we're going to jail now." That guy, he had to laugh, it was so ridiculous. Wahoo was always doing something. He'd go up to Joe Namath's and play poker and cash his game check. One night I think all he had left was $100. Lost his whole game check. Then he took a hundred-dollar bill, set it on fire, and lit a cigar with it. He said, "Ain't no use going home with a hundred."

BAKE TURNER: Wahoo had been on Dainard Paulson's case for a few days. They got into a scuffle one day in the locker room. Now, Dainard was a defensive back about my size, six feet, 180. He pinned Wahoo, and everyone was amazed this rassler who had already been doing some pro rasslin' was pinned by Dainard.

WAHOO McDANIEL: In 1966, the AFL was expanding to Miami, and the Jets drafted a linebacker from Oklahoma, Carl McAdams. Weeb Ewbank said, "We're going to have to give him a chance. Miami wants you bad. You can probably get more money there, but you don't have to go if you don't want to." Stupid as I was, I said, "I don't mind. I'll go." I played there three years. And wrestled there for a long time, '95, '96.

10

One Tough Cookie

On August 4, 1962, the Bills acquired Canadian Football League standout fullback Cookie Gilchrist from the Toronto Argonauts. Gilchrist's talent was unquestioned. He never played college ball and played two years in the Ontario Rugby Football Union before unleashing his talent upon the CFL. In six seasons there, he displayed an array of skills possibly unmatched by anyone in the game at that level—he played fullback, offensive tackle, defensive tackle, and linebacker, and he returned kicks, kicked off, and kicked PATs and field goals. He was a 1,000-yard rusher. He had 10 interceptions. He was named to the divisional All-Star team as a running back five times—once as both a running back and a linebacker.

But it was also telling that those six amazing seasons took place with three franchises. He was made available for all of $5,300 after he and five teammates were caught breaking curfew by Toronto coach Lou Agase. The team's general manager, Lew Hayman, was quoted as saying he tore up a series of four one-year contracts and allowed Gilchrist to fly south because Gilchrist "gave me a headache."

Gilchrist's activities included a busy business schedule—renting out binoculars at the Woodbine horse track, running a maid service, selling light globes—that sometimes got in the way of football. He once concluded a business deal in Toronto around noon on a Saturday with a game scheduled that night against the Hamilton Tiger-Cats. Gilchrist was about halfway to Hamilton when it dawned on him that the game was in Toronto; he arrived at the stadium with barely enough time to get into uniform. There was the time that he contended that a Toronto newspaper had maligned him and was paid $5,000 by the paper to abate his mental anguish. Shortly thereafter, he tried to convince the purchasing manager at that paper to buy his line of light globes. No sale.

FRANK TRIPUCKA: I only played one season with him in Canada, '58 in Saskatchewan. He was one of the finest football players I ever saw. He'd run back punts and kickoffs. He didn't mind blocking people. He'd bone-rattle 'em. The unfortunate part of it, nobody could control him. He'd run two or three plays and say, "I know this play. I'm not going to run it anymore." And he'd tell the coach that. He'd practice for maybe 10 or 15 minutes and say, "I've had enough." He didn't care if they fined him.

JACK KEMP: Built like Arnold Schwarzenegger. Handsome guy. Great personality. Never went to college—smart as heck.

LOU SABAN: Cookie had a tryout with the Cleveland Browns straight out of high school, but I guess they felt they couldn't put up with a young guy, and he went to play in Canada. Our personnel director, Harvey Johnson, said he might be available. I told Harvey, "Why don't you have him come in?" He said, "Well, he owes some money." I said, "Tell me what we have to pay to bring him in." We arranged whatever had to be paid for him to get out of Canada. Harvey said, "He'll be here on . . . such and such a date . . . he'll be here by 12:00." Well, on that date, it got to be five minutes to 12:00. "Where is he? If he doesn't get here by 12:00, the deal is off." And I'll be darned, at 12:00, there was a knock on the door. Cookie opened the door and said, "Are you looking for somebody?" What an entrance!

CHUCK BURR: Cookie was the Bills' second catalyst, along with Jack Kemp. We got him slightly after his heyday. There was nothing the guy couldn't do. In addition to being a great runner, he was a great pass catcher. And a great blocker. In the Canadian league, he played both ways and was also a good kicker. What a lot of people don't realize about Cookie is that he couldn't see very well. Off the field, he wore glasses. The ball always came to him in a blur.

AL BEMILLER: The first day that Cookie came to our camp, we all loaded buses to go an exhibition game. We all came down dressed in shirts and ties. Here came Cookie dressed casual. He might have had shorts on. And Saban told him, "Get your butt up there. Get dressed like the rest of the ballplayers." And he did.

That first exhibition game in New Haven, the man had never played with us. Before the game, he was very, very verbal. We were looking at each other: "Who the hell is this guy?" He was going to kick off. He kicked off, went down, and made the tackle.

JOE COLLIER: He started screaming as he was going down to cover. He knocked two guys down and made the tackle. Right then, our whole damn team thought, "He's our guy." He turned out to be the best blocking fullback I've ever seen. He was the first *big* fullback. He was 250. And he was the toughest sucker I'd ever seen come down the pike. He wanted to play linebacker, too. I don't doubt he could have. But he wanted to get two salaries.

Gilchrist might have been a bargain at twice the price, serving as Buffalo's starting fullback and placekicker for the '62 season. He wasted little time in proving he was worth all the attention. In the second game, he broke the club rushing record with 131 yards at home against the Broncos despite pulling a hamstring that contributed to two missed field-goal attempts. That mark lasted five games, erased by a 143-yard effort against Oakland at War Memorial. Gilchrist rushed for 100 or more yards six times, shattered the league rushing record for a season in the penultimate game, finished the season as the AFL's first 1,000-yard rusher (1,096), and was named Most Valuable Player.

JOE COLLIER: We were getting beaten in Denver. Frank Tripucka threw about four touchdowns. I was visualizing the headlines the next day in the paper: "Collier's Defense Stinks." Cookie caught a screen pass right in front of the bench and took it about 60 yards. And I ran right down the sideline with him: "C'mon, Cookie!" We won, and they didn't say a thing about my defense.

BUTCH BYRD: One time, the Oilers were beating us when they shouldn't have been. Cookie went around to everybody, yelling and screaming: "You've got to play now, or I'll kick your ass!" To everybody. No one told him to sit down, and we won that game. I don't know if it was because of his vocalness, but that certainly played a part in it.

BILLY SHAW: He was the best football player I've ever played with or have seen. Not the best athlete, the best football player. He was 252 pounds, but he was built so different. His calves behind his knees were deerlike legs. He was so strong in his upper body.

BOOKER EDGERSON: He had all the confidence in the world. It was like he was made to play the game. Whoever'd run up, he'd run at him and then run over him. A lot of guys said, "Why don't you sidestep and run around?" He said, "I want to teach them a lesson. If I run over 'em, they won't come up anymore."

We were roommates that first year along with Monte Crockett, a tight end, and Cookie wasn't around a whole lot. He more or less stayed up in Canada his first two years. We practiced in the morning in those days, so he would go back and forth to Canada. Toronto was about an hour and a half away, and the speed limits weren't enforced that much. So Monte and I benefited from his big salary. Cookie bought all the furniture other than the bedroom stuff. We used to go up to Toronto and have parties from time to time, play cards. He was the social director.

And before the 1963 season began, Gilchrist displayed more numbers that were reminders of why he often quickly wore out a welcome. In February, he filed for bankruptcy, listing $59,000 in debts and $7,400 in assets. In May, five officers escorted him to a jail cell, where he spent about 12 hours following his arrest initially for running a stop sign. He produced neither a driver's license nor registration for the car, decked an officer, and was eventually charged with seven offenses. The charges were all dropped more than a year later, citing double jeopardy.

VAN MILLER: Cookie was the worst card player in the history of the world. We flew then in old DC6Bs, prop jets. On those West Coast trips, you're talking maybe seven hours. We played seven-card stud. Cookie'd always try to fill the inside straight. He would never drop out of a hand. If we took off from Buffalo, by the time we were over Chicago, Cookie would be borrowing money. But he always paid it back.

JOE COLLIER: He had all kinds of schemes. Outside the stadium, he sold Christmas trees. He was always selling something. He sold stock in a gold mine in South America. He got Lou and Ralph Wilson to buy some. He was always involved because he was always running out of money. One year, he came in and got an advance on his salary—you didn't have bonuses in those days. He went out with another guy and bought an airplane. The guy got in the plane, took off, and Cookie hasn't seen him since.

ELBERT DUBENION: One time Cookie went to get a haircut and saw a parking space close to the barbershop. By the time he got there, somebody had gotten it. So he wanted a space about two spots back that he passed, but there was a whole line of cars behind him. He wanted people to back up their cars so he could get the other spot. They wouldn't do it, so he locked his doors and stayed there until the law came. He thought he was right.

LOU SABAN: He was tough to handle. He and I had a great understanding. At the same time, he didn't quite understand he wasn't the only person on the ballclub. He wanted to become the greatest who ever was. And I said, "You *can* be, Cookie, but let us handle things."

BUTCH BYRD: It was clear that Lou didn't know Cookie, and Cookie couldn't have cared less. One game we came in at halftime, and Cookie started taking off all his stuff. I'd never seen that before. It turned out, that was Cookie's ritual but no one seemed to notice until that game. Lou was beside himself because he thought Cookie was taking off.

Gilchrist's second season in Buffalo began in a different gear after he suffered a rib injury during the exhibition season. It took him nine games to register his first 100-yard performance, but he turned it on in the last two games when the Bills swept the Jets to finish in a first-place tie with Boston. He rumbled for a pro-record 243 yards at home, breaking the mark set six years earlier by Cleveland's Jim Brown by 6 yards, and added another 114 the next week at the Polo Grounds. But in the cold and snow at War Memorial in the divisional playoff game, he mustered only seven yards on eight carries as the Patriots won. He finished third in the league in rushing with 979 and was so insistent that he was underpaid that he asked for a trade—in writing, copies of which he sent to local reporters:

> It unfortunately becomes necessary again for me to formally request that you make efforts to trade me to some other football club in the AFL. My attorney, Mr. Messina, and I have made these requests since

April of 1963 without, I feel, adequate response from you. Therefore, in the best interest of the Buffalo fans—who have been exceptionally kind to me—and in the best interest of the team, and, frankly, in my own best interest, may I ask you to give serious consideration to the trade offers made for me by other AFL clubs.

Very truly yours, Carlton C. Gilchrist

CHUCK BURR: We set up a press conference in June to announce his signing a new contract. We had the press, local radio, and television down in our offices. No Cookie. Where was Cookie? He was up in Canada. He and a group of prospective investors had hired helicopters to stake claims for what they considered to be uranium deposits up in the wilds of Ontario. He called the next day. He apologized, but by then the damage had been done.

BILLY SHAW: Cookie liked to be the center of attention. Jack Kemp was a master at handling Cookie's temper tantrums. When Cookie got mad, Jack had a way with him. But on Sunday, Cookie was always ready to play.

That "ready to play" fail-safe took a beating with the Bills at their zenith late in the 1964 season. A franchise that had never before stood more than a game above the .500 mark won its first nine games, most of them in impressive fashion. The Bills could virtually clinch the Eastern Division title when Boston came to visit on November 15. The Patriots, though, were no pushovers, leading 14–13 late in the first half. Buffalo was pushing downfield with the prospect of at least kicking a field goal to grab the lead at intermission, when the most significant substitution in Bills history took place.

CHUCK BURR: All of a sudden, Cookie took himself out and sent in his backup, Willie Ross. Saban had no knowledge he did it until he saw Willie Ross.

Kemp had attempted 22 passes in the first half, completing 10 for 168 yards. Gilchrist had carried five times for 23 yards. Buffalo quarterbacks had averaged 28 passes per game during the season. Gilchrist had averaged 16 carries per game.

LOU SABAN: We didn't give him the ball much, not for any specific reason. We just felt we had to attack in a different way. We wanted to get in position to kick a field goal. Cookie walked by me. I didn't say anything. At halftime, I said, "Cook, why'd you do it?" He said, "You haven't given me the ball." I said, "You're going to have to play under our rules, not your rules."

The Bills came to life early in the third quarter, taking advantage of a Patriots fumble on a kickoff return to score two touchdowns in a matter of seconds and go ahead 28–14. But Boston hung tough and scored three consecutive touchdowns to build a 36–28 cushion—the last TD set up by a fumble by Kemp—midway through the final quarter. Saban then benched Kemp for young Daryle Lamonica with no success. The loss eliminated thoughts of a perfect season and slapped the Bills into the reality of being concerned about winning the division, Boston having pulled within a game and a half with four games to play.

And there was another problem—how to deal with Gilchrist's latest transgression. To Saban, the answer was as simple as the waiver wire, where Gilchrist landed on the Tuesday morning after the game. Oakland, New York, and, ironically, Boston placed claims for the enigmatic star the next day; Oakland, by virtue of having the worst record of the three, would be entitled to his services—except that a group of Bills players interceded on behalf of Gilchrist.

LOU SABAN: The players came up to me and said, "Coach, we've had a great team. We've hung in there together. We want Cookie back. We know he was out of line, but we've got a really strong club." I said, "Do you want him back 'cause you want to win, or do you want him back 'cause you want to help him?" They were very dedicated to giving the guy another shot.

JACK KEMP: I felt kind of responsible. I called my own plays, a lot of them at the line of scrimmage. I might have overdone it, didn't run him enough. He walked out on Saban, but he was really mad at me. And we were very good friends. We came to practice on Tuesday, and he wasn't there. So I took it upon myself to go over to his apartment and had a long talk with him.

BILLY SHAW: Hey, we weren't stupid. But Cookie had to ask his way back on the team, humble himself.

CHUCK BURR: It took Billy Shaw, Jack Kemp, half a dozen other players— I got into that act a little bit, too—to talk Lou into recalling the waivers. He finally did but only after Cookie went on television that night on Channel 4 and issued an abject apology for his actions.

All appeared well the following week, when Gilchrist carried 21 times as Buffalo won a showdown of division leaders at San Diego. The Bills still needed to win their season finale at Boston to claim the division crown—and did so, 24–14. And Gilchrist was among the stars in Buffalo's championship win over the Chargers, rushing for 122 yards. But that performance ended his Bills career. He had three seasons, more than 3,000 yards, and a ticket to Denver in a straight-up swap for fellow fullback Billy Joe, the 1963 Rookie of the Year. Three years and two more moves later, he was out of football.

LOU SABAN: He carried us for two years. We were building while he was carrying. He could mesmerize a crowd. He was a great speaker, very thoughtful. He was fun! Clever! Entertaining! People loved him! But all of a sudden, he'd come to a curve in the road, and he'd become another person.

AL BEMILLER: He didn't do anything close to what these people do today. He didn't beat up his wife, get caught with drugs. He didn't kill anybody. It was just a discipline problem.

BUTCH BYRD: I thought Cookie was the heart and soul of the team. Sure, he was controversial. And he had some run-ins with the law. But when it came down to playing, it was a comfort to have him there.

JACK KEMP: He came to maturity at a time that coincided with the Civil Rights movement. Face it: none of us white guys had any inkling of what it was like to be a professional athlete and be treated as a third-class, third world citizen. And Cookie was a very proud guy. Guys today talk about racial profiling, getting stopped. He got stopped all the time. Here was a big, good-looking African-American football player driving a white Cadillac in the streets of Buffalo or Toronto. He didn't take any guff from anybody. To his credit, it's remarkable that his career was as unhindered as it was.

11

The Weakest Link

The surest bet going into the AFL's maiden season was that the Oakland Raiders were the shakiest team in a shaky league, problems affixed to their entry like barnacles. They were technically the last club to join, the league awarding the orphaned Minneapolis franchise only in late January. The Raiders were one of three AFL clubs that would face direct NFL competition in their market, from the San Francisco 49ers across the bay. And compounded to all this, not only was there "no there there" in Oakland, as Gertrude Stein famously wrote, there was certainly no adequate pro football stadium there. Like George Bailey groveling to old man Potter in *It's a Wonderful Life*, the AFL's Oakland team suffered the indignity of having to ask for at least temporary shelter over in San Francisco's Kezar Stadium, already home to the 49ers. This couldn't be likened to the Los Angeles Chargers' sharing of the L.A. Coliseum with the Rams. The Coliseum boasted a storied history and initially provided the Chargers some "big-league" identity, though the "big" really described how massive the structure looked when barely occupied for a game. Anyone who dared to pick Oakland above last in the AFL West really hadn't paid attention.

Even coming up with the team nickname required much more time and attention than necessary because the fix was in on the initial appointment. One of the club's many owners was in the habit of addressing acquaintances as "señor" and rigged a name-the-team contest to result in the club's being called the Oakland Señors, with the lucky winner receiving a trip to the Caribbean. The contest was conveniently won by a woman who was very close to said owner. The club's name was announced at a cocktail party, with an informal mascot making a grand entrance clad in sombrero and serape. Soon after, someone decided such a moniker was not in the best interest of the city, and the nickname Raiders was eventually adopted along with the helmeted pirate and crossed swords logo.

It was into such an atmosphere that a veritable football hayseed like Jim Otto arrived. Undrafted by the NFL, the University of Miami lineman reached the San Francisco airport with two cardboard suitcases, a rare size-8 helmet, a pair of cleats draped over his shoulder, and absolutely no idea of how to get to Raider camp in Santa Cruz, north of the Bay Area. But he did have a keen ear and heard an announcement that all Oakland Raiders players were to report to a certain area to catch a bus.

JIM OTTO: Our first camp was at the Palomar Hotel. The first day of practice in pads, I lined up and said, "Well, this is it." I took a couple deep breaths and went at 'em like a wild man. When I got through, I said, "Well, this isn't bad at all. I can do this." Every time I lined up, I just sucked it up and kicked their butt. I started getting a little bigger and lifting weights. We always had to go where they had some weights, so I teamed up with a friend of mine on the offensive line named Don Manoukian.

To say Don Manoukian was cut from a different cloth would require apology to the entire textile industry. Enrolled at the relatively sedate bastion of learning that is Stanford University, Manoukian compiled a personal résumé that indicated his mind wasn't always on his studies. He and a teammate were kicked from the squad after tossing some garbage cans on top of a theater while on a trip to play Ohio State. Then there was the time that he rode his motorcycle through the school library wearing only a jockstrap and a grin—though it wasn't his idea. Oh, and his initial foray into a sports career was as a pro wrestler.

DON MANOUKIAN: I had secured the plumb athletic department job, marshaling the Stanford golf course, keeping all the local high school kids and residents from sneaking on. I talked the greens keeper into letting me marshal it on my motorcycle. So it became a pretty well-known thing that this guy on the motorcycle was a little bit goofy. Scared people to death. Stopped the sneaking on immediately. And then the guys put up a $20 bill for me to ride my bike into the library wearing only a jockstrap. That was a lot of money at that time.

We played at Ohio State, and John Brodie was our quarterback, and it was Ohio State's homecoming. He hit a receiver in the end zone with no time left, and the kid dropped the ball and we lost. It could have been an incredible upset. We were at the Deschler Hilton in Columbus. Curley Carswell and I had a few cocktails and commandeered the service elevator and thought that we, in our own mature way, would get even. We dumped these garbage cans full of champagne bottles, which the Buckeyes emptied celebrating the homecoming victory, in the theater next door. We thought we were bulletproof. Of course, we got nabbed with greasy hands, and they threw us in the slammer until sunup.

I finished up at Stanford in December of '57, played in the East-West Shrine Game, and was voted the outstanding lineman. So the 49ers felt pressure to get a local boy signed up. They had some fine offensive linemen. I went through the exhibition season, and they elected to keep the experienced guys. I was five eight, about 255. Even at that time, they liked big guys. I wound up playing the rest of the '58 season with the Salinas Packers in a semipro league that came and went. It involved the Tucson Cowboys, the Orange County Rhinos, the Eagle Rock Athletic Club in L.A., the Petaluma Leghorns—those are chickens—the South San Francisco Sea & Ski Windbreakers, the Bakersfield Spoilers. Their quarterback was Tommy Flores. I was very disappointed in not playing in the NFL and became a wrestler, Don "the Bruiser" Manoukian. I wrestled in Japan. I was contacted by Brodie, who was the Niners' quarterback at the time, and by Paul Wiggin. They said, "Hey, you can still play. There's a new league that would be just right. You ought to come back to the States and play." So I came back.

The Raiders brought home a native to coach in Eddie Erdelatz, who led Navy to 50 wins in the period 1950–58, including a Sugar Bowl win over Ole Miss and a Cotton Bowl victory over Rice. The Oakland game program was effusive in its praise for him: "Mr. Imagination . . . Mr. Success . . . Mr. Oakland Raider—that's Eddie Erdelatz, popular coach of our Raiders!"

To the surprise of many—or at least those paying attention to the first season of AFL football—the Raiders were not the worst team in the league. Flores and Babe Parilli provided leadership at quarterback and guided Oakland to a 6–8 finish.

BABE PARILLI: Eddie really didn't know pro football. We had 10 plays. All we did was run. We had two teams, Flores on one team and me on the other. We'd run on the field in practice, run a play, and sprint off the field. Eddie and I didn't get along too well.

Home games at least featured the added bonus of relief from aggravating traffic delays and parking problems. The original Raiders didn't play in front of a home crowd of as much as 13,000, with the finale against Denver luring in 5,159. And to save money, the team's seven road games were arranged so only the short trip down to Los Angeles was a one-game trip. The three East Coast stops (Boston, Buffalo, and New York) and the three other ports (Denver, Dallas, and Houston) were made on two huge round-trip flights.

TOM FLORES: We started out in Kezar Stadium. There was nowhere else to play. We had more seagulls than we had people.

DON MANOUKIAN: Partway through the season, we lost our rights to play there because the field was just too torn up. Poly High School, across the street, would practice there. They'd play junior college games in there. And that was the Niners' home field. So Candlestick Park was the next choice.

TOM FLORES: You talk about wind. We actually had a punter at Candlestick who punted a ball for minus-three yards. It went up in the air and came down out of bounds three yards behind the line of scrimmage.

We would usually follow the Chargers on the road or they would follow us. And in '61, we played those three games in the East and went from there to Dallas before coming home, to play on Thanksgiving. We ate canned turkeys.

Such perks weren't enough to keep Manoukian, who continued to hear the siren call of turnbuckles and step-over toeholds. When the season ended, he disappeared into the north woods with no intention of returning to the Raiders.

DON MANOUKIAN: I was wrestling in Oregon in the middle of the summer just before I went to Japan. I was in Portland, and the 49ers were up there playing an exhibition game on a Saturday night. And a bunch of the guys came to the matches on Friday night. They were at ringside, and they came in like they didn't know me. These were guys that I'd worked out with, played with, drank beer with. And they started giving me the business, getting the people behind them and saying, "Hey, that guy's a dirty wrestler. Let's get him!" Those sons of bitches wound up having a riot there. The people didn't know who the hell they were and were going to support them when they attacked the ring. Yeah, that was a great time.

The owners sent up Otto, my old roommate, and his instructions were, "Bring that guy back to camp." Otto ended up traveling with us, Shag

Thomas and Luther Lindsay and a couple of other characters. Goddamn Otto—he fit right in. He just loved it. Wrestling on the road, driving back in the middle of the night, drinking beer. Shoot, it was terrific. And we almost got him except we ran out of time to break him in, to get him as a big German. We could have made some money up there with him—a lot of Germans up in the Northwest. He decided he'd better get his ass back to camp.

I came back to Oakland before leaving for Japan, and we had a party in Jackie Jensen's bar. He and an old quarterback from Cal named Boots Erb had a restaurant in Jack London Square called the The Bow and Bell. Wayne Valley came up to me and made me a financial offer to play. I really felt bad that I couldn't accept. I had a moral and contractual obligation to go to Japan and wrestle. And I knew the wrestling engagement would be more long term than the football career. To do it over again, I probably would have had more fun playing another couple of years with Oakland.

Otto, having resisted the temptation of becoming "Herman the German," reported to the second Raiders camp and experienced a life-changing event— or at least an event that would put his stamp on professional football. All thanks to an imaginative equipment manager named Frank Hinek.

JIM OTTO: The first year, I wore number 50. Now, a lot of guys would call me "Ott," which sounded like "aught," which is zero. Frank got the big idea that I should have a different jersey. "Why don't we put an 'aught' on Otto's jersey?" Someone said, "No, Johnny Olszewski is wearing that with the Redskins. That's Johnny O." Then someone said, "Why don't you have 'aught-o' put on the jersey?" They asked me what I thought, and I said, "I don't know. It seems kind of weird." They said, "We'd like to do that, for recognition." The first three or four games that year I played with number 50, and then they got permission from Joe Foss to wear the double zero. He thought it was a neat idea.

The '61 season was a step back. Parilli was traded to Boston, and the reins of the offense were handed over to Flores exclusively. The Raiders began with the unenviable task of playing the two division champs on the road. They opened with a 55–0 loss to the Oilers. The subsequent 44–0 defeat at San Diego must not have been recognized as progress, because Erdelatz was fired and replaced by one of his assistants, Marty Feldman. The Raiders were 1–6 at midseason and cracked 10,000 for a home crowd only when the division champion Chargers came up the coast. Feldman's main contribution was fashioning a second consecutive home victory over the oddly attired Broncos, but even that wasn't enough to avoid a 2–12 showing that was the worst in the league. And, without its own stadium, rumors of the Raiders' relocation were more frequent than victory celebrations.

JIM OTTO: Eddie Erdelatz treated us all like we were plebes in the navy. He really worked us hard and wanted us to do certain things. In 1961, the coaches were arguing with each other all the time. There was no loyalty. And Marty Feldman got very close to the owners and made them think he knew something about football. He was not a football coach. He was a rugby coach.

The second year, we heard that someone from New Orleans was talking to the Oakland people about moving the team there. And there was talk about Seattle wanting a team. Our owners would always cry poor; we didn't have any money or this, that, and the other. I got married in 1962 and wanted to buy a home. My father-in-law said he'd loan me some money for a down payment but said, "Please, don't do it now because you might be moving to New Orleans."

And a team desperate for players cashed in the first pick in the college draft for some established veterans. That's why Lance Alworth didn't become a Raider. It reached the point that the AFL arranged for a special internal draft through which the two teams that were obviously sucking wind to keep up—the Raiders and Broncos—were allowed to choose three players made available by the other six clubs. Somewhere amid the gloom, Oakland could look on the bright side. The end of the '61 campaign meant no longer having to cross the Bay Bridge to play a home game. Construction of the Raiders' own home stadium in Oakland was complete. The bright side, in this case, was gleaming steel from a bare-bones facility that accommodated about 20,000 fans right off the Nimitz Freeway. What humble Frank Youell Field lacked in opulence was made up for in the fact that, well, it was finished and ready for play.

TOM FLORES: It was like a little high school stadium, almost like a little erector set. It wasn't much, but it was home. There weren't many fans, but you could turn around and talk to 'em.

LARRY EISENHAUER: Hey, I loved every second of playing pro football, so going to Frank Youell Field to play the Raiders was like playing in Yankee Stadium. Just to be there.

It didn't take long for misfortune to hit the '62 team. Flores was diagnosed with tuberculosis, and Oakland hastily acquired Cotton Davidson from Dallas. New stadium? Same old team. A crowd of 17,053 greeted the Raiders when they played their first home exhibition game against San Diego, but that number wasn't reached the rest of the season. The 1961 campaign took on the aura of the "good old days" when the Raiders threatened to go through the full season winless. They stood at 0–13, disposing of Feldman in favor of assistant Red Conkright going into the finale at home against Boston. Lucky for Oakland, it faced a Boston team that had seen its chance to win the Eastern Division disappear the previous day when Houston clinched the title with a victory at New York. The listless Patriots became the first Raiders shutout victims ever, 20–0 in the rain and mud before 8,000. The victory was celebrated with blaring car horns in the parking lot and was chronicled, as was every Raiders game that season, in the "Monday Morning Quarterback" column in the *Oakland Tribune*, written by Tom Flores.

TOM FLORES: I had a fever and a spot on my lungs. I don't know if it was life-threatening, but I was in isolation for 10 days. There was no medical coverage in those days. We had twin boys, only two months old; I was feeling pretty good about my career in spite of winning but two games in '61. Then I'm without a job, without any funds at all. We had nothing. If it hadn't been for my in-laws, I don't know what we would have done.

TOM YEWCIC: We were a half game behind Houston. And when they won in New York on Saturday . . . Babe Parilli had gotten hurt, and I quarterbacked the last five or six games. So when the game meant nothing, everybody went into Frisco except me. The next day, we got in the huddle, nobody wanted to play. Back then, nobody was even playing for contracts. We lost, and I got clobbered. I got a black eye, and my face was swollen.

Red Conkright was thanked for ending Oakland's 19-game losing streak and then relieved of his coaching duties. (Actually, nearly all of the Raiders' coaching staff was out scouting during that last game and only victory. Defensive assistant Walt Michaels was left behind as caretaker.) Oakland ownership, to its credit, sought to emulate the success achieved in the AFL West by San Diego and listed young Chargers assistant Al Davis among those whom they would interview for the vacancy. The AFL All-Star Game in San Diego provided a convenient opportunity for interviewing Davis. A meeting was arranged that included owners Wayne Valley and Ed McGah; Davis; and two members of the *Oakland Tribune* sports staff, sports editor George Ross and football writer Scotty Stirling. The owners excused themselves at one point, which gave Davis the opportunity to tell the two newspapermen, "These guys don't even know the right questions to ask!" The club offered a one-year contract, and Davis immediately turned it down. The offer was extended to three years. Davis said he wanted to be general manager as well as coach. Ten days later, he was in command of Oakland's football fortunes.

WALT MICHAELS: When Al Davis came in, there were three of us left— myself, Conkright, and Ollie Spencer. Al said he was going to make new moves. I hired a U-Haul.

JIM OTTO: We didn't know what to expect with Al. But the first day we got to camp and thereafter, we worked and we worked and we worked and we worked. He wanted to see who the football players were. We wore pads in the morning. We wore pads in the afternoon. We hit, morning and afternoon, all the time. We were excited because we finally had a real football man.

TOM FLORES: Right away, you could see and feel that it was being run a different way. The offense that was put in was very enjoyable. Being a quarterback, I liked it. We threw the ball. Some of the players that he brought in helped us, and we were able to get on a roll.

FRED WILLIAMSON: Al Davis was a con man. He could con you into believing you could walk through a wall. We knew Al Davis was coaching Lance Alworth down in San Diego. We figured we had someone who could choose the right players and take us all the way.

And Williamson happened to firmly believe he was one of the "right" players. He came into his own, joining Jim Otto as a Raiders All-Star in 1962, after being cut by San Francisco and spending a nondescript year with Pittsburgh. As a Raider, he became a topic of conversation among football fans with his white shoes and style of playing defensive back that included use of "the Hammer," a thunderous forearm usually addressed to an opposing player's head that also became his nickname.

JIM OTTO: A lot of people put the tag "showboat" on him. He was always a pretty boy. He played hard. For the type of football in those days, he was part of the recognition that the league was trying to get. He was an average cornerback.

TOM FLORES: He was a lot of braggadocio and very confident in that day and age and played well. He was probably ahead of his time. Nowadays, he'd probably be one of the calm ones. He was one of the first big defensive corners. In those days, you could beat a guy up on the line of scrimmage if you could get a hold of him.

FRED WILLIAMSON: The nickname came when I was with the 49ers. They put me at cornerback after drafting me as a flanker. I couldn't cover because I didn't have the experience of having to run backward. After embarrassing me for two weeks, coach Red Hickey came over and said, "Son, you're not going to make this team." I'd never been a loser at anything. No way I could go back home and tell 'em I didn't make the team. I decided since I was bigger than everybody I was covering—six three, 200—I started knocking everybody down in practice. I would never let 'em get more than five or six yards downfield. After about five days of this, Hickey said, "Listen, will you stop hammering my players so I can get some pass offense in?" And the name stuck.

Davis changed the franchise inside and out. He junked the black and gold color scheme for black and silver, ditched the uniforms' rounded numerals and sleeve stripes for block-style numbers and no stripes at all. Gone were the black helmets with nothing on them, looking like a bargain pickup from the nearest five-and-dime. In were the silver helmets with logos on the sides—all of which remain today. Oakland was the surprise of the league, going from 1–13 to 10–4, sweeping Davis's old Chargers team and coming within a game of edging out San Diego for first place.

COTTON DAVIDSON: The final week of training camp, Al cut two offensive tackles that had started all camp and kept the one that had played sparingly. His philosophy was, if they can't win for you, don't keep 'em. Frank Youso and Dick Klein came in that Monday and played every down when we opened the season on Sunday. We had very few people around at the end of that first year that we had at the beginning of it.

We beat everybody in our division twice that year. The first time we played San Diego, Al's old team, I threw an interception and Al met me on the 10-yard line and let me know he didn't appreciate that. I threw a touchdown with just seconds to go to win the game. Beating Sid Gillman in San Diego was a big, big victory for him, and that was the first time I really saw Al emotional. When we played them in Oakland, we scored 30-something in the last 11 minutes and beat 'em. It was rainy and misty. Sid had on a topcoat and a hat. Every time we'd score, he was taking something off. By the time the game was over, he was in his shirtsleeves.

Trumpets did not blare when the Raiders brought in Ben Davidson after the beginning of training camp in 1964. No football blue blood, Davidson didn't play football in high school and had to be shown how to buckle his pants when he went out for the team at East L.A. Junior College. But in his first game, he got clipped and responded by gouging the opposing player's eye— confirming his attraction to the sport; he eventually earned a scholarship to the University of Washington. But he lasted only three weeks in New York Giants camp in 1961 and did little to distinguish himself, benchwarming for a year with Green Bay and two with Washington.

BEN DAVIDSON: I was a Raider all along. I didn't fit in with the Redskins. They had me playing backup offensive tackle, backup defensive end. Abe Gibron, five nine or so, was the offensive line coach. He was in charge of weight. When I got there in '62, he poked me in the chest and said, "268." And I said, "What's 268?" He said, "That's your weight. Don't go above it." Training camp 1964, big weigh-in. I never even went and weighed myself before the weigh-ins because I thought I weighed about 230. The scale went to around 270. Abe looked at the chart, and he started screaming at me: "It's guys like you that don't care and blame all their misfortunes on me." That's when they released me.

The week before, I knew that was going to happen because they evidently put me on waivers to see if anyone in the NFL wanted me. I got a call on the pay phone on the wall at the dorm where we lived: "This is Ron Wolf, Oakland Raiders. Ben, the Redskins have you on waivers, and we'd like you." I said, "Well, they haven't told me anything." He said, "Maybe they're shopping you around, but we'd like to have you." When the Redskins got rid of me, they said, "We know the Jets are interested in you, and you might want to talk to them." Since I had started my career in New York, I was pretty excited. I could go back and show Allie Sherman and prove myself. Well, the Raiders called again, and I said, "No, I'd rather go to New York." And Ron Wolf said, "We have your rights, so you gotta come with us."

Davidson developed into one of the AFL's most feared defensive linemen and one of its most recognizable figures, thanks in part to a handlebar mustache that he grew shortly after joining the team. The league had its first marquee villain.

TOM KEATING: Nobody wanted to sit next to him on the bench. Fans used to throw shit at him. He loved it. He would just revel in it. Ben was always so different. I'd never seen anybody like him. The first year of the Coliseum, they were having a lot of trouble with the drainage because the field was actually below sea level. We went out for warm-ups, and the end zone was soaked. The defensive linemen, of course, were in the end zone, and the coaches said, "Don't worry about getting on the ground. Just stretch." What did Ben do? Got on the ground. Did his sit-ups. Rolled around in the water, covered with mud. I thought, "What do those people on the other side who have to play against this guy think?" But with Ben, it was him against 21 other guys on the field. You had to look out. I would be tackling the quarterback and *wham*, he'd run right into you. Ben always thought a late hit was hitting the guy in the parking lot when he was going home with his girlfriend. If the guy was anywhere near the field, he'd hit him. He'd hit him high so he wasn't trying to wreck his legs or anything. He was an offensive lineman for a long time, and he was great to play next to 'cause he knew all the offenses. Ben knew all the calls. He'd be on the line of scrimmage and say, "They're gonna run this way." Sure enough, they would.

Davidson was only one of the personalities on the Raiders that didn't quite fit a chamber of commerce mold, most of whom played defense. Another was Dan Birdwell, a lineman from Texas who amazed teammates with his vast collection of activities on and off the field.

TOM KEATING: He played center for a while at Houston, so he knew all the offenses. He was six four and weighed about 265. He had the biggest hands I've ever seen on a player. You could drop a quarter through his ring. His hands were so big that he couldn't put his hands in his pants pockets. He'd use his first two fingers and his thumb to get his wallet out. And his feet were the same way.

BEN DAVIDSON: Dan Birdwell was a legend. I'd go to All-Star Games, and other players would want to hear Birdwell stories. He was the beast of Big Spring, Texas, kind of a prototype Texan. His head was somehow . . . part of his ear would stick out below the helmet. We could never figure it out. Keating one time went to an official and said, "Make him put his ear in his helmet!" We had a defense that called for Birdwell, the defensive tackle, to cover the tight end. He could backpedal, but the last thing Birdwell wanted to do was have to run downfield with the tight end. To solve this problem, Dan decided that the best thing was to hit the tight end in the head with his fist. And twice, Dan Birdwell hit tight ends in the head with his fists and knocked them out at the line of scrimmage, through their helmets. If you can imagine a bunch of guys like the Raiders looking at film of one of their guys dropping a guy with one punch, it was like carrying him around the locker room on your shoulders.

DAVE COSTA: The first day I walked into training camp as a rookie, I saw this guy sleeping in the bed. All I saw was this big, hairy back. I was tiptoe-ing since I was a rookie. I made a little noise, and he jumped out of bed and said, "How ya' doing? Dan Birdwell!" He was shaking my hand and had the biggest hands and was the strongest guy. His face had cuts on it. His nose was broken. I thought, "God, is that what I'm going to look like in 10 years?" I said, "How long have you been playing?" He said, "I was a rookie last year!" I thought, "Oh, God. That's what I'm going to look like *next* year!"

In between practices, we'd always rest because it was so exhausting. Lie in the bed and put our feet up against the wall, try to drain the blood out of them. So we'd always pass out. One time I passed out, got up, and was going to the afternoon practice, and Dan wasn't there. I started to walk over to the training room. In Santa Rosa, it was about 100 degrees. I saw these feet hanging out from under his beat-up car. I kicked the feet and said, "Dan! Dan! We've got to go to practice!" He said, "Aw, I'm just changing the brakes!" He came out from under the car, and he didn't have a shirt on. It was a gravel parking lot, and he had big pieces of rock stuck in his back. He just walked over to camp like nothing had happened.

TOM KEATING: Physical pain wasn't even on his radar. He was one of those guys that I thought was literally indestructible. I got to the team when we were in Houston, and Ben said, "C'mon. You've got to watch Birdwell shave." Birdwell was standing in front of the mirror with a can of shaving cream and, in those days, a razor with the blade that popped out. He put in a new blade. Then he took the shaving cream—it looked like a cream pie—and smeared it all over his face, part of his nose. Then he ran the blade in this huge basin of hot water. Then—he did this without stopping—he went *wham, wham, wham* on one side, *wham, wham, wham* on the other. Underneath his chin. Then he closed his lips together and went right across his mouth. When he was finished, he threw water all over himself. There were big puddles on the floor. He'd turn around, grab a towel, and wipe himself off. Then he'd start to bleed. There were nicks and cuts. And Dan would wear a short-sleeve white shirt and a tie and a sport coat. Blood stains all over the shirt. That went on all week, the same thing every week.

COTTON DAVIDSON: Our training camp in Oakland was the back section of a motel. There was a little quadrangle, and we were chipping golf balls. Dan wasn't a golfer, and he hit one right through the door of the game room; it bounced around and broke up a card game. All of a sudden, guys came flying out of there.

BEN DAVIDSON: He and I were roommates. They thought maybe I could civilize him. They cut one of his best friends, a linebacker named John Robert Williamson, just kind of a journeyman. Dan got so upset he went out and drank I don't know how many screwdrivers, came back and threw up in the bathroom. The maid refused to clean it, and it dried. We had to keep the door closed, and I had to go out back and piss in the bushes. But he knew his football. The defensive line coach would give us tests, and we always wondered what would happen if you failed your test, if you wouldn't have to play in the game: "Coach, if we don't do good, will Carleton play the whole game?" Our defensive line coach had no sense of humor, so Birdwell would ace those tests. Another one of Dan's roommates wondered why his toothbrush was always wet in the morning. He thought it was condensation from the window in the bathroom, so he closed the window. And his toothbrush was wet again. Never could figure it out. It turned out Birdwell had been using his toothbrush. Raiders roommates sharing.

Even with new personnel and the new Davis attitude, there remained signs that the Raiders, like every other team in the AFL, were far from Easy Street. Sometimes, it was as evident as noticing who was parking your car at Golden Gate Park.

JIM OTTO: I didn't park cars like some other guys, but at $7,000 a year, you had to have another job. I'd make $150 a week selling ready-mix concrete. I'd go out speaking every night. I'd get $15 a speaking engagement. I'd speak to anybody who'd hear me speak. And I could eat for free, so my wife didn't have to make me dinner.

BEN DAVIDSON: The Raiders ticket office had probably been a gas station in the '50s. It had a canvas awning out in front that was torn. I never understood why no one had gone up and cut down the rest of the awning. When Al Davis went into the Pro Football Hall of Fame, a young reporter who had no idea of the meager beginnings of the AFL wanted to do an interview with me about the class organization of the Oakland Raiders, the mighty Raiders mystique, pride, and poise and all that. I thought briefly of talking about torn awnings at the gas station that was the Raiders ticket office, but I didn't want to rain on Al Davis's day.

I loved to go with Jim Otto to banquets in the Bay Area back then. If there were 49ers players, they invariably would bad-mouth the AFL and the Raiders. Jim was real serious about being an original Raider. Jim would stand up right there and challenge the 49ers: "Let's go! Right here! C'mon! We'll see who's minor league!" The 49ers players would really enjoy that, so they would egg him on. It *was* kind of minor league, and that's what was fun about it. I think we all knew we had to try harder.

12

The Hit

Ralph Wilson began to put together Buffalo's organization, and the Detroit-area resident's club quickly began to take on the look of Lions East. Its uniforms were a virtual pickup, put-down with blue jerseys, silver helmets, and silver pants. And, for the first head coach, the Bills turned to a former Lions assistant, Buster Ramsey. Buster brought with him, if nothing else, the lion roar.

LARRY FELSER: Buster was from Maryville, Tennessee, and he was a mountain guy. He was a wild man. Twice the first year, he attacked guys on the sidelines. One was Al Dorow, the quarterback for the New York Titans. Dorow got driven out-of-bounds in front of the Bills' bench. Richie McCabe, one of the Bills' defensive backs, hit him out-of-bounds. Dorow turned around and threw the ball in his face. Richie didn't do anything, but Buster did. Buster pounded him, hit him in the chest and drove him back about three feet. There was a big melee. Then later, Buster got in an argument with the best defensive player he had, middle linebacker Archie Matsos, one of the guys he had in Detroit. He ended up plugging him on the sidelines.

Being a Tennessee mountain man, Buster had the team doctor, Dr. Jim Sullivan, carry in his medicine bag a bottle of Buster's Maryville-brewed moonshine. Buster was so high-strung, right after the game he'd say, "Doc! Give me a bottle of that stuff!" He'd knock it off in the dressing room. By the time he got on the plane, he was roaring. On one trip in 1961, the coaches were in the back rehashing the game with Buster and there was a big argument over whether drafting Stew Barber, a high draft choice from Penn State, had been a wise thing to do. They drafted him as an offensive tackle and were trying to make him into a middle linebacker. Barber had a hell of a game, and they were rehashing the argument. Buster was drinking even more regular booze. He ended up firing two of his staff. This was when the press flew on the team plane. Jack Horrigan from the *Buffalo Evening News* and I were look-ing at each other. My deadline had already come and gone. Jack went to Buster and said, "If these guys aren't rehired by the time we land, this is going to be on the front page." Buster thought about that for a while and rehired 'em. That was life with Buster.

CHUCK BURR: Buster was a very, very gruff coach, but he had a big heart. He often took losing better than he did winning. In the second year, we won in Dallas and went from there up to Denver. On the plane up, he and Breezy Reed, his offensive assistant, got into a little bit of an argument. The next thing you knew, Breezy had quit, only to be rehired the next day. Of course, Buster could be difficult when he lost, too. I was in charge of getting play-ers aboard the plane. If the charter was scheduled to leave at 7:00, he wanted that thing off the ground then. I got into a jam once with him 'cause I was looking for one ballplayer who had stopped to loiter in the airport. A guy named Gene Grabosky, a big tackle from Syracuse, made the trip, and I don't think he'd ever gotten out of western New York. I wouldn't let the plane take off, and we had to finagle a way to keep the plane on the ground while I finally got the guy about 7:05.

ED ABRAMOSKI: Buster used to say, "All you have to do is play one-on-one and you'll see who will hit and who won't hit." When he wanted to prove a point, he would get in a three-point stance, turn his baseball cap backward like the kids wear now, and tell the guy to either fire out on the defensive player or have the defensive player hit on *him*. The guys were reluctant to swing at him because he was an older guy. And he'd say, "Goddamn it, hit me! Hit me! Get off the ball!" If we lost, all the players would fake being asleep because he would berate them after the game on the plane. He loved to play liar's poker on the plane. He used to have our team doctor always get 100 one-dollar bills to play poker. They used to carry one kid on the roster who could play spoons.

AL BEMILLER: Buster was a tough old fart. He came from the old school. He played hard, and he coached hard. I loved the man. I knew exactly where I stood with him. He had an old gimpy leg, but many times, he'd get down in the trenches himself and make you block him.

CHUCK BURR: With Buster, everybody in the organization was a friend. You were invited to go out and party with him. But if you partied with Buster and you were out until the bars closed at 4:00 A.M., he was in the office at 8:00 and he expected you to be there. But everybody liked Buster. Even the players swore by him, though they used to curse him out during heavy practice sessions and when he started screaming.

AL BEMILLER: He would sit in the back of the plane, where all the coaches would sit. It was a semicircle. They would discuss the game. At a certain moment, he would come up through the plane and pick out somebody and get into his face pretty good. I saw some players cry.

BILLY SHAW: Going from Bobby Dodd at Georgia Tech to Buster Ramsey was quite a difference in character, like the difference between the North and the South. I was one of the players who came in from the College All-Star Game and joined the team before an exhibition game in Canada. He did not like the fact that we missed part of camp. We had to catch the bus on the way to Hamilton. We got on the bus, and Buster said, "Well, here are the saviors."

LARRY FELSER: Buster scared the crap out of the players and was tougher than any one of them. The first training camp, they had a decent-looking receiver from Georgia by the name of Norman King. They trained in East Aurora, New York, an incredibly charming town, stayed at the Raycroft Inn and trained at the Knox polo fields. Buster was very enthused with this kid. Here was Norman King, first guy up for breakfast, first guy going out on the field. What Buster didn't know was you could sneak an elephant out of the Raycroft Inn. Norman and his friends were going over the roof and down a drainpipe, going into Buffalo about 15 miles away. When he was coming down to breakfast, he hadn't even been to bed. Norman and a friend of his, Ed Coffin, a fullback from Syracuse, ended up in this hangout called the Elmwood Strip, all sorts of restaurants and bars and entertainment places. The fabled place was called Cole's, still going strong. It was owned by a guy named Jimmy Parker, who was the first big season-ticket holder for the Bills. King and Coffin ended up at the bar in Cole's looking for women. King made an unwanted pass at a girl. She was with a little guy, and King kept it up. The guy turned out to be one of the better local actors. King gave him a shove, pushed him out of the way. He was going to take over this girl. The actor decked him. The next morning, the first person that Buster heard from was Jimmy Parker: "Two of your guys came in here, started a fight." So Buster cut King and told him, "I might have kept you, but you got decked by an itty-bitty actor."

ELBERT DUBENION: People said he liked me, but he scared the devil out of me. He'd rant and rave, my goodness, with a lot of profanity. Bluffton, my school, was a church school. Couldn't cuss there. He used to grab me by the collar and shake me. Man, today, he'd be in prison.

LARRY FELSER: Buster would go out of his mind if he couldn't practice. I drove out to practice one time when there had been a huge rainstorm not 10 minutes before. I told Art Baker, a fullback from Syracuse who was a rookie, "I'm amazed you guys are even out here. Didn't it rain like hell here?" He said, "Yeah, it did, but Buster just stomped his foot, said, 'Goddamn, son of a bitch.' It stopped raining."

VAN MILLER: The Bills played in Denver the first year after coming up from Los Angeles. I went to the Colorado–Air Force game in Boulder the Saturday afternoon before. It was 85 degrees. I got up on Sunday morning, went to church with one of the players—it was 56 degrees and thickening clouds. We kicked off in a snowstorm. The Bills got ahead 38–7 in the third quarter, and Denver came back and tied the game. It was three and out, and Billy Atkins was punting into a monsoon, a 10-yard punt, and it went on like that. I had a rental car. Buster rode with me to the airport. He wouldn't ride with the team, he was so angry: "That Billy Atkins'll never punt for me again!"

For a home field, the Bills took advantage of War Memorial Stadium, which had housed the former Buffalo Bills in the All-American Football Conference. Located at Best and Jefferson Streets, a lot about the stadium could be learned simply in its nickname—the "Rockpile."

BOOKER EDGERSON: It's like they say about your first home. It wasn't your dream house, but it was a place to lay your head and call yours. The paint was peeling off the walls. The place was dingy. You didn't have enough showers for everybody. They said, "OK, we're going to fix it up eventually." And it never got fixed.

ED ABRAMOSKI: The roof on the stadium would leak down on a big tile roof underneath the tar paper, then come out on our end on the second floor because our end was a little tilted. Still, they could never find the leak. They tarred all around and never found the leaking. We'd use buckets to catch the water. The stadium manager would get mad at me, but he really had a losing battle. Our equipment manager let a newspaper photographer take pictures one time, and the city was *really* mad about that.

JOE COLLIER: We'd meet right below the toilets, and urine would run down the walls. We didn't even have chairs. We had to sit on beer-case boxes. And they never did anything to the field. They hired winos off the street to come in and work on the field. They'd cover the field after we'd get done practicing, but there wouldn't be anyone there to roll the damn tarp off the field. We had to get players to do that.

LARRY FELSER: The first time the New York team came in, columnist Jimmy Cannon came with 'em. He was at War Memorial Stadium for the first time and said, "This is the new improved War Memorial Stadium? They spent money to do this? It's like putting rouge on a corpse."

AL BEMILLER: The showers didn't work. It was very crowded, especially for exhibition games when we had 100, 125 ballplayers. But we loved playing there. The people were very, very close to you. They knew you, and you knew them. It was very, very verbal. They were from an old working town. They loved their football. If you were on top or you were on the bottom, they let you know it.

BILLY SHAW: I got my nose broken in a home game and was bleeding like a hog, and a group behind the bench got concerned. Several of them called the team office or my home to see if I was OK.

CHUCK BURR: It was a great place to watch a football game if you weren't behind a pole. The press box was very cozy. As we progressed and got more demands for seats from the press, it got very crowded. All we put out there were hamburgers, hot dogs, and soft drinks. We gave free tickets to the writers for their families. The families weren't supposed to get the free hot dogs and so forth, but they passed 'em out the windows to members of their families.

Ramsey endured more occasions to lose his temper through the 1960 and '61 seasons than he probably wanted. The Bills got off to a 1–4 start the first season and stumbled through an odd campaign in which they scored victories over each of the division winners yet finished 5–8–1 and in third place. The

'61 season brought only more of the same, a 6–8 mark that landed them in the Eastern cellar. The worst indignity was suffered on a trip to Boston in late October for a standard Friday night date on the Patriots' home schedule.

VAN MILLER: It was a beautiful Friday morning. I was sitting in Billy Sullivan's office with Dick Gallagher. Billy said to Dick, "I'm going to postpone this game tonight." I said, "It's a beautiful day. Why are you doing this?" He said, "We've got a hurricane alert up the coast." I said, "Billy, you can't do that. You've got 8,000 season-ticket holders. . . ." And he threw me out of the office.

JACK GRINOLD: Billy Sullivan recalled the same thing happening when he was at Boston College. They delayed the game a day or two, and everything worked out hunky-dory. So he did the same thing.

ED ABRAMOSKI: And there was no hurricane. We just waited. We took the players out and bought everybody some underwear. Buster had the club pay for it.

VAN MILLER: That night in the Boston area—and I don't know how many high schools there are—there might have been 70 games in the area, and they were played in 67-degree temperatures with a nice, gentle breeze.

JACK GRINOLD: All the teams we played stayed at the Hotel Kenmore, which was only one block from our office. The Bills were hanging around the office, coming in and trying to date our secretaries.

VAN MILLER: And we kicked off Sunday afternoon at B.U. in a monsoon. It was horrible. And the Bills got drubbed 52–21.

RALPH WILSON: Buster blamed me for blowing the game. I said, "Baloney! The team played terrible. It had nothing to do with it." You know the coaches, if everything isn't right on time . . . if the steaks weren't served right on time, medium rare and all that baloney.

Having apparently had his fill of baloney and two losing seasons, Ralph Wilson dismissed Ramsey in early January. He replaced him a few weeks later with Lou Saban, the former Boston coach who had been on the Buffalo pay-roll since midseason as a scout and consultant. Maybe he told them they needed a new coach. The deal was consummated at a dinner to which Wilson summoned Saban and Bills general manager Dick Gallagher.

Lou Saban: We talked for a couple of hours. Nothing was said at the time that made any sense. As I walked out of the dining room after our conversation, I looked at Dick and said, "What are we here for?" He said, "I don't know. I guess he wanted to talk to you." And that was it for the moment. As Ralph came back in, he said, "How would you like to take over the club? I know what you did in Boston, and I know what you did at Western Illinois." So we had a handshake. It was just about that quick. I said, "OK. We'll do it."

Buffalo's 1962 season was highlighted by the acquisitions of quarterback Jack Kemp through the waiver mistake by San Diego and running back Cookie Gilchrist after he wore out his welcome north of the border. Kemp took over the club late in the season after fully recovering from the hand injury that had sent him to the waiver wire in the first place, and Gilchrist became the AFL's first 1,000-yard rusher. The initial improvement to the club was minimal in the won-lost columns; they achieved a 7–6–1 record that inched them back into third place. The same record was good for a tie for first the following year and the disappointing loss at home in the Eastern playoff game against Saban's former Boston club.

The Bills' most important roster move going into the '64 season involved the smallest player on the team. Pete Gogolak didn't know much about football when he entered high school in Ogdensburg, New York, on the St. Lawrence River. His family had moved to the United States from Hungary when he was 15 in the wake of the Soviet invasion. He was an avid soccer player, but few high schools then—including Ogdensburg—fielded soccer teams. So he tried out for football though he had never seen the game. The coach said they needed some kickers, and a bunch of players lined up to try out. But when it came time for young Gogolak to kick, he didn't back up directly behind the ball.

Pete Gogolak: I lined up from the side, in a 45-degree angle. And I had these high boots on, so everybody started laughing. "You're going to kick the ball into the stands. You're supposed to kick it straight." Nobody wanted to hold for me, thinking I was going to kick them, so I couldn't get the ball up in the air. The ball went about three feet off the ground. Everybody said, "Send this guy back to the old country." That's how it started.

Gogolak eventually found a holder and showed that soccer-style kicking could work on field goals. He began watching college games and was convinced he could succeed at that level. College coaches, though, didn't share his enthusiasm. He received no scholarship offers and decided to attend nearby Cornell of the Ivy League. He kicked three field goals in his first freshman game against Yale and became, if nothing more, at least a novelty for the rest of his Big Red career. But would any pro team be willing to at least allow him to audition? With the size of pro rosters, it was unthinkable to occupy a slot with a player who was only a specialist.

PETE GOGOLAK: Harvey Johnson came to Cornell about a month before the draft and said to the coach something like, "I heard about a guy who kicks the ball sideways. Geez, I've got to see this." We went up to the football field, and I kind of swallowed my pride and hit a few balls for him. He said, "I've seen enough. I think we'll see what we can do." They took a chance on me, in the 12th round. Back then there were no specialists at all. Nobody from the NFL touched me. So I went up to Buffalo, up to training camp. Jack Kemp was the quarterback; Daryle Lamonica was the holder. Jack never wanted to hold for me because he said somebody once kicked his finger. I basically made the team because I kicked a 57-yard field goal in the first exhibition game, against the Jets in Tampa, Florida. I think Ralph Wilson said, "We're going to keep this guy. He might bring some people to the stadium."

BUTCH BYRD: Pete came from Hungary. There was a semirevolution with the Russians, and the Russians had overthrown it. And one of the things the Russians did was shave all the people's heads. One of the hazings we had was that rookies that made the team got their heads shaved. Maybe half a dozen of us made the team, and they got us. And Pete was really putting up a stink about it but never really said why. Apparently, Lou Saban knew about the Hungarian incident and went berserk.

DARYLE LAMONICA: The ball would just explode off Pete's foot. He was very temperamental, as most kickers are, about the way he wanted the ball positioned. If it was a short field goal or extra point, he wanted the laces away, straight and up. The farther you got away from the goal posts, he wanted the ball tilted back toward him so he could get the leverage that he needed, get the compression. He helped us win a lot of games, and it opened the doors for soccer-style kickers.

Things looked brighter only a week into the 1964 season by virtue of winning on opening day against Kansas City, something the Bills had failed to accomplish in the four previous openers. And off they went, capturing nine consecutive victories until stumbling against the Patriots. They passed an important test the following week, rebounding to score their second win of the season over the champion Chargers and rolled to a 12–2 finish, best to date in the AFL.

The Chargers did not resemble the AFL champions, did not resemble the team that methodically dismantled Boston in the championship game, in the early weeks of the season. They split a pair of home games against Houston and Boston, then headed for their annual three-week road trip to the Northeast. The sojourn began with a 30–3 loss at Buffalo and a 17–17 tie with the New York Jets. Next up was Boston, a rematch of the '63 title game.

JOHN HADL: We were kind of up and down early. We were staying in Bear Mountain, New York, for 10 days on that trip. We had a quarterback meeting one night. I really got ready and prepared 'cause it was game plan night. Tobin had been out drinking a little beer, and he was tapped a bit. In the meeting, I just did what I was supposed to do. After that, I took over and took the team to the championship game. Hell, Tobin was 38 or 39 by then. Then, the day before the championship game in Buffalo, Sid told me he was going to start Tobin because of his experience in championship games. I went haywire. We had a big fight about it. He was the boss, and Tobin started. I played most of the second half.

JOE COLLIER: Sid Gillman was fit to be tied because our field was in terrible shape. That was the only practice field we had. We just wore it out. In Buffalo, New York, of course, you're not going to get good weather. So we were always practicing in the snow and rain and mud. So the field was not very conducive to the Chargers, who were based on speed. Gillman was threatening to call the game off. He called the commissioner. We had bigger guys on the defensive line in those days than most teams. Ron McDole, who was 290 to 300 pounds. Jim Dunaway was 270. Tom Sestak was 270. And Tom

Day was only about 250, 255. And our linebackers were big. We played in the mud and the snow a lot, and big guys have a little bit of an advantage.

But when talking size, there was no presence on the field that day bigger than Chargers defensive lineman Ernie Ladd, at six nine and weighing somewhere in the neighborhood of 300 pounds. The "Big Cat" they called him, a player who caught his breath in the off-season by wrestling. He was the assignment for Bills guard Billy Shaw.

BILLY SHAW: Ernie and Kansas City's Buck Buchanan were the largest in the league at that time. Ernie was a mammoth presence. He was so big and strong, he didn't have to be mean. I played against Ernie in practice before the College All-Star Game. One of the coaches, Dick Stanfield, showed me something. Ernie put his right hand down all the time. Before he delivered his forearm, he cocked it a bit. Stanfield said, "That gives you time to get set before he's able to deliver the blow." I never told a soul about that in all the years that I played. When the lineups were introduced before the championship game, they must have introduced both defenses because I was on the sidelines. He came to the middle of the field and pointed at me. People said it set me on fire. I just know I was scared.

VAN MILLER: I remember going in the locker room before that game, and Billy said, "Van, you have that ring guy ready. I have a good feeling about the game."

JOE COLLIER: We had a little bit of an advantage in that Lance Alworth was out. He was hurt. They went right down the field and scored on the first damn series. Tobin Rote was the quarterback.

The Chargers needed less than four minutes to take a 7–0 lead. Keith Lincoln rumbled for 38 yards on San Diego's first play from scrimmage, and the four-play possession ended quickly on a 26-yard touchdown pass from Rote to Dave Kocourek. The Chargers forced Buffalo into a quick punt when the course of the game changed with 6:41 to play in the first quarter. San Diego faced a second-and-10 at its 34-yard line when Rote dropped back and lofted a screen pass for Lincoln, who happened to be the responsibility of linebacker Mike Stratton.

BUTCH BYRD: I saw it develop 'cause Mike played right in front of me. Rote dropped back. Don Norton came out and ran some sort of in pattern, a deep hook or a deep in. I ran with him, and I saw Lincoln float out. There didn't seem to be anyone covering him. I saw Rote look over at him. If Lincoln caught that ball with no one around him, he might have scored. Then Mike stopped and started up the field. Rote lofted it out there, I guess to make sure he made the completion. You could see the ball coming toward Lincoln. I was maybe 10, 15 yards behind Mike. I could see what was going to happen. And Mike hit him.

MIKE STRATTON: They always ran kind of a curl pattern to the wide receiver and would run a flair with the back. It seemed as if the quarterback would take his cue from the linebacker. If the linebacker was in the line of fire and far enough back, they would dump it off to the running back. They'd already run that once or twice, so I decided, "I'll try something new." When I saw the pattern develop, I just turned my back to the quarterback and took several steps to the wide receiver, then stopped and turned back and went back toward the quarterback. If they caught me, the most they could do was throw to the wide receiver. I started back for Lincoln, and I saw they were throwing to him. It was just, put your head down and try to dig the dirt because, golly, if Lincoln caught the ball in time to give me a juke, hell, he could have been gone. I was trying to get there just as he caught it or after he caught it, when I could get a hand on him. But it worked out a little differently.

KEITH LINCOLN: We were in split backs. The halfback, Lowe, was to the left, and I was to the right. Lowe ran like a wheel pattern, deep going down. I came across like I was going to block on the side that he vacated, then I looped out of the backfield, stayed behind the line of scrimmage like three or four yards. Then I was the primary receiver. Tobin had Lance run like a post. For a split second, he thought Lance was open. He looked at me and looked at me, then looked at Lance again, then came at me. Well, the first time he looked at me, Stratton was about 20 yards downfield. He saw me out there, knew I was his man. So he started coming. In the meantime, Rote decided he was coming to me; the rush was in on him; he threw the God-damn ball to me like you'd throw a snowball down the chimney. And just as the ball got to me, Stratton hit me. He separated my sternum, rib cage. It was a good hit, a clean hit.

BUTCH BYRD: It was probably one of the hardest hits I've ever imagined. And Lincoln was done.

MIKE STRATTON: You just kind of get up and go back to the huddle. I didn't have any idea what was happening. When we got back to the huddle, all of us looked over there. I think Harry Jacobs, the middle linebacker, went ahead and called the defense that we were going to run for the next play. We were getting ready to break the huddle and Lincoln was still down.

JOE COLLIER: I later told a writer from *Sports Illustrated* that a thrill went up and down the bench. When that was in the magazine, I got 10 or 15 letters from people saying I was a sadist: "How could you say that after he got hurt!" It turned out it wasn't that bad of an injury, happens all the time. Anyway, after that happened, the air went out of their bubble. Our offense was a ball-control offense. They did a great job keeping San Diego on the bench. From then on, we controlled the game.

LARRY FELSER: As soon as it happened, you knew it was a monumental play. It was probably the greatest open-field tackle that I've ever seen. It was one of the most famous plays in AFL history, and it did turn the game around. All the Chargers were walking over, taking a look at Lincoln on the field writhing in pain. And he was a tough guy. The Chargers knew it was a turning point. You could see. Body language told you.

KEITH LINCOLN: I went in and tried to get 'em to doctor it up a little bit and tape me up. I came out and tried to kick off to start the second half. That was the end of that one.

MIKE STRATTON: In the locker room, it got a lot of attention. There were a lot of folks who asked about it. Sportswriters more than anything, who had a view from overhead. And, of course, Paul Maguire, because he was such a cheerleader for all of us. But we didn't watch any film of it. By that time, it was gone.

JERRY MAGEE: They called it "the hit heard 'round the world," but a week later, Lincoln played in the AFL All-Star Game. He was a very tough guy.

RON MIX: They say the Bills are still fond of saying that they won because Mike Stratton broke Keith Lincoln's ribs. But as valuable as Keith was, he wasn't our whole team. We played many games without him. We played a lot of games without a lot of our stars and kept winning. The Bills were just a good team, period. They probably would have beaten us whether they knocked Keith out of the game or not.

The teams met again in the 1965 AFL Championship Game, marking the Chargers' fifth appearance in the title game in six seasons. It was a different Buffalo team, at least a different offensive unit, by both choice and necessity. Billy Joe had replaced Cookie Gilchrist in the backfield. At tight end, Ernie Warlick was relegated to second team in favor of Paul Costa of Notre Dame, who proved his mettle in the season's second game, at Denver. And the wide receiver rotation was stripped cleaned when Elbert Dubenion was lost with a knee injury in the third game against New York—a game otherwise known as Joe Namath's first pro start—and Glenn Bass by an ankle injury the following week. At midseason, Buffalo found help at wide receiver in Bo Roberson.

BILLY JOE: There wasn't really a lot of pressure on me because I knew that I had the ability to play real well. Nobody came up to me and said, "We traded for you, and you're going to have to supercede anything that Cookie Gilchrist did here." I was going to play my game, and that's what I did.

PAUL COSTA: The first series of plays in the second game, at Denver, I caught a pass over the middle. Somebody cut my legs out, and I came down on my head. And I'm out, not out cold. I got back in the huddle, and Kemp called the same play. We were breaking the huddle, and I said, "Well, what do I do?" He said, "Run the same play from the other side." So I ran the same play, ran out and caught the ball. Got back in the huddle. He called another play. I said, "What do I do?" I had a concussion. Nowadays, they get you on the sideline and like four doctors look in your eyes, your ears. We came off the field, and I heard Kemp talking to Saban: "Hey, Paul is out of it. He doesn't know the plays. He's gaga." Saban said, "Well, tell him what to do!" I played the whole game, and they had to tell me every play.

ELBERT DUBENION: That would have been my greatest year. I had like 18 receptions in three games. Then I got hurt on a flanker slant in the end zone.

I took two steps, drove off the slant, and the ball was behind me. I reached back, and Willie West, who was my roommate with Buffalo, crashed into my leg and knocked it in the wrong direction. But I caught the ball for a touchdown. Then the trainer came out there. My leg was looking funny. Medial collateral. They operated on Monday evening. The next week, our other receiver, Glenn Bass, had the same type of injury. He went to Buffalo General and was in the room next to me. I heard him crying and moaning. So I got on my crutches, went over there, and said, "What's the matter, Glenn?" He said he couldn't play. I said, "Are they still paying us?" He said, "Yeah." I said, "Whew! I was afraid we wouldn't get paid." They went out and got Bo Roberson, from Cornell, and he did a great job.

The Bills retained their Eastern title without gaudy individual statistics. Running back Wray Carlton, an original Bill, had his best rushing season with the club and combined with Billy Joe to give the team a potent, if not Gilchrist-like, ground game. Roberson, playing eight games, led the club in receiving, as Kemp sprinkled the ball around to backs and the tight end as well. The Bills faced no competition in the division and wrapped up the title on Thanksgiving weekend.

It was difficult to gauge San Diego's worth given the odd presence of three ties on its record to go with nine wins and only two losses, tying the league-record low. There was no confusion, though, regarding the weapons in the Chargers' offense. Paul Lowe topped the league in rushing with 1,121 yards. John Hadl, San Diego's starting quarterback from day one, led the AFL in passing yards with 2,798. Lance Alworth was tops in receiving yards with 1,602 and boasted a phenomenal 23.2 yards per catch. Even the league's best punt returner was a Charger, the aptly nicknamed "Speedy" Duncan. The Chargers soundly defeated the Bills in Buffalo early in the season, 34–3, and tied them 17–17 in San Diego. Combine those results with dangerous offensive stars and the game being played at Balboa Stadium, and there were the makings of San Diego's being established as a seven-point favorite over the defending champion.

PAUL COSTA: In San Diego, we were out every night, drinking beer, having a good time. Not staying out late. We were going to the same places as the San Diego players. And they were giving us the business: "We're gonna kill you guys. We're gonna mop you up." But it was like friendly stuff. And that whole week, we took it from them.

Lou Saban: The press came out and said the Chargers this, and the Chargers that. And, oh, yes, they're playing the Buffalo Bills. That was all they said about the Buffalo Bills. They beat the Chargers last year, but that was going to change. I didn't think we had much of a chance.

Larry Felser: The teams had met a month before, and Keith Lincoln barely played. He had a beef with Sid. It was probably over money. Sid, as great a coach as he was, would undo a lot of the stuff when he put his general manager's hat on. I knew Lincoln and talked to him after that game. As we finished, I said, "You'd always be welcomed in Buffalo." He said, "I'd *love* to play in Buffalo." So I wrote it.

The Chargers were favored in the championship game. The *San Diego Tribune* had a cartoon of Ernie Ladd, this monstrous form, hovering over this freckle-faced kid with a Bills uniform on that looked like it was too big for him. It was supposed to be Jack Kemp, number 15.

The Friday night before the game, there was a party at a Hilton in a private little dining room. I was talking to Esther Gillman, who was a Hall of Fame wife. All of a sudden, I heard a guy hissing in my ear, and he said, "You are no longer welcome in the San Diego Chargers' dressing room." I turned around, and it was Sid. He was going on about the Lincoln story. Well, it was a party. Everybody had been drinking. I got up and told Sid, "You may tell the San Diego press what to write about, but you'll never tell *me* what to write about." I was rather loud. People were looking around and saying, "Hey, there's Sid Gillman and some guy in an argument!"

By that time, Sid was trying to calm me down: "Larry! Larry! Let me buy you a drink!" We went up to the bar. He bought a round. I bought a round. After a while, he was telling me, "There's no way we can lose this game. Jack Kemp has the maturity of a 10-year-old girl." He went on and on. A couple of friends helped me to my room. I woke up at 6:00 A.M. the next day with the mother of all hangovers when I got a call from Sid: "Larry, about that conversation we had last night . . ." To which I replied, "What conversation?" Then he said, "Go back to sleep." Click.

Butch Byrd: The night before the game, Paul Maguire and several other Bills were out at a party, and Don Norton, one of the Chargers' receivers, told Paul what he was going to do to me the next day. I was incensed. Norton never had a good day against me. And Paul told Joe Collier, the defensive back coach at the time. Before the game, Joe called me in for a special one-on-one and said, "I don't want you to get too excited out there. I want you to play your game." I said words to the effect of: "Not a thing to worry about."

RON MCDOLE: We went out there, were supposed to get slaughtered. They wrote up how Billy Shaw was playing against Ernie Ladd, and Shaw got knocked out on the first play. And George Flint, who was a backup guard, my roommate, went in and played the whole ballgame and controlled Ernie like nothing. I wouldn't have bet on that.

JOE COLLIER: They had all their weapons. Alworth was there. Paul Lowe. Keith Lincoln was healthy. They had a new starting quarterback, Hadl. We knew it was going to be a hell of a lot more difficult. Two years before in the championship game in San Diego, they beat Boston and rolled up 600-something yards and Lincoln had an unbelievable game. It rained the day before, and Sid Gillman hired helicopters to dry out the field. If I had all that speed, I'd want a dry, fast field, too.

BUTCH BYRD: The game was going back and forth. I was so focused on Norton. Hadl threw a sideline ball over his head, and I just blasted him as hard as I could. Those were the days that, when the ball was in the air, you could hit the wide receiver. He looked at me. His eyes were huge. We were running down the sidelines later, right in front of Sid Gillman. Hadl still had the ball, and I blasted Norton again, knocked him right into Gillman. I jumped up and looked at Gillman and said, "You'd better get him out of this game or I'm going to kill him!" Gillman looked at me like I was crazy.

The Chargers' offense was surprisingly quiet in the first half. After a scoreless first period, the Bills got on the scoreboard first on an 18-yard touchdown pass from Kemp to Ernie Warlick, who caught only eight passes all season after being pushed behind Costa. Late in the period, Buffalo increased its lead to 14–0 when Byrd returned a punt 74 yards for a score.

MIKE STRATTON: We went to the locker room at halftime and were looking at each other saying, "Hadl, he doesn't have a clue." He didn't know whether to call timeouts or wind his watch. We changed some looks and things. We could do anything we wanted to.

JOE COLLIER: Our offense did the same thing that it did against them the year before, controlled the ball and didn't do anything fancy. We played one of the best defensive games that we played all year, in a number of years. I think the closest they got was the 25-yard line, and they missed a field goal. Paul Lowe busted off a run for about 30 yards early, and that was about it. We doubled Alworth wherever he was.

LOU SABAN: It was a defensive struggle with a couple of great catches, one by Ernie Warlick and the other by Paul Costa. A lot of our players were beat up, but they hung in there. It was just a remarkable game, the most memorable game of my lifetime.

RON McDOLE: San Diego put like three or four guys in the Hall of Fame during that era. We didn't have anybody until they put Billy Shaw in. We couldn't figure it out. It dawned on me, that's probably the way our team was. We had a good defense, good offense, but everybody had to play to make it work. Every week, somebody else got the job done.

AL BEMILLER: We didn't have any big stars. Jack Kemp was probably the biggest star. Cookie, maybe. But none of us ever dreamed of doing that. We all got together and loved each other. Even to this day, we get together and know each other like it was yesterday. Jack Kemp came into the airport on a private plane when he was campaigning, and all of us were there to greet him. As he came down the gangplank, I turned around and made out like I was snapping the ball to him. And he yelled out, "That's gotta be Bemiller! I recognize the butt!"

13

The Bright Lights

At the outset of AFL play, it was arguable that the teams were simply grateful to have their games shown on network television. The $1,785,000 total annual payoff from ABC, which increased gradually each year over the balance of the five-year contract, didn't provide the kind of revenue that meant a large difference in the operations of the clubs.

But the stakes were raised in January 1962, when the NFL's young TV-minded commissioner looked to make the league television contract a significant source of revenue. The deal that Pete Rozelle struck with CBS brought in $4,650,000 annually, not to mention the additional $615,000 received for the rights to televise and broadcast the NFL Championship Game alone.

And in January 1964, Rozelle pushed the TV pedal to the floor and began to leave the pups from the AFL in the dust. When the ink dried, the latest NFL-CBS pact upped the annual take to $14.1 million for the 1964–65 regular-season games.

The newly created difference in the leagues' TV income might have made it impossible for the AFL to keep bringing in top young talent. Joe Foss, World War II flying ace, adjusted his goggles and set out to get the AFL back in the television game once the initial ABC deal expired following the '64 season.

RALPH WILSON: ABC was televising our games, and every team was getting about $100,000 in the deal that was going to expire after the '64 season. We had come up with the idea of splitting the TV revenue equally, not the NFL. They copied us about the fifth year of our existence. NBC did not have pro football on Sunday, and CBS was killing them. They wanted pro football to compete. Sonny Werblin and I became the closest of friends, and Sonny knew Bobby Sarnoff of NBC. So Sonny talked to him.

JOE FOSS: I was dealing with Carl Linderman, NBC's vice president in charge of sports. I was holding out for $36 million. Some of the owners wanted to settle for $32 million, which is what NBC was offering. And I said, "No way. I'm the one who has been talking to them over there. We've got to get more if we're going to get off dead center here. We need it so that we can get the type players that we need." So I kept talking back and forth to NBC. Of course, Sonny Werblin, having been in the business before, knew all the ins and outs on it. He was in a big rush to get the thing settled. I kept holding out on it. Finally, we got up to $34 million. So then we had a meeting, and some of them were really owly at me over the thing. Sonny said, "Well, I know that business, and I know those people over there. They aren't going any higher." He was close friends with a guy at NBC named Kintner, the big dog behind Linderman. Nothing scares me, anyway. So I just went back to Linderman some more.

RALPH WILSON: The NFL had just gotten a new contract from CBS that was over a million per team. Lamar and I were at the '64 Winter Olympics in Innsbrook. He was there on his honeymoon, and I was over there by myself, and I got a call from Billy Sullivan. He said, "You know, NBC has offered each team $600,000, $700,000." He was ecstatic and wanted us to go with them. I said, "Billy, we can't compete." He said, "What do you mean?" I said, "We need more." And I told Lamar that, though I'm sure it kind of shocked Billy.

JOE FOSS: Sonny was speaking over at a dinner in New Jersey where ABC and all the rest of them wanted to talk about contracts. You can't talk at a deal like that and make much sense out of it. I came back to New York the next day to meet with Sonny. I read in the paper that Billy Sullivan was going to come down and get this whole thing settled. I just laughed 'cause he didn't have a darn thing to do with it. He might have thought he did, but he sure didn't. I went and met with NBC in person for the first time, with Kintner, Linderman, and their lawyer and one other man. They said, "Where's the rest of your crew?" And I said, "There aren't any. I'm it." I didn't have to have somebody looking over my shoulder. I didn't need any lawyer there to get in there and screw it up. That sort of startled them. And when I came up with the big figures that first time, they said, "What makes you think that you need that kind of money?" I said, "It's simple. I know you need football, and you want the quality of players that will compete with the NFL. In order to get that, it takes money. Actually, you're the winner in the long run." "Well, that makes sense." And that's where we were haggling from. I had been talking to Tom Moore over at ABC, a very good friend of mine. They were interested in only three years, and I wanted five to let everybody know we were going to be here a while.

So Carl Linderman and I were haggling back and forth. Every few hours, we'd talk back and forth. Finally, I believe it was a Wednesday, he said, "All right. We're going to give you your $36 million. But it's got to be $34 million for the existing teams and $2 million for the expansion teams." I said, "That's all right. We'll go that way." So he read me the contract over the phone, and he said, "I'll meet you at Toots Shor's." I got there first, and there was the whole ABC crew. I just said hi to 'em, shook hands, then went back out looking for Carl. I met him right outside the door and said, "We don't want to go in there. All your friends from the other network are in there. There's a telephone booth right down the street here. We can go down there. There's pretty good light, and I can take a look at the contract." Carl, a big guy, and I went in the phone booth. I know people came by and thought we were rather odd. I read it, so we just signed it. He said, "Well, let's go down to 21." We went down there, and right at table number one, who was there but Sonny Werblin. He invited Carl and me to sit down, which we did. We were going to have dinner. Carl and I were sort of laughing to ourselves. We knew that Sonny was going to say something, and sure enough he did: "When are you guys going to get together? We've got to get this thing settled." He expected Carl to say, "Well, the commissioner's too high on it." We just let Sonny talk away. Finally, I pulled out the contract and handed it to him. Oh, he was one happy guy.

Then, who buzzed through the door but Billy Sullivan. Sonny invited him to join us. He had a drink, and we sat there and visited back and forth. Then he slid over next to me, sitting on my right shoulder, and he said, "Commissioner, we've gotta get that contract done. We're going to lose it." I said, "Yeah, we've gotta get it done, all right. But we've got to stick to where we want it." "Well, we're up there as high as they'll go." "That's according to you. I don't agree with that." I just let him suffer a while, let him talk for a while and think he was getting something done. Then I pulled out the contract and handed it to him. He got red as a beet. He was a fast-talking, very nice guy. And to think that it was all done after what I had read in the paper . . . it read like there was nobody else in the world who could get the dang thing signed but him.

RALPH WILSON: We got $900,000-something per team, which was pretty close to the NFL. I really think the close contact that Sonny had with Sarnoff did it, not to discredit Joe Foss.

LAMAR HUNT: Sonny Werblin was the key negotiator on the NBC contract. I think ABC would have liked to have stayed with us. They had carried the AFL for four years and had one year to go. I can't tell you how seriously they looked at it. But I'm sure they looked at it because it was their principal sports property at the time. But NBC made a really substantial offer that put us on the map.

Bolstered by the NBC ammunition, at least some AFL teams suddenly became more dangerous in the signing war with the NFL. Boston couldn't take advantage and lost the top AFL pick overall, quarterback Jack Concannon from nearby Boston College, to Philadelphia. The NFL's first selection, end Dave Parks from Texas Tech, was the 32nd player taken in the AFL, by San Diego, and he signed with the 49ers. But Houston scored a Lone Star coup by signing first-round pick Scott Appleton, a revered lineman on the University of Texas' 1963 national championship team, away from the Dallas Cowboys. The Chiefs and Detroit Lions went head-to-head over USC quarterback Pete Beathard in the first round, with Beathard eventually heading to KC.

One of the more intriguing early battlegrounds was the first serious hand-to-hand combat between the two New York clubs. And the prize was none other than a former Long Island high school star, Matt Snell, a bruising back from Ohio State. Snell was tabbed in the first round by the Jets and in the third round by the Giants, who made Oklahoma running back Joe Don Looney their first-round selection. The AFL's impact on Giants signings to date was minimal, really just a couple of offensive linemen from the previous draft—Dave Hill, a fifth-round tackle from Auburn who went to Kansas City, and Dave Herman, an eighth-round guard from Michigan State who signed with the Jets.

MATT SNELL: I got a call from Woody Hayes's office that Tim Mara, the representative of the Giants, was in his office. Woody didn't allow agents on campus at that point, so I went over there and met with Tim Mara. He said, "We know you've been a Giants fan for all of your life. We'd like to offer you a contract—$12,000 with a $5,000 bonus." Woody said to me, "You've got to wait to see what the Jets will pay. They drafted you in the first round." OK, but I was thinking, "Jeez, a $12,000 contract with a $5,000 bonus! I'm rich!" A couple weeks later, Weeb Ewbank and Clive Rush came out. Weeb said, "We think you can come in and play right away. We're going to give you a $15,000 contract and a $10,000 bonus." Tim Mara apparently got word that the Jets were in town and returned with Emlen Tunnell, a legend with the Giants and an assistant coach: "Emlen really thinks you can help our team. It's going to be a couple years, but we'll groom you. Joe Don Looney will probably get the first shot, but we think you can hold your own. This is our final offer: we're going to give you a $20,000 contract and a $20,000 bonus. That's good money for a third-round draft choice." I was sitting there thinking, "Wow!" Woody said, "That sounds like a very good offer. Let me talk to Matt about it, and we'll get back to you." Emlen stayed over and took me out to dinner. We had drinks, nice big steaks. And he was telling me how great the Giants organization was. I didn't sign anything.

The next day, Woody said Sonny Werblin was flying into town. "The guy is the owner of the Jets," Woody said. "I think we should listen to what he has to say." This big, long, black stretch limousine was sitting out front of Woody's office. I walked in the office, and there was Sonny Werblin, all tanned, dressed to kill. He said, "Here's what we're gonna do. We want to sign you. We feel we're in a position to build this franchise, and we want to start with you. We're going to give you a $20,000 contract, but we'll give you a $30,000 bonus,"— I figured I had died and gone to heaven—"and if it takes anything else to close the deal, what have you always wanted most in your life?" I said, "Man, I've always said if I ever got myself some money, I was going to get a new Thunderbird." He said, "You got it." I said, "You're taking it out of the bonus, right?" He said, "No, no. That is my gift to you if you'll come with the Jets and sign now." I said, "I'm not looking for you to make a down payment on the car." He said, "No, no. The Thunderbird is yours. The car will be delivered to you. I can't put it in writing because it would have to be part of your contract and we'd have to give you a 1099." Woody said, "Don't hit him with taxes." Sonny said, "We'll find a way." I said, "I don't want a lease." He said, "No, we'll find a way to do it." They delivered the car to me at school, and I never heard from the Giants again.

Two years later, the Jets were able to secure Snell's partner in the New York backfield thanks to assistant coach Walt Michaels's willingness to dig deep into his own pockets, at least in the short term. Had that not happened, Emerson Boozer might instead have been in the uniform of the Pittsburgh Steelers.

MATT SNELL: I talked Boozer into coming to the Jets instead of Pittsburgh. I told him, "As long as the money is somewhat similar, you come here. You can play right away. You're better than any halfback we have on the field right now."

WALT MICHAELS: When I went down to sign him, I was told, "Pittsburgh's got him. You know they're down there." Good. I took off in the middle of everything—no clothes, no nothing—went down to the Princess Anne Hotel in Maryland and met him. "Emerson, you want to be in New York or you want to be in Pittsburgh?" One thing led to the other, and he said, "I'd like to be in New York." As we got negotiating, it got up to about $110,000. I called back to the team and said, "Hey, these Pittsburgh guys are running around this campus like crazy. I've got to give him a bonus." I talked to the president of Maryland State. He was more interested in New York for Boozer than Pittsburgh. Finally, I wrote out a personal check for $20,000 as his bonus. I didn't have the money, but I called Sonny Werblin: "If you don't get that $20,000 in my bank account, we won't have Boozer." The check was fine. I also signed Earl Christy from that team as a free agent. I don't think I gave him a bonus.

Dollar signs weren't always the most memorable aspect of AFL-NFL contract negotiations, though they usually weren't far behind in any case. Defensive tackle Tom Keating of Michigan was a fourth-round choice of Minnesota and a fifth-round pick belonging to Buffalo who discovered that greenbacks and blue language could cross paths when wooing a young man's contractual affection. He was introduced to the bedside manner of Vikings coach Norm Van Brocklin, who wasn't known as "Stormin' Norman" for nothing.

TOM KEATING: I was coming out of the locker room after playing against Michigan State and waved up at my dad. And there was a guy behind who was waving at me, too. My dad said, "There's a guy here to see you. His name is Ralph Wilson. He's the owner of the Buffalo Bills." Then the fun began. The Vikings were coached by Norm Van Brocklin, "the Dutchman." They sent down a guy, Walt Yowarsky, not a bad guy, to sign me. Took me out to dinner on a Monday. I said, "I told Ralph Wilson I was going to talk to him, and he's not going to be able to see me until Friday." Walt said, "Aw, you can't do that. Boy, the Dutchman's really going to be mad at me. You've *gotta* sign!" I said, "I can't. I told my mother and father I would wait." He said, "Aw, who's making the decisions around here?" Boy, I was really pissed at that guy. I went back to my apartment, and Walt proceeded to take my roommates out the next two nights. He took 'em out drinking, bought 'em beer. He tried again with me Thursday night. Same deal. He said, "Jesus, I don't know what to tell Norm. God, this is terrible."

So Yowarsky left. And on Friday afternoon, about 5:00, Ralph Wilson showed up at the apartment. He offered me a car for my parents, $20,000 in cash, $15,000 a year for two years guaranteed. I just kept sitting there, and he kept offering me more stuff. I said, "I'm going to talk to my mother and father, and I'll get back to you." The next day, Wilson called: "You know, you'll need a car for yourself, too. Pontiac's got a small car, the GTO. How 'bout one of them?" "Sure! Sure!" We met at the old Willow Run Airport, and we brought along a family friend who was a lawyer to make sure everything was in order. We went in, shook hands, and signed the deal. The next morning about 7:00, the phone rang at my apartment. The guy said, "Hey, this is Norm Van Brocklin. What's this fuckin' shit I hear about you signing with those fuckin' pussies in Buffalo?" Those were the first words he said to me. He just went on and on. I said, "I'm sorry." I hung up the phone.

A year later, I was back at Michigan watching the spring game that my brother Bill was in. And after the game, who was in the locker room but Van Brocklin. Bill knew the story of what happened between him and me. Van Brocklin was talking to him about playing football, and Bill said, "Aren't you the guy who said to Tom, 'What are you doing signing with those fuckin' pussies?'"

Then there was the unique case of America's favorite young seaman, Roger Staubach. The Navy quarterback won the Heisman Trophy as a junior in 1963, leading the Middies to a number two final ranking behind Texas. When he came eligible for the pro drafts in 1964, teams had to grapple with the fact that a four-year military commitment would mean Staubach wouldn't see his first pro action until 1969 at age 27.

Ironically, it was the two old backyard rivals—the Chiefs and the Cowboys—who decided to gamble on Staubach . . . well, the word *gamble* might be a tad dramatic. The Cowboys selected him in the 10th round and picked another "future" quarterback—Tulsa junior Jerry Rhome—three rounds later. Kansas City chose Staubach in the third round of the AFL's separate futures draft.

ROGER STAUBACH: When I went off to the Naval Academy, I really didn't have thoughts about a pro football career. That didn't happen until I played in the College All-Star Game, spending three weeks with the top rookies that were going into pro football. Kansas City contacted me right away to see if I would sign a contract, that if I ever did leave the service I'd play for them.

GIL BRANDT: I went to visit him at his home in Cincinnati in the summer between his junior and senior years. We also had an assistant basketball coach whom we had known, a young guy named Danny Peterson, that was kind of our unofficial scout at the Naval Academy. We made sure that Roger knew through Danny how interested we were in him.

ROGER STAUBACH: I went back to the Naval Academy and was on staff there for about six months, mostly as a plebe coach, assistant coach. They kind of kept a number of ensigns back there to help with the athletic department. Lamar Hunt came to see me at Annapolis. We talked it through, had dinner at our house. He said he'd come back with a contract that would pay me some money then, pay me while I was in the service, and then, if I ever left the service, I would have a contract with Kansas City. Anything that they paid me previous to that, if I stayed in the service, was just mine.

A navy legal officer named Captain Paul Borden went up and met with the Cowboys in Philadelphia; they happened to be playing the Eagles around that time. He told them about the contract and asked if they had any interest. They said they sure did and basically gave me the same type of contract with similar money: $10,000 bonus, I think it was like $500 a month while I was in the navy, which was more than I was being paid by the navy.

GIL BRANDT: Paul Borden came to our hotel, and we made a deal that night that gave him a signing bonus that was his to keep whether he ever played.

ROGER STAUBACH: Because they were an NFL team, I agreed to sign with Dallas. I called Lamar back. He said, "Well, I sure wish I could have negotiated more with you." I said I really didn't want that: "I was very surprised I had this opportunity. And if I leave the service, I want to play for Dallas."

The only glitch with the Cowboys occurred when Brandt made the mistake of speculating about Staubach leaving his commitment early—like basketball star David Robinson would do years later—to Momma Staubach.

ROGER STAUBACH: That was a big mistake. My mother was . . . we didn't think of any kind of negotiating with the service. That was during the Vietnam era, too. I just didn't feel good to even try to think about giving up something that I had committed to. David Robinson made a deal where he'd only have to stay in two years and have a six-year reserve tour. He outgrew being a pilot. It was a great thing for the academy to do. That was the right deal at that time. For me, that was never in the cards.

14

Taken for a Ride

Pro football of the early '60s was unique in American pro sports because it was the only sport operating franchises in the South—in Dallas with the Texans and Cowboys and in Houston with the Oilers.

While the other sports dealt with segregation only when passing through the region before the season, football stared it directly in the face. And what it often saw was particularly disturbing, whether it was in a theater, in a hotel lobby, in a dining room, or even in the stands of a team's very own stadium.

KEITH LINCOLN: We always went to the movies the night before a game, home or away. We were in this huge theater in Dallas. The bus pulled up out back. We didn't go through the lobby. We went in and were like in the second balcony. And they wouldn't let the African-Americans go down to get concessions. Then a white guy came in with his date, and they wanted us to move to another level while the movie was going on. That's when Sid Gillman said, "We've had enough. Let's get out of here."

RED MILLER: One year with Buffalo, we got to the hotel in Houston. Lou Saban was starting to check in players. I overheard the man at the desk tell Lou, "Coach, the black guys stay across the street." All of a sudden, it was kind of quiet. And Lou said, "We're out of here." He called Wally Lemm, who was coaching Houston, and we got one of the nearby college dorms that had some empty space.

ERNIE LADD: We went into Houston my first year, and [the African-Americans] were still sitting in the end zones. There was a sportswriter, Lloyd Wells, who was calling us every name in the book because we went ahead and played with our brothers and sisters sitting in the end zones. He said, "You have no nuts. You Chargers have no nuts. Big Ernie Ladd, I see you." That was an embarrassing moment for me. But Lloyd Wells was right.

JACK KEMP: My father came to the '60 championship game in Houston. My dad sat on the 45-yard line, and the black families had to sit in the roped-off part. Black guys were sitting outside the stadium telling the black athletes not to play. My heart just went out to those guys. They were going to play, but you know they had concerns having their parents sit in a roped-off part of the end zone while my dad was sitting on the 45-yard line. I think about that and what that does to a person's psyche.

HOUSTON ANTWINE: When I first went to Houston in 1961, we didn't stay in different accommodations, but we stayed at some motel outside of town because they couldn't find anywhere where we all could stay together. I was impressed with the fact that they didn't want to split the team up. The years after that when we went in to play, it seemed as though they had corrected that situation.

We were going to New Orleans in 1962 to spend a week there and play an exhibition game. The team didn't let the ballplayers know what the situation was in New Orleans until we left Buffalo: "Look, we can't stay as one team in the hotel." They put the black ballplayers in some hotel way across town.

SHERRILL HEADRICK: Abner Haynes and I ran together. He went wherever I'd go in Dallas. They'd say, "Sherrill, that guy can't come." I'd say, "What guy?" "That black guy." And I'd say, "Black guy. What black guy? . . . Abner, are you black?" He'd say, "No, I'm not black." Back then it was separated quite a bit, but I could go with him in his part of town.

He and I and Jon Gilliam, who also played with us in Dallas, went out to the All-Star Game after the 1961 season. We went in Abner's car because he had a Thunderbird and I think Jon and I had Volkswagens. We went down through El Paso and started getting hungry and ready to sleep. We pulled into a restaurant. They brought two glasses of water and just turned to Abner and said, "You've got to go outside." So we just got up and left. We finally got some sandwiches at a grocery store. We stopped at a motel, and they wouldn't let us in. I said, "Abner, I'm about to give out. Get in the trunk." Jon and I went ahead and checked in. When we got over to the room, I went in and got a bedspread and took it out there and covered Abner. He still swears that was the fastest 40 he ever ran, into that room so he could get some rest.

DAVE GRAYSON: Before getting an apartment in Dallas, I stayed in one of the hotels in East Dallas. I remember the Chargers coming in, and that's where the black guys were, too. Growing up in the West, it was something I read about happening to blacks in the South. To experience it, it was something that . . . not alarmed but intrigued.

With an eye toward future expansion, AFL owners decided to hold the annual All-Star Game that followed the 1964 season in a nonleague city as an audition of sorts. The game was scheduled for Tulane Stadium in New Orleans, where Lamar Hunt had nearly moved his Dallas Texans two years earlier. Dave Dixon again was the primary New Orleans contact, and the game was scheduled to be played two weeks after the Bills defeated the Chargers for the AFL championship. With Buffalo and San Diego playing for the title, that meant Bills coach Lou Saban would guide the East All-Stars while Chargers coach Sid Gillman would lead the West.

All-Star games in general are seen by many as a necessary evil, popularized by the Major League Baseball version that began in the early 1930s and was started by a Chicago newspaperman. Football All-Star games are probably the least regarded of all—pushed to the end of seasons rather than played as a "midseason classic" as touted in baseball, basketball, and hockey. It's often regarded simply as an another opportunity for injury in a competition that means nothing. Even exhibition games can be interpreted as preparing coaches and players for the coming season and therefore meaningful even if the outcomes aren't.

So as league officials, coaches, and players prepared to head to New Orleans, there was limited anticipation for the coming week's events. At best, it was a chance to experience a new town, one that might become an AFL city. Surely, no one expected to attract the nation's attention to what turned out to be one of the most significant mixes of sports and social consequence of the 1960s.

DAVE DIXON: I thought having the All-Star Game in New Orleans could lead to getting an AFL franchise. I also thought it would light a fire under the NFL. After Lamar had moved his team to Kansas City, I had worked out a deal with the AFL owners. We tried to buy the Raiders. And Lamar was for it. He wanted a team in New Orleans. We went out there thinking we had a deal with Wayne Valley. There was a slipup from our political adviser. Somehow, his office told someone in the New Orleans media he was out in Oakland with me. There went our cover, and it became a front-page story in Oakland. So Wayne Valley went to Senator Nowland, a very prominent

Republican, and got some sort of commitment that they would do something in Oakland. That's one of the reasons the Oakland Coliseum got built.

New Orleans is a different kind of a city. New Orleans was a better city about race than any other Southern city because of a long tradition of people living right on top of each other. I lived in a pretty nice home, and we were never more than two or three blocks from black families. We had no problems in New Orleans at all.

BOBBY BELL: I had been down in New Orleans prior to the All-Star Game, for the Black America beauty pageant. I noticed some things that were different from what Kansas City was. I had to stay in an all-black hotel that was on the other side of the tracks. All the functions were all-black. When the All-Stars went there in January of '65, they said they had worked it out 'cause New Orleans wanted to house a pro team. They guaranteed that the black players could stay in downtown New Orleans, French Quarter, Bourbon Street. Eat. Do whatever. That was cleared.

The players came from wherever they were, flew into New Orleans, and many of us ran into each other when we arrived at the airport. White players, black players. The white players were going out, getting in cabs, and taking off, going to the hotels. When the black players would go out to get a cab, the white cabbie would say, "No. Can't go." I guess we were out at the airport a couple of hours. Finally, one of the porters came up and said, "Hey, you guys have to call a colored cab. They have to come from the city to get you."

ERNIE WARLICK: Two of my teammates with the Bills, Mike Stratton and Jack Kemp, said, "C'mon. Let's go down to the French Quarter." Being a little skeptical, I said, "No, you guys go ahead." "No, c'mon, let's go." So we headed to the French Quarter. We started to go into a place. Jack went in. Mike went in. And I started in, and then: "Naw, we don't serve your kind." So I was standing outside. They came back out, and I said, "That guy won't let me in." "We'll go some other place." We tried another. We were standing inside. Somebody with the management called over to Kemp and Stratton, pointing at me. "C'mon, we'll find another place." We got back outside, and I finally said, "Look, you guys go on ahead. I'm going back to the hotel. There's no point in all of us not being allowed to go in." So I got a taxi. A black taxi.

ERNIE LADD: I flew into New Orleans, got a cab with Dick Westmoreland and Earl Faison, two of my teammates from the Chargers. A white cab. No problem. Took us to the Roosevelt Hotel, where the West All-Stars were staying. We got ready to go down to the French Quarter. It was close enough to walk, though we didn't know it. And the same cabdriver wouldn't pick us up and take us. When it was really noticeable was when we tried to stop a white cab in the French Quarter to take us back to the Roosevelt and no cab would stop. They told us we couldn't get in.

Earl was my roommate, and I told him, "I don't need to take this crap." And Dick Westmoreland said, "I'm taking my black a' back home. I'm not playing." And Earl said, "If you're not playing, I'm not playing." Back at the hotel, Earl said he was going to call Sherman Plunkett of the Jets, a former Charger and his best friend over on the East team: "I'm going to make sure that Sherman goes."

HOUSTON ANTWINE: I was staying at the Fontainebleau Hotel with the Eastern squad. Cookie Gilchrist and some of the other guys came in and wanted to go over and visit with the guys on the Western team. We couldn't get cabs to go over to the Roosevelt. The cabdrivers said, "We can't haul you guys. We're going to call you some colored cabs." And Cookie raised a whole bunch of noise. We eventually got over to the Roosevelt, and it seemed like the black ballplayers there were having the same problems. During the course of the evening, the problem persisted. Late in the evening, everybody was comparing notes: "You couldn't do this, and you couldn't do that, and you were insulted here."

ERNIE WARLICK: Cookie called me up the next morning and said, "All the guys ran into some discrimination. We're having a meeting. We need to decide whether we're going to play." So we had a meeting. There were a couple of our white teammates there. They couldn't believe it, either.

RON MIX: We were sitting on the bus to go to our first practice. Sid Gillman, the West coach, was taking roll. "Bobby Bell!" No answer. "Earl Faison!" No answer. Somebody said, "Hey, all the black guys are missing!" And somebody from the back of the bus said, "They're all meeting back at the hotel." Sid said, "What about?" "When they arrived at the airport, they couldn't get cabs. Then they wanted to go out to eat and were turned away at restaurants. They're thinking about boycotting the game." So I got off the bus and went to where they were meeting. Cookie Gilchrist was leading the discussion.

JERRY IZENBERG: Cookie Gilchrist, who was always trying to make a buck from something, called me and said, "I have an exclusive for you. I want to sell it." I said, "If you really have a good story to sell, call the *Star* or the *Enquirer*. I don't have any money! And I wouldn't give it to you if I did!" He said, "I'm here in the hotel room where the players are meeting to see what they're going to do about this taxi thing. . . . Just a minute. . . . Stand by. I've got to make a broadcast." Then I heard, "This is Cookie Gilchrist speaking to you from the Roosevelt Hotel . . ." I was sure it was a fake. And he went through this thing about the angry mood of the players. Then he came and told me, "I can't hold 'em off, Jerry. If you want this piece, you'd better tell me." I said, "I don't want it!"

BUDDY DILIBERTO: I was working in the sports department of the *New Orleans Times-Picayune*. I was scheduled to help cover the All-Star Game that week. We got a call at the office. The news department put me on the story and told me where all these people were meeting. I headed over to the hotel. It was difficult to get players. By that time, the city had marshaled all the movers and shakers—the mayor, the presidents of the black universities, everybody that you might say had clout. I was outside of the room. It was very easy to hear what was being said. Some wild talking was going on.

JACK KEMP: We all got in a room, West and East players. I remember Cookie talking, Abner Haynes talking, Art Powell talking. I said, "Well, we've got to do something. We can't just accept this. What do you think we should do?" I wanted the black guys to decide.

RON MIX: I said, "I've heard what's happened and that you're thinking of boycotting the game. Maybe it would be more important if you stayed and we played the game but we talk about what has happened to you all week and bring national attention to it." But the consensus was it was really time to take a stand about treatment like that and that they were going to leave. I said, "OK, then count me with you."

HOUSTON ANTWINE: They were promising us cars. They were promising us everything, if we just stayed there and played. But if we did that, we would be accepting the conditions. Everybody made plans to leave.

ERNIE WARLICK: They tried to convince us that all this money had been spent: "Please! You've got to play the game! You can't walk out now!" "Hey, you should have thought about that beforehand. We're not going to play."

ERNIE LADD: Sure enough, they brought in a black guy. Then we agreed not to play. Earl and I were definitely not going to play. And Dick Westmoreland. Then all the white guys sided with us, Kemp and Mix and the others. They said, "It's all or none." We chose to go.

ERNIE WARLICK: We needed a spokesman, and Cookie said, "It's not going to be me because everybody thinks I'm the instigator," which he was. ". . . We need one of the older guys. Ernie, you be the spokesman." Then everybody started walking out. So I proceeded to try to put something together because the media had gotten wind of this and they were standing outside the door. I just gave my statement, and that was it. I still have it:

> The American Football League is progressing in great strides and the Negro football players find they are playing a vital role in the league's progression and have been treated fairly in all cities throughout the league. However, because of the adverse conditions and discrimination practices experienced by the Negro players while here in New Orleans, the players feel they cannot perform 100 percent as expected in the All-Star Game and be treated differently outside. With the exception of the hotels where the squads have been quartered (the West in the Roosevelt, the East in the Fontainebleau), recreational facilities and transportation were not available to the Negro players and service was refused.

So we all left town. "Taxi!" "OK." Jumped right in. Any taxi. At least we broke that barrier while we were there.

CHUCK BURR: I was sent by the league to advance the game. I wound up having to call Chicago, where the owners were meeting, and inform Joe Foss.

By that time, it was all said and done. The blacks had left. The game was off. We were under tremendous heat.

BUD ADAMS: I talked to some of the other owners. It was a general opinion that we couldn't afford a strike. I thought we could do pretty good in Houston. I said, "We'll take it on." It was kind of a last-minute decision.

ERNIE WARLICK: I got home to Buffalo that night and got a call either that night or the next morning: "Get on a plane and go to Houston."

The gathering at Houston's Jeppensen Stadium on Saturday, January 16, numbered all of 15,446 for the hastily arranged game. Five West players scored touchdowns in the 38–14 victory over the East. With the West boasting a 5–0 record in the game, the league owners later voted to change the All-Star format the following year to match the newly crowned AFL champion against All-Stars from the other seven teams.

There are no plaques, no citations that note the action taken in Room 990 of the Roosevelt Hotel that led to the All-Star Game leaving New Orleans. So the following notation will have to do. Twenty-two black players made the collective decision; some have said since that the decision was unanimous while others have indicated there was at least some dissent and disagreement.

HOUSTON ANTWINE: A lot of the ballplayers were still ticked off when we got to Houston, and their attitude was shown when we were practicing. I think the coaches couldn't get across some of the stuff they wanted. You had ballplayers with attitude. All they wanted to do was get the game behind them.

DAVE DIXON: I went over to Houston and met with the guys. By then, all the AFL owners were very much on our side. And the players. Even Cookie came up and apologized: "Look, you're a good guy. I'm really sorry." I think Cookie arrived in New Orleans with a slight chip on his shoulder. If you're a black guy and you arrived like that, you're going to find trouble. That's the only criticism I would make, and it may be unfair. That soured New Orleans on the AFL, and it wasn't the AFL's fault.

HOUSTON ANTWINE: It didn't get the publicity that I think it should have. We didn't feel it was properly addressed. Back in Boston, there was one little blip in the paper showing me with my bag leaving the hotel. That was basically it. The hostility and the treatment that we received in New Orleans was never, never really publicized. I've talked to Cookie, and he was really ticked off about it. Right now, if you ask somebody, "Do you remember the AFL All-Star Game that was supposed to be played in New Orleans?" nobody remembers what happened.

15

Planes, Strains, and Automobiles

Armed with a larger war chest thanks to the new television contract with NBC, the AFL became more of a threat to sign a greater number of top college prospects during the mid-1960s. And a business that was constantly evolving and adjusting to strategy changes led to an unlikely innovation in pro football—the baby-sitter.

In this case, the workforce consisted mostly of respected businessmen and other allies of the NFL who contributed their services to help make sure that top talent wouldn't be snatched away under cover of darkness. Their duties often required a touch of espionage, a flexible schedule, and a piece of plastic with a high credit limit.

GIL BRANDT: Burt Rose with the Los Angeles Rams assembled this corps of baby-sitters for the whole league. They had businesspeople in different parts of the country. One was the governor of Oregon. Burt would submit a list, and the baby-sitters would cover about 50 players. You might have one or two players. And, basically, you had carte blanche for what the baby-sitter wanted to do. The whole thing was a clandestine affair. If he wanted to take the player to Las Vegas, that was fine. Hawaii? Fine.

Coincidentally, Las Vegas and Hawaii ended up on the itinerary of one Harry Schuh, an All-American offensive lineman at Memphis State. In the weeks before the leagues held their first simultaneous drafts on November 28, 1964, Schuh drew the attention of the Los Angeles Rams, Green Bay Packers, and Oakland Raiders. And, before it was all over, maybe AAA, too.

HARRY SCHUH: When I was in the ninth grade in Neshaminy High in Langhorne, Pennsylvania, I was practicing the shot put on a cold spring day. I was almost six two, 190 pounds, and ran a 10-flat hundred. Two gentlemen in big cowboy hats came up and asked me where the coach was. One guy said, "Are you a senior this year?" When I told him I was a freshman, he said, "Well, we're from West Point."

I played in the "Big 33" All-Star Game in Pennsylvania in the summer of '61 with Joe Namath from Beaver Falls and Freddie Biletnikoff from Erie and Marty Schottenheimer. First I signed with Tennessee, but back then you could sign with as many schools as you wanted and my cousin had played football in high school with the coach at Memphis State, Bob Patterson. I went back and forth and ended up going to Memphis State.

My senior season, a gentleman came across the field one day after practice and asked me how I was doing. "You probably don't remember me," he said. "Wait a minute now. I recognize the face. I think you were at Army." And he said, "You have a good memory." That was John Rauch, who was then with Oakland.

The Raiders kept in touch with me, and the Rams and Packers said they were interested in me. Before our last game, about a week before the draft, one of our coaches told me, "After the game, the Raiders want to fly you to New Orleans. They'll get your wife and daughter and fly them down there." And that's what happened. When I got there, I ran into Oakland's Ron Wolf. They decided they weren't going to tell me much before the draft. We spent the night, and then they said, "Let's go to Vegas." So I met my wife and daughter, who was about three months old, and went to Vegas.

RON WOLF: It was all segmented by Al Davis, so you only knew what you were responsible for.

HARRY SCHUH: The first night was fine. The second night, we went to a Dean Martin show and then played blackjack. My wife was tired and went up to our room. These two gentlemen came up to me at the blackjack table. After about 20 minutes, one of the guys said, "Harry, you're doing really good." I recognized them but couldn't place 'em. Then one guy put down his business card, and it said "Los Angeles Rams, Hamp Pool." They asked me to meet them for something to eat. I said I would. I looked around and knew all the Raiders scouts and coaches were in the next room. I figured I'd show them the card. Next thing I knew, I was in a closet waiting for a car to show up to take me across the desert to Los Angeles to catch a plane to

Hawaii. My wife didn't know where I was. They just told her I was safe. She flew to Oakland and stayed with John Rauch's wife.

Ron Wolf: The Rams' people were down in the lobby, calling all the time. They didn't know who I was. I got a call from Leon Hart, who won the Heisman Trophy in '49, telling me that when we met, he was going to obliterate me. He probably could have just reached out his arm and done that.

Gil Brandt: Hamp sent a telegram to the other NFL teams: "Boo, hoo. I lost my Schuh."

Harry Schuh: By this time, my parents had moved to New Jersey, and Vince Lombardi's brother was in charge with the New Jersey state troopers. The Packers were looking for me and had a police officer go to my house. But Al Davis was pretty quick. He had already called my high school coach, told him to tell my parents that I was fine, that I wasn't kidnapped. But he couldn't say where I was. I was in good hands. On draft day, I got woken up in Hawaii. After the Jets took Joe Namath, the Raiders took me. Joe got all the money, and I got the change. We played together at the Senior Bowl. He was sitting having a drink and a cigarette right in the lobby, coaches walking by and saying hi. But that was Broadway Joe.

John Rauch had remembered me after all that time from high school. You have an instinct that if you know somebody . . . I signed with the Raiders right there in Hawaii. Then I flew to Denver the next day, where the Raiders were playing the Broncos. I sat on the bus with "the Hammer" after the game. He wound up getting traded to Kansas City, so I never got to be his teammate. But I got to listen to him. That was pretty good.

Sometimes, it wasn't even clear who was trying to sign whom. Miller Farr left Wichita State with a year's eligibility remaining and moved to Los Angeles, where his family had moved from Texas after his younger brother, Mel, began playing for UCLA. He was surprised that he attracted attention going into the 1965 draft since he had left college early.

Miller Farr: When the draft was coming up, a radio announcer in L.A. named Brad Pye came to my house. He was affiliated with Al Davis from when Al coached with the Chargers. Pye said, "I'm going to take you up to Oakland. The draft will be in a week, and we want to make sure we keep you in the AFL." I had heard of this guy, so I told my parents where I was going, went up to Oakland, and stayed about a week. When I got up there, there were quite a few guys. I was in a hotel when my brother called and said the Dallas Cowboys had offered him a thousand dollars to tell them where I was. I left the hotel and caught a cab to the airport.

RON WOLF: I signed Miller Farr in a restroom at L.A. International for the Raiders. Lo and behold, he got drafted by Denver. That contract disappeared.

Otis Taylor was a little-known wide receiver at a small predominantly black college near Houston, Prairie View A&M. The Chiefs picked him in the fourth round in 1965 while he went undrafted in the NFL. But Gil Brandt's scouting machine rarely stopped with the draft. To the contrary, the team would gain a reputation well into the 1970s for being able to find top talent under some relatively unlikely rocks—wide receiver Bob Hayes out of Florida A&M, lineman Jethro Pugh at Elizabeth City State, lineman Rayfield Wright from Fort Valley State.

But by the time the Cowboys discovered Otis Taylor, they were actually about seven years behind the Chiefs.

OTIS TAYLOR: When I was 14 years old, I met Lloyd Wells, a professional photographer in the Houston area for 30, 40 years who started working with Hank Stram. Because I played at a small college, there was not real great interest in me from pro football. Lloyd Wells was the one who really encouraged me to get ready and look for a chance to play pro football. I was drafted only by the Chiefs and first heard from the Cowboys right before the draft when I was at Prairie View. I was interested in them, because they were the Cowboys from the NFL.

The Cowboys' serious pursuit of Taylor began with a gift to . . . Mom—with a turkey for Christmas. Wells, not to be outdone, followed by sending Otis's mother a turkey plus a $100 bill. Wells was confident enough in Kansas City's situation with Taylor that he left Texas for Nashville, Tennessee, for a few days before the draft to check on some other players that the Chiefs were interested in. That was the break that the Cowboys needed. They sent a baby-sitter to

Prairie View to bring Taylor and teammate Seth Cartwright, a senior lineman, up to Dallas.

GIL BRANDT: We had one of the stockbrokers in town, a guy named Reed, with Otis and Seth Cartwright at the Continental Hotel out on North Central Expressway.

OTIS TAYLOR: The Cowboys had a guy, nothing very strenuous, sit in front of my door, who was supposed to be my shield from the other league. And I had promised Lloyd Wells that I would give the Chiefs a chance to talk with me. My whole young life, Mr. Wells was focused on me. He was an up-and-coming black man getting into the scouting world and would do a lot of good for the black schools.

By that time, Wells learned that the NFL fox had raided his henhouse back in Texas. He left Nashville as soon as he could, catching the next plane to Dallas without knowing where Taylor was being stashed. His wallet became his weapon as he raced from motel to motel using $20 bills to help interrogate a bellman here, a desk clerk there. He desperately called his list of Taylor's girlfriends back in Houston. As a last resort, he phoned Taylor's mother and told her that something had come up and that she needed to call a female friend that Taylor had in Dallas.

Bingo. Mom learned that Otis was at the Continental. The next challenge for the resourceful Wells was to get Taylor away from the Cowboys' grip. He entered the lobby with a camera and, with the aid of another $20, learned from a black bellboy that a young black man who fit the description of Taylor was staying in a room near the pool. Wells knocked on the door, which was answered by the baby-sitter, and said he was from *Ebony* magazine and wanted to do a story on Taylor. The baby-sitter asked to see Wells's press card—how was he to know Wells was practically carrying a warehouse of different business cards for various emergencies? Wells was admitted, chatted a few minutes with Taylor, and managed to get word across that he would try to spring him later.

Wells couldn't come through the lobby again. In fact, while trying to determine his next move, he was told to hit the road by a night watchman. So he later made his way to the room's poolside entrance, tapped lightly on the sliding glass door, and was greeted by a young black woman. He passed along his phone number at the Dallas Sheraton and asked to have Taylor call him there. It was 3:00 A.M. when Taylor finally made the call. It was time to make the escape.

GIL BRANDT: Our guy either had a little too much liquid libation, or he didn't have the staying power of Taylor and Cartwright. So he fell asleep.

OTIS TAYLOR: I climbed out and slipped off, got on a plane, and went to Kansas City. After a couple of days, I went over and signed with the Chiefs. I never did hear from the Cowboys. I don't think they wanted to say anything to me.

A year later, the Chiefs resorted to some baby-sitting of their own—and didn't fool around when it came to deciding who would do the sitting. The Pittsburgh Steelers had their eyes on Minnesota defensive end Aaron Brown, who was a freshman when the Chiefs' Bobby Bell was a senior with the Gophers. As the draft approached, the NFL sent representatives to Brown's home in Port Arthur, Texas—only to discover that Brown wasn't there. And when Pittsburgh's time to draft during the first round arrived, the team couldn't even get Brown on the phone. That's because he was on a Kansas City–to–New York flight, sitting next to Chiefs owner Lamar Hunt. While Hunt was often ridiculed through the years for wearing shoes with holes or not having change for cab fare, he had the foresight on this trip to at least carry a pen enabling Brown to sign a contract as soon as Kansas City drafted him.

There were other occasions when NFL baby-sitters weren't exactly like Canadian Mounties in getting their men. In 1966, a group of them escorted three players from the University of Illinois—safety Ron Acks, linebacker Dan Hansen, and halfback Sam Pierce—to New York. But they mistakenly allowed the players to have their run of the big city. They chose to run over to the AFL office and declare themselves available and even brought along an associate professor of business law to negotiate their contracts.

Lowell Perry was an NFL baby-sitter whose mission was to hang with Michigan defensive tackle Bill Yearby in Nashville before the '66 draft. That irked the New York Jets, who had been assured by Yearby that he would stay put in Detroit with his lawyer. The Jets insisted that Yearby come to New York. That he did, with Perry in tow. Jets assistant coach J. D. Donaldson met them at the airport and displayed his speed. He directed Yearby into a waiting limousine and quickly shut the door before Perry could get in. "What are you plans, Lowell?" were Donaldson's parting words. New York made Yearby the answer to a trivia question—who was the Jets' top pick the year after Joe Namath?—and quickly signed him . . . with Lowell Perry wandering somewhere around the city.

And, sometimes, baby-sitting just wasn't necessary. Such was the case of Tom Mack, a tackle out of Michigan whom the Los Angeles Rams chose with their first pick in 1966—even ahead of Mike Garrett, the Heisman Trophy–winning running back and hometown hero from Southern Cal. Did the Rams sequester Mack away at some hunting lodge in the Upper Peninsula or some beach house on Catalina Island? No need. For when Mack completed his college career with the Wolverines playing in the Rose Bowl, it seems he made the acquaintance of a young local lady named Anne Tollefson. They became engaged soon after, and Mack made it known that he intended to play his pro ball in L.A.

For all the clandestine meetings and 3:00 A.M. phone calls and sneaking around baby-sitters, there was one big "baby," one biggest prize, in the signing war between the leagues. That was a quarterback from Pennsylvania by way of the University of Alabama who boasted the ability to release a football quickly and stay at a bar past last call. No, Joe Namath didn't win the Heisman Trophy in 1964. That honor went to John Huarte, who quarterbacked Notre Dame to the number three ranking in the nation. But there was little disagreement that Namath, despite a history of knee injuries that had all but eliminated his mobility in the pocket, was the best player available in the drafts before the 1965 season.

CHUCK KNOX: I was an assistant coach with the Jets. I had known Joe's family since he was in high school. I'm from Sewickley, Pennsylvania, right on the Ohio River, within five miles of Joe's hometown of Beaver Falls. I coached at Ellwood, and we played Beaver Falls all the time.

Namath's older brother played for Kentucky, and Namath initially intended to play his college ball at Maryland until he learned that he didn't qualify academically there. An Alabama assistant coach named Howard Schnellenberger had coached Namath's brother at Kentucky, heard that Joe wasn't going to Maryland, and brought Joe to Tuscaloosa, where Bear Bryant had quickly turned the program around in three seasons. The Crimson Tide's 1960 team finished 8–1–2. When Joe spent 1961 on the freshman team, he watched as the Tide varsity won the national championship. Expectations weren't lacking when Namath took over as the starter the following year, and Bryant wasn't about to coddle his young talent.

JOE NAMATH: We were playing Georgia my first game in 1962, my sophomore year. Coach Bryant would take the quarterbacks for a walk after the pregame meal around the block at the hotel. Mal Moore, Carlton Rankin, Jack Hurlbut, and myself. Coach Bryant said, "Joe, you got the game plan?" I said, "Yes, sir. I think so." "You *think* so!" God, he jumped all over me with both feet. I learned to say, "Yes, I know." He taught me how to be prepared, which carried over into my professional career.

Namath nearly led Bama to a second consecutive national title as a sophomore. At 8–0 with two games left before going to a bowl, Alabama fell short by a point at Georgia Tech when it failed to convert a two-point conversion in the fourth quarter. Namath's junior season was a peculiar one, preceded by the *Saturday Evening Post* story by Atlanta sportswriter Furman Bisher that charged Bryant and Georgia coach Wally Butts with conspiring to fix their teams' meeting in 1962. The season was far from a disaster, but Alabama suffered losses to Florida in Tuscaloosa and to Auburn in Birmingham.

The 1964 season, Namath's last at Alabama, provided him both his greatest college triumph along with a development that would define his pro days. The Tide finished the regular season 10–0 and, as was the practice at the time, was named national champion before meeting Texas in the Orange Bowl. The unblemished mark was accomplished despite a scare in the fourth game of the season, a 21–0 victory over previously unbeaten North Carolina State. On a rollout play in the second quarter, Namath cut to his right and crumpled because of a knee injury. He never again displayed the mobility that had previously complemented his powerful arm so well. The injured knee prevented him from starting in the Orange Bowl, which Texas won, 21–17.

Bad knee or not, Namath was made the number one priority of Jets owner Sonny Werblin, who recognized a combination of talent and flair that he considered a perfect fit for New York. His partner in making this happen was the Houston Oilers. They also wanted a rookie quarterback, but their sights were set on Tulsa's Jerry Rhome, who led the nation in passing in '64. New York had acquired Rhome's rights a year earlier in the redshirt portion of the AFL draft. Houston, with the top two picks in the draft, was more than happy to trade the second pick to the Jets for Rhome and take Baylor end Lawrence Elkins with the top pick. The New York Giants owned the first pick in the NFL draft thanks to a trade with Pittsburgh and selected a player from Alabama's archrival, Auburn, running back Tucker Fredrickson. Giants coach Allie Sherman proudly proclaimed Fredrickson the "best football player in the country regardless of position." The Giants signed Fredrickson that day in Birmingham, where he was attending the wedding of a teammate. Namath was picked in the first round by the St. Louis Cardinals, now owned by Violet Wolfner's son, Bill Bidwill.

MICKEY HERSKOWITZ: The AFL was constituted in part with the idea that the quickest way to attract a following was to emphasize the players from your own area. And the Oilers were *always* trying to sign guys from the University of Texas and Texas A&M and even Rice and Houston. Jerry Rhome played at Tulsa, led the nation in passing. They played the University of Houston almost every year. While Namath was already a national figure in college, the papers of the '60s—at least in the Southwest—were so parochial. People in Houston knew Jerry Rhome. Getting Namath would not have been a P.R. coup. As great as he was, he still played on a Bryant team that was basically a running team. Joe had the bad knee his senior year, wasn't up there in contention for the Heisman Trophy. Rhome was second to John Huarte. Houston fans were delighted to have the guy who was the leading passer in the nation.

MIKE BITE: I had been a student manager of the Alabama football team [in the '50s] and later became acquainted with Joe playing golf, and we became friends. I went into law, and Joe asked me to help him with his pro negotiations. Chuck Knox came to Birmingham shortly after the draft, the night that Alabama had their senior awards banquet, and then went to California to meet with Sonny Werblin.

CHUCK KNOX: We were going to play at San Diego on Sunday. My job was to make sure Namath got there. I rousted Joe out of bed on that Saturday morning. We hustled to the airport, carried our bags on, and just made it out there.

MIKE BITE: Before we really talked business, we went to watch the Jets play at San Diego. Mr. Werblin had connections at Universal Pictures and sent for a limo for us. They took us to the San Diego Zoo and, finally, to Balboa Stadium for the game. Lo and behold, we were sitting on concrete benches. Our high schools in Alabama played in better stadiums. I looked at Joe and said, "I don't know what we're getting into." The Jets had Dick Wood from Auburn out there at quarterback. I remembered when he played for Auburn and we beat 'em—he threw it a thousand miles an hour. If he didn't knock you on the turf, it was a reception. When we got back from Balboa Stadium, we ended up having dinner up at Trader Vic's with Jane Wyman, Ronald Reagan's ex-wife. Lovely lady. Mr. Werblin, of course, was one of her agents at one time, so that was very impressive. He knew how to punch the right buttons.

When we got back, Joe called me and said, "The Cardinals want to talk. They're coming to Tuscaloosa." I always want to talk to the other side. We met with Bill Bidwill and his right-hand man, O'Shea or something. I started throwing out some numbers. I couldn't get a feel right off the bat. They were always, "Oh, no . . . uh . . . uh."

JOE NAMATH: We were upstairs at my dorm in my room. I was sitting on a bunk bed, and these two guys were on a bunk bed, and we're negotiating. They said, "What do you want?" I told 'em, and they both almost had heart attacks. They were writhing. And then I said, "I need a new car, too." "Oh, sure. Yeah." They were very put off by what I asked for, but before they left the room they wanted me to sign. Well, a quarterback under Coach Bryant is not *that* slow. I told 'em, "No, sir. I can't do that."

MIKE BITE: I was expecting to talk to the New York Giants. Whether the Giants felt like they had it worked out with someone else to trade for Joe, I'm not privy to that. But I asked the Cardinals, "Where are the Giants?" "Oh, no. We're the only ones."

WELLINGTON MARA: We had intended to draft him number one. When we learned that Houston had the first pick, we switched to Tucker Fredrickson because Houston had gotten another player into the oil business. When the Jets traded for the pick, we tried to make a deal with St. Louis but were unable to.

MIKE BITE: I got the feeling the NFL wasn't going to pay anything to Joe. I ran into Harry Gilmer, an All-American at Alabama who was coaching at Detroit at the time. He said, "I think you're making a mistake if you don't send Joe to the NFL." I just nodded and said, "We'll take everything into consideration." With the Cardinals, we were always talking about, "Does Joe pay for his shoes?" Nickel-and-dime stuff. Mr. Werblin kept alluding to Joe's persona, his presence when he came into a room. And when we talked bucks, Mr. Werblin didn't have to go to a committee.

JOE NAMATH: Coach Bryant told me, "Get to know the people you're working for." And when I met Weeb Ewbank and Sonny Werblin and Leon Hess and Chuck Knox, I wanted to work with those guys. It didn't make any difference what league it was or what town it was. I can't tell you how much weight Chuck Knox carried. He was from home. That was special. And Weeb Ewbank had coached Johnny Unitas and had won championships with the Baltimore Colts.

Coach Bryant told me what to ask for, which was double what I thought about asking. When I first met with Mr. Werblin and the Jets' representatives in California, we didn't really negotiate a whole lot. He opened up offering me a third more than I was asking for. Then, after a while, we added some things.

MIKE BITE: I never discuss his contract [widely reported to be between $400,000 and $427,000—a staggering figure at that time], but I will say this: we asked for a clause from day one—three years, no cut. I had a basic number, then I came back [for more] for his mother, his father, and everybody else to get as much as we could. And the car.

CHUCK KNOX: We had the deal set with Joe. He was playing in the Orange Bowl, and I went down there with my wife. She was looking after Rose Namath, Joe's mother, to make sure nothing would disrupt what we had done.

MIKE BITE: I had the Jets' signature, but they didn't have our signature because Coach Bryant and the NCAA had a rule that you couldn't sign. In fact, when we went to California, my law firm paid for Joe's flight, his room, everything. I did get reimbursed from the Jets later, but I made sure that we had checks to show we paid our own way because I wanted Joe to be eligible for the Orange Bowl. I could look Coach Bryant in the eye and say, "We didn't break any rules."

It was a done deal after the Orange Bowl. I had the Jets' contract in my little hand. All I had to do the morning after the game was, "Hey, Joe. Wake up. Put your X here, baby." The first news conference was held in Miami. Then we went up to New York.

Namath was one of five players selected in the first round by each league during the first simultaneous drafts. Well, the AFL got an hour's head start, at 8:00 A.M. Eastern. The negotiations that went into fighting off each other for eight hours resulted in the AFL's getting through five rounds but the NFL only two. Twelve first-round picks were signed that day.

Though the Chicago Bears didn't own the NFL's number one pick, they quickly planted themselves at the center of the bidding war by acquiring two additional first-round selections to go along with their own choice. With the number two pick overall, acquired from the Steelers, they picked Illinois linebacker Dick Butkus. They soon added Kansas running back Gale Sayers and, on a pick from Washington, Tennessee tackle Steve DeLong.

In the AFL draft, Denver took Butkus in the second round as something of a consolation prize, ditching its initial plan of taking Fredrickson upon learning of his impending signing with the Giants. Sayers was made the top pick of the Kansas City Chiefs, just down the road from his college home. And DeLong was picked sixth overall by San Diego.

GALE SAYERS: Dick Butkus, an All-American from Illinois, was going to play with the Chicago Bears. Simple as that. Case closed. Since I went to Kansas, I knew Lamar Hunt very well. Don Klosterman was the Chiefs' general manager and came to see every game I played my junior and senior years. And I went to see the Chiefs play.

My baby-sitter was Buddy Young, who worked in the commissioner's office in the NFL. When draft day came around, my wife and I were at his home in Baltimore. Lamar Hunt and Don Klosterman couldn't find me. We went to the All-American banquet that weekend after Thanksgiving. That's how they caught up with me and talked with me about being drafted and how much money they would give me.

I think many people thought I would go with the Chiefs, but I really felt that, in order to better myself as a football player, I had to play against the best. And I felt at that time the best football was played in the National Football League. When it came down to talking contract, Lamar Hunt had billions of dollars back then and I thought the Chiefs would offer me much more money than the Bears. Lamar offered me a four-year contract for $27,500. I signed a four-year contract with the Bears for $25,000.

While Bite says all precautions were taken to ensure that Namath's eligibility for bowl season would never be questioned, similar episodes weren't as delicately handled. Exhibit A was the case of three Oklahoma players, including Ralph Neely, headed to play Florida State in the Gator Bowl on January 2, 1965. Neely was drafted by Houston in the AFL and Baltimore in the NFL.

GIL BRANDT: Bud Adams signed Ralph somewhere around the first of December. I went to visit Neely and his wife at the time in Norman. They told us he had signed but, in thinking about it, they thought they made a mistake. If they had an opportunity to go to Dallas rather than Baltimore, he would rather play in the National Football League in Dallas. Neely's father-in-law, Bob Forte, and I worked out a deal to be signed after the Gator Bowl. On the night prior to the game, Coach Landry got a call from Gomer Jones, Oklahoma's coach. I was in Jacksonville with Forte. The topic of the conversation was that we had signed Neely and he was going to be ineligible, which we hadn't done. It turned out four or five OU guys had signed and four or five Florida State guys had signed. The Oklahoma kids, including Neely, told the truth, and the Florida State kids played in the game. We came back to Dallas 'cause Neely was on his way to the Hula Bowl. We signed him in the Admiral's Club at Love Field.

A guy named Bob Brightenstein had gone to school with Neely in New Mexico. Brightenstein's uncle was a circuit court appellate judge and said our contract wasn't valid. We went to court in Oklahoma City, and the Oilers turned down a proposal to settle in the judge's chambers. The judge awarded Neely to us because of the fact that Neely was a naive individual and didn't know what he was doing. The Oilers appealed, we went to appellate court, and Judge Brightenstein was one of the three judges. It was a two-to-one decision for the Oilers, and Judge Brightenstein supposedly voted against us. The settlement was made, which included draft choices and three preseason games.

16

The Handsome New Prince

The franchise that once rattled around the near-empty stands of the Polo Grounds was now the flagship of the new league. Shea Stadium was the place to be, for both the AFL and New York football. Up in the Bronx, the bottom fell out on the Giants in 1964. After playing in six NFL Championship Games in eight years, they suddenly plummeted to the bottom of the Eastern Conference. By the mid '60s, most of the core stars either retired (Frank Gifford, Y. A. Tittle, Andy Robustelli, Rosey Brown) or were traded (Sam Huff to Washington, Erich Barnes to Cleveland). Suddenly, it was New York's NFL football team that lacked exciting, talented players and was operating out of an aged facility.

As Joe Namath reported to training camp in Peekskill, New York, the town was for the taking—if he could put his mouth where his money was, starting with his new teammates.

LARRY GRANTHAM: I was at the All-Star Game, and Weeb called me, told me he wanted to get together. The whole gist of the meeting was the fact that we had just drafted and were going to sign this quarterback named Namath, and we were going to have to give him a lot of money. [He came to me] as one of the team leaders; he wanted to go ahead and sign next year's contract so we could tell all the other ballplayers that we were going to negotiate in good faith with them, too. So I jacked my price up, and he met it. So Joe Namath getting drafted by us, getting ready to sign with us, helped me.

JIM HUDSON: I first met Joe the week of the Orange Bowl. That's how we ended up rooming together during training camp and on the road with the Jets. What surprised us at Texas was how quick he would get rid of the ball. We'd never played against any quarterbacks like him, and we had played some pretty good ones—Don Trull, Roger Staubach.

WALT MICHAELS: The contract that he got was split so many ways. He had a couple of dollars going to his sister, couple of dollars going to a brother, couple dollars going here and there. I was scouting and ran into one of his brothers-in-law who said, "I've got to be here in order to get some money." Joe came in with everybody thinking it was all his, but from what I understand he tried to help God-knows-how-many people.

FRANK RAMOS: We introduced Namath the day after the Orange Bowl. The next week, we signed John Huarte, Heisman Trophy–winning quarterback from Notre Dame. Within months, we sold like 18,000 season tickets. So the Namath and Huarte contracts were paid for immediately.

DAVE ANDERSON: Namath came to New York right after the Orange Bowl for his first knee operation. Werblin invited the beat writers to see him at Toots Shor's. There was a restaurant and a bar, then a banquet room downstairs. Upstairs, there was a room for private parties. There must have been six or eight or ten of us there, just the pro football writers, to get a chance to visit with Joe. Lou Effrat, a writer from the *Times*, said, "Joe, you're making all this money. What if you don't make it?" Joe just sat there and finally said, "I'll make it."

FRANK RAMOS: Before camp, Joe had already been on the cover of *Sports Illustrated*. Bill Hines from *Life* magazine, who had done the book on the Green Bay Packers, *Run to Daylight*, arrived with Namath at training camp at Peekskill. That's how it started. It was that type of attention from the get-go.

CURLEY JOHNSON: We didn't know what kind of guy Joe was, just what we heard and what we read in the paper. When camp began, everybody was watching him like a hawk. He made a big entrance in his big Lincoln.

GEORGE SAUER JR.: I remember strong resentment from the veterans. Not that they disliked him. They resented the situation. Some of them were with the team when a lot of them didn't get paid: "Where are the checks? . . . There's no towels because nobody paid the laundry bill." All of a sudden, hundreds of thousands of dollars were being thrown around. But a lot of guys understood that Sonny Werblin had come from show business. He wanted to promote Joe publicly to get a lot of interest in the team. And there was $200,000 for John Huarte from Notre Dame.

JOE NAMATH: Some veterans were more understanding than others. Some were not getting paid what they thought they should, and it was justifiable for them to figure, "How can a guy just coming in be getting more money than me?" The game was changing, and Weeb tried to explain it to the team. We had some misunderstandings, but we cleared the air. We had a meeting, and it basically came down to, on the field, we're here for the same reason. Off the field, I don't care if you like me or not. Even on the field one day, we were running a lap and a linebacker ran up behind me and knocked me down, jumped on my back. I had to have some words.

DAVE HERMAN: Guys wouldn't talk to Joe about it. They would get into someone else's face, talk behind the doors. They grew out of it as they got used to it. Some of them took it like I did, glad to have a football player of that caliber.

CURLEY JOHNSON: We always had a warm-up drill at practice called "pat and go." The receivers and the backs would get in a line and run and quarterbacks would throw the ball. Had one quarterback at one end of the field and another at the other end—then, it was Joe and Mike Taliaferro. When we saw Joe throw, we thought the guy was unbelievable.

MIKE TALIAFERRO: My relationship with Joe was excellent. I had the highest respect and regard for Joe. John [Huarte] was more of an introverted, quiet individual. I think, to some extent, he suffered from being in the College All-Star Game. It was kind of hard for him to catch up with the offense. Joe and I were really a lot better friends, and John just kind of showed up three weeks later.

DAVE ANDERSON: That first preseason, the Jets played a preseason game in Allentown, Pennsylvania. It was a downpour. And Joe threw the ball through the rain like an arrow. He would just flick it. That was the first time I knew he was the real thing.

BAKE TURNER: Namath was so far above anybody we'd ever seen as far as delivery, knowledge, and toughness that Huarte didn't stand a chance. Mike Taliaferro was battling Namath, and he had an arm so strong that he'd really have to let up to keep from throwing the ball too hard.

DON MAYNARD: He wanted to make the ballclub on his ability, not on the fact that he had a guarantee and all that. That was just the type of guy that Joe is. And I told him, "I'll help make you a better quarterback, and you'll make me a great receiver."

MATT SNELL: Every day, we had this hoard of press. It was a real circus atmosphere. John Huarte was a good athlete, and he was a good runner, but he wasn't a professional quarterback. I could throw better than John Huarte. And he got $200,000. But Sonny decided, "If that's what I need to get him to come in from Notre Dame, that's what I've got to pay." But you knew Joe was the man.

JIM HUDSON: I wasn't surprised by the attention Joe received. I was surprised by my new teammates and the way things happened in pro ball as opposed to what I was used to with Texas and Darrell Royal. The first team meeting we went to, George Sauer and Namath and I—all rookies—went together. When we walked in, those old veterans were sitting around. There was a table of 'em playing cards. Some of them were sitting around drinking coffee and smoking. Another group of them were over telling what happened in the off-season. And when Weeb came into the room to start the meeting, nobody quit. They kept playing cards. They kept reading the papers. They kept smoking. Joe and I looked at each other. If Coach Royal or Bear Bryant walked in the room, everything stopped and you looked forward. And in camp, there wasn't but four or five showers for the whole team. You had to wear your jersey and pants the whole week. At Texas and Alabama, we were used to getting clean uniforms every time we went to work out.

BILL HAMPTON: We trained at Peekskill Military Academy, which had no air-conditioning. The players bought screens to put on the windows. The training room was an old coal bin. The commander of the academy lived adjacent to the parade grounds, in front of the dorms. One time, one of the players was throwing firecrackers out the window at midnight. The commander got pissed off and went to Weeb and said, "You've got to cut that stuff out."

PETE LAMMONS: Sonny Werblin's boys had gone there, and I'm sure it was cheap. Sonny had put a lot of money into it, but what a god-awful place that was. I think we had to wash our own clothes. And we called back to school to get equipment—shoes and pads.

BILL MATHIS: Mark Smolinski brought to camp something like a mink, so fast it could catch a snake in midair. He had it in a cage that was wood with wire mesh on top where you could see the tail through a hole. When guys wanted to see it, he would get them to take a pencil, rub the wire, and it would come out. That door would fly open, and the tail would fly out on the person who was watching. He showed it to Emerson Boozer one time, and Boozer almost went out a second-floor window. Sprained his ankle. At a meeting after that, Weeb said, "Smolinski! Get up and read rule number eight—no pets in camp!" Paul Rochester said, "What about Namath's dog?" That dog would come up and eat off Weeb's plate. And Weeb said, "Uh . . . uh . . . everybody knows . . . that's our mascot."

WALT MICHAELS: We were in a city where the Giants were number one. As a result, when Namath did anything, he was immediately compared to Y. A. Tittle. "Well, Y. A. Tittle wouldn't do that!" Well, no. Y. A. Tittle, in all fairness, was a good quarterback, but he couldn't throw the ball like Joe. When you get into certain categories, you've got fair ones, good ones, great ones, and fantastic ones. Joe had a whole ballgame. And he was as streetwise as anybody. Joe was a guy who could play a symphony without being able to read a note of music. He was gifted. And you have to be gifted when you come up to a team with knees as damaged as [his were] when we got him.

Ewbank and the Jets brought Namath along relatively slowly, naming Taliaferro as the starter coming out of camp. The excitement of Peekskill seemed long ago and far away when New York immediately fell into an 0–2 hole with losses to Houston and Kansas City. Before the Jets headed to Buffalo to face the unbeaten league champions, Ewbank announced that Namath would get his first start. Joe Willie connected on 19 of 40 passes, including touchdown passes of three yards to Bill Mathis and nine yards to Dee Mackey, in the

Bills' 33–21 victory. Judgments of the star rookie's play ranged from a compliment from Buffalo defensive end Tom Day ("He's worth the $400,000") to a complaint from Buffalo quarterback Jack Kemp ("I was getting a little tired of watching our guys pick up Namath after they knocked him down. None of their guys picked me up.").

And, after that, the American Football League was never the same, on—or especially off—the field.

BAKE TURNER: He was the biggest thing in New York, even above Mickey Mantle and Roger Maris and all those guys. The attention he was getting from people and the press was boggling. He didn't have any time for the players. He was either at an interview or a commercial or with some of his cronies. A couple of players kind of buddied up to him. Jim Hudson was close to him. I wish I could have known Joe better. There were a lot of team functions, and Joe attended those. But he was in Manhattan, in the high-rise, and most of us were out by Shea. He was really just like some of the rest of us—young, wanting to have a good time. He was having a good time.

JIM HUDSON: It was a good adventure. Wasn't ever bad. On one road trip, Joe and I were out late, and I said, "Joe, I've got to go in." He was playing pool for money. He said, "I'm not going in until I get through playing." So I left. Weeb and them came by our room: "Where's Joe?" "I don't know. I don't know where he is." They knew I was lying. Well, they sent the equipment manager, Bill Hampton. He knew all the guys. Here was Hampton: "Tell me where he is. I'll go get him, and I won't tell Weeb anything." I said, "Aw, bullshit. You'll tell Weeb. I know you have to. But here's where he is. . . ." Hampton got down there with him, and he got to have a drink or two. He got betting on the pool game. And both of them stayed out all night.

We'd room together on the road. He'd register under his name, then we'd move to another room. Because the phone never quit. People knocking on the door. We were playing an exhibition game in St. Louis. About 3:00 in the morning, somebody started banging on the door. We thought it was one of the teammates coming in drunk. I was in the bed nearest the door. I opened the door, and a guy said, "Where's Namath? I want to kill that son of a bitch!" "Are you crazy? Get the . . ." The guy started to push into the door. I didn't even see the second guy. I slugged the first guy, and when I did, the other guy cut my throat, I don't know what with. When it happened and that blood started squirting out, I started hollering at Joe. He started hollering. He got a towel and some ice. Never did find those guys.

FRANK RAMOS: It was like a rock star. The fans in the opposing cities treated him like royalty. We would come out of a stadium, and there would be 5,000 people waiting by the buses just to see him leave the stadium.

MERLE HARMON: Traveling with the Jets then was like traveling with a three-ring circus. After a game in Buffalo, they had the team buses parked on the street. War Memorial Stadium was in a neighborhood. There wasn't any parking except for people's front yards. People were lined up outside. John Free, our business manager and traveling secretary, jumped on the bus and said, "OK, bussie. Let's go." "Wait a minute! Joe's not here!" John said, "Let's go, bussie. Move it." We went about two blocks down the street and made a right turn, pulled over and parked. Pretty soon, here came an ambulance up alongside. Joe got out. They had backed the ambulance right up to the stadium.

JOHN FREE: Every road game, I would scout a way to get him out of that stadium and to the buses. An ambulance. A reporter's car, where he laid down on the floor. I don't know how many things I did. The laundry truck in San Diego was my favorite. I couldn't figure out how to get him out because the buses were down in a tunnel. The people just jammed the tunnel. I saw this laundry truck and went over to the driver and said, "I'll give you 25 bucks if you let this man in the back of your truck. Go down that highway exactly one mile, pull over to the right, and wait for this first bus to come to you." The guy opened the door to the back of the truck, and Namath got in with his little suitcase. The driver's girlfriend had snuck into the stadium in the back of the truck. The driver said to his girlfriend, "You come up here with me. I don't want you back there with him."

JOE NAMATH: It was so crowded, you couldn't just stop and visit. It was a safety factor. Plus, we had a team and a schedule to leave. It was an efficiency thing to try to get to the airport. But it was fun. It was nice. It was a good feeling.

FRANK RAMOS: He received incredible attention, but he knew how to handle it. He had his moments and had certain battles with the press. But I spent

39 years in P.R., and I've seen very few players that could touch him as far as being accommodating. When we went to the West Coast, we would travel a day early. We would do a news conference on a Friday or a Saturday before a game and let the media have availability to him. Then after a game, most games he spoke for 45 minutes to an hour. There's not a player today who does anything close to that.

JOE NAMATH: I remember when I got to meet Mickey Mantle for the first time. We were in a nightclub in New York called the Pussy Cat. It had wonderful ribs. I was sitting over at the bar, and the night manager came over to me and said, "Joe, you know Mickey Mantle, Billy Martin, Whitey Ford?" "Well, yeah." "You wanna meet 'em?" "Wanna *meet* 'em?" "Yeah, they're sittin' over here." He took me over there and sat me down with those three guys. Boy, it was great. And later on, Mickey and I were in business together with Mantle Men and Namath Girls. And that was fun.

The first few years, I would go out to dinner with Mr. Werblin—and Mrs. Werblin, Leah Ray—at least a couple times a week. He'd been around, and he knew how to deal with people. I wouldn't call him a father figure, but he was a friend and a leader, someone that I looked up to, someone who constantly tried to help me. We were at dinner one time, and I was upset about something that was written. Leah Ray just leaned back and said, "Joseph! That's show business!"

MIKE BITE: They have the Gridiron Banquet in Washington every year, president of the United States and everything. We went the first year he was a pro. The banquet was in the same hotel where we were staying. Secret Service everywhere. Couldn't even leave the room. It was late. I fell asleep. All of a sudden, Joe said, "Get up! We gotta catch a plane right now!" So, hell, I just jumped up, didn't look out the window. You know how hotel rooms are dark, shades pulled. So I took a shower, got dressed, and that son of a bitch was lying in bed. It was maybe 1:00 or 2:00 in the morning. So I said, "The hell with this." I just sat in the chair with my coat and tie on.

The NFL had all the players. All of a sudden, Joe Namath is playing for the New York Jets. Joe Willie. Women started saying, "The old man is watching 'cause he's got a bet on the game. . . . You wanna watch football? You watch the Jets. I wanna see Joe Willie." Women, in my opinion, began to make an impact on NBC's ratings. And NBC learned real quick they would try to put the Jets on to the biggest part of the country.

BUTCH BYRD: We had an exhibition game against the Jets. Joe had a roommate at Alabama named Ray Abruzzese, who had played for the Bills and had gone to Alabama. Ray and I were good friends. He and a couple of guys went up to see Namath. I went along really just to see what a $400,000 ballplayer looked like. To my surprise, this guy was natural and likable, nonassuming. I shouldn't say surprise. It was more gratifying that he was a normal guy. He and I and Ray and two or three other guys went over to Canada for the horse races. We had a great time.

AL WARD: I was in New York in '65 in the league office when Joe was a rookie. I was with him at the All-Star Game in Houston after the season. I never got to visit with him. He was always busy. Turns out he had Mamie Van Doren up in his room the whole week at the old Shamrock Hotel. He was supposed to have a roomie, but I don't know what he did with him. And then he went out and played a great game, threw three touchdown passes.

JOE NAMATH: When I was a rookie, like November, our orthopedist, Dr. Nicholas came to me and said, "Where are you going during the off-season?" I said, "Well, I'm going to go see my mother in Pennsylvania." He said, "You need to go where it's warm. The arthritic condition in your right knee will feel better in the warm weather." He didn't have to tell me twice. We first played in the Orange Bowl my sophomore year. I couldn't believe what it was like in late December and early January. Then we went back and played Texas in the '65 Orange Bowl. At home, it was snowing. Back then, you had to walk off the plane onto the steps. And the heat hit me. "This is wonderful." Flowers and things like that. I needed Florida for my health.

BILL MATHIS: I roomed with Joe in the off-seasons in Miami. His first off-season in Miami, he had two DUIs, so Werblin got me to go down and stay with him after his first year. I'm three or four years older than Joe. We played golf and went fishing. I didn't keep him in check at night. I just drove. But we never had anything that was negative publicity. And that's what we did for the next four off-seasons.

JOE NAMATH: I had two roommates, Bill [Mathis] and Joe Hurst with the *Daily Racing Form*. They were trying to help me. Bill's a good citizen and a great guy. We got along great. He was good for me. We went out. There weren't drugs. Drinking was the only thing. There was really not that much to get in trouble for.

BILL MATHIS: One of Mr. Werblin's friends that Joe and I met had a horse farm between Miami and Fort Lauderdale, and the guy gave Joe this Irish setter. The dog was named Pharaoh. He got him as a puppy and took him everywhere he went. That's the dog Joe took to training camp. Riding around in a Cadillac convertible—everywhere. One day, Joe and I were out in the yard playing catch. We threw the ball and said, "Let Pharaoh get it." It went in the bushes. We went inside and started getting ready to go out, just left the door open wide enough for the dog to get in. We came back downstairs, and it looked like a mass murder had taken place. When Pharaoh picked up that ball, he cut his tongue on a piece of glass. We had white furniture and white carpet, and everything in there was red.

FRANK JACKSON: In Miami, I ran with Joe and Marty Schottenheimer. Joe was a different kind of guy when we went out somewhere. One summer I was with [Baltimore Orioles pitcher] Jim Palmer a whole lot when he was recovering from a shoulder injury. We'd go out drinking, and women would come up and approach Joe. He'd put his hand on my leg and say, "I'm with him."

LEROY NEIMAN: I was the Jets' artist in residence from the time Namath came. Sonny Werblin used to buy paintings from me, and we became good friends. I could go anywhere with the Jets. Team buses. Team flights. The locker room. The sidelines. Weeb didn't take too much to me being around, didn't think I was necessary. And he was right, but it was a fun time.

Joe's apartment was a big deal. They made a lot about the chandelier and the llama rug. We had a lot of fun, nothing I care to talk about.

BILL MATHIS: One Monday, Joe either had a real good game or a real bad game the day before 'cause [Howard] Cosell was coming over to interview him at his place in Manhattan. He couldn't talk Joe into coming to the studio. That's when Joe and Ray Abruzzese had those blackout curtains and llama-skin rugs and all that stuff.

JOE NAMATH: Howard and Dick Schaap and I were sitting in my living room. Ray was in the bedroom sleeping. Ray came walking out in a T-shirt and these nylon shorts, wiping his eyes. He looked up and saw Howard: "Oh, Howard!" In his Philadelphia accent. "I thought you were on television! I was just coming out to turn you off!" Schapp and I died. Howard sat there, just staring, his mouth agape. After about 10 seconds, Howard started in on every Italian in the world.

Howard was a big put-on, boy. We were leaving ABC one day, and we were on an elevator. I was standing in the back. Howard was in front of me. Guy got on. Howard said to him, "Did you hear about that Namath kid last night?" Guy said, "No, what happened?" "The kid was drunk. They found him in the gutter downtown. Whatta ya think of *that?*" The guy didn't say anything. And there was Howard: "Heh, heh, heh."

MERLE HARMON: Joe once said, "If I'd done everything I was given credit for doing, I would have been dead when I was 26." One time he supposedly jumped the club before an exhibition game. Well, they thought his brother had cancer and he was going back home to be with him. He really loved his family.

CURLEY JOHNSON: All the things that Joe did and all the things that he was accused of doing probably were true, but we really didn't care. We didn't run with him. The only guy he ever associated with back in the early days was Jim Hudson. He wasn't the easiest guy to meet. A lot of guys tried to get next to him. He'd be late to meetings. Weeb would fine him. But nobody really gave a shit. We knew that potentially, he could take us to the championship.

As a rookie, Namath threw for 2,220 yards as New York again fell short of posting its first winning season. His sophomore season resulted in a league-high 3,379 yards but an alarming number of interceptions, 27, as the Jets finished third at 6–6–2. And the 1967 season produced the most yards ever thrown for by a pro quarterback at that time, 4,007—George Sauer Jr. and Don Maynard combining for 146 catches—to go with 26 touchdowns and 28 interceptions. But the club lost three of its last four games to fall a game behind division-winner Houston, and critics began to chirp that this strong-armed, gimpy-legged wild child might not be the player who could lead New York to the top.

GEORGE SAUER JR.: Yeah, he threw some interceptions, but we were forced into a throwing game. We lost Matt Snell and Emerson Boozer. We were playing the second half of the season without our top two running backs. How else are your receivers going to come out one-two in the league? I screwed up a pattern once, and Joe threw it right to Butch Byrd, Buffalo's cornerback. The safety blitzed, so I was supposed to change the pattern. We got over on the side, and Joe said, "You didn't see the safety." I said, "No, missed it." He said, "Well, you'll get it next time." He could have chewed me out, but he didn't. I think the fact that he didn't made me feel more guilty.

BUTCH BYRD: We were getting ready to play the Jets, and Namath had the bad leg. He always had a bad leg. Our defensive coach, Richie McCabe, suggested if we blitzed, we could take a shot at his leg. And the defensive team as a whole said they would not do that. It wasn't mandated. And after that two- to three-minute conversation, he was a little embarrassed that he even mentioned that 'cause he had no takers. And I heard other teams had similar conversations.

CURLEY JOHNSON: When he came to workouts with those knees and you'd see him hurt and soak 'em in ice, you knew he was a competitor. He had some hits during games that a lot of quarterbacks would have come out from. He played hurt, and sometimes it would just make you sick.

RON McDOLE: One time we were playing in New York, and the Jets were struggling. I hit Namath and Tom Sestak hit him and Jim Dunaway hit him, all three at the same time. Joe used to backpedal all the time instead of turning and running. He was lying down and looking up at us and said, "Did you happen to pass anybody up there in a green-and-white uniform? Didn't you even fall over anybody? Did you jump over anybody?"

BAKE TURNER: If it had gotten worse in '67 than it was in '66, there would have been some major doubts. But he got better and became totally confident with Maynard, myself, Pete Lammons, and George Sauer.

17

War and Peace

By the spring of 1966, the Namath contract numbers that had shaken the very financial foundation of pro football were obsolete. Tommy Nobis, the talented linebacker from the University of Texas, commanded a package worth about $600,000 to turn away from his home-state Oilers and sign with the team that made him the top selection in the NFL draft, the new Atlanta Falcons. And the scary part was that the money waved in the faces of rookies would only continue to mount under pro football's competitive two-league structure.

Like a race-car driver pushing hard on the accelerator, the AFL owners had to ask themselves whether they had the stomachs—and the wallets—to continue to collectively floor it. And if so, the AFL camp was divided between those who sought to gain admittance into the NFL and those who wanted to achieve parity with—or even superiority over—the established league.

RALPH WILSON: After the Namath contract in early '65, merger stuff started behind the scenes. There was a meeting at Barron Hilton's. Sonny Werblin and I were appointed to talk to Carroll Rosenbloom, owner of the Colts. Sonny was against it and never came to the meeting. Carroll had a little cottage on the beach in South Florida, and we discussed a merger. There was such hostility between the leagues that you couldn't merge and just start playing each other. Here was his format of how it would work: "We'll spread all the money between the AFL and the NFL. We'll have a four-year hiatus when AFL and NFL teams will play exhibition games, and we'll have a common draft. After that, when things have cooled down, we'll have realignment." I must have had seven or eight meetings with Carroll. One time I met with him and Pete Rozelle and Tex Schramm at the Sea View Hotel. The NFL wanted money to let us in. I said, "How much?" They said, "Fifty million." I said, "Forget it!" We began to work things out, and I told Sonny, "This sounds great." He said, "No, I want to fight." And so did Wayne Valley in Oakland. But the rest of us in smaller cities thought this was our salvation. In the long run, the NFL would put us out of business because they had the big cities. They were going to get much more television money. I talked to Sonny and Wayne on the phone, and they came around a little. We had a meeting at Monmouth Park in New Jersey, but we couldn't put the thing together and it didn't go through that year.

The next battleground came in the person of a soft-spoken West Texas half-back named Donny Anderson, who was actually drafted a year earlier. He was eligible for the 1965 drafts, being held shortly before the end of the 1964 college regular season, although he was playing only his junior season at Texas Tech. Because he had been redshirted in 1962 following his freshman season in Lubbock, he was eligible for the regular NFL draft while the AFL conducted a separate selection phase for redshirts.

Donny Anderson: The draft was around Thanksgiving, and I was home in Stinnett, Texas. Gil Brandt told me the Cowboys were going to draft me in the second round, after picking Craig Morton. The morning of the draft, I got a call: "My name is Tom Miller with the Green Bay Packers, and we're considering drafting you in the first round." Then all of a sudden, I heard, "This is Vince Lombardi. We've just drafted you in the first round. What do you think about that, young man?" I was shocked. Houston drafted me in the AFL, and I went down and visited them. I told both teams I was going to finish my senior year. I discussed it with my family, and I just didn't think it was right to leave my teammates. And they left me alone because they still had my rights. The next year, the Packers were trying to sign two first-round choices—Jim Grabowski and Gale Gillingham—plus me. Grabo was the first player picked in the AFL draft, by the Miami Dolphins, who were new.

The big part of the story was that my father worked in Borger, Texas, for Phillips Petroleum Company. So that became kind of an automatic with Bud Adams. My dad got transferred to Nebraska before my senior year, so Bud made sure to pick up my father every week in his personal plane and fly him to my games. It was kind of a bidding war. Bud's stuff wasn't as much cash, which, looking back at it, didn't make any sense to me. The Packers were all cash. Bud offered four service stations, and I'd rent 'em back and get royalties. Then there was a huge house down near Houston thrown in. I had uncles in Beaumont and Port Neches and Houston. One day on a plane flying back to Lubbock I met Bobby Layne. In his infamous way, he said, "I'll tell you how to handle your contract. Take the cash." That's all he said. I said, "Well, I've got this . . ." He said, "Take the cash." Even though the Packers didn't offer as much, it turned out to be much more in cash. The hardest part was telling Dad that I was going to Green Bay instead of Houston because of all his brothers and family. I just said, "The Packers are the best football team, and Lombardi is the best coach." I had not agreed to [anything] going into the last week in December '65, and Bud brought the stakes up to about $900,000. But he didn't bring any cash to the table. The Packers' bonus was $300,000 and a guaranteed contract for three years. We were playing in the Gator Bowl on December 31, 1965. I signed right after the game. My brother was working at the time to become a CPA, and he was doing all the work.

TEX SCHRAMM: We always signed who we wanted to sign. Before the '66 draft, we were trying to sign Grabowski, a fullback from Illinois. He had an agent, the first agent that I can remember. And Green Bay was after him. What I didn't realize was that Green Bay had a lot of cash because, when they were founded and formed a corporation, there were no dividends. All the money had to be used to improve the team, so they were sitting there with cash in the bank. They wound up signing Grabowski before the draft. I said, "If that can happen to us, then we've got a big problem."

LAMAR HUNT: There were merger conversations on and off going back to before the AFL ever actually played a game, all the way back to the fall of 1959. People would get together and say, "Well, there shouldn't be a second league. Take an expansion team in the NFL." And in '62 or '64 there may have been a meeting here or there. Really, merger was not something that drove our thinking. We wanted always to be successful financially. But a championship game, much like baseball had with the World Series, was something that a lot of people really wanted to see happen.

TEX SCHRAMM: The baby-sitting was one of the things that eventually led to the merger. The teams that had the most resources available were the teams that were winning the war. Or the teams that were the smartest. A good example of one of the tough persons to compete against in those days was Al Davis. He didn't have the resources like Lamar Hunt, but he knew how to do it and was so competitive. The Jets could compete. They had the money. But it had gotten to the point that some teams were drafting players only because they knew they could sign them. The Steelers drafted a guy in the first round, Dick Leftridge, a running back from West Virginia, who would have been fortunate to go in the third round. It had gotten to the point where you had to sign early. I told Rozelle, "I've got an idea of how to do the merger and what I want to do. Only on the basis that nobody in the league except you knows that. I'm going to first talk to Lamar." I knew if there had to be any little shenanigans done in their league, he'd be the one that would be able to do it.

LAMAR HUNT: I had a conversation with Tex Schramm around April 6 or 7, when I was on my way from Kansas City to Houston for the league meeting where Joe Foss was going to resign. Tex called and said he had something he wanted to visit about, would it be convenient to get together. I said, "Sure. Any urgency to it?" He said, "It's important." I said I'd be happy to stop off in Dallas and maybe we could meet there and visit for a couple of hours at the airport. We met at the statue of the Texas Ranger inside Love Field that evening and went out to his car in the parking lot. It was just a feeling that there would be a little more privacy if we did that. It looked very suspicious to have two guys out in the parking lot in the dark.

TEX SCHRAMM: I outlined it. It involved moving of teams—the Jets and the Raiders—and it was not a totally simple thing.

Within hours, the face of the AFL would be changed drastically. It had been decided who would floor the league's gas pedal. Certainly not Joe Foss.

JOE FOSS: I wanted the merger in a different way. I didn't want to pay anybody a nickel. I didn't want to give any money to the 49ers and the Giants. I wanted the leagues to remain with their separate identities just as baseball had with a National League and an American League. Actually, there were five owners that agreed with me 100 percent and four that were sort of thinking, "Maybe Joe's too slow on this stuff." So I just figured, "Nuts, I don't have to hang around here. The league's going. I'm ready to get busy in something else."

LAMAR HUNT: Joe Foss had brought major prestige to the league in a sense that few people could. His name really meant something nationwide when the name American Football League didn't mean anything. Joe was a battler. He had done a good job in the early years, but I think he felt the time was there for a change. We felt we needed more of a hands-on person.

The AFL owners met in Houston in April 1966 to determine who would succeed Foss in shaping their league and, in essence, the future of all of pro football. The consensus pick turned out to be far from a Foss, far from a schmoozer who would tell funny stories at banquets and glad-hand from coast to coast. The owners selected a so-called football person, just the opposite from what Foss represented when he nurtured the league in its infancy. The owners handed the keys of the AFL over to none other than Al Davis, whose drive and dedication to purpose as an assistant coach under Sid Gillman with the Chargers and in turning around the Oakland franchise as head coach had become almost legendary.

And Davis's first act as commissioner? How about breaking up a brawl between Oilers owner Bud Adams and *Houston Post* sports columnist Jack Gallagher?

BUD ADAMS: Gallagher was sort of a negative writer. He was looking for a way to get to the bottom of things but not being nice about it. He was always looking for something sensational. We had the press conference to introduce Al, and Jack wasn't there. I went home afterward, and they said I had to come back to the Shamrock Hotel to sign some papers. I was about to go to my ranch and had changed into my ranch clothes. Meanwhile, Jack Gallagher and a photographer showed up. He said he was sorry he missed the press conference, was out of town or something. The photographer said, "I want to get you all over here in the picture." And Jack said to me: "Well, Bud, you're not really dressed." The more I thought about it, the madder I got.

RALPH WILSON: They weren't friends by any means, and Bud said something like, "Don't talk to me, baldie."

BUD ADAMS: I called him a couple of names, then he said something back to me. I'd had enough by then, so I just went over and coldcocked him. When he was down on the floor and I was standing over him, I said, "You'd better stay down there or you're going to get hurt." And, with that, he kicked me in the nuts. So I jumped on top of him.

RALPH WILSON: Bud was a big, strong, burly guy. He was pummeling him. I was on top of Bud, and Al Davis was on top of me. We finally broke it up.

The niceties of the commissioner's job out of the way, Davis set out to do whatever he could to prove that the AFL was at least the equal to the NFL. The battle of public perception would be a critical theater of operation, which is why Davis decided to bring in three men to fill what typically had been a single job description.

MICKEY HERSKOWITZ: Al brought in three guys to work on P.R.—myself, Irv Kaze, who was the public relations director for the California Angels, and Val Pinchbeck from Syracuse. I had met Al in 1962 through Don McMahon of the Houston Colt 45s when I was covering baseball. There was something about him the moment I shook hands with him. He just had a personality that embraced everything around him. We ended up someplace and had a drink or two. Before Al left Houston after being named commissioner, he said he was going to call me at the sports department of the *Houston Post* and offer me a job: "I'm going to call you Tuesday at 7:00, and I'm going to need your answer on the phone." He had big plans, and he was going to move fast. I took him seriously, had no reason to doubt him. I had just been named the sports editor of the *Post* at 26 and had a show on the NBC affiliate that the paper owned in Houston. I thought about it pretty steadily over the next few days. Al basically told me what the job was and what the money was. It was liaison with the television networks, though it was called director of public relations. And I said, "Al, I'll take it. I'm coming with you." And then there was a long pause. He was having second thoughts! I said yes too fast! The next thing he said was, "Can you name the offensive line of the Denver Broncos?" And I said, "Al, can *anybody*? I have a little press guide in my office. I can look it up for you in two minutes." He said, "No, never mind. I'll see you in New York."

VAL PINCHBECK: I was the publicity man at Syracuse University. Al wanted to put together a group to go to war with the NFL. He brought in Ron Wolf. Mel Hein, who had been with him at Southern Cal, an NFL Hall of Famer, headed up officiating. That was sort of throwing something in the face of the NFL people because Mel was an ex–New York Giant household name then. Al's style is different from most. He's not an early riser, not a guy in the office early. But he's a guy in the office late. He was a guy behind closed doors a lot of that period of time.

RON WOLF: I went as talent coordinator of the entire league. We had a pretty good group of guys lined up to scout. What we were trying to do—and this was all Al's idea—was get mainly evaluators and signers. We wanted people who could sign players. One of those guys went on to become one of the more successful general managers in the history of the National Football League, Bob Beathard.

JOANNE PARKER: One of the things that Ron Wolf and I did when we went to New York was find new offices. Al Davis said, "I want to be on the top floor of a building. I want the entire floor, and I want the elevator to be such that nobody else can get to that floor. I want a corner office with windows." He actually tried to give us the layout, and we had to try to find it. Neither of us knew anything about New York. I contacted somebody at the Jets who gave me names of Realtors. I don't think we looked at more than two or three places. We found a place at 555 Madison Avenue on the 32nd floor, the whole floor. I looked at the layout and said, "I'm sure this is going to be exactly what he wants." I called him that night, described the layout—where his office would be, where the P.R. department would be. He said, "We'll take it." We took that space sight unseen as far as Al Davis was concerned. We got rid of everybody from the AFL front office except for one girl, Maxine Isenberg. And Al Davis wanted to get rid of her, too, but I convinced him that she would be an asset to us. Al Davis stayed back in Oakland, and Ron and I went in two weeks ahead of him to, among other things, get to know every important person who ran every restaurant in New York, find a good limousine company.

MICKEY HERSKOWITZ: My office was just to the left of Al's. When he walked in from the hall, he passed my doorway. So every day, I tried to get there before him. No matter how early I got there, I could never get there ahead of him. It was always so discouraging to get there and know he was the first one in the office. He just took pride in that.

JOANNE PARKER: When Al Davis got to New York, a man called up and asked to speak to him. Al Davis's office was right next to mine, and he could hear everything I said on the phone. I told the man, "I'm sorry, he's not in." And he was. At the end of the conversation, Al Davis said to me, "Who was that on the phone, and how do you know that maybe I might have wanted to talk to him?" I looked at Al Davis and said, "Let me tell you something. You brought me to New York. You respect what I can do, and I know who you want to talk with, who you don't want to talk with. I'll make those decisions, and if you don't like it I'll leave." He didn't say a word, just looked at me, walked back to his office, and we never had a problem again. You have to stand up to him.

MICKEY HERSKOWITZ: I was there almost a week with nothing to do because Al hadn't had time to meet with anybody, although he liked for people to figure things out for themselves. I got a call from Steve Perkins, who was covering the Cowboys for the *Dallas Times Herald*. The paper ran a full-page layout every Sunday called the "Witness Stand." They interviewed one guy, question and answer with a little bit of text to open it up. It was an enormous amount of exposure. "They want to do it with you this week," I told him, "and they asked me to get back to them on what would be a good day to call you." Davis leaned across his desk and said, "Are you crazy? They're the enemy!" I was sort of startled by that and said, "But that's why it's important for you to do it. If they say good things about you—and I certainly have enough confidence in you to know you'll come off well—it's going to mean an awful lot more than having somebody do it from Houston or Buffalo or Kansas City." And Al thought about it: "All right. Tell them to call me. . . . But if he screws me, I'll never take your advice again." If that failed, I was going back to Texas anyway 'cause I already saw what a pressure cooker it was going to be.

The story was going to run in the next Sunday paper. I'd already done a little homework and knew that the Dallas papers got to the nearest Big City Newsstand at 11:00 A.M. on Monday. I got in and within a minute Davis was in my doorway saying, "How did that story turn out?" I said, "Oh, I haven't seen it yet, Al. But I called the newsstand. They get the Dallas papers at 11:00 A.M., and I'll be the first one in line to get one and I'll bring it right to you." He said, "When you get a minute, come in my office." So I got up and followed him into his office. He walked behind his desk, pulled open the middle drawer, and pulled out this incredibly long sheet of Western Union paper. He had a friend wire the story to him Sunday morning. He said, "It was terrific. It worked out just like you said. But if this ever comes up again, you don't wait 'til Monday to find out what's in it. You have some friend of yours call you and read it to you on the phone."

Only five weeks into Davis's term as commissioner, the pro football war took an unlikely turn—from the side, so to speak. The man who had made pro football history as the first sidewinding placekicker two years earlier made an even greater impact when he became the first frontline player to move from the AFL over to the NFL. This wasn't a subversive, under-the-table deal. It was merely a free-agent signing. Pete Gogolak, after two years with Buffalo, was simply looking for another team to sign with. No one, though, ever dreamed it would be with an NFL club.

PETE GOGOLAK: When I originally signed with the Bills, it was a standard one-year contract that included a one-year option. I had a very good year as a rookie in 1964, and we won the AFL championship. I was making $11,000 as a rookie, which was nice money in those days. I said, "Since I proved myself and didn't get a big bonus like some of the other guys received, I'd like to get $20,000 for next year." They offered me $13,500. I was kind of a hardheaded Hungarian, so I said, "In that case, I'll go play out my option." That meant I took a 10 percent pay cut. My second year, I played for $9,900. Helped win another championship, was the second highest scorer again. Gino Cappelletti always beat me out because he was also a receiver. On May 1, 1966, after my second year, my contract was up. A week before, they offered me $20,000, and I said, "No thanks." And after May 1, the Giants contacted me.

WELLINGTON MARA: His agent, Fred Corcoran, was a fellow member at Winged Foot Golf Club. He told us Pete was available.

PETE GOGOLAK: I was surprised that I didn't have 20 teams call me. I proved the soccer-style kick worked. I realized that nobody from the AFL was going to contact me because the owners agreed that they weren't going to raid players from their own teams. The NFL, I don't know the reason. Maybe they heard the Giants were interested and that was that. I thought this is a free country, you put your goods out on the table, and you find out what they're worth. That's one reason we left communist Hungary to come to a country like this. In every other profession, that's what happens. The Giants gave me $35,000, and I signed a four-year contract.

TEX SCHRAMM: We had an unwritten understanding that we didn't go after players that were signed by other teams. When Wellington Mara signed Pete Gogolak, it was "open sesame" for the AFL to go after our players. Al Davis didn't know anything about the merger plan. He immediately started an offensive, which at the time was exactly the worst thing.

RON WOLF: I was in the process of moving my family back east. I got on an airplane in San Francisco to fly to New York, picked up the *San Francisco Chronicle*, and there it was. The Giants had signed Gogolak. I thought, "Oooo, jeez. Do they know what they've done?" By the time I got to New York, Al had his plan all ready to go.

VAL PINCHBECK: Pete Gogolak signed with the Giants the day I came to New York. Good timing. I immediately thought, "I wonder how long I'm going to be here." Al came in flying. He was going to have his guys go out and sign the Brodies, sign the Ditkas, the hell with the price. He was certainly anxious to get into the fight. The idea was, "We're going to whip the NFL. We're going to wind up as the better of the two leagues."

The AFL hit list focused primarily on skill-position players. Three of the most prominent were Roman Gabriel, the promising young quarterback of the Rams; John Brodie, quarterback of the 49ers; and Mike Ditka, tight end of the Bears.

BUD ADAMS: I was for going after the NFL players, and I don't think Lamar and Ralph Wilson were too active doing that. We signed Ditka, and we went after Brodie. There were several others where we were close, but we didn't have the money to get it done. Some of the NFL guys were really starting to hurt 'cause we were outfoxing them on ways to get around the corner and shoot 'em in the rear when they weren't watching.

MIKE DITKA: I was drafted by the Oilers in '61 but signed with the Bears. Not that I had anything against the AFL. I wanted to prove I could play in the best place, and at that time the NFL was a little bit better. I never made more than $25,000 with the Bears—played pretty damn good and was never really rewarded for it. So I signed a contract with the AFL to play for the Oilers. They gave me a $50,000 bonus, and the contract would have called for like $183,000 over three years, which was unbelievable money in 1966. Don Klosterman, the Oilers' GM, was the guy who first got in touch with me. I talked with Don, and I talked with Al Davis, who was the commissioner then.

JERRY IZENBERG: I went to see Scotty Stirling, by then general manager of the Raiders. He unlocked his filing cabinet and pulled out a folder that said "CONTRACTS" on the front. He held up—and I don't remember what the name of the quarterback was—Davis had gone out and signed quarterbacks from the NFL. He showed me this contract and said, "This thing will be over within two years."

MICKEY HERSKOWITZ: Al was signing players and assigning them to the teams that needed the most help. Al gave me a list of guys to call that I knew from Texas A&M and Texas. The first guy I called was John David Crow, who was with the St. Louis Cardinals. He was the first 1,000-yard rusher in Cardinals history, won the Heisman Trophy for Bryant at A&M. The deal we were offering was what Al called the "three 50s." It was a $50,000 bonus, then a three-year salary at $50,000 each for a $200,000 package. I think at the time Crow was making $30,000, and I think his bonus when he signed with the Cardinals was like $10,000. He was ecstatic when we talked on the phone: "Just let me know when you want me to sign something." He was coming.

ROMAN GABRIEL: The Raiders sent a friend of mine, Claude Gibson, whom I had played with at N.C. State, and Scotty Stirling, the general manager, down to my house in Granada Hills. I think I was making $22,500, and they offered me a three-year contract for $100,000 a year and a $100,000 bonus check. I had never heard of that much money. I told them I had to call Elroy Hirsch, the Rams' general manager. And, of course, Elroy said, "We're not able to do that." I signed, but I would have to play out my option year in '66. I wasn't quite sure what to do with the bonus check. So I carried it around for probably a month in my wallet.

Harland Svare got fired as coach of the Rams, and George Allen was hired from the Bears. He found out about what I'd done and came by my house and said, "Here's what I'll try to do for you. I'll get you $32,000, but I'll get you $100,000 when you retire. You'll probably need it more then than you do now. But you've got to send that check back." I probably could have kept the money and still stayed with the Rams, but I did what I was told. About a week later, the check came back. George said, "You've still got to send it back or you won't be our property." I mailed it back again, to Scotty Stirling. Everything that George said—his word was gold. I never regretted it.

JOHN RAUCH: I worked on signing Roman Gabriel with the Raiders. It was a credit that he sent that money back. A lot of guys that were contacted by the AFL, just out of a promise of some kind of contract, never played for the AFL but they got paid.

Veteran San Francisco quarterback John Brodie was mulling over what he considered a disappointing contract offer—especially considering the Namath numbers—when Houston's Don Klosterman told him the team was prepared to give him a deal that could confine his postfootball responsibilities to playing golf, drinking beer, and gambling. He nobly informed the 49ers that he planned to look into the offer and headed to Houston with a financial adviser, "Sonny" Marx. The two of them met up in a hotel room with Klosterman and Oilers owner Bud Adams, who was resplendent in leather boots, Stetson, and string tie.

Houston's offer was $500,000 over three years, considerably more than the Jets' contract with Namath. With Brodie relatively numbed by the numbers, Marx coolly said his man was worth a full million. Adams countered, and when the financial smoke cleared, the parties settled in the middle— $750,000. Marx uttered words that became extremely significant down the road: "Let's see how that looks on paper." What was handy at the time was a cocktail napkin, and Adams wrote, "The AFL agrees to pay John Brodie $250,000 a season for three seasons." And both parties signed the napkin. Brodie said he would give the 49ers a day to match the offer and hadn't heard back from San Francisco the next morning. But when Adams and Klosterman returned for what Brodie thought was a simple formalization of the deal, the Houston contingent was suddenly backpedaling. Frantic calls from other AFL owners to Adams indicated that signing Brodie would damage the ongoing merger talks. Adams tried to water down the situation, saying that business agreements are routinely broken. Marx and Brodie weren't interested in Adams's version of Business 101 and convinced the Houston owner that he couldn't go back on his word.

Meanwhile, the sides grew closer to a merger.

Lamar Hunt: My recollection is that there was an AFL meeting in Sonny Werblin's condominium in New York, nine people from the AFL teams at the dining room table. We had two that were really not favorable toward a merger, New York and Oakland. They didn't like the playing conditions for the teams in New York and Oakland. But we continued to try to work those things out. From my conversations with Tex, one of the earliest criteria was that all teams would stay in their same locations. I can't say what might have taken place on the NFL side. What was asked was the AFL would pay $18 million over a 20-year period. We were not told where the money would go. As it turned out, it all went to the 49ers and Giants. But it was never presented that our teams were paying a territorial thing, but I guess it was a price that they had to get from the 49ers and Giants to get them to approve it. I was in New York when Tex asked me to come down to Washington to meet with him and Pete Rozelle. The idea was the merger would be announced the next day.

Jerry Izenberg: Jim Kensil, the P.R. guy for the NFL, and Pete Rozelle were going to go meet in Washington with Lamar Hunt the day before the announcement. They decided they were going to go anonymously—put on sunglasses at LaGuardia—and registered under a phony name. Instead of taking a limo, they took a cab to be less ostentatious.

Don Weiss: They forgot to tell Lamar where to meet them. He knew he was supposed to be at the Sheraton Carlton. Nobody told him it was Ralph Pittman's suite. As luck would have it, Rozelle and a couple of lawyers happened to walk in the lobby about the same time Lamar was approaching the front desk to try to figure out where he should go.

Jerry Izenberg: They were rehearsing the press conference, and every time there was a tough question, Rozelle said, "Well, I think I want to defer to Lamar on that one. . . ."

Tex Schramm: Pete Rozelle came down under another name and spent Memorial Day at our house, where we drew up the final wording. It was what Lamar agreed to. The Washington meeting was where I had made the deal. My understanding was the Jets were going to go to Memphis and the Oakland Raiders were going to go to Portland. Wellington Mara got up and said, "We're going to get sued. It's going to be a terrible mess." We were going to receive $20 million from the AFL. So everybody started thinking, and we gave the Giants $10 million and the 49ers $8 million.

DON WEISS: The first really extensive conversations that took place involved the Jets and Raiders relocating. There was a lot of discussion about that. I think from a legal point of view, the attorneys, at least the NFL attorneys, liked the idea of no franchise relocation.

EDWIN POPE: I broke the first story on the merger, on June 4, 1966. But I can't take any credit for it because I got a tip from the *Detroit Free Press*, which couldn't use the story because of some sort of confidentiality type of thing from where they got the story. It said the NFL and AFL owners had reopened peace talks; they were working toward a merger, a common player draft, and an interleague championship game.

JERRY IZENBERG: I knew the merger was set the day before, and I didn't want to write it. The reason was simple: what did I have? "They will meet tomorrow. They will merge." Then, I'd have 28 paragraphs of background. I called Rozelle, whom I was very friendly with: "I know it's tomorrow." He said, "If you write that, we'll have some problems. We have four guys who do not want to be merged." Wellington Mara, Sonny Werblin, the guy with the 49ers, and Wayne Valley. I said, "I will make a deal with you. If you will sit alone with me after the merger is announced and tell me everything that I ask, everything about what happened, all the maneuvering, I'll hold off." He said, "Not only will I do that, I'll bring Tex Schramm." So that's what I did.

JOANNE PARKER: The day before the press conference took place, the *New York Post* headline was something about the merger was going to take place: "Werblin Sells, Davis Quits." Al Davis was not in the office when I saw it. He came in later, and I put the paper on his desk and said, "What does this mean?" He just looked at me and said, "You know as much as I do." Whether he knew more and didn't want to tell me at the time, I don't know. Our phones were ringing off the hooks. He wasn't talking to anyone at that point.

MICKEY HERSKOWITZ: Al kept saying, "There's something going on, and I'll fill in you guys the first chance I get." Weeks went by with that being the only kind of nourishment that we were getting. Then the night before the announcement, about 7:00, Al dropped a two-year contract on everybody's desk. He put one on mine and said, "Sign this." I said, "What's this about?" He said, "It's about nothing. Just go ahead and sign it. Trust me. It's for your protection."

VAL PINCHBECK: Al came out of his office at one point early in the afternoon, and I said, "Are you going to the press conference?" And he said, "What press conference?" "It seems that there's an announcement being made by the NFL and the AFL over at the Warwick in a couple of hours." He looked at me and said, "Do you remember Yalta?"

PAT SUMMERALL: I had advance notice of the press conference through my friendship with Mr. Rozelle. But by the time I got to the Warwick Hotel, there was a mob scene. They were on the second floor, and I knew what room they were in. There was a guy outside painting or washing windows, so I accosted him on the sidewalk and said, "I need to use your ladder." I gave him $20 or some exorbitant amount of money at the time and climbed up the ladder. Rozelle spotted me and opened a window.

MICKEY HERSKOWITZ: All the AFL guys went to the right, and all the NFL guys went to the left—like a wedding. Rozelle made the announcement. Cosell put a question to Lamar like he was breaking a story at the United Nations: "Lamar, the American people want to know, the American people have the right to know, the American people *need* to know, was this a sellout? Is this a defeat for the league?" Lamar, in his low, humble voice, said something about how it wasn't a defeat, it wasn't a sellout. Cosell immediately sort of chastised him for his meekness and timidity. And Lamar actually apologized for talking too softly.

The details disclosed in the news conference at New York's Warwick Hotel on June 8, 1966, have become part of the pro football landscape. The leagues agreed to form one unit beginning in 1970, the thinking being that existing contractual agreements prevented them from totally merging before then. There would be one common draft of college players, ending the escalating signing war. Teams were free to schedule exhibition games with clubs from the opposing league immediately, which meant starting with the 1967 preseason. And the intent was to initiate a world championship game between the winners of the NFL and AFL at once, the first one to be played in January 1967 at a site to be determined.

Oh, and Pete Rozelle was named the commissioner of all of pro football.

LAMAR HUNT: Al was not in on the merger discussions. After the announcement, to use the expression, he was a general without a war. The AFL paid him for the full term of his contract as commissioner, which I believe was a five-year contract.

BUD ADAMS: I'm sure Al was disappointed with the merger agreement. He was looking forward to being the commissioner. Al's always been one to go with whatever it takes to get it done. I don't believe in his way of business, but to each his own.

VAL PINCHBECK: Al felt that if they had left him alone, he could have accomplished what the original plan was. On the other hand, leaving him alone, in most of their minds, meant going out and spending an untold amount of dollars when, really, the reason Lamar started the league was he couldn't get a franchise in the NFL.

MIKE DITKA: The league bought out my new contract. I was traded to Philadelphia, mostly because I had signed with the AFL. I made a normal salary in Philadelphia. Then, after the end of my career, the league paid me $17,000 a year for 10 years.

MICKEY HERSKOWITZ: I never did get back to John David Crow 'til I saw him two or three years later.

Through all of the merger frenzy, John Brodie stood firm in the figurative pocket when it came to the $750,000 napkin contract that he signed to play with the Oilers—although he lost the napkin. Since the pirating of NFL players was done by the AFL and not by its member teams, the subsequent merger meant that Brodie's legal adversary in the case wasn't the Oilers, wasn't even the AFL but all of pro football. In August 1966, Brodie settled for what he reported was—when tossing in legal fees—$910,000.

LAMAR HUNT: After the merger was announced, Pete Rozelle suggested that each league appoint a committee of three to be the merger committee to work out the details. That committee was Wilson, Hunt, and Sullivan from the AFL and Schramm, Rosenbloom, and Dan Reeves from the NFL. And Pete sat on that committee, also. We met three or four times during the summer and fall of '66, and the first order of business was to work out the details for a championship game. The two championship teams the year before had been Buffalo and Green Bay. Nobody could envision wanting to play in Buffalo or Green Bay in January, so we explored the idea of playing at a neutral site. That was very revolutionary at the time.

DON WEISS: Rozelle's first inclination was to play the game in the Rose Bowl because of its size, but they weren't interested. They were very protective of their own January 1st game. They set the rent very high, almost half a million dollars under the terms of the gross sales.

LAMAR HUNT: The L.A. Coliseum was kind of a mecca for big sporting events because of the market. Miami had certainly not proved itself in its first season of AFL football. The weather and the Los Angeles market and the big stadium—those were the things that led us to the L.A. Coliseum.

During one of those meetings, we were sitting in a hotel room talking about scheduling and I said, "Well, do we want to have an extra week before the championship game?" "Well, what do you mean by the championship game?" "You know. The last game. The final game. The Super Bowl." And everybody kind of looked at me. Obviously, the word *bowl*, like the Orange Bowl, the Cotton Bowl, and the Rose Bowl, was a big football game. I think Super Bowl came to mind because my three children at the time had a toy ball called a super ball, a high-energy ball that you bounce on concrete and, like a golf ball, would bounce over a house. Thereafter, this committee began, rather than going through all this awkward language, to refer to the game as the Super Bowl.

Everybody thought that was a hokey name and we couldn't call it that. But Pete felt strongly that the game needed to have a quality name. The name NFL-AFL World Championship Game was on the trophy and the program and the tickets, but it wouldn't fit in a headline. So the media, for the most part, seized on the name Super Bowl.

Lamar Hunt poses in his red team jacket as his Texans work out for the first time in public, July 23, 1960. *Dallas Morning News*

Introducing the new Buffalo Jills cheering squad for 1962.

Photo copyright © by Robert L. Smith Photography, Orchard Park, New York

Lance Alworth, nicknamed "Bambi" by teammate Charlie Flowers, became the first player to begin his career in the AFL to be selected for the Pro Football Hall of Fame. Copyright © AP/Wide World Photos

Abner Haynes of the Dallas Texans (28) just told referee Red Bourne that, having won the coin toss going into overtime in the 1962 AFL Championship Game against Houston, he elects to kick off. Coach Hank Stram had instructed Haynes, if he won the toss, to defend the north goal. Instead, the Oilers got both the ball and the wind at their backs to start overtime. The Texans eventually won in double overtime on a field goal with the wind at their backs. Also present are Oilers captains Al Jamison (70) and Ed Husmann (82) and Texans captain E. J. Holub (55). Kansas City Chiefs

"It ain't much, but it's home." In 1962, the Raiders finally played their first home game in Oakland following the opening of Frank Youell Field.

Oakland Tribune/ANG Newspapers

Sid Gillman, with familiar pipe and bow tie, prowls the San Diego Chargers' sideline. Gillman's team won five of the first six Western Division titles plus the 1963 AFL championship.
Copyright © AP/Wide World Photos

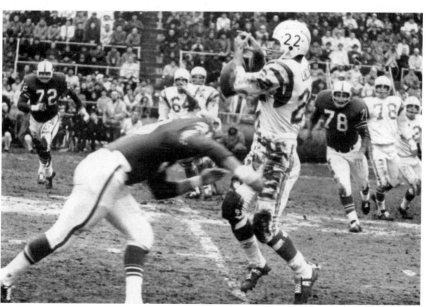

Bills linebacker Mike Stratton is about to crunch Chargers running back Keith Lincoln during the first quarter of the 1964 AFL Championship Game in Buffalo. Lincoln, San Diego's leading rusher during the season, suffered numerous injuries and didn't return to the backfield that day. The Bills went on to win 20–7. Copyright © Robert L. Smith Photography, Orchard Park, New York

Al Davis (right) visits with Bills owner Ralph Wilson shortly after Davis's introduction as the AFL's new commissioner, April 8, 1966.
Copyright © AP/Wide World Photos

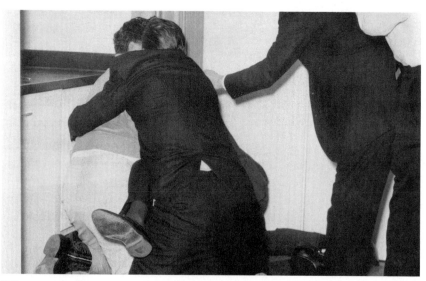

Who says it's all passing in the AFL? Here's some contact. Oilers owner Bud Adams (you can tell Adams by the boots) grapples with *Houston Post* sports columnist Jack Gallagher while newly appointed AFL commissioner Al Davis (foreground) tries his hand at negotiations.
Houston Post, Dan Hardy/Houston Public Library

Bills tight end Paul Costa makes an acrobatic catch over Patriots defender Ron Hall (23) during Buffalo's 23–7 victory at Fenway Park in 1965.

Photo copyright © by Robert L. Smith Photography, Orchard Park, New York

In addition to popping the pads, some members of the Broncos, like Jerry Sturm (overcoat) and Bob Scarpitto (far right), go out and press the flesh to try to increase ticket sales. Photo by Orin A. Sealy, courtesy of the Denver Broncos

A couple of heavyweights: Cookie Gilchrist (left) and boxer Sonny Liston. Photo by Duane Howell, courtesy of the Denver Broncos

On the day that the Dallas Texans announced their move to become the Kansas City Chiefs, someone failed to update the message board in front of the team's ticket office. Note the Cowboys' billboard just down the street.

Dallas Morning News

There was no mistaking the early Denver Broncos with any other AFL team, thanks to their cut-rate uniforms featuring vertically striped socks. Here, halfback Don Stone (34) follows a cadre of linemen against the Oilers in Houston during the Broncos' season-ending, seven-game losing streak in 1961. Copyright © Lou Witt, courtesy of National Football League Properties

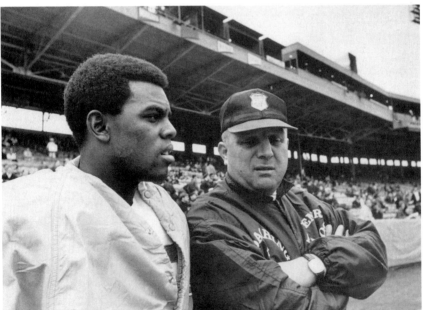

Broncos quarterback Marlin Briscoe confers with coach Lou Saban during the November 3, 1968, game against the Boston Patriots at Fenway Park. Briscoe played quarterback for the Broncos for much of the 1968 campaign but was traded to Buffalo following the season. Copyright © AP/Wide World Photos

It's not exactly a skybox, but some Denver fans are willing to stand on the snowy hillside outside Bears Stadium to watch the Broncos battle the Kansas City Chiefs. Photo courtesy of The Denver Broncos

O. J. Simpson heads out onto the field as a Buffalo Bill for an exhibition game against the Los Angeles Rams at the L.A. Coliseum. O.J. wore number 36 for a few exhibition games before reclaiming his familiar number 32 following the roster cut of Gary McDermott.

Photo copyright © by Robert L. Smith Photography, Orchard Park, New York

The Chiefs' Len Dawson is looking for running room during Super Bowl I against the Packers in Los Angeles, January 15, 1967. Green Bay went on to win this first AFL-NFL World Championship Game, 35–10.

Copyright © AP/Wide World Photos

Donny Anderson's two-yard touchdown run gives the Packers a 23–7 lead over the Raiders in the third quarter of Super Bowl II in Miami, January 14, 1968. The Packers went on to win 33–14. Copyright © AP/Wide World Photos

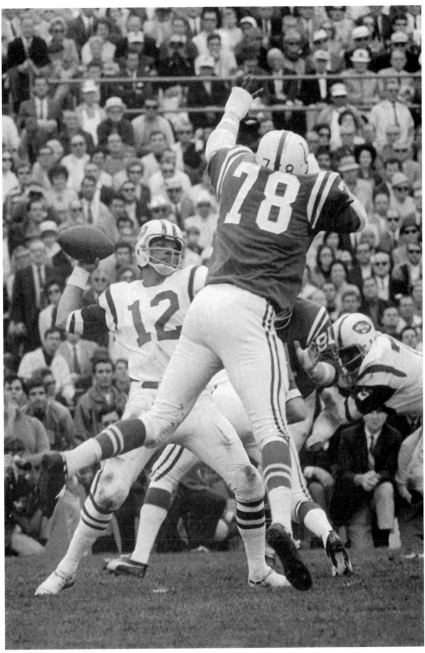

The Jets' Joe Namath lets one fly while Colts defensive end Bubba Smith tries to
get to the New York quarterback during Super Bowl III in Miami, January 12,
1969. The Jets won the game 16–7, becoming the first AFL team to take home
the world championship. Copyright © AP/Wide World Photos

Chiefs coach Hank Stram gets a free lift following his team's 23–7 victory over the Minnesota Vikings in Super Bowl IV on January 11, 1970, in New Orleans.
Copyright © AP/Wide World Photos

18

No Day at the Beach

At their June 1965 meeting, AFL owners committed to expanding by two franchises for the '66 season. Likewise, the NFL was looking to increase its membership for the first time since it hastily moved into Dallas and Minneapolis at the beginning of the decade in response to the creation of the new league.

The AFL owners stated their goal confident in the fact that they could plant new clubs in Atlanta and Philadelphia. At the same time, they were hoping that the instability of the Denver Broncos, owned by the Phipps brothers, could soon be resolved. A number of groups outside Denver had expressed interest in buying and moving the Broncos, including one group in Atlanta.

FURMAN BISHER: The NFL came into Atlanta and threw a block on the AFL. Leonard Reinsch, the head of Cox Broadcasting in Atlanta, came close to making a deal with one of the Phippses. The franchise was going to be sold to Atlanta. He was not able to stick around to see it out because his wife had a very delicate heart operation that could be performed only in New Zealand. The day after he made the tentative deal, they had to catch a plane to New Zealand for the surgery. In the meantime, Rozelle had gotten wind of it and got in touch with the governor of Georgia, Carl Sanders. Pete made a swooping raid into town and lined up Rankin Smith, who was an old college mate of the governor, and two or three other potential owners. Atlanta had a sports commission then, headed by the Coca-Cola bottler named Arthur Montgomery. This all happened in the course of about three or four days. All of a sudden, Leonard Reinsch's franchise got lost in the shuffle, and the NFL had a new franchise in Atlanta.

On June 30, 1965, the NFL announced that the Atlanta Falcons would begin play in the city's new stadium as the league's 15th franchise beginning in

1966. The AFL was forced to regroup, having lost Atlanta in a manner similar to the Minneapolis heist in 1959. The league also learned that the Philadelphia group had withdrawn its bid. The chances of cranking up two new teams in 1966 were dimmed, but the league at least had a new owner lined up.

Lamar Hunt: We then looked around and came up with Miami. It was not easy to get them to agree. It was not something where they came and sought us. We found Joe Robbie and Danny Thomas, who were willing to take on the leadership to put a team there.

Larry King: I was working in Miami in radio and television at the time that the Dolphins began. Miami was a college town—the University of Miami owned that city—and I didn't know how well the Dolphins would do. Every year, the NFL had that game there between the two runners-up, the Playoff Bowl. I thought Miami had a better shot as a baseball market 'cause of the Latin influence. I didn't think there was a great deal of Cuban interest in football.

Edwin Pope: Joe Robbie was just a lawyer from Minneapolis. He and Joe Foss went back a long way together. I understand he borrowed about $30,000, and that's what he started the franchise on. I never knew Danny Thomas's involvement in exact financial terms. I think he gave them a little cash infusion, but mostly it was by using his name as a partner that Robbie utilized him. And Thomas was really a great asset because he was such a personable guy. He would come around, and everybody knew him and fell all over him. He was Lebanese, like Robbie. When anyone would ask him why he got into football, he said, "Well, doesn't every Lebanese kid from Toledo want to start in the AFL?"

The Dolphins and Falcons were born the same year. I had a bet with Rankin Smith, the Falcons' owner, whom I went to the University of Georgia with, that the Dolphins would win their first exhibition meeting. The Falcons won it, so I had to jump in the Miami River. I didn't really jump in there, though. I took a picture of the Miami River and had 'em superimpose my head on it.

Chuck Burr: I left Buffalo and went to Miami as executive manager for administration, although in the press book Joe Robbie told Charlie Callahan to list me as business manager and that started us off wrong. No consideration was given to how we were going to operate the franchise until our first season started. I was sitting in Miami, and Joe was in Minneapolis practicing law. We didn't have any money. We were on cash on delivery for just about everything. I went to Miami in the February preceding our first year and ran into a hornet's nest. The only bank account I had in Miami was a transfer account. Every dime we took in on the sale of season tickets—we sold only about 9,000 or 10,000 the first year—was put into that account and was transferred to the Bank of Minneapolis Trust Company, from whence Joe borrowed all his money to keep the place going. I've got to give the guy credit. What he did later, after he took control of the club, how he did it I don't know. But he built a stadium without putting public money into it.

He was sometimes very difficult to get along with. You could go out and have dinner with him one night, have a completely enjoyable time. Next morning, he wouldn't speak to you. I was there only a year and a half, and we ended up in court over my contract.

EDWIN POPE: Robbie was just a difficult person, one of the nicest guys that ever burned down an orphanage. He wasn't bad at first, but then his drinking sort of increased exponentially. He just got on everybody's nerves. But he was a great trailblazer. You have to give him that.

The Dolphins were allowed to pick four players from each of the existing eight AFL franchises. Twenty-three of the 32 picks made the roster, led by tight end Dave Kocourek from San Diego, fullback Billy Joe from Buffalo, cornerback Dick Westmoreland from San Diego, offensive guard Billy Neighbors from Boston, offensive tackle Norm Evans from Houston, and linebacker Wahoo McDaniel from New York. And Frank Jackson was left unprotected by Kansas City because he was planning to leave football to pursue a career in medicine.

FRANK JACKSON: I was at Kansas City College of Osteopathic Surgery, in medical school. I already said I was retiring so that the Chiefs could protect another player in the expansion draft. And I think Miami indicated they weren't going to touch me. I was in gross anatomy dissection laboratory hacking up a cadaver. I think we were doing the abdominal flap at the time, had my hands up to my elbows in cadaver. One of the secretaries came to the lab, where we probably had 50 cadavers laid out on dissection tables. I was in my lab coat, had cadaver and formaldehyde all over me. I got called for an emergency call. If you miss five minutes of a dissection lab, you practically have to start the whole semester over. I was really pissed that someone would call me and that it was critical. It was Hank Stram. He said, "Frank, I'm sick. Just sick." I said, "Coach, I'm just in my first year. I don't know if I can treat you." He said, "No. No. You're a Miami Dolphin now. They just picked you up. They weren't supposed to do that." The next day, I announced my retirement. I was just going to finish medical school. I finished my third quarter before summer hiatus about the time camp started. I was scrubbing on surgeries in the morning and helping deliver babies. But I kept getting calls from Joe Robbie. Nearly every day. I kept putting him off. I was polite. I had another career. He kept insisting. I was bored to death in the summer. He said, "We'll fly you down first class. We'll pay your expenses. Just come down for a few days and enjoy yourself." I figured, what the hell. He said, "Incidentally, if you come, bring your shoes." Like a dummy, I put my shoes over my shoulder, got on a plane, and went to Florida. I went to the first workout. Boy, I started smelling that grass. We spent some late-night sessions hammering out a two-year contract. At medical school, they said, "We'll give you a one-year leave of absence. But if you're out more than one year, you have to start over."

Robbie took a reverse approach to building his new team, first selecting players—through both the expansion and college drafts—and then deciding upon a coach. And to lead the new Dolphins, he hired George Wilson, whose eight-year term as head coach of the Detroit Lions began in 1957 with him winning an NFL championship over the Cleveland Browns, the Lions' last championship to date. Wilson produced five winning records, Detroit's best finish following the title year being second place, and left after the 1964 season. He served as an assistant in Washington in 1965 before accepting Robbie's offer to come to South Florida.

EDWIN POPE: George was known as a very solid coach. He'd worked as an assistant coach with the Detroit Lions in the '50s. He was at the team banquet late in the summertime in 1957 when Buddy Parker said, "This team is uncoachable." And he quit on the spot. Wilson took over the team and won the NFL championship the first year. The Fords, who owned the Lions, fired five of his assistants in the early '60s. George told 'em if they didn't want his assistants, they didn't want him, either. He was perfect for a new franchise. He didn't have the kind of heroic temperament or discipline that it takes to win championships very often, but not having it also sort of gave him the patience it took to be a coach with a new franchise. People always say, "You don't want to be the first coach of a new franchise." George came in and loved everybody, and everybody loved him. He had been in the NFL as a player and a coach for 29 years. And 24 hours after he got to Miami, he was calling the NFL "the other league."

HOWARD TWILLEY: George was a great player's coach. He was, "OK, let's go out and beat those no-good SOBs." If there was a fight, the coaches would fight their coaches. The coaches always liked to drink before practice, and sometimes they had a little more to drink than they probably should have.

LARRY KING: I joined the Dolphins' broadcast crew the last year that George was there, in 1969, after they'd tried a lot of unusual things. Red Barber and Mel Allen from the Yankees did it one year together, not generally known. I did a weekly show with George, and he was a terrific guy. He and Robbie had one thing in common—they both were alcoholic. Wilson was too much one of the guys.

The Dolphins' first training camp was held in St. Petersburg Beach . . . sort of. It became evident quickly that whatever the team was saving financially by bunking and chowing down at the Blue Dolphin Inn was instead being spent less tangibly in frustration and anxiety.

CHUCK BURR: Robbie met a young promoter by the name of Charlie Proper. When I got to Miami the preceding February, Robbie wanted me to go over and talk with Charlie about putting training camp in St. Petersburg Beach. The mayor was there, and we hammered out a deal where we would have a free training camp with provisions outlined. We had to have a field. We had to have a place to stay. We had to have set menus, everything a training camp has. In those days, you're probably talking about $150,000. The quid pro quo was that Danny Thomas would give a free concert. Just where, I don't know. I reported this to Joe Robbie, who said, "Oh, we've got to grab this." Joe Thomas, who was our director of player personnel, had a place all picked out in Boca Raton, at some school. This superceded Joe Thomas's plan.

DAVE KOCOUREK: The first Dolphins camp was a joke. We stayed at a beachfront motel. No locker rooms. No nothing. We would practice, go back to our rooms, take our stuff off, turn in our socks and jocks. And next door was an aquatic marine land. At all hours of the night, there were things going, "Urp! Urp!" It was unbelievable.

EDWIN POPE: They didn't have anything like a nutritionist. They were subject to eating a combination of what the motel wanted to give them and what the Dolphins could afford. Wahoo McDaniel said, "If we have chow mein one more time, I'm going to come to practice pulling a rickshaw." One week, Robbie couldn't make the payroll and, as I recall, George Wilson and Joe Thomas combined to advance him the money to make the training camp payroll. It wasn't that huge, about $3,000 or $4,000, but it was touch and go all the way.

CHUCK BURR: When we got to the Blue Dolphin Inn, the menu turned topsy-turvy. It was heavy on carbohydrates, not enough protein. Very few steaks. Plenty of spaghetti.

DAVE KOCOUREK: We walked to the field, which was about three-quarters of a mile away. The field was grass laid on top of sand. Well, the guy who set up the deal with Robbie was hoping his kid would make the cut with the team. His kid was a lousy football player. So when they cut the kid, they stopped watering the field. Then it was grass laid on top of sand without being watered. It was just terrible. The only good thing was we were near the water. When you're getting all those nicks and bumps and scrapes, salt water does wonders for that.

CHUCK BURR: We found out the field was roughly 75 yards long and about 40 yards wide. Of course, there was hell raised about that. I suppose I'd have to take some responsibility because I accepted the contract as written. I never checked the dimensions of the football field.

DAVE KOCOUREK: I had the honor of living with Rick Casares, who was a great fullback with the Chicago Bears. I walked into the room, and Rick said, "Hi, pal. I'm Rick. That's my dog, Josie, on your bed. And she likes your bed." I said, "I hope she doesn't like it too much because I'm going to throw her ass out of here pretty soon." We had a very good relationship.

CHUCK BURR: The Blue Dolphin Inn was not fulfilling its part of the deal because they were supposed to get money from St. Petersburg Beach, which was going to get money through the Danny Thomas show that never materialized. George Wilson said, "We can't operate on this." After our first preseason game in San Diego, we moved the hell out of there, to Boca Raton. . . . We did get the field cut to normal length.

JOE AUER: That whole first year with the Dolphins was kind of hand-to-mouth. We used to go down to the Dolphins' office in the morning for a meeting, then we'd have a lunch break and then have practice. One time during the lunch break, Joe Robbie's secretary said to me, "You live in Coral Gables, don't you? Would you run by the Coral Gables cleaners and pick up the game uniforms?" So I went by the dry cleaners and told 'em to load 'em in my car. And they said, "Well, they haven't paid the bill yet." So I had to pay them, and I had a hell of a time getting that money back from the Dolphins.

GENE MINGO: I was picked in the expansion draft from Oakland, and we had to find places to live. My wife had come down to Florida with me, and I had my son. Wendell Hayes and his wife and my wife had looked in the paper to find a place to live. They called this one place in Miami, and the lady said, "Yes, we have this room." They assured her that they would be there to put down a deposit. Evidently, the lady thought she was talking to a white person. When they pulled up in front of the apartment, the sign in the window said "vacant." When they got out to go in, she took the vacancy sign out of the window, opened the door, and told Donna and Irma, "Oh, I'm sorry. We rented it."

This kept going on, and I just lost it: "You've got damn people who say they want a football team in this city, and I can't even get a room for my wife and my son. I guarantee you, there won't be an AFL team playing in this city." "Oh, you play for the Dolphins? Just a minute. My maid's upstairs. Let me see if there's anything that she's cleaned up. . . . Oh, she said there's a suite available with a stove and a refrigerator. You can have that." If I hadn't told that man that I was a member of the Miami Dolphins, I wouldn't have gotten a place to stay.

The Dolphins frightened few during their initial preseason, losing all four games and pegging out offensively at 16 points. Their only home exhibition game was something of a moral victory at the turnstiles if not on the score-board. While the Chiefs ho-hummed to a 33–0 win, a crowd of 36,366 greeted Miami's first pro football team since the Seahawks of the old All-American Conference.

And as the preseason drew to a close, the roster that would face the Raiders on opening night at the Orange Bowl began to take shape. Miami's initial sea-son would bookend with a free spirit who played high school football in the Orange Bowl, started his college career at the University of Miami before transferring to Georgia Tech, and worried teammates along the way with his taste in pets.

JOE AUER: I had a pet lion my last year in college, a cub that I just kind of bought on a lark. Had it in the dorm when it was still kitten-sized. He was a lot of fun, but he grew almost daily. I had relatives in Decatur, Georgia, which is a suburb of Atlanta. They kept him in an indoor-outdoor bird dog run. I ended up donating him to a circus after about a year. I was a redshirt at Georgia Tech and was eligible for the draft with one year of college eligi-bility left. I was drafted that year by both leagues, by the L.A. Rams and by the Dallas Texans just before they moved to Kansas City. I decided to go with the Chiefs and spent most of the '63 training camp with them.

I felt like I had a spot on the team made. Right toward the end of the exhi-bition season, Hank Stram called me and said I was traded to Buffalo. I said, "Well, I don't want to go to Buffalo. I like it here." He said, "Let me explain how it works, son. You signed a contract with the American Football League, and there's only one of those. We sent your contract to Buffalo. By the way, you need to catch a plane right away because you need to be in Buffalo and they have a game in a couple of days. They want you to play in that game to see if they like you." I called my bride of six months and said, "We've been traded to Buffalo. Rent a U-Haul trailer. Put the TV and whatever you can in it and drive to Buffalo." It never occurred to me I wouldn't make the team there. And she said, "Where's Buffalo?" I didn't know anything about geog-raphy and said, "Drive to New York City and ask directions." The amazing thing is, that's what she did, without looking at a map. And this guy said, "Go up the Thruway here. Turn left. Drive 430 miles. Get off on Exit 1. You're in Buffalo."

I played with Buffalo through 1965, then spent most of the '66 training camp with the Rams in L.A. I played both ways in college and was drafted by the Rams as a defensive back. When I got out to the Rams, they said, "Oh, you're a cornerback." I said, "No, I'm a running back." I could play corner-back, but it wasn't my idea of a great time. Right at the end of camp, I thought, "This is stupid. Why am I out here when I've got a team in my hometown?" I called up the Dolphins and said, "Hey, perchance could you use a running back?" They said, "Well, maybe." There was an airline strike at the time, so I had to do a combination hitchhike and take trains from L.A. I got there just before an exhibition game in Jacksonville. It was like, "Hi. How ya' doing? Get on the bus." I don't know how they chose me to be on the return team other than I was one of the fastest guys in camp.

BILLY NEIGHBORS: Joe used to talk to that Flipper in that tank in the end zone. He talked to that damn dolphin all the time: "Hello, Flipper. What are you doing? Are you enjoying yourself?" He's a little weird. He liked animals. Maybe he could talk to 'em.

Orange Bowl turnstiles didn't exactly overheat when Oakland came in for the Miami opener on Friday night, September 2. The announced crowd was 25,188, with presumably all of the Dolphins' 12,503 season-ticket holders that season in attendance. If they were lucky, they were in their seats for the opening kickoff that Auer fielded at the 5-yard line.

JOE AUER: I was the return man on the left. I took it at the 5, went upfield. There was a gap that opened on the left, then I just outran their safety. There was only one guy that kind of had an angle on me. He caught my foot right about the 5, but I made it into the end zone before I fell down.

TOM KEATING: And the last 25 yards, Danny Thomas, who was standing on the sideline with a cigar in his mouth, was chasing him. Got to the end zone, and Danny ran up and kissed him, big cigar in his mouth. I said, "Boy, is this great or what?"

There was only one problem for the original Dolphins—they had to keep playing following Auer's touchdown. When it came to offense, defense, and other special teams play, there weren't many opportunities for smooching in the end zone the rest of the season. Miami scored only one other touchdown in the opener, which the Raiders won 23–14. The Dolphins lost their first five games, only once managing more than two touchdowns. Paramount among the shortcomings was the output at quarterback, matters not helped by the fact that they couldn't find one to start most of the season. They began with AFL veteran Dick Wood and finished with John Stofa, who began the fall playing for Daytona Beach in something called the Southern Professional Football League. They had hoped that Rick Norton, a first-round pick from Kentucky, could earn the position on a regular basis, but that didn't happen. The most starts at quarterback ended up going to, of all people, the son of the head coach.

CHUCK BURR: We drafted an All-American quarterback, Rick Norton from Kentucky, but he had a bad leg when he was drafted. Even after the injury, he never did fulfill his potential. Dick Wood was another one of our quarterbacks. Tall—six foot five, six foot six—with bad wheels. Then we wound up with George Wilson Jr., who was actually a backup at Xavier University. But George brought him in, and he played credibly. Then I got a guy who had played at the University of Buffalo, John Stofa.

GEORGE WILSON JR.: Buffalo had my rights and traded them to the Dolphins. It was me and Dick Wood and Rick Norton. I was pretty much going to be the punter. The first three games, we switched quarterbacks. Nothing was ever really set. Dick started the first game. I forgot which game it was when I was designated as number one, and we went on to beat Denver the sixth game of the season for our first win. And then we beat Houston. We were looking for the championship then. It was very awkward to be the coach's son. You've got to mind your p's and q's, just make sure you did everything right. You didn't want to make him look bad.

FRANK JACKSON: Bill Brubaker, who covered the Dolphins for the *Miami Herald*, said it best: we were a collection of flotsam and jetsam. And our quarterbacks were just journeyman-type guys. Dick Wood, who was a good football man, had average talent. John Stofa. George Wilson Jr. We went through quarterbacks like offensive linemen. George Jr. was a really good kid. It's hard to be harsh with him, and he wasn't any worse than what we had. I'm saying it in sort of a critical way 'cause being on the receiving end of those quarterbacks was really difficult. A great quarterback knows how to lead you away from traffic. Len Dawson would never throw a ball where you'd have to go right into a defensive back, headfirst, kamikaze. Well, those quarterbacks would throw the ball five feet over your head . . . in the dirt . . . behind you. You were always going right into the teeth of the defense. Every game was like a suicide mission.

EDWIN POPE: The Dolphins got Cookie Gilchrist in late 1966. Anything about Cookie was always different from anybody else. He had started out in Canada in the '50s playing for about $6,000 a year, and he was always bitter about that. By the time he got here, I think he was making $35,000. Part of the deal was that Robbie was going to give him a new Cadillac. Robbie, instead, gave him *his* Cadillac. I was having lunch one day with Cookie, and he seemed to be pretty sullen about the whole thing: "Joe Robbie promised me a new car. He gave me his damn old clunker, and it rattles." So I wrote a column. The next Sunday, Cookie glowered at me and said, "You did me wrong! You did me wrong!" I said, "What are you talking about?" He said, "What you wrote in the paper!" I said, "Hey, Cookie. That's what you told me!" He said, "Yeah, but I didn't know how it was going to sound when it came out in the paper!"

Miami's 2–5 mark following wins over Denver and Houston led to excitement that was short-lived. The offense went back into hibernation, and the Dolphins topped their maiden five-game losing streak with a six-game slide. It required an outstanding performance in the last game of the season by Stofa in his only start—and Joe Auer scoring the final touchdown of the Miami season in the closing seconds of a 29–28 triumph over Houston—for the Dolphins to close on a positive note. Their 3–11 mark equaled the best by an NFL-AFL expansion team, though that distinction isn't quite as impressive when considering that three of the four expansion teams to date achieved that (Minnesota in 1961, Atlanta and Miami in '66; the only first-year club unable to reach that level was the Cowboys in 1960, at 0–11–1). The reception by the Miami community was, uh, lukewarm. Only games against Joe Namath's Jets and the defending champion Bills swayed more than 30,000 to the Orange Bowl with fewer than 20,000 venturing to the stadium for either of the last two home games.

GEORGE WILSON JR.: The reception was not that great. We might have averaged 20,000. They were a very tough crowd and still are. They're not really that loyal. You go to some teams who haven't won in a number of years, they still have all the backing in the world.

EDWIN POPE: You have to understand Miami was a barren place back then. Now, there are *too many* professional sports. Back then, there were none. There was University of Miami football and horse racing and dog racing and jai alai. It was pretty much virgin territory. The stories are greatly exaggerated that the players could look around and count the number of people. They didn't draw as well as they hoped to, but they didn't play in seclusion by any means.

Miami patiently began to gather the parts over the next couple of years that would come together and quickly evolve into a championship-caliber team in the following decade. The Dolphins owned the fourth pick in the first round of the 1967 common draft and had their eyes on the Heisman Trophy winner from up in northern Florida, quarterback Steve Spurrier of the University of Florida. He and Purdue's Bob Griese, the Heisman runner-up, were considered the class of the incoming crop of signal callers.

Quarterbacks made their imprint throughout the top of the 1967 draft, the first in which NFL and AFL teams picked together as one unit based on their records for the '66 season. The NFL's incoming expansion team, the New Orleans Saints, was awarded the top pick. That selection went on to Baltimore, acquired through a trade for Gary Cuozzo, considered a budding star quarterback stuck on the bench behind Johnny Unitas. The Colts selected defensive end Bubba Smith from Michigan State. The second pick was also traded, from the team with the worst record in pro football—the New York Giants—to Minnesota in the deal that sent veteran quarterback Fran Tarkenton to New York. The Vikings took another Michigan State Spartan, running back Clint Jones. With the Dolphins and Atlanta Falcons each finishing 3–11, a coin toss determined that the Falcons got to pick third. Again, the choice was traded in advance of the selection, to San Francisco. If Dolphins fans had visions of Spurrier in their dreams, their team was within one pick of making that happen.

LARRY KING: Spurrier was the choice of Joe Robbie real bad. Griese was rather unknown in Florida. But Joe Robbie was smart enough never to interfere with the football thing. He was smart enough to give his general manager, Joe Thomas, carte blanche. Joe Thomas really knew personnel and did a sensational job. He did that with the Vikings, too, before he got [to Miami]. Joe Thomas met with Spurrier and Griese and told me, "As I was talking with Spurrier, he was looking out the window. Griese was asking questions about the city, the people in the city, the surroundings, what the Orange Bowl was like." And he thought, "That's the kind of guy I want."

As it turned out, Miami never had to decide between Spurrier and Griese. The 49ers, despite the presence of one of the NFL's star quarterbacks in veteran John Brodie, tabbed Spurrier at number three. And the Dolphins—having juggled quarterbacks through their first season—placed their fortunes in the hands of a quiet son of a Midwestern plumber.

BOB GRIESE: I never expected to go to college to play football. I was a small-town kid from Evansville, Indiana. My father died when I was 10. When I was All-American my junior and senior years at Purdue, everybody said, "You're going to play pro ball, aren't you?" "Well, I don't know." I was planning a career getting my degree in industrial management. When I got drafted in the first round, I thought, "This'll be fun for a while. Then I'll get on with my life's work."

FRANK JACKSON: You could tell Griese was going to be the real deal. He had a lot of talent. He had a great touch on the ball. He was quiet and contemplative—not like he is now when he gets on television.

EDWIN POPE: Griese was very quiet. Actually, people thought of him as aloof and arrogant, and he wasn't. He was just a guy that did not like people making a big to-do over him. He shunned any kind of attention or controversy. When he first got to Miami, it wasn't long before he took the starting job from John Stofa. I was out drinking with Stofa one night, and he said, "I know when I was hurt, George had to use Bob Griese. Now I'm OK. Why won't he start me again?" I said, "George says he doesn't want to hurt Griese's confidence by taking him out of the starting job." And Stofa said, "Griese's confidence! How 'bout *my* confidence?" Stofa never got his job back.

BOB GRIESE: I roomed with Jack Clancy in camp at St. Andrew's. Two beds to a room, right under the window opposite the door, linoleum floors.

We had curfew, and I think we were the only ones who came in on time. Late one night, there was some pounding on the door. It was Wahoo McDaniel. The door opened, and he slipped something into the room. You could hear something scratching on the hard floor. It was an armadillo. I don't know how we got that thing out.

BILLY NEIGHBORS: I never did see Wahoo wrestle, but I saw him put a kid to sleep in practice one day. On Saturday mornings, we used to have practice and people would bring their kids out there. This kid was making fun of Wahoo 'cause he was rasslin', called him, "Fake! Fake!" Wahoo waited around and put that sleeper hold on him, and the kid fell out. I thought he'd killed that boy.

BOB GRIESE: You did a lot of scrambling. You did a lot of running around. When Don Shula came in, in '70, the first thing he said was, "Hey, I want a quarterback to stay in the pocket." I thought, "I'd love to stay in the pocket, but there was never a pocket."

In 1968, following another 10-loss season in Griese's rookie year, the Dolphins drafted a handful of players who would contribute to the club well into the '70s—running back Larry Csonka and tackle Doug Crusan in the first round, safety Dick Anderson in the third round, running back Jim Kiick in the fifth round. With multiple picks in most of the first nine rounds, they were in position to gamble in the sixth round by taking Olympic sprinter Jimmy Hines, whose football résumé was confined to little Texas Southern. And there was the surprising opportunity to acquire All-AFL linebacker Nick Buoniconti from Boston before the '69 season. No one started printing playoff tickets yet in South Florida, but the 5–8–1 and 3–10–1 seasons that closed both the Dolphins' AFL days and George Wilson's coaching career pointed the franchise in the right direction.

EDWIN POPE: The guy who never gets any credit for the Dolphins because the team had sort of declared him a nonperson was Joe Thomas, the first personnel director. Some of the first players didn't turn out very well—Rick Norton, the quarterback from Kentucky, and Frank Emanuel, a linebacker from Tennessee. But Joe Thomas was the guy who went out and really built the team so that things were in place.

Csonka came in bursting with confidence, rah-rah spirit. You couldn't call him a teddy bear, but he was a very warm and lovable guy who always had stuff to say. He might tell six writers six different stories, but he would never let you down. You'd go up to Larry and say, "Do you have any idea what Marv Fleming is making?" And he'd say, "No, but I'll run down and find out for you." He was a physical phenomenon, Paul Bunyan come to life in a football jersey. When he was in college at Syracuse, he was home in Ohio visiting his folks and got fired up talking to his father about some game they were going to play. He hit a wall with his forearm and broke the door join. The house almost collapsed. He was an animal who did not give in to pain. He and Kiick were sort of like the Mickey Mantles of football. They would play with holes in their sides and their hips. They'd stay out late at night, but they'd be the first ones in there the next day.

HOWARD TWILLEY: We had this thing where you had to prove to George that you were a man. And if you could, he loved you. We had this rookie party. They had these skits and afterward, George said, "We're going to scrimmage tomorrow, but none of the veterans are going to." But he didn't tell the rookies that.

LARRY CSONKA: They'd take two or three veterans and select one rookie as their "champion." Then they'd pit us against each other to drink shots, beer, kind of a fraternity-type thing. They tormented us that way until we got so abusive toward them it wasn't worth the fight anymore. You fight back, and there's a bonding thing there. After keeping you out drinking all night, then they throw you into that 90-degree heat.

HOWARD TWILLEY: They took Zonk out, and I don't know how many shots of tequila he had. A lot. He dove off the pier in Delray Beach. There was no water under the pier. He dove off the pier into the sand. Csonka came in at 5:00 or 6:00 in the morning. Then they had this scrimmage around 11:00. It was hot and just awful. The veterans were all suited out, but then we just kind of went over to the side. Now, we had a lot of rookies in camp then, and, I mean, Csonka just ran over everybody.

LARRY CSONKA: I never dropped. Was close to it, though. I quit drinking not too long after that.

HOWARD TWILLEY: Csonka could come back from drinking and just run over people. That endeared him to George Wilson. He's the toughest guy I've ever met. One time he had turf toe, where you bend your big toe back. I had one, and I know how painful they are. I used to have to get shots before every game to play, right in the ball of the joint. Well, Csonka wouldn't do that. He would jump on his toe for like 30 minutes before the game so the pain finally was deadened.

LARRY KING: Csonka and Kiick were very different individuals, but they became great friends. Kiick was this guy from Wyoming who was kind of a hick. Didn't speak very well, didn't handle the media well. Csonka, on the other hand, was an A student at Syracuse, academic All-American. But it was like ham and eggs. They were just perfect together.

LARRY CSONKA: I hooked up with Jim Kiick in the Chicago All-Star Game. I was roommates with him from then on. Jim was a good guy, quiet. We liked a lot of the same things. We weren't all that flamboyant. We just liked to go our own way and have a good time, shoot pool, hang out different places.

JIM KIICK: At Wyoming, I was 215 and bigger than a lot of my linemen. Larry was huge, 250, bigger than *all* my linemen. I looked at him and couldn't believe he was a running back. We met in Chicago, sneaking up the fire escape at 3:00 in the morning.

EDWIN POPE: I was the first president of the Pro Football Writers Association from the AFL. We would present the winner of the championship with a big trophy at halftime of the game between the College All-Stars and the pro football champions. So I had to present it to Vince Lombardi after the second Super Bowl, in 1968. Lombardi wasn't a guy who engaged in a lot of idle shop talk. For want of anything else to say, I said, "What do you think of Csonka?" He'd been drafted by the Dolphins, and that was his first appearance, against the Packers. "Too slow." I said, "Oh? How's that again?" He said, "Too slow. Too damn slow." That was his comment on Csonka, Hall of Fame fullback.

LARRY CSONKA: Contrary to what a lot of other people will say, I remember a core of about 30,000 fans that sat through that dismal first year. What

I really enjoyed, I got to know those people. We parked in the same parking lot, got to know a lot of our fans because they were down there commiserating with us. I know it sounds crazy, but I still remember a lot of those people that I met in the community or knew or saw on a regular basis.

JIM KIICK: Since then, I've run into approximately 200,000 people that had original season tickets, but there were only about 25,000 people in the stands. Where the other 175,000 were, I don't know. As it has been proved today, if you don't win in Miami, you're not going to bring out the people.

It was a lot of fun in those early days. I was pretty much taken under the wings as a rookie by Wahoo McDaniel and John Bramlett, which was pretty scary. We went to a hotel bar in Buffalo. It was getting close to curfew, and since I was a rookie I was getting a little concerned. There was another guy there who had been a wrestler. Bramlett was egging him on, saying, "We hear that wrestling's fake, and they've got glass in their fingers to cut." As this guy was agreeing with it, I could see Wahoo's eyes getting bigger and bigger. I knew he was going to tag this guy, and I was going to miss curfew. Sure enough, this guy provoked him enough that Wahoo leaped across the table. I just shook my head, and there was Bramlett, smiling. He accomplished what he was trying to do.

19

Setting the Stage for the Big One

The streets of Buffalo had barely been swept up from the Bills' second consecutive championship celebration following the 1965 season when Lou Saban dropped a bombshell. On January 2, 1966, less than two weeks before the Bills were scheduled to play the AFL All-Stars in Houston, Saban announced that he was leaving the club to become head coach at the University of Maryland. Team owner Ralph Wilson, stunned by the news, promoted 33-year-old defensive coordinator Joe Collier four days later, making him the youngest head coach in pro football.

LOU SABAN: There were a couple of things that weren't working out, but basically I figured, "We've had two great years." And about that time, the Maryland job came open. I just felt pro football was too difficult on the family, to go through those situations where bottles were thrown and things of that nature. Being close to Washington, it might be great for the kids.

RALPH WILSON: He just came in and said, "I'm leaving."

CHUCK BURR: I was in a restaurant called the Goalpost, owned by one of our players, Glenn Bass, and I got a call from Lou: "You'd better come down to the offices. I'm planning a press conference." I was envisioning a big trade. He said, "You'll find out when you get here." I headed downtown and Dick Riefenberg, a sports announcer for WBEN radio, came on the radio with a bulletin that Saban would be announcing his resignation. I thought I was going to drive the car right off the road.

JOE COLLIER: I didn't go back to Buffalo after that '65 championship game in San Diego. My wife was back in the Midwest while we were in California. Larry Felser from the *Buffalo News* got me at my brother-in-law's and told me about it. It was a big shock. Lou never mentioned it to any of us. Mr. Wilson talked to three assistants—Jerry Smith, Johnny Mazur, and myself. I guess he decided on me and asked the other two to stay on.

Going into the final weekend of games in 1966, the Patriots owned a half-game lead over the Bills with both clubs favored to win their finales. Boston, 8–3–2, headed to Shea Stadium to face the reeling Jets, whose 4–0–1 start had eroded into a 5–6–2 mark. And Buffalo, 8–4–1, welcomed a 4–9 Denver team that had lost on its last three trips to War Memorial.

The Patriots, by virtue of their game in New York being scheduled on a Saturday, could clinch the division title before the Bills ever took the field the following day. Instead, a stunning 38–28 victory by the Jets put them in the excruciating position of returning to Boston and counting on the Broncos to win at Buffalo.

GINO CAPPELLETTI: We had just won three in a row, over Miami, Buffalo, and Houston. And right before that, we tied the Chiefs in Kansas City 27–27, so we felt pretty good about playing Kansas City. We had everything in our favor.

WILL MCDONOUGH: The Patriots had a hell of a team. The 27–27 game in Kansas City was one of the best games I ever saw. Tommy Yewcic, who was a hell of a punter and a backup quarterback, was back to punt at a crucial moment. Just as he was punting, Bobby Bell broke through to block it. Tommy missed the ball and, of course, all hell broke loose. Guys were diving around on the ground. I said, "That's the worst thing I ever saw. How did the punter miss the ball?" After the game, I went to Tommy in the locker room. He said, "I did it on purpose. I saw Bobby coming in. If I kicked that thing, he was right above me. He'd block it; they'd run it in for a touchdown. So I just missed it." Now, how many guys would think of that? And they ended up 27–27.

We were out in a little motel by LaGuardia Airport, walking out the door to get the bus. I said to Houston Antwine, "Whatta ya think? How many points are we gonna need to win this game?" He said, "If we get a field goal, we've got it covered."

GINO CAPPELLETTI: We went to New York, and, boy, were they ready with a great game plan. Boozer and Snell just tore us apart, getting into the open field. Namath was working Bake Turner and Don Maynard. Snell and Boozer were also catching passes. That was a real downer.

WILL MCDONOUGH: Joe Namath tells the story how he was drinking all night the night before the game and was so drunk he was sick. He only had a couple hours' sleep on Saturday morning. He was thinking of calling in and saying, "I'm not gonna play." He went to the ballpark. He was still half in the bag. He was sick and said, "I think I'll go out there and give it a shot." Well, he killed them.

We were on the charter coming home. You can imagine how everybody felt. In those days, you got off the plane and walked down to the ground. It was about 8:00. There was the Boston Fire Department band playing. They thought we were going to win the division, so the mayor sent them out. They had about three guys. *Ooom-pa. Ooom-pa.* They didn't want to be there. Nobody wanted them there. Nobody was in the terminal.

As if the stakes of Buffalo's last game against Denver weren't enough, another bizarre twist was added a few days before the game when the Broncos announced that former Bills coach Lou Saban would become their coach for the 1967 season. Ray Malavasi's final Denver team offered only token resistance on the season's final day. Buffalo built a 17–0 lead in the second quarter. Two second-half defensive touchdowns by Tom Janik on an interception and Mike Stratton on a fumble recovery provided a 38–7 cushion before the Broncos had a pair of late scores that made the 38–21 final appear somewhat respectable. Bottom line: the Bills, new coach not withstanding, were in the championship game for the third consecutive year to host Kansas City; the Patriots were out.

GINO CAPPELLETTI: Bill Sullivan had gotten us fitted for blazers. We were going to wear them on the trip to California.

It took little time to set the tone in the AFL championship game that would send the proud victor on to meet the challenge of the NFL—one play. The kickoff by Kansas City's Fletcher Smith might have carried all of 25 yards and was fumbled by an upback, Dudley Meredith, at Buffalo's 31-yard line. The Chiefs moved in for a touchdown in three plays and, thanks to an interception by Johnny Robinson, turned what appeared to be a tying touchdown late in the half into a Kansas City field goal. KC romped over the Bills 31–7 in stunningly easy fashion to earn the initial Super Bowl berth. Jack Kemp was intercepted twice and also lost a fumble on a play on which he was knocked out. That was Buffalo—knocked out—after having won the previous two AFL titles but with no avenue for testing its mettle against the NFL's best in those seasons.

LEN DAWSON: Going into Buffalo for that game, the weather was terrible. We might have been the last plane or the only plane to land in Buffalo. Today, they probably wouldn't have attempted it. Back then, we weren't that valuable. Part of the field at their wonderful War Memorial Stadium was frozen; part of it was all right. Part of it was sloppy, depending on where you were when the sun hit it.

BUTCH BYRD: I got up that day just *knowing* we were going to win. And two things happened. Dudley Meredith got the ball on the kickoff. And instead of just getting on the ground with it, he picked it up and they hit him. Second, strong safety Tommy Yanik, who had maybe eight or nine interceptions that year, did his normal thing. He used to undercut the tight end. Dawson threw it right through Tommy's hands on their 15-yard line, and he dropped it. Those two plays set the tone. Then, it was Katy bar the door.

LEN DAWSON: Butch Byrd was a real hitter, stocky guy, maybe 200 pounds, which was pretty good size in those days. When he hit, you didn't go forward. Otis Taylor made a catch inside the 5-yard line, and I remember the collision between those two. Otis was able to shake it and get into the end zone, which I hadn't seen anyone do against Byrd all year. Second, Jack Kemp threw one into the end zone. Instead of them catching, Johnny Robinson caught it and raced back until he ran out of gas and we kicked a field goal. That was a 10-point swing at halftime.

FRED WILLIAMSON: We knew, man for man, we outmanned Buffalo. The only thing they had going for them was Kemp, a very good quarterback, good arm, good leader. Their passing attack was Dubenion. He was just a speed guy. The guy had no moves. There was no way he could run all those pass patterns on me. All he was going to do was come off the line and try to run by you, and I wasn't going to let that happen.

ELBERT DUBENION: We didn't go toward "the Hammer" too much. I think we were kind of afraid of him. I know I beat him on a long touchdown pass. I was in the clear another time, and the quarterback overshot me. "The Hammer" grabbed his leg like he had a pull. And when the ball went over my head, he jumped up.

BOOKER EDGERSON: It was a disaster from the get-go. If Lou Saban had been our coach, there's no doubt in my mind we would have won not only the championship game but the first Super Bowl. The man knew the game, in and out.

BILLY SHAW: It was *not* from not being prepared because Joe Collier wouldn't let you go on the field not prepared. He was a great head coach. It was really my only frustration from football. Still is.

MIKE STRATTON: It's never the correct thing to say the better team lost, but I certainly did feel that was the case. I think we would have made a much better showing in the first Super Bowl. There was no fear on our team of any offense.

LAMAR HUNT: I didn't get thrown in the shower, but I had champagne poured on me. That was one of the few times that happened.

DENNIS BIODROWSKI: Lamar got fined for having champagne in the locker room because we weren't supposed to do it. The trip back to Kansas City was fantastic. All the fans were at the airport. It was a good feeling.

The champion Chiefs awaited the outcome of the NFL Championship Game, played later that day at Dallas' Cotton Bowl. The Green Bay Packers were seven-point favorites to claim their second consecutive NFL title and fourth in six years. The matchup pitted the former assistant coaches of the New York Giants staff of the late '50s, Vince Lombardi of the Packers and Tom Landry of the Cowboys. A Dallas victory would create an ironic story line for the Super Bowl, which would then pit Lamar Hunt and his Chiefs against the organization that forced his Dallas Texans to move to Kansas City.

The NFL Championship Game turned out to be more of an offensive shootout than expected, four touchdowns scored in the first quarter. The Pack tried desperately to hold onto a 34–27 lead as the Cowboys earned first-and-goal to go at the Green Bay 2 with only 45 seconds to play. But Dallas was thrown into reverse by a five-yard offside penalty. On fourth down, Dallas quarterback Don Meredith was practically wearing Green Bay defender Dave Robinson when he tried to find Frank Clarke. Instead, the ball found a home in the hands of Packers defensive back Tom Brown.

Next stop, California and pro football history.

20

Mickey Mouse Gets His Shot

With two weeks between the league championship games and the Super Bowl, Vince Lombardi elected to house his Packers in Santa Barbara. Hank Stram took the Chiefs to Long Beach. The most newsworthy event of the pregame period proved to be a Fred Williamson interview in which he promised to introduce the Packers to the wrath of "the Hammer."

MICKEY HERSKOWITZ: I stayed with the AFL 'til the end of the year and was the second guy that Rozelle sent out to the Super Bowl, staying about three weeks setting up the arrangements. I had to get 120 cars, and Pete said there was one rule: "You can't do anything for one league or one sponsor that you don't do for the other." Well, we had CBS and NBC, and we had Ford and Chrysler. Ford was represented by Young and Rubicam in New York, so I went there to get my first 60 cars. The guy laughed in my face: "I can't get you any." I said, "You can't get me what, any Lincolns?" He said, "No, I can't get you *cars*. Our big game is the Rose Bowl, and your game comes two weeks later. We can't pull those cars in and wash 'em in time to get 'em turned around for your event. Besides, this game doesn't mean anything to us. We don't know how it's going to turn out." On my way out to Los Angeles, I stopped in Detroit to talk to Chrysler's agency and a guy named Jack Barlow: "Rozelle said don't do anything for one sponsor that you won't do for the other. But the week after the game, I'm leaving this job and going back to Texas, anyway. So if you want the whole sponsorship, you can have all 120 cars."

Rozelle gave me $250,000 to spend in L.A. and said, "I don't care how you spend it. But when the news media leaves, I want them to be talking about all the things we did that they don't do at the World Series." It was amazing how hard it was to spend $250,000 when you hadn't thought about it. To every room I sent a bottle of Pinch scotch and Jack Daniels bourbon and flowers for their wives and special friends. I had cuff link and tie clasp sets made for all the people that covered the game. And they got the date wrong.

JERRY IZENBERG: I got in a car with the late Jack Murphy from San Diego, and we drove up the coast to Santa Barbara. We turned into the motel where the Packers were, and Lombardi was standing there with his arms folded, hollering at us: "What are you doing here?!" I said, "Well, it was a great day for a drive. . . . What do you mean, what are we doing here?" He said, "Well, I don't want anybody to be late for practice, and I don't want . . ." He went through this long thing. As he was talking, I looked over his shoulder; up on the second floor were Fuzzy Thurston and Henry Jordan and Jerry Kramer, and they were waving. Lombardi couldn't see that, of course. I waved back, and Lombardi turned around. He looked up there and said, "I don't want to see any of you guys in the pool at any time today!" He couldn't think of what to say.

LEN DAWSON: We were a very young team. The Packers were a veteran team, and a lot of the Packers were guys that our players looked up to when they were in college or high school or junior high. They were kind of in awe of the Lombardi legend. We were uptight all week long. One of the reasons, I think, was because we were accessible and the Packers weren't. I don't think Lombardi would let the media hang around. We were the new kids on the block and said, "Heck, come over and see us." They had to get stories, so they were rapping on our doors. They were getting us in the coffee shop. Of course, our theory was, "Let's not say anything to get them riled up." Then, there was "the Hammer." There went our psychological advantage.

FRED WILLIAMSON: The press was following me around like I was the Pied Piper. They were writing everything that I was saying. And my teammates said, "Hey, man. You're going to make the Packers mad." I said, "Man, the Packers know we're here. We ain't hiding from them, and they ain't hiding from us." It was like I fired up the Green Bay Packers, which was obviously total bullshit. Over in the Packers camp, little Willie Wood had a sock full of sand running around hitting people in the helmet saying, "Hey, 'the Hammer' gotcha! You've been hit by 'the Hammer.'" They were making a joke out of it.

BILL CURRY: Guys chuckled because we'd had other people who talked big before playing us. And what it said was, "We're scared." At least some of them.

JERRY IZENBERG: One night, I decided I wanted to talk to Max McGee. I just called the hotel, and they put me through to the room. His roommate, Zeke Bratkowski, answered the phone. "Zeke, is Max there?" He said, "No, it's only 10:59." I said, "What time's curfew?" He said, "Eleven. Call back in the middle of the night."

BART STARR: Typical of our coaching staff led by Coach Lombardi, it was business as usual that week. Good practices, very much detail oriented and fundamentally sound. He just never, ever varied. In the films, we could see the quality of the Chiefs. They were bigger and stronger than we were. I think the greatest advantage we had was overall team maturity and experience because they were very, very talented.

JERRY IZENBERG: I had breakfast two days before the game with E. J. Holub. We were talking, and he reached across the table and said, "Feel my hands." His palms were sweaty. And I said, "Is this because you're going to be the first team . . ." He said, "No. Do you realize if we win the game, I can take out $15,000?"

DONNY ANDERSON: After being in Santa Barbara for a week practicing, we went into L.A. Everybody there said, "Why does anybody want to watch the Packers play Kansas City? They're just going to kill 'em." Now, Lombardi had been beaten by the College All-Stars in 1963, and, boy, I heard he made the biggest fuss. He went crazy, screaming about how we were not going to lose this game. It went from our $1,000 curfew fine to $5,000 if you had a girl in your room.

BILL CURRY: Vince got us down on a knee in the Coliseum the day before the game. He said, "I want you to understand two things. If you're out tonight, it's going to cost you $2,500." Well, my salary was $13,500. "And one other thing. You'll never play another down in the National Football League." I know I was in my room at 8:30.

JERRY IZENBERG: Wellington Mara got Vince Lombardi the job with the Packers and prevented him from going to the Eagles 'cause he thought Green Bay would be a better job when it opened up. Before the game, he wrote a little note to Lombardi saying, "This is a war, and we cannot think of anyone better equipped to carry our standard into battle than you."

E. J. HOLUB: They called us a Mickey Mouse league. Hank always tried to be a motivator in some way. He went out and got a bunch of Mickey Mouse caps and had guys wear them around the locker room before the game. Still, we were young men and we had guys . . . before we went out on the field, hell, they were pissing in their pants, throwing up. It was real emotional because the Green Bay Packers were somebody you watched all the time. Here we were playing against them.

HANK STRAM: I told our equipment man, Bobby Yarborough, to go out and find a 10-cent store and get some Mickey Mouse caps and also the song. Just the guys who worked in the locker room put the hats on. I thought we'd have some fun with it. I didn't know how it was going to go over. Then, when everybody was in, ready to go out on the field, we played, "Mickey Mouse . . ."

JERRY IZENBERG: This is how I made my Super Bowl pick, even though I knew I was going to pick the Packers. I said to Fuzzy Thurston, "Do you know anything about these guys?" He said, "Nothing." I said, "Well, you must be spending a lot of time with film." He said, "No, I'm not." I started to say, "Why . . ." He said, "Because we're going to win this game." I said, "What makes you so damn sure?" He said, "We have the best coach who ever lived."

Then I was over in the other camp, talking to Junius Buchanan, who was an old friend I knew from Grambling. I said the same thing to him: "What do you know about these guys?" He said, "Well, I don't know a lot, but I'm learning now. I went to a bookstore, and I bought a copy of [Jerry Kramer's book about life with the Packers] *Run to Daylight*. Right now, I'm getting ready to read about the Lombardi sweep." I looked in the book, and there was a quote from one of the players who had to make this impossible block. One of them said, "The way we're coming at them, you can see the linebacker's eyes pop." I thought, "This is what the guy's going to read two days before the game." It had to be the Packers big.

EDWIN POPE: There's a terrible misconception that the game was not known as the Super Bowl then. It wasn't *officially* known as the Super Bowl—like, on the program, it said "NFL-AFL World Championship Game." But "Super Bowl" was used in the newspapers. I wrote a column that was a whole take-off on super this, super that. And there were more than 700 media credentials given out. Even though the game wasn't sold out, it wasn't played in privacy like some people like to say. I will say an awful lot of writers missed that first one and never missed another one.

FURMAN BISHER: Our very wise editor said, "Nothing will ever come of this game. There's no point in going out there. It's too expensive to send somebody all the way to Los Angeles." He was a man of extraordinary vision.

JERRY IZENBERG: The guy in charge of the pregame show had arranged for these doves of peace to be released. The Grambling band was there. And they couldn't find the doves! They were running up and down looking for them. They were in a packing crate and Dr. Ralph Waldo Emerson Jones, the president of Grambling, was sitting on the crate. He just assumed it was something that came with the band.

And there was another big matchup. In the hastily convened negotiations to get the world championship game off the ground within a matter of months, it was agreed that both networks that had contracts to cover the leagues—CBS with the NFL and NBC with the AFL—would be allowed to televise the game. It was the only time the odd arrangement occurred, with an alternation between the networks beginning the following year and continuing until ABC and later Fox were added into the mix.

CURT GOWDY: Rozelle was like King Solomon when he was going to cut the baby in half. He decided to let both networks do the first game and get double fees. We were just taking the feed from CBS. They called all the shots, then we announced what we saw on the screen.

BOB DAILEY: I was the producer-director for CBS, and I worked with a producer on that show named Phil Creasy. We fed NBC. If I remember correctly, I had about 12 cameras and four replay machines. NBC had a producer named Lou Kusserow. Harry Coyle, who was a great baseball director, was there. He had the output of our cameras, but he was not allowed to punch 'em up. For commercial purposes, they had their associate producer in our truck. They were a little unhappy with the situation, but it worked out well for them. And when we went to a commercial, he called his truck to go into a commercial, too.

CURT GOWDY: We could have done the game in Cheyenne, Wyoming. Just give us a monitor and a couple of mikes.

VAL PINCHBECK: All the announcers got along, the Summeralls and the Giffords and the Gowdys. But the technicians didn't. They eventually had to build a fence between the compounds.

The game officials—six from each league—were decked out in specialized contrived uniforms that included white caps and short black sleeves with white numerals to prevent them from wearing their particular league outfits. The Packers won the toss and elected to receive, and the first possession of the game was significant despite the fact that it resulted in no scoring and a net loss of three yards for the NFL champs. On Green Bay's third play from scrimmage, veteran wide receiver Boyd Dowler led a sweep in front of full-back Jim Taylor and separated a shoulder trying to block Johnny Robinson. With Dowler lost for the balance of the afternoon, the Pack turned the position over to 34-year-old Max McGee, who had announced his intention to retire after the game and had to scramble to find his helmet when summoned. What attracted more attention before kickoff were stories that McGee, known as a live wire off the field with running buddy Paul Hornung, might not have retired at all the night before the game.

BOBBY BELL: I don't think [McGee] had his jockstrap on. He was sitting on the bench, and they said, "Hey, you've gotta play!"

DONNY ANDERSON: Max said he went out with the little girls and drank his whiskey. I don't know that. Max was such a great storyteller. I think he has embellished that story a little bit. Max was a great athlete, though. Whether he had one scotch or 20, I don't know. And whether he stayed up all night, I don't know.

BILL CURRY: What's true and what's—how shall I say, a product of the mythology—I can't say. Max was going to retire anyhow. He might have found something that was worth $2,500 to him. I don't know. It was not uncommon for Max and Paul to observe their own training rules. Vince loved to catch 'em so he could fine 'em incredible amounts of money.

The Packers official who was in charge of bed checks was assistant coach Dave "Hawg" Hanner. The Hawg, who retired to Florida in 1996, told the *Milwaukee Journal Sentinel*'s "Packer Plus" in August 2002 that the stories of McGee's antics the night before Super Bowl I are just that—stories. "I can promise you, he was not out before the game," Hanner said. "I checked him three times that night. And I can guarantee you, if he got out, Lombardi would have been on my butt. If he got out and I didn't catch him, I would have been on the ropes and Max would have been sent home."

Sober or stupored, rested or rusty, McGee became the unlikely first hero of Super Bowl lore with a game that eclipsed his receiving output for the previous two seasons. He stunned the Chiefs with a one-handed grab at the KC 23-yard line late in the first quarter that he turned into a 37-yard touchdown for the game's first score. He added a second TD reception in the second half and finished with seven catches for 138 yards in Green Bay's 35–10 triumph.

There was actually drama at halftime, when the Pack arrived with a 14–10 lead into the locker room. But Green Bay's Willie Wood intercepted a pass intended for tight end Fred Arbanas near midfield on the Chiefs' fourth play of the second half and returned it to the KC 5-yard line. After Elijah Pitts carried over the left tackle to give the Packers a 21–10 advantage, Super Bowl I had effectively come to an end less than three minutes into the third quarter.

BOB OATES: It was no surprise that a Lombardi team pulled away in the second half. He was as far ahead of the other coaches as anybody I can remember. Teams would play the Packers close in the first half, and then they would just kill 'em.

BOBBY BELL: Max was catching balls behind him, one-handed, close to the ground. He'd jump up, and the ball would just stick. He was just fantastic that day.

LEN DAWSON: Before the game, we all said the same thing: "If we play errorless ball, we've got a chance." I really thought at halftime, when it was 14–10, we could win. We were on the move in the second half. It was third-and-five near midfield, and the interception I threw killed us. They hadn't blitzed the whole game. We hadn't seen any film of them blitzing. They just happened to guess right, blitzing from my weak side when I didn't have any protection. My arm was hit, or the ball was hit. They scored, and then we were playing catch-up against that defensive team when they didn't have to worry anymore about the run. That's not the situation you want to be in offensively.

Donny Anderson was involved in the most significant event of the fourth quarter, maybe the only memorable play following Wood's interception. It provided an answer to the question: where was "the Hammer"?

FRED WILLIAMSON: They hadn't thrown to my side, except two times. I dislocated Boyd Dowler's shoulder, and I knocked Carroll Dale up in the bleachers. They decided to run a sweep at me. I said, "Oh, I've been waiting for this famous sweep." I went flying up. I went under the pulling guard, which I think was Fuzzy Thurston. I went to tackle Donny Anderson and tried to bury my head in his nuts, and his knee caught me right in the head. I went down.

DONNY ANDERSON: I did not anticipate getting to play, but some of the young guys like me got to play mid-third quarter and got to play nearly half the game. I had a collision with "the Hammer." It was a pretty good collision, and he got knocked out. If you look at some of the old film, Willie Wood on the sideline said, " 'The Hammer' is out! 'The Hammer' is out!" And you can hear somebody in the background say, "Well, who did it? Who did it?" And Max McGee said, "Anderson. I think Anderson hit him with his wallet."

FRED WILLIAMSON: I was a little woozy, but I wasn't hurt. I was embarrassed 'cause I was down. I knew I had been the Pied Piper and I was supposed to be invincible. I set myself up for that situation. They came over and asked me if I was all right. I said, "Yeah, but I'm a little woozy." And they said, "C'mon. Get up." I said, "No, I'm not getting up. Pick me up. Carry me out."

So we had like a 10-minute conversation. Finally, they got me up, dragged me over to the sideline, and tossed me over. I got up and waved to my fans, let 'em know I was OK.

I knew I could cover Boyd Dowler. If he ever caught a pass on me, he was going to be a great target. Six six, 230 pounds or 220 pounds. If he caught a slant-in on me, I'd put him to sleep. They moved Carroll Dale to me and brought in slow-ass Max McGee over on the other side. Lo and behold, he became the hero of the Goddamn game, caught two touchdown passes on Willie Mitchell. So, again, it was my fault. I hurt Boyd Dowler.

HANK STRAM: We thought we were very capable offensively, but we needed help defensively. When you play in the Super Bowl, any shortcomings you have are going to be exposed. I was fearful of that and worried about our defense. Chuck Hurston was a terrific player, great heart, but a small defensive end. We just were outmanned in that particular category.

JOHNNY ROBINSON: We very seldom ever blitzed, and we did that because Chuck had been sick with some kind of virus, weighed about 210 and was over Bob Skoronski, who weighed about 280. When the Packers took their halfback out of the backfield, my responsibility was with him. That took me up to the line of scrimmage and out of the middle of the field. We blitzed the weakside linebacker and left the middle of the field open for a slant-in with Max McGee. He caught two touchdown passes on two blitzes. The first touchdown they threw, the linebacker went right into Bart Starr, just a hair from hitting him.

I don't know if we were the best team to go against Green Bay. It was cold turkey. If we had played an exhibition or another game against an NFL team before, we would have been settled. Some of that unknown factor was there. And you have to understand Green Bay wasn't just the NFL. They dominated the NFL. You were playing the greatest team, maybe, in the history of the NFL. Lombardi was the greatest coach. And Kansas City had not necessarily dominated the AFL. It would have been logical had Buffalo gone since they had won the two years before.

The television war was officially won by CBS with a rating of 22.6, compared to NBC's 18.5. And the first and only double-network, shared telecast of a Super Bowl game did feature some awkward moments during and after—

including a different kind of TV "replay" that none of the network executives could have envisioned throughout their many pregame meetings.

Bob Dailey: There was a screwup coming back from halftime. We had gone to a commercial, and NBC was doing something else. We said, "You'd better get back because they're going to kick." They didn't believe us, and they kicked. Then all hell broke loose.

Pat Summerall: They told me to ask Lombardi to kick off again because NBC had missed the second-half kickoff. I said, "You've got the wrong guy. I ain't doing that."

Bob Dailey: Finally, Tommy Bell, the referee, called an offside, and they kicked over again.

Pat Summerall: During the postgame show, one of the concessions CBS had to make was to let the NBC reporter, George Ratterman, in the winners' locker room. And we had to let him ask one question, so I handed him the microphone. One of the secrets anytime you're doing a postgame show is, don't let go of the microphone. When I handed it to him, Bob Dailey yelled at me, "Get that microphone out of his hands! Get it in your hand!"

The lights were hot, and I had on a coat and tie. I was sweating like a hog. I had Elijah Pitts, Jim Taylor, and Bart Starr up on the platform. Jim Taylor looked at me and said, "Man, you're sweating like you played instead of us." And he had a can of Coca-Cola. Bob Dailey said to me, "We're not giving away free commercials. Get rid of that can of Coke." I wasn't about to tell Jim Taylor he couldn't drink that. I couldn't think of what to do. And Bob told me, "Coming to you in 15 seconds. Get rid of that Coke." About that time, Jim Taylor said, "You want some of this?" So I took it. I had solved my problem. I had the Coca-Cola can. But I didn't want to insult him, so I took a big slug of it. It was straight whiskey. He had poured the Coke out and put whiskey in there. Then Bob said, "You've got it. Go." So I asked Bart Starr the first question because I knew his answer would be long while I got my breath.

Bob Dailey: Hank Stram was in the other locker room with Charlie Jones from NBC. Charlie wanted us to go in there to interview him, and both trucks elected not to go into the losers' locker room. Charlie got pissed off over that. He had no control over it.

MICKEY HERSKOWITZ: I was back in Texas in July, writing for the *Houston Post*, and I picked up the phone. It was Jack Barlow: "Mickey, I just thought you'd like to know. We found the last rental car from the Super Bowl at the airport in Phoenix." It never crossed my mind that the writers and the TV guys would drive 'em home!

21

The Broncos Carry the Banner (Really?)

By 1967, the Broncos had survived the near move to Atlanta in 1965, a bizarre arrangement in which they "borrowed" quarterback Jacky Lee from Houston for the 1964–65 seasons and, of course, the uniforms from hell during those first two seasons. And they stood face-to-face with yet another crisis then. The club's future in the merged NFL wasn't assured because its playing facility, Bears Stadium, could not accommodate the minimum 50,000 paying customers. The pro football boosters in Colorado hoped to eliminate that problem in March '67 with the passage of a $25 million bond issue that would pay for a new football stadium in Denver. Waiting in the wings was a group in Birmingham, Alabama, that hoped to acquire the team and move it to Legion Field.

Just when things looked their bleakest in Denver—and that was saying something, given the Broncos' history—the team put together what was arguably its most successful offensive drive ever, though it came off the field.

FRANK THOMAS JR.: I was involved with the Kiwanis trust funds in Birmingham, which for several years sponsored an NFL preseason game. Back then, so many of the pro football teams played in baseball stadiums that they had to play exhibition games in other cities. Birmingham always seemed to turn out an excellent crowd. We would average probably 40,000-plus. That's why an AFL team looked at Alabama and Birmingham as a very prominent site for moving one of the teams that was having financial difficulties.

LARRY VARNELL: Art Modell had indicated he would not bring the Cleveland Browns to Denver to play. He said he couldn't make enough money with the present stadium to pay his hotel bill. I was chairman of the sports committee of the Denver Chamber of Commerce. When the voters turned down the new stadium, the head of the chamber came to me and said, "If we don't do something, we're going to lose the Broncos to Birmingham. What do you think we can do?" So we got together a group and we raised a million, eight hundred thousand from just contributions, people who wanted to make sure we kept the franchise in town.

LOU SABAN: People didn't think it was going to go over. We just went ahead and established a situation whereby we would go out and see if the community could help us raise funds to keep the team in Denver. They had seen what pro football had done in other cities. But it came really close because the Phippses were strapped. They were on the verge of making a decision. Some of the big people in town came forward. I look at that as probably one of my happiest moments. We had a nothing operation. We didn't have enough money to send some of our scouts out. We had to go borrow money, and it was tough to borrow money when you've got a loser. But once they thought maybe they'd quit losing, with the changes we had in personnel and coaching, they said, "Let's go ahead and do a job."

LARRY VARNELL: We bought the stadium from the owner, Gerry Phipps. We gave it to the city, and the city was able to issue revenue bonds that didn't require a vote of the people. As a result, we were able to expand the stadium from 34,000 to 54,000. And the National Football League said that was acceptable, so we were able to keep the Broncos in town.

One cloud that had hung over the Broncos since their inception was almost certain to change—the fact that they had never signed a first-round draft choice. With the first AFL-NFL common draft, the only competition in the '67 draft came from north of the border. The Broncos had the sixth pick in the first round.

VAL PINCHBECK: Lou had decided they were going to pick, if available, lineman Gene Upshaw, because he would be a great player for 15 years. But at the 11th hour, Lou decided that maybe we ought to draft a guy who could come in to the community and captivate it by his college background. Three or four days before the draft, he said to me, "I want to talk to you." We left his office, where everybody was gathered, and went back to my office. He said, "If we draft [running back] Floyd Little from Syracuse, could he come in here and be a captain? Could he be that kind of leader, even as a rookie?" I had spent 10 years working at Syracuse. We had Jimmy Brown, Ernie Davis, Floyd Little, Larry Csonka, John Mackey, Jim Nance. I said, "I have no doubts at all, but you're going to draft Gene Upshaw." He said, "If he's available, we're going to draft Floyd Little."

Despite the lack of competition from the NFL for the first time, little did the Broncos realize that their pick might not be a sure signee after all.

Floyd Little: I had a talk with Sonny Werblin and Weeb Ewbank, who were big-timers then. They had come to our games against Army and Pitt at Yankee Stadium and Shea Stadium. I had a very good friend named Andy Marciano, a Syracuse grad who was friends with those guys. He talked with Weeb, and they were very hot on drafting me. I had calls from Vince Lombardi and Jim Finks. I told them I had already committed to the Jets.

Lou Saban: We drafted him, and I called him: "Floyd! Lou Saban calling!" "Yeah, Coach." "I've got news for you! You've been drafted number one by Denver!" He said, "Where the hell is that?" I think he was in a state of shock. I said, "Floyd, you'll like it! We're going to build. We're going to start with the running game, and we're going to get ourselves a strong defense."

Floyd Little: I was angry. I was irate. I did not even plan to talk to Denver. The only choices I had were the Broncos and Canada. Lou got a hold of Marciano, who got a hold of me and said, "We ought to go out there and just see what they have to offer." I thought Denver was a place where you could get attacked by Indians. The only people who went to Denver were in a Conestoga wagon. We flew out, and it was the most gorgeous thing I'd ever seen. They came to a deal where I would get more than Steve Spurrier, so I held out until Steve signed with the 49ers. And I got 50 cents more.

When I got there, the team was on the verge of moving. I was the first first-round draft choice ever to sign, which created a big deal for the city. I traveled all over the area that was Broncoland—North Dakota, South Dakota, around New Mexico, up to Wyoming, over to Nebraska. We caravanned—

Stan Jones, the defensive line coach, and Sam Rutigliano. They were able to build the beginnings of Mile High Stadium.

The Broncos, the least successful of the AFL's eight original franchises through seven seasons, found themselves on the front line of the next skirmish with the NFL—the impending rivalry of interleague exhibition play. Most of the AFL teams were eager to finally get their first shot at NFL competition, allowed by the merger agreement in the three seasons remaining before the convergence of regular-season play beginning in 1970. Every AFL team took advantage of the new option at least once for a total of 16 games, with the Chargers topping the list with three such games. Some of the matchups were predictable naturals—the Raiders and San Francisco 49ers, the Chargers and Los Angeles Rams, the Oilers and Dallas Cowboys. The Patriots brought the Redskins, who were founded in Boston before moving to Washington, back for a game in The Hub. The Dolphins took whacks at the NFL's new teams, both based with them in the Southeast—the Atlanta Falcons and New Orleans Saints. But New York's teams, the Jets and Giants, were unable to get together until the '69 preseason. Some matchups required some background to understand. The Chiefs elected to bring in the Chicago Bears, who for years were the dominant pro football team for the entire Midwest. The Rams brought the AFL-champion Chiefs back to the Coliseum.

And the first AFL team to defend league honor against the overlord NFL, the first team provided the opportunity to answer for Kansas City's shortcoming in the first Super Bowl, was the meek and humble Broncos. Denver, in fact, was one of four AFL teams that scheduled two NFL opponents to prepare for '67 league play. Following an exhibition opener against the Dolphins in Akron, Ohio, the Broncos welcomed the Detroit Lions to the University of Denver's stadium on August 5 and then the Minnesota Vikings on August 18.

Lou Saban did all he could to make sure it would not be the same old Broncos taking the field. Out went Lionel Taylor, Goose Gonsoulin, Jerry Sturm, Willie Brown . . . in all, 25 players listed as at least costarters from the '66 club that finished 4–10 were either sent packing or demoted below that status the following season.

GOOSE GONSOULIN: We had heard from other players that what Lou Saban normally did was cut all the old players. As far as the team was concerned, it was probably good because he would shape up and stand up to management. In the motel just before camp started, some of us were up talking one night, and I said, "Well, I want a no-cut contract." Somehow that must have gotten back. The next day, Jack Gehrke called up and said, "Goose, they're putting you on waivers." I said, "Waivers! I was in the All-Star Game last year. I was captain of the team! This guy doesn't even have the decency to talk to me?" He said, "No, he doesn't want to talk to you. That's just the way he's doing things. And there're going to be a lot more heads to roll around here."

JERRY STURM: Lou told me I was over-the-hill. I said, "I'll outlast you, you son of a bitch." They were trying to get two or three guys for one good guy. They traded Lionel Taylor and me to Oakland in a five-player deal. They did get Rich Jackson, but he was the only one that made the team.

LIONEL TAYLOR: I was too old to go through a building process with Lou. He was a good man coming in, but I just didn't think that was for me. I had a no-cut, no-trade contract unless I said so. I had to come to camp, and I said, "Well, I'll be there the day before the league opener." So he had to trade me.

But Saban's task was trying to provide what Denver had lacked since the desperate Frank Filchock told assistant coach Frank Tripucka to dress out for the second half of the franchise's inaugural intrasquad game—a young, talented quarterback. The answer, Saban thought, was to acquire Steve Tensi, who was sitting behind John Hadl on the San Diego bench. Saban was so convinced of Tensi's potential that he traded Denver's first-round draft picks for the next two drafts to the Chargers.

LOU SABAN: We had a good running team, good defense, and I couldn't find a quarterback. By this time, the fans wanted to go ahead and get a winning team. They were tired of this business of buying time. I felt like I had to make a move. Steve had a great career at Florida State, so I made the trade.

Forget playing the NFL: the Broncos painfully learned in their exhibition opener that they weren't ready to play the second-year Dolphins. Miami defeated Denver 19–2 with former Bronco Jerry Hopkins, traded only weeks earlier, returning an interception for a touchdown and former Bronco Gene Mingo kicking two field goals. The opening performance left Saban in such a dither that he considered taking new running back Cookie Gilchrist, acquired in the summer trade with Miami, and moving him to middle line-backer—a curious option considering Denver's offense didn't score in the opener. But the Broncos' lackluster performance against Miami didn't dull the local appetite for the historic visit of the Lions. With temporary bleachers increasing the stadium capacity to 32,260, the prospect of a Saturday-night near sellout appeared likely by that Thursday afternoon.

DAVE COSTA: I was a captain, so I walked out for the coin toss. The Lions had Mike Lucci, Alex Karras, and somebody else. I put my hand out, and Alex Karras just looked at it. He looked around the stadium and said, "If we lose this game, I'll walk back to Detroit."

Karras didn't even make it to the end of the game. The Broncos first dazed the Lions by taking a 10–0 halftime lead, and they held on for an improbable 13–7 victory that shocked and delighted the 21,228 in attendance—OK, so much for a sellout—but also stunned the football landscape from coast to coast. In Oakland, where the Raiders were playing the Chargers, players on both sidelines began slapping teammates in the pads with joy when the final score was announced. The key play in the defensive battle came when Broncos punter Bob Scarpitto tucked the ball and ran on fourth-and-11 at the Detroit 44-yard line for a 28-yard gain to the 16. Gilchrist scored the game's only touchdown on a 1-yard plunge. Shortly before the TD, Karras was ejected from the game for kicking Broncos guard Pat Matson in the head.

LOU SABAN: After that game, Denver felt like, "We can beat the people in the National Football League!" I said, "People, don't get excited." We might have been the worst team in the league, but we had an identity. We belonged. And on the radio, they started giving reports every hour: "Alex Karras has now reached . . . Des Moines, Iowa."

The Broncos even won their next tussle with the NFL, beating the Vikings 14–3. But the next red-letter matchup between AFL and NFL clubs came on August 23 when the Bears traveled to Kansas City. Chiefs coach Hank Stram always took exhibition games seriously, so it was hardly surprising that the team had followed its Super Bowl defeat with impressive victories over the Oilers, Jets, and Raiders. But Stram and the rest of the Kansas City organization were especially eager to make a good showing against the Bears. Aside from the big picture of the interleague rivalry, longtime Bears owner and coach George Halas stood as a symbol of the NFL's disdain for the AFL. And there was also the matter of how the Chiefs, and their loss to the Packers, were about to be portrayed in the upcoming Super Bowl highlight film.

HANK STRAM: I got the film from NFL Films. I didn't want anyone else to look at it. I wanted to look at it myself to see what it was like, and I was really pissed off about it. It was terrible, demeaning. The day of the game, we were at Liberty College, going to take the bus to Kansas City. I didn't say a word. I just called them in a classroom and put the film on. Nobody said a word. Smoke was coming out of their ears.

CHRIS BURFORD: I was working at a television station in Kansas City. We were behind at the end of the first quarter, but at halftime we were ahead 24–10. Someone at the station said the AP sent back, "Please send corrected score." They didn't believe we were ahead. When we went in at halftime, all the people were standing, and it didn't stop the whole 15 minutes for halftime. Then, we killed 'em. We scored every way you could. This was a game when the starters did not go out. Late in the third quarter, Richie Petitbon was playing safety and said, "When are you guys going to let up?" I told him, "Not tonight, Richie." And that shut up a lot of that crap about the AFL. In those days in Kansas City, both teams were on the same side of the field at Memorial Stadium. When we were going off the field, I was watching George Halas walk by. He had tears in his eyes.

The 66–24 final score is listed among the historical highlights in the Kansas City media guide. Likewise, the 66 points is mentioned as the most ever allowed by the Bears, though that will never make it into the Chicago record book since it was a game that didn't count—except in the minds of the Kansas City players and staff.

GALE SAYERS: We knew it was going to be a tough game, but we didn't think that they would beat us like that. The horse that they had running around the track after each touchdown almost died. It was awful.

HANK STRAM: We coached it just like we did a regular-season game. We wanted to make sure we won the game, but we played all preseason games that way. You hear coaches say, "We've got to look at these people." I don't know what the hell they're looking for. They've got minicamps. They've got tryouts. Why do they have to try to figure out if they can play in exhibition games? We played every exhibition game with the idea that we were going to win.

Success was in the eye of the beholder following the completion of the exhibition schedule. The AFL had won the first game. The Chiefs' demolishing of Chicago had turned heads and brought a measure of revenge to the Super Bowl losers. But it and the two Denver victories were the only triumphs for the AFL. The Dolphins couldn't beat first-year New Orleans. The "battle of L.A." was no battle at all—Rams 50, Chargers 7. The best thing that the AFL could say about the "battle of Texas" was that it was closer—Cowboys 30, Oilers 17. And even the embarrassed Lions dusted themselves off in the wake of the disaster in Denver to beat the Bills and the Chargers.

If only the Broncos could have played Detroit more often. Their three remaining seasons in the AFL, all under Saban, resulted only in the same kind of frustration that the franchise had previously suffered through. A victory over the Patriots to open the 1967 season was quickly swallowed up by a club-record nine-game losing streak that began with a 51–0 loss at Oakland. The final record of 3–11 marked Denver's fifth consecutive season weighed down by double-digit losses. The Broncos' fortunes in 1968 improved only slightly with a 5–9 record, but the long-term prospects might have looked bleak with doubts raised about Tensi's being the answer at quarterback. Saban replaced Tensi at midseason with Marlin Briscoe, pro football's first black starting quarterback and the first to play at all since Willie Thrower relieved George Blanda during one game with the Chicago Bears in 1953.

LOU SABAN: The first year, Steve looked bad. I figured, hey, that's the way it goes. The second year, I felt like we were coming on. After one practice, there was this youngster walking down the highway by our practice field. This kid wanted a long pass thrown to him. I always hated to leave the practice field until everybody was gone. Steve revved it up and threw. Grabbed his shoulder. I was walking out of the locker room and said, "Oh, my God! Two first-round draft choices. What a kick in the tail."

Marlin Briscoe was drafted in the 14th round that year out of Omaha University, where he played quarterback. He decided to play college ball at his hometown school instead of at any of the well-known predominantly black schools of the day like Grambling or Florida A&M in part because he assumed the opportunities to get an engineering degree at such schools weren't as good. His nickname was "Marlin the Magician," and the Broncos listed him as a running back on draft day.

MARLIN BRISCOE: I got that nickname because I used to pull out games that seemingly were impossible to win. A couple of games, people went home. They thought we had lost. I threw three touchdown passes in a few minutes one time, and we won. When I got to a party afterward, they were telling me how sorry they were that we lost. They missed the best part of the game.

I was a starting cornerback when I went to camp. They were getting ready to dismantle their secondary and were willing to start all rookies. I acquiesced to their wishes to play defensive back but told them that before I'd sign, I wanted a three-day trial at quarterback. I knew it would be open to the public, open to the press, that at least I'd get an opportunity to showcase my skills. A lot of people didn't know I was black because I went to a predominantly white school.

I excelled during the three-day trial even though I didn't get the fair amount of reps like the other quarterbacks. But I knew that going in, so I made the best of the opportunity. After the trial was over, I went to cornerback. Then Steve Tensi suffered his injury. The quarterbacks that they used at the end of preseason didn't put any points on the board. The fans and the media remembered me from the three-day trial. I got some publicity from Nebraska, too, being close to Denver, and I played basketball in Denver in college. They said, "Why don't you give him a try?" That's how I got a chance.

LOU SABAN: Everybody thought it was a touchy situation. It wasn't with me. First, what choice did I have? He was about five foot eight or nine. You've not seen quarterbacks that size make it in big-time football, but he was exciting. I said, "You could become a great, great receiver as well." Well, he got upset about it. I said, "This is where I think you belong." He wanted to play quarterback. I said, "I'll let you play." At the same time, if we got someone that had more size and stature . . .

Saban made another memorable personnel decision late in the '68 season, one that wasn't preceded by a lot of forethought. In fact, the cutting of Floyd Little during the course of a November home game against Buffalo came and went almost within a matter of minutes. Little fumbled in the final minute, resulting in a 17-yard field goal that capped an 18-point fourth quarter by Buffalo to grab a 32–31 lead.

FLOYD LITTLE: We had the game won. We were trying to run out the clock, going from sideline to sideline. I was running the sweep. You never let a guy who's right-handed run left. It was stupid to call that kind of play. I got tripped, tried to maintain my balance. The ball came loose. Either Butch Byrd or Booker Edgerson picked it up. There was like 20 seconds left, they kicked a field goal, and we were down by one point. On my way off the field, Lou was yelling at Fred Guerke, the general manager: "I want him out of here! He can take the Valley Highway! He can take I-70! I don't care, but he's through! He'll never play for the Broncos again! He's fired!" So I said, "Well, the hell with you." And I started into the locker room during the game. Then I said, "The hell with that!" I turned around and ran back.

MARLIN BRISCOE: I went back in the huddle after the kickoff, and Lou was yelling and screaming. Lou had sent in Fran Lynch for Floyd. I looked up, and Floyd pulled Fran Lynch off the field and came in.

FLOYD LITTLE: I told Fran, who would be my roommate for nine years: "Get out!" "No. No. I'm not going anywhere." The referee, Jim Tunney, came back and said, "You guys have 12 on the field." I said, "I ain't leaving. Fran, you need to go." The coach was on the sidelines with his hands on his hips yelling at me to come out. Then Fran starting walking toward him with his hands up in the air, saying, "What the hell do you want me to do out there? There were 12 guys on the field." I told Marlin, "I need one favor. We've got one play. I don't care where you throw the ball—the South stands, on the highway. Anywhere you want to throw it, I'll get it." He said, "What kind of pattern do you want to run?" I said, "Don't worry. Just throw the ball as far as you can." He threw that thing into a prevent defense. I went up between John Pitts and Butch Byrd and George Saimes. I grabbed the ball out of the air, and they beat the shit out of me all the way.

The gain was 59 yards, though the pass went across the field and traveled farther than that. Little came down at the Buffalo 10-yard line, and a half-the-distance penalty against the Bills gave Denver another 5 yards that it probably didn't need for kicker Bobby Howfield. He set up for a 12-yard field goal instead of a 17-yarder.

FLOYD LITTLE: When Bobby was coming in, I stopped him and said, "Make it happen, my friend." He said in his English accent, "Floyd, this one's for you." He kicked the field goal, and time ran out. Lou was standing on the side where you go into the locker room. He said, "Come here a minute!" I said, "What the hell you want, Goddamn it?" He said, "I'm going to give you one more week!" I loved him.

The last-second win over the Bills gave the Broncos a 5–6 record with three games to play and kept alive their mathematical chance to end with a winning mark for the first time. The math didn't work out; losses to San Diego, Oakland, and Kansas City resulted in yet another losing season . . . and the end of the brief Marlin Briscoe era. Saban refused to leave him at quarterback, and Briscoe was traded to Buffalo.

MARLIN BRISCOE: I thought my performance was excellent. I started only seven games and threw 14 touchdown passes. Namath threw 15. That record, most touchdown passes for a Denver rookie, still stands, over John Elway and all the quarterbacks that came after me. I had no preseason preparation from the cerebral level. The three-day trial was basically foot drills and throwing. To be able to do that and get the offense in gear, we scored a lot of points.

I was featured in *Ebony* magazine. But that was the only one. None of the so-called white publications gave me any publicity. It was mostly the black tabloids that were proud that I played and played well. They let the world know that a black man could think and throw and lead. In 1968, I could not have pulled that off in any other city. Denver always had a reputation for racial tolerance and harmony during those tumultuous times.

FLOYD LITTLE: The little guy was a scrapper. He was a good injection of opportunity for a young team. He was a guy that demanded more money. I knew about the situation because Lou was saying, "Hell, the number one draft choice is only making this much. I can't pay Marlin twice as much as I'm paying him." Marlin said, "Pay me or trade me." So they traded him.

LOU SABAN: I did what I thought I had to do. He went down to Miami a year later and played receiver and did very well. People said, "You were right." You've got to look out for the product, what's best for the team.

22

Bombs Away

In looking to finally put themselves ahead of Kansas City and San Diego, the Raiders made a bold move going into the 1967 season. They sent starting quarterback Tom Flores, the league's third-leading passer in '66, to Buffalo in a multiplayer trade that brought them Daryle Lamonica, Jack Kemp's young backup. Lamonica was a 24th-round draft pick from Notre Dame in 1963 who had on occasion seen some significant playing time with the Bills. Even as a rookie, Lamonica started and led Buffalo to its two final victories to tie for the division title before Kemp returned for the playoff game.

JOHN RAUCH: We needed a young quarterback. Tom Flores had some injuries, and you never knew when he was going to be knocked out again. Buffalo had been calling. Lamonica evidently didn't fit into their plans. We had Kenny Stabler coming up. He had a bad knee and some marital problems. He wasn't ready to play. We sent him up to Seattle in the Continental League. Buffalo wanted Art Powell, who was a leading receiver in the AFL. They would get Powell and Flores, and we'd get Lamonica and Glenn Bass. He was a very swift receiver but had broken his ankle.

RON WOLF: It was one of those things where you have a belief about a player. The player I had a belief about was Lamonica. We just felt he could be the kind of guy to turn you around. Eventually, Al got the deal worked out. I was surprised they let him go even though he was going to be a backup there.

JOHN RAUCH: It came down to the day of the draft. Joe Collier called and said, "This is it. If we don't hear from you in half an hour . . ." something like that ". . . this deal's going to be off." At the last minute, Collier threw in a request for a draft choice. Al wasn't going to do that. We said, "Who cares about the draft choice?" The trade was made.

DARYLE LAMONICA: The night before I was traded, Ralph Wilson and Ralph Wilson Jr. both told me I was going to be their starting quarterback. I was so pumped up when I hung up the phone at home in California, I could have run through a brick wall. The next day, I went to see a buddy of mine, and he said, "Hey, you've been traded to the Raiders!" I said, "Yeah, yeah, yeah. Right." He said, "No, you have!" I had to call the *Fresno Bee*, my hometown paper, and they confirmed it. I was crushed. I was shocked. "Hell, I talked to the owner the night before." So I called Al Davis, and he said, "Hope you're happy about the trade." I said, "Well, I'm in a state of shock right now." The next day I met everybody, got a playbook. The first thing I looked up was the schedule. The fifth league game was at Buffalo. I started to get ready right then and there. Nobody, to this day, has ever called me from the Bills organization and ever explained that to me.

There were other important introductions to be made before Oakland's season began, at least one other that played in concert with an opponent's desire to retool. Lou Saban wanted to do everything he could to mold the Denver franchise to his liking on and off the field, which included sprinkling many a Bronco on other AFL rosters. The Raiders acquired Willie Brown, a four-year starter at cornerback in Denver, in exchange for lineman Rex Mirich. To provide a fallback for Lamonica, Oakland picked up 39-year-old George Blanda after Houston considered his seven years as its starting quarterback and kicker enough. And there were changes on Rauch's coaching staff. Offensive assistant Bill Walsh, who had come from the Stanford staff, wasn't sure he wanted to make the personal and family sacrifices that came with being a big-time pro coach and left after one season to take over the Continental League's San Jose Apaches. One of the new assistants to come on was a relative fuzzy face, 31-year-old John Madden, who came from Don Coryell's staff at San Diego State.

The pieces were set in place for one of the most unforgettable seasons ever put together by a pro football team. A lopsided opening win over Denver meant little, and even a convincing victory over a Boston team that nearly won the East in '66 was only somewhat satisfying. But more than 50,000 Oakland faithful crammed into the Coliseum the following week and saw the Raiders prove their worth against the champion Chiefs, 23–21.

The Raiders came back down to Earth the following week, dropping a 27–14 decision to the Jets in front of more than 63,000 at Shea Stadium. From then on, Oakland showed no mercy, took no prisoners, and refused to accept another defeat. In going 13–1, the Raiders flaunted the league's most dangerous offense and most aggressive defense. They scored five or more touchdowns in seven games, totaling 60 more points than the next highest scoring team in the league. Lamonica took on the persona of "the Mad Bomber," throwing for more than 3,200 yards and 30 touchdowns. The vertical passing game featured a pair of talented young split ends in Fred Biletnikoff and Warren Wells. Biletnikoff, finally coming into his own following two tepid seasons, averaged an incredible 22 yards per catch. Wells was a pickup from Kansas City and caught only 13 passes, but 6 were for touchdowns. Yet Lamonica's most frequent target was actually a running back, Hewritt Dixon, with whom he connected 59 times. Defensively, Oakland had its cake and ate it. The hell-bent defensive front set a pro record with 67 sacks and led the AFL with 30 interceptions. And Blanda took advantage of all the Oakland weapons to lead the league in scoring for the first time.

JOHN RAUCH: It was an amazing thing. Everything fell into place. The Raiders' system basically came from Sid Gillman and the San Diego Chargers that Al brought in, and Sid was ahead of most people in the passing game. A big part of Al's philosophy was there were certain times when you got a defensive team into man-to-man coverage on receivers as well as backs, and that was the time to go for the jugular. Lamonica could throw the ball 50, 60 yards on a straight line, and he was pretty accurate. A big part in coaching him was to recognize when the other team was going to blitz to put him in a man-to-man situation.

DARYLE LAMONICA: I went in with the idea that I'd earn the respect of my teammates. I roomed with Cotton Davidson, the senior quarterback. I kept him awake all night saying, "What would you do if you faced this defense?" And he walked me through it. And George Blanda and I talked, too. We had a lot of different personalities, but every one of us was a bona fide football player. A lot of people thought we weren't in shape, but we used to pride ourselves on playing hard for four quarters. I knew if I could keep the score close, we could beat anybody in the fourth quarter.

BEN DAVIDSON: Daryle came in, and he was kind of a different guy. Not a real warm person, but since I didn't play offense I didn't care. There was a real division between offense and defense, and I think Al liked that because we had some serious scrimmages. We got in fights, and there were bodies flying through the air. We were really in competition. We took great pride sometimes when the offense was floundering and we'd have to pull a game out for 'em.

TOM KEATING: The only regular-season game we lost was in New York on a Saturday night. In those days, the goal post was on the goal line. I hit Joe Namath and knocked him right into the goal post just as he was dumping the ball. Just mashed the shit out of him. I thought I'd killed the guy. He stood up. He was OK. And Dave Herman was yelling at me. I didn't do anything! They didn't take him out. The next play, he threw like a 60-yard pass to Bake Turner. Now, what does that tell you? And Ben Davidson loved to get him. Ben would just salivate with Namath. And Namath really took it kind of seriously. We were at an All-Star Game one time and Namath wouldn't get a picture taken with Ben.

BEN DAVIDSON: I liked Joe because he was relatively immobile, and that was right up our alley.

JOE NAMATH: We used to have a saying: the one-eyed monster never lies. Talking about the projector. If you looked at the films, big Ben did things that were uncalled for. The Raiders were always a little extracurricular.

The only reason not to assume that the AFL Championship Game matchup against a 9–4–1 Houston team was a formality was the fact that the Oilers statistically had the best defense in the league and held the Raider offense to a season-low one touchdown in a 19–7 Oakland victory. So much for that prospect. The Raiders raced beyond the pregame betting line of 10½ points in the second quarter and never looked back. Lamonica didn't need to grab for his holster much of the day—one of two touchdown passes came on a fake field goal—as the Raiders rumbled for 263 rushing yards and crushed the Oilers 40–7.

DARYLE LAMONICA: We were primed. We were ready. We were explosive. I'd like to say you win championships with offense, but you really don't. You win with defense. We clicked on all cylinders.

MILLER FARR: I went to the Oilers in '67. I went to high school in Beaumont, Texas, with Warren Wells of the Raiders. In high school, we had a group called the "zook" team that we practiced against. I looked over at Warren on the sidelines, and he said, "Man, you guys look like our 'zook' team."

JIM NORTON: It finally came out in that game that we had no offense. But the Raiders were notorious for holding. They could not have run the patterns that they ran. Starting the second quarter, they ran a sweep with that big back, Hewritt Dixon. He went 60-something yards down the sidelines. There wasn't anybody over there! They tackled everybody! Including Cannon! And he'd laugh about it!

Super Bowl II was arguably the least compelling, the least memorable of the four played before the full merger of the leagues. It didn't boast the historic significance of the first game. It lacked the shock value that rose from the last two. After Green Bay's convincing win over Kansas City in the first meeting between the leagues, there wasn't exactly a clamoring among cities to even host the game.

DON WEISS: The agreement with Los Angeles and the Coliseum had some options that we could automatically renew at the same terms after the first year, but nobody was really interested after only 62,000 people showed up. Miami was a very strong choice that year. The AFL had just established a team playing there in '66, so they had a lot of contacts. There was some discussion of New Orleans but very little of going back to Los Angeles. In fact, Dan Reeves, the Rams' owner, didn't even push it very hard himself.

The Packers were again heavy favorites, coming off another last-minute victory over Dallas in the NFL Championship Game in almost subhuman cold in Green Bay. The "Ice Bowl" triumph, with Jerry Kramer digging his cleats in the frozen turf and creating a path for Bart Starr to sneak in with the winning score, became the stuff of legend as Vince Lombardi claimed his fifth league championship in seven seasons. Sure, the Raiders had compiled the AFL's best record ever at 13–1 and had manhandled Houston to win the league championship. But the AFL was, after all, just the AFL. The most dramatic element emanated from whispers that Lombardi would end his storied coaching career in the glow of a second Super Bowl triumph.

BART STARR: If anything, there was a very strong push going into that game to ensure that we were maintaining the same type of feelings and positioning that we did in the first one.

DONNY ANDERSON: There was actually more pressure on me. Hornung and Taylor were gone. Jim Grabowski was hurt. Elijah Pitts was hurt. We'd just gone through the Ice Bowl and, thank the good Lord, had a great defense. We were really struggling offensively 'cause we had so many people hurt.

DON WEISS: There were strong indications at that time that Vince was perhaps interested in a political career. He had been making a lot of motivational speeches, talked a lot about freedom and integrity. I tried to get a transcript of one of his speeches, and he blew me away, like I was trying to steal his household goods.

DONNY ANDERSON: The older guys, the guys who'd been under Vince for his nine years, felt that he was going to retire. It was in the air, emotionally, the way he was talking. So, being a starter, I wanted to do really well. Even though I was a second-year player, I could see what it meant to all the players.

BART STARR: Maybe in the Super Bowl week, there was maybe a hint or two that might have heightened someone's comments or feelings about it. He wouldn't have said or done anything that would have been any kind of indication. There was one meeting in which Coach Lombardi became very emotional and teared up, but I'm sure some of that was due to the fact that we had a very, very difficult year. There were serious injuries; I had been injured. We had to really struggle because everybody wanted a little extra piece of you when you're going for a third consecutive championship. And I'm sure it had taken its toll on him as well.

JOHN RAUCH: I made a comment before the game out of respect for Vince Lombardi and the Green Bay Packers. They had been in existence a lot longer than we had. They'd been under fire more than we had. This was kind of a Southern tradition. You always try to lull your opponent into falling asleep on you. Davis didn't like that and played it up like I was quitting before we started.

JIM OTTO: 'Cause I grew up in Wisconsin, it was a game that I wanted to win the worst way. In Florida, I got real sick. I had pneumonia and didn't know it. I went in the hospital two weeks later, after the All-Star Game. But it was great. I wanted to beat the Pack. We were a young team probably not knowing how to handle some of the hoopla. The Packers had been in those games before.

BEN DAVIDSON: Being a former Packer, the reporters were trying to egg me on and get me to say bad things about them. I was sitting by the pool one day reading, and it turned into a press conference. Some guy from New York said, "Ben Davidson holding court at poolside," and all I wanted to do was read my book. Then, I was very insulted. Someone said "an insect of a mustache."

We practiced on a field at Florida Atlantic University. It had a swamp adjacent to the field. They told us strictly not to go after any football that went over there because there could be some animals lurking. Fortunately, being a lineman, I didn't have to deal with much of that.

JERRY IZENBERG: The Packers stayed at a place called the Galt Ocean Mile, very nice place in Fort Lauderdale. Al Davis put his team in an abandoned army barracks or military school. It was a place you really had to drive to get to. There were no ocean comforts. The players shared rooms that were very small. I can't remember whom I had gone to see on the Raiders, but there was only so much you could write. But they were so hungry. Dan Connors chased me down the hall saying, "Why don't you speak to us? Because we're linebackers? Don't you think linebackers have feelings?" He grabbed me by the arm and pulled me into a room. There were four or five guys with him, and he said, "Interview us." I thought he was nuts, so I wasn't going to argue with him.

On that Saturday morning, there were six or eight of us around Al Davis at the press headquarters in Miami Beach. There were these Japanese stairs with big spaces that you could look up. And Al was pontificating: "We can stop the sweep." As he was talking, you could hear *click, click, click.* The heads started to look up. There was this hooker—maybe she wasn't, she had no underwear on as she was walking up those open stairs. Davis was saying, "As the tackle pulls . . ." and he had no eyes looking at him at all. He looked up and saw the same thing. He looked at us and said, "You guys are disgusting. Don't you know tomorrow is game day?"

BEN DAVIDSON: We went to the Orange Bowl to practice the day before the game. It was not in the best area, and the neighborhood kids would climb the fence and play there. Al Davis was all concerned that the field was full of kids and asked the cops: "How are you going to get all of these kids out of here? . . . How are you going to keep them back? . . . How are we going to end up with enough footballs to practice?" One of the cops in charge was pretty nonchalant about the whole thing. He said, "Oh, that's easy." All of a sudden over the loudspeaker came: "Clear the stadium! We will be releasing the dogs in five minutes!" And all the kids screamed and ran back over the fence. He said, "How easy was that?" We had our field.

TOM KEATING: The championship game in Oakland was a real wet field. In the second half, I slipped and Walter Suggs, Houston's offensive tackle, jumped on the back of my right leg. I thought I just pulled a calf muscle. We were winning, and they kept me out after that. We came back to practice on Monday, and my ankle was all swollen up. We had two weeks before the Super Bowl, and right before we went to Miami I took some cortisone shots. Got there, and I still couldn't practice. Two days before the game, George Anderson, the trainer, built me a shoe with a heel lift in it to take the pressure off my Achilles tendon. Then he taped my foot with the toe down, so it looked like I had a high-heel shoe on. I could run. He said, "I can give you something to block it." This is a euphemism for freezing it so you can't feel it. Some guy told me he did that once and ended up tearing a tendon and didn't know it. I didn't want to do that. The day of the game, the *Oakland Tribune* said, "Keating out for Super Bowl, won't play." I ended up playing the whole game.

DONNY ANDERSON: The fanfare was a lot bigger. It seemed like it was a championship game. The first one never did 'cause the writers had kind of said, "Well, the Packers are going to win." They didn't make a big deal out of it. I went out to practice punting, and there were these two huge balloon figures. One was the Raiders, and one was the Packers. They seemed like they were 50, 60 feet tall.

TOM KEATING: Ben Wilson was a fullback for the Packers. We tackled him near the sidelines. He got up, and he couldn't see. He lost his contact. They stopped the game, brought over the camera guys with the floodlights. Here was Wilson on his hands and knees, two referees, and they were looking for his Goddamn contact lens! You'd think he had a second pair, but I guess not. That was a real beauty.

The game fell into something of the same mold as the Pack's conquest of Kansas City the year before, though it lacked the spice of an unlikely character like Max McGee bursting into the spotlight. Green Bay's first two possessions resulted in field goals by Don Chandler and a 6–0 lead early in the second. Twice in three possessions, the Oakland offense couldn't scratch out even one first down. And when the Packers added a touchdown on a stunning 62-yard pass from Starr to Boyd Dowler on first down, the 13-point difference had the look of another Green Bay rout. The Raiders responded with a touchdown drive of their own, the score coming on a 23-yard pass from Lamonica to tight end Bill Miller. Chandler added another field goal on the final play of the half to give the Pack a 16–7 lead.

The second half provided no dramatics, serving mostly as a chance to speculate on the margin of Green Bay victory and whether Lombardi would walk the Packers sidelines again. In the third quarter, the Packers scored more points than the Raiders ran plays (10 to 9, including punts). The fourth quarter produced the most big plays of the day, though they wouldn't affect the game's outcome. Oakland suffered two turnovers, including a 60-yard interception return for a touchdown by Herb Adderley that gave Green Bay a 33–7 cushion. Lamonica answered with his best series of the game, passes of 41 yards to Pete Banaczak and the final 23 yards to Miller for another Raiders score.

DONNY ANDERSON: They were in a 5-2 defense, which was very rare in the NFL. We had to do a few things differently. Playing for Lombardi, you concentrated because you knew the key was to not make mistakes. If you did, you couldn't hardly stand him chewing your ass out. You had an option, usually—get better or catch the bus out of town. You weren't going to beat us deep, and their concept was to throw long touchdowns instead of short, control passing. Eventually, our defense just wore 'em down. When you're behind like that and you're playing the world champions, the Packers, it's so deflating.

BEN DAVIDSON: Having been a Packer, I thought I was in a unique position to know what to expect. And I tried to keep in mind that I'd seen every one of those guys naked—there were a few new ones—and they were just the same as us in the shower room. I thought we had every chance to beat them. But we had a young kick-return guy who bobbled one, and the offense gave up a touchdown. We were not quite prepared for Bart Starr and his third-and-short long passes.

DARYLE LAMONICA: I remember shaking hands with Bart Starr after the game. He said, "Daryle, you've got a real good football team. You're going to be around a long time." And that meant a lot to us. Anytime you come in second best, you think you're the worst team in the world. It takes a while to get that out of your craw.

JOHN RAUCH: We played a good game except for three situations. Twice, the Packers had short-yardage situations on us, and they had play-action passes. One they threw to Boyd Dowler for a touchdown. They threw another touchdown pass off a play-action pass, on which we messed up our coverage. The third thing was, the score was 13–7 with less than a minute to go in the half. They were punting near their own end zone. Donny Anderson was the punter, a left-footed punter, and we didn't have anybody left-footed to practice against. Rodger Bird was our return man, had handled 40-something punt returns during the season. We tried to get left-handers to throw the ball out there with a left-handed twist. Rodger was going to field that thing about our 45-yard line. I was thinking, "If we could make a first down or two, we can get a field goal." Unfortunately, he fumbled, they recovered, and Chandler kicked another field goal. Then we gambled in the second half, had a pass interception they ran back for a touchdown. We just didn't have the moxie, if you want to put it that way, that they had. We made the key mistakes, and they cost us the game. We were kind of immature for that game.

When it was over, there were no Mickey Mouse ears to talk about, no Hammer histrionics. Just the knowledge that, if Vince Lombardi's illustrious career was indeed over, he had closed it with convincing Super Bowl victories that left some people wondering if this merger business really was a good idea after all. Green Bay never trailed at any point throughout the two games. When mistakes were relatively even, the Packers dominated the flow of play: in Super Bowl I, with each team committing one turnover, Green Bay outgained Kansas City 361 yards to 239. When yardage was relatively even, the

Pack was superior in the turnover battle: in Super Bowl II, Green Bay out-gained Oakland by only 322 to 293 but committed no turnovers to the Raiders' three, two of which were turned into 10 points without so much as adding a single first down.

BOB OATES: I didn't think the NFL was the better league at that time. The difference for the first two years was simply Lombardi. He was the best coach up to that time. Since the AFL was presumed to be a minor league, the big game was the NFL Championship Game that put the Packers in the Super Bowl. And, both years, that was the Packers against Dallas. Those were the two biggest games in the minds of everybody throughout the country except in the AFL cities. Dallas had the better team both times, and Lombardi slick-ered 'em. The championship game in Dallas before Super Bowl I, Lombardi knew he couldn't win his way. Lombardi was a running coach, didn't believe much in the forward pass. He thought that was basketball on cleats. It was a very simple-minded offense; you hit the other guy harder than he hit you. But he built his team in a short period of time into as good a passing team as there has been. They just barely won by outscoring the Cowboys. To this day, the game in Dallas was the best football game I've ever seen.

On February 1, Vince Lombardi made it official. He stepped down as coach of the Packers though remaining on as general manager. His first act in that singular role was to promote assistant coach Phil Bengtson to fill the coaching vacancy.

23

The Old Master Returns

The 10th and last AFL franchise was established in May 1967, and the move marked the return to pro football of one of its most legendary figures. The league admitted Cincinnati and awarded the club to Paul Brown as part owner, general manager, and coach. Brown had brought his Cleveland Browns into the NFL in 1950 when the league absorbed them along with the San Francisco 49ers and Baltimore Colts following the collapse of the All-American Football Conference.

The failure of that league could probably be traced to the dominance of the Browns in its four seasons. Cleveland won every league title and barely lost any games at all along the way. The Browns were amazingly popular for a new team in a new league, even from the outset, in a town that had just seen its NFL champion Rams flee for Los Angeles. The team's opening game at Municipal Stadium in 1946 attracted more than 60,000 fans.

But what Brown and his Browns accomplished afterward was even more impressive. They swaggered into the established league and won the championship that first season (against the Rams, no less) in beginning one of the most impressive runs in sports history. Cleveland played for the NFL championship in each of its first six seasons, claiming three titles.

Enter Art Modell, a young businessman from Brooklyn who acquired controlling ownership of the Browns in 1961, when Cleveland was still a perennial contender for the conference title though not as dominant. Modell and Brown coexisted awkwardly almost from the beginning, when Modell began guaranteeing an NFL championship. The new owner saw that as simple huckstering, almost required salesmanship, to drum up interest and ticket sales. The old coach saw it as a noose around his neck in the event that the Browns didn't win a title and fans demanded an explanation. The division between them degenerated during the events that followed the drafting of running back Ernie Davis before the '62 season. The Browns considered Davis the perfect complement to Jim Brown—another Syracuse product, even—in a backfield that demanded power and stamina as seasons would wind down into the harsh winters on the banks of Lake Erie. But only days before joining the squad for preseason camp, Davis was diagnosed with acute leukemia, and team insiders were informed he had only a few months to live. Yet, according to Brown, Modell insisted on giving the impression that Davis might be able to play at some point that season, in the name of selling tickets. It reached the point that, the coach said, Modell told him, "If he has to go, why not let him have a little fun?" Shortly after season's end, Modell called Brown into his office and told him he was fired as coach and general manager, that he and not Brown would be considered the dominant image of the club as long as he remained.

TOM GRAY: I started with the Browns in the '50s as a volunteer equipment helper. I was a volunteer, but I was paid under the table. I don't know if "P.B." ever really wanted to be an owner. He was given a certain percentage of the club by each of the first two owners. Art was a younger man, and the situation between them was building for a while. Art did things that were against the grain of the way Paul did 'em. I think Paul's record indicates he might have been doing things the right way.

D. L. STEWART: The story for publication, at least, was that Modell thought he knew something about football. And, apparently, Art Modell and Jimmy Brown sort of got closer together. As you can well imagine, Jimmy Brown and Paul were not thick. Jimmy Brown, even back then, had a little more militancy than Paul expected, from a black player especially. The buzz was that Jimmy had Modell working for him, and Paul took exception to that. Basically, it was a power struggle: "Who's in charge here?" Paul, for years afterward, would always use the phrase, "That shows you what happens when nonfootball people try to run a football team." That was always a direct reference to Art Modell.

By the late '60s, Brown was ready to return to pro football, and he spearheaded the effort to bring a second team to Ohio, to Cincinnati, on the state's southern border with Kentucky. Previous overtures made from the city, including an inquiry about the Denver Broncos in 1965, weren't taken seriously because of the town's lack of a suitable pro facility. That changed when the city pledged to build a multipurpose stadium that could house Cincinnati's longtime baseball club, the Reds, and a pro football team. The AFL admitted Cincinnati beginning with the 1968 season knowing that the new team would have to play at least two years at the University of Cincinnati's diminutive Nippert Stadium, seating about 25,000, before being able to occupy new Riverfront Stadium. The Bengals' organization was also small, with Paul Brown's family at the core.

AL HEIM: It had to be the smallest. Of course, a lot of other teams didn't have a whole lot of people, either. But we seemed to do all right with what we had. We knew each other. You were never working with a stranger. I had been executive sports editor of the *Cincinnati Enquirer* and had worked there probably 10 years before that. I was kind of overwhelmed when he offered me the position in public relations.

AL LoCASALE: When Paul Brown retired, he lived in LaJolla, California. Milt Woodard, our league president, called me one day and said, "Paul Brown called me and asked if you were free and available to talk to him." I was ready to leave San Diego for a number of reasons. I called Paul and went up to his home with my wife because Paul always said, "I want to meet the wives." Spent a delightful day, four blocks up off the ocean. You could sit in the backyard and hear the surf. He had these small tomatoes with a bowl of salt mixed with peppers. You just rolled 'em in there, pop 'em in, and wash 'em down with scotch.

He was wonderful to work for. Before I got there, we went over our budget. I told him I wanted three full-time scouts and I would be a super scout. He came back from a league meeting and said, "We've got a problem. They're not going to give us the full TV share the first two years, and I can't afford what I had budgeted. You're going to have to do it." About 10 days later, I got my first paycheck and there was a raise. His answer: "Now you have to do the work for three more people, and I felt I had to compensate you for that."

TOM GRAY: I came down to Cincinnati and applied to "P.B." I never asked him, but I think if I had been on the payroll as a paid Cleveland Browns employee, I probably would have not been employed by the Bengals. But I was a part-time guy, and I knew exactly how he liked things done.

That familiarity extended to the look of the new Bengals, who borrowed the nickname that previous Cincinnati pro football teams had used during brief tenures in short-lived leagues early in the first half of the century. The team's uniforms were strikingly similar to those that the Browns had worn since Paul Brown brought them into the NFL. The Browns sported brown, orange, and white; the Bengals would wear black, orange, and white. The Browns wore orange helmets with no logos on the sides, a unique look in the NFL; the Bengals' helmets were orange without a logo, only the word *BENGALS* printed on each side. Paul Brown later said that the near-identical color combination was a coincidence, the Bengals' scheme picked to go with the nickname. As for the helmets, he always preferred simple, almost bland designs as a means of self-defense. To Brown, there was nothing worse than a bad football team that attracted attention by the way that it was dressed.

AL HEIM: We never talked about it much, but I don't think it was a coincidence. Paul liked to go by things that he did before. After all, he founded the Browns, he owned the Browns, and he coached the Browns, won a lot of championships with the Browns, so he was going to take a little bit of everything he could with him. In molding his new team, he went back to the team that he molded before, even down to the colors.

D. L. STEWART: I was the first guy from the Dayton papers assigned to cover the Bengals. I had grown up in Cleveland worshipping Paul Brown. I was 25, 26 years old. To prepare for meeting him the first time, I read a book, *Return to Glory*, about the rise and fall of Paul Brown, what happened in Cleveland. I said, "I grew up in Cleveland, a Browns fan. I'm going to have some mixed emotions the first time you play the Browns." He said, "Well, what do you think *I'm* going to have?" I told him, "I was reading in *Return to Glory*," and started to ask a question. He said, "I never read that book." I said, "It was about you." He said, "I never . . . read . . . that . . . book, young man." He just stared at me. I realized at that point there were no questions he was going to broach about Cleveland. I quickly realized the bitterness that he felt. And he never, ever got over that.

BOB TRUMPY: The first time the team met, it was the night before training camp. We had a three-hour talk from Paul Brown. And in 1968, remember, there were no roster limits. We had to have 200 guys in one room. And all the coaches, too. Paul used to refer to the "eternal verities," and I'm thinking, "When do we get to the football?" One of the first things we used to practice before we went on the field was how to line up for the national anthem. "Helmet under your arm. Stand at attention. Find out where the flag is. Face it. I don't want anyone screwing around. You stand there at attention." And I'm thinking, "That's not going to help us win or lose. Why is he saying this?" Then we learned the huddle. It was very difficult to play for Paul Brown, but I didn't know any different. The longer I've been away from it, the more I've learned the good things. The more routine, the better. The longest I ever practiced with him as my head coach was an hour and 15 minutes on the field. If we had coaches who wanted their players to stay out longer, he was thoroughly disgusted: "If you can't coach 'em in an hour and 15 minutes, there's something wrong with you. Get 'em off the field. That's it."

SAM WYCHE: Paul always had the team assemble in a classroom before every practice. He would put white athletic tape on the desks with your name on it. You always had the same seat. It was a classroom building, so you couldn't wear your old, metal-tipped cleats 'cause you'd tear up the tile hallways. He would basically tell the practice schedule, what he hoped to get accomplished. You'd have to carry your shoes into the classroom for a meeting that lasted a minute and a half, two minutes. Paul's favorite word was *why*. If you knew why we were going to do something, then you wouldn't forget it in the heat of a game. He wanted you to know why we did calisthenics, why we did certain drills, why we called a certain play, why we blocked a certain way.

As was the case when the Dolphins were added in 1966, the AFL held an expansion draft to make veteran players available to the new Bengals. But the Bengals were given an advantage that the Dolphins didn't enjoy—a hoard of additional picks in their first college draft. The team was granted multiple picks running from the second round through the seventeenth and final round—nine in the sixth round alone! The result was an inaugural training camp at Wilmington College that featured a mass of humanity.

AL HEIM: We probably had 125, 130 guys come through that camp, one right after another. First you had the draft, where we got two or three people at each position. Then we got four or five players from every team in the league. Then other teams would cut down their rosters, and we'd bring those guys through. Some of them went so quick, you hardly knew they were there.

TOM GRAY: We sometimes were bringing in 20 people some days, just to try and find somebody. We had people who got there in the morning and didn't make it to lunch. We used to take 'em down to the local bus station with a ticket and drop 'em off. There was a boxer who tried out, and we could not get him to run. As he would go down the track, he would kind of shadow box. He was one of the guys who didn't make the next meal.

SAM WYCHE: I broke three vertebrae and two transverse processes in my back with four minutes to go my last game as a senior at Furman. I would not have been drafted high, but I think I would have gotten a shot. I played one year of minor league football for the Wheeling Ironmen of the Continental Football League. After one year, I came back and became a graduate assistant with the University of South Carolina. Paul Dietzel was the head coach, and I was assigned to help a young coach named Lou Holtz. I still wanted to play. I was a scout squad quarterback. When the scouts would come and look at the Gamecock players, I'd leap in front of them and throw the ball around. Lou made a phone call to Cincinnati and Rick Forzano and got me a tryout, right in the middle of some term exams. They signed me to a contract for $16,000. I stood on a street corner at a pay phone calling my wife to let her know we were rich. Of course, we hadn't made a dime yet. You had to make the team to make that.

With the second overall pick in the draft, Cincinnati chose All-American center Bob Johnson from Tennessee. In all, the Bengals made 41 selections in 17 rounds. They included two quarterbacks—Vanderbilt's Gary Davis and Tennessee's Dewey Warren—to join in the battle for the starting position with former Miami Dolphins starter John Stofa and free agent Sam Wyche. They included a tight end who thought he had been inducted into the military service. They included Western Michigan's Dale Livingston, whose college résumé included kicker, punter, and member of the marching band. They included a defensive back from Michigan State named Jess Phillips whose most recent address was a state prison in Michigan after he had been convicted of passing bad checks.

JOHN STOFA: At the end of the '67 season with the Dolphins, I found out that Paul Brown was down for a few days in Miami. Honestly, everybody thought he was looking at Rick Norton. We found out he was checking to see how my leg had responded and how well I was throwing. I found out I was going to be traded to Cincinnati the last week of the season.

AL HEIM: John Stofa was our first player. With Paul, he always wanted to get quarterbacks early.

SAM WYCHE: In training camp, I was struggling every day to stay alive. I thought it was embarrassing if you got cut right away. I thought I had made the team, and we rented an apartment. Then I saw my picture on the news and they said, "released today by the Bengals." I was released then immediately assigned to the cab squad. Then injuries came, and they activated me.

JOHN STOFA: Sam didn't have the strong arm. He didn't have quickness. Where Sam really made his mark was that he had a coach's mind. That carried him forward.

SAM WYCHE: I wasn't a very good player, but I was a "hard-try" guy. That caught their eye as much as anything else. Plus, I must have taken real good notes. Every year, Paul Brown would pick out one player and keep his playbook from training camp, and he chose my book.

D. L. STEWART: They had John Stofa, who was a good guy but about as mobile as a fire hydrant. They had Dewey Warren, and he got hurt. And then there was Sam. I believe I'm the first guy who ever interviewed Sam. He was rooming with Stofa in training camp. I knocked on the door, and Sam said, "John's not here." I said, "I'm not here to interview John. I'm here to interview you." And he said, "Why?" He was the most self-effacing, modest, quiet guy. He was not the same Sam that, when he was a coach in Cincinnati, grabbed the microphone and yelled, ". . . you're not in Cleveland!"

BOB TRUMPY: I started for the University of Illinois as a sophomore and led them in receptions, then left for the University of Utah. I left Illinois because they had a big slush-fund scandal. Half the athletes left. By then there were scouting combines that apparently had my name on a list somewhere. I spent a period of time in the navy. My wife is from southern California, so when I got out of the navy I went back to L.A. and figured my best chance was to sign as a free agent. The Rams were there. San Diego was there. I took one of those junior jobs at Beneficial Finance, and I was collecting bills.

My wife called one day and said, "We just got a telegram. You've been drafted." "That can't be true. I just got out of the navy." She said, "No, you got drafted by a team called the Cincinnati Beagles." "What? Read that telegram again." "Congratulations. You were drafted in the 12th round by the Cincinnati Beagles." I said, "It's not Beagles. It's *Bengals*." She said, "Oh, yeah. It is *Bengals*. But it's in Cincinnati." I said, "Who signed it?" She said, "Paul Brown." "Are you sure?" She said, "Yeah." And I walked in to my boss and said, "This is the worst fucking job on the face of the earth, and I just got drafted by the Cincinnati Bengals. Good-bye." And I left. Six weeks later, a guy named Tom Bass showed up at our $85-a-month apartment in California with a contract for $15,000, a $1,500 signing bonus, and $1,000 if I made the team. Done deal. No negotiating.

AL HEIM: Dale Livingston was a pretty good punter. He came from Western Michigan, where he was also in the marching band. Every once in a while, he'd get trapped—a bad snap or he fumbled the ball—and he'd have to run. A time or two, he got away for a first down. He'd get a lot of cheers for that.

SAM WYCHE: Dale pulled one punt down that he could have gotten off and chose to run and did *not* make the first down. He was kind of slow getting up, right on the Bengals' sideline. Paul Brown looked at him and said, "You'd *better* be hurt!"

D. L. STEWART: They picked Jess Phillips up literally at the door to a prison in Michigan. He was in for a white-collar crime, a bad-check rap.

AL HEIM: Mike Brown went up to Lansing and got him. It went very smooth. Today, the media would probably want to know everything about him. It wasn't a real big deal.

TOM GRAY: I think it was common knowledge among the staff what had happened, but there wasn't a lot said. Again, we were looking for talent. Paul'd have gone to any lengths to get a player back then to be competitive. Jess was the toughest kid I ever met, the most polite and nice kid.

D. L. STEWART: He was a defensive back in college, and they converted him to a running back the second year. And he was probably one of the nicest guys I met in the years I covered the Bengals. He invited me home for dinner one night. His wife cooked a lovely dinner. Just a sweetheart of a guy.

SAM WYCHE: He was not a bad actor, not a criminal element at all. I'm sure Paul Brown knew that or he wouldn't have brought him in.

And there was a relatively unknown third-round pick from Arizona named Paul Robinson. The source of his anonymity was the fact that he had played only one year of football for the Wildcats, attending the school initially on a track scholarship.

AL LOCASALE: Paul had been a good track man, a quarter-miler. He had used his eligibility in track, and somebody said to him, "You still have a year of eligibility in football." And he hadn't graduated yet, so he went out for football. We were impressed. We had a good feeling about him. We figured his best football was in front of him because he had so limited an amount of college experience.

PAUL ROBINSON: I was raised in a little town near Tucson called Marana. My father was a cotton-picker contractor. He would get pickers from Texas, and they would stay in little tents behind our house. In '64, I went to Eastern Arizona Junior College on a basketball scholarship. I also ran the hurdles and ended up running hurdles at the University of Arizona. I needed a fifth year to get my degree after I finished with track and went to the football coach, Darrell Mudra, to see if I could get a football scholarship. He was nice enough to tell me if I made the team that he would give me a scholarship. So that was my goal—any position, as long as I made the team. I wasn't thinking about pro football. The only thing I wanted to do was try to be the first out of my family to get a degree.

The original Bengals lost their opener in San Diego as expected but delighted the small but zealous Nippert Stadium faithful by beating Denver—coached by Paul Brown disciple Lou Saban—and Buffalo in the team's first two home games. But Cincinnati couldn't keep its quarterbacks healthy. Stofa gave way to Warren, who gave way to Wyche. It became obvious early that the ground game would be Cincinnati's only chance for success. The first year of AFL football in Cincinnati soon became a showcase for Paul Robinson. As the Bengals compiled a 3–11 record, equaling the best by an expansion club in the AFL or NFL, Robinson rambled for 1,023 yards to lead the league in rushing and easily capture the Rookie of the Year award.

BOB TRUMPY: Nippert Stadium was awful, terrible. The field was so bad that, late my rookie year when we played the Jets, they painted the dirt green. Guys had it everywhere, and they had to throw uniforms out. But I don't think any of us cared. We were playing teams like the New York Jets, the San Diego Chargers. And we had our names on the backs of our jerseys. Geez, my parents were in the stands. I ran up to see my dad and said, "I've got Carroll Dale's number on! Eighty-four! Man, this is really cool!"

SAM WYCHE: Our dressing room was a gymnasium, an open area, and we had to lay our clothes on folding chairs. The stadium was intimate, and the crowd was into it those first years. We had some surprising wins early, and everybody was excited. We could have played on the rec department's last field and we'd have been as excited.

D. L. STEWART: They had drafted Warren McVea out of the University of Houston and thought he was going to be their big deal. Warren played well, but Paul Robinson came from nowhere. He was an innocent. He had this bewildered look on his face and a big, big grin. Everybody in the world loved him.

PAUL ROBINSON: Joining the Bengals was the perfect situation for me. There were no stars, no set positions. The slate was open for anyone hungry enough to get that position. My first goal was making the team. Then coming out of training camp, I had worked myself up to the starting position. The first professional game that I saw in person was the exhibition opener that I started, against the Kansas City Chiefs. Buck Buchanan and those guys—oh, gosh—10 times bigger than they were on TV!

Bob Trumpy: We had to wear suits or sport coats, dress shirts, and ties on road trips. "Straight Runner"—that's what we called Paul Robinson—came up to me in the locker room and said, "I need your help." I said, "What's up?" He said, "Come here." And he took me back in this storage room where there was nobody else. He was wearing his pants, his shirt and had a necktie in his hand. He said, "This is the first suit I've ever owned. I don't know how to tie a tie." I said, "You're kidding. Well, you're on." So I tied it around my neck and put it around his head, pulled it up straight and said, " 'Straight Runner,' you look great." He was there for four years. He wore the same suit with the same shirt with the same tie for four more years. The knot I tied in 1968 was still in that tie in 1972.

Sam Wyche: Everybody loved Paul. He was a smooth, gliding runner. He had a terrific knack for setting up his blocks. We used to run a sweep with him a lot where we'd pull both guards. Paul would give a move one way, set the block up, then go the other way.

Tom Gray: Everybody in the league knew that the only thing we could do was run, and we did it anyway. I think we did it by having so damn few plays. We did it in practice until it just had to work.

Paul Robinson: I wanted to be the leading rusher, which would automatically mean I was going to be the Rookie of the Year. Kansas City had a rookie I was competing with, Robert "the Tank" Holmes. I lucked out and ended up with 1,023, which was enough to lead the league in rushing and the first rookie to rush for 1,000 yards in the AFL. And I had a Bengals record, an 87-yard run, that Corey Dillon finally broke in 2001. I kept that over 30-something years. That was pretty neat!

Bob Trumpy: After the first season, he and I had an engagement to go out and sign autographs. I was first in line, and Paul was second. All of a sudden they're stacking up after me. I looked over to Paul and I said, "What the hell are you doing?" He said, "Man, I don't know how you're doing it so fast." I looked over, and on every picture he was signing: "No. 18 . . . Paul Robinson . . . 1968 AFL Rookie of the Year . . . Straight Runner." I said, "Just put '18 Paul Robinson' and let's get the hell out of here. We'll be here until your next birthday."

SHERRILL HEADRICK: Paul Brown thought we were going to have a Super Bowl–champion team. We had only about two or three real players. We won two exhibition games, won two of our first three games, and he said, "Well, we'll just do it this year." I turned to Bobby Hunt—he and I made about 80 percent of the tackles—and said, "If we win it this year, he'll be doing it without us because I'm just about broke in half now." Sure enough, it was a couple more weeks before I got hurt, ended my career. And now I have metal knees and metal hips and a broken neck.

JOHN STOFA: We won three games, as we did with Miami. If I try to compare the two, Cincinnati probably started jelling a little bit sooner. A lot of that is because the way that Paul Brown orchestrated the way he wanted things to work.

SAM WYCHE: We were well received in Cincinnati. Expansion teams are, though. You've got a year or two before the losses start to make you unpopular. It seemed like it was me or Bob Trumpy or Bob Johnson at every banquet along with two Cincinnati Reds named Pete Rose and Johnny Bench. We had equal footing from that standpoint.

The Bengals headed into the second year still looking for players at many positions, especially quarterback. There was still room to welcome far-flung free agents, but there was also the fifth pick in the first round, around which a team could be molded.

AL LoCASALE: Paul knew I was going through a divorce. I was on the road in the spring of '69, and Paul came back from a league meeting and said, "What are your future plans?" I said, "Being on the road all the time has contributed to the unhappy situation in my home life, but I love scouting. Why?" "At the meeting, Al Davis asked if he could have permission to talk to you about heading up his administration." I said, "Yes. Not because I want to leave

Cincinnati but because I want to get off the road." An offer was made, and I told Paul I was going to take it. He wished me well. In fact, we went to the Queen City Club for a final lunch.

BRUCE COSLET: I was an undersized tight end, so I was never drafted when I graduated in 1968. I signed before the draft in Canada, with the Edmonton Eskimos. I got about halfway through the season and got cut. I'm from California; a lot of my college friends were living in the San Francisco area, so I went back there and got a job at Uniroyal Tire and Rubber. I was selling Tiger Paws. Out of the blue in 1969, I got a call from Bill Walsh. They were looking for a tight end. He had me go over to Stanford. I ran patterns, and Jim Plunkett threw me the ball, and I ran a 40. And Bill signed me the next day by phone. They didn't have any minicamps then. I didn't meet anybody with the Bengals until the day I showed up for training camp.

PAUL ROBINSON: Wyche and Coslet, I can't see how these crazy guys become head coaches. They'd put turtles in your thigh pads. You're running and all of a sudden you see this thing moving in your pants. You had to jump out there in front of everybody and take your clothes off. And they became head coaches.

TOM GRAY: The start of the second year, I think we had 11 people on the staff. Paul and Mike and Pete Brown and the coaches, couple others of us. And I know all of them wanted to draft Bobby Douglass. Paul Brown wanted Greg Cook. And he made the right pick.

BOB TRUMPY: Strangely, none of our players recognized the ability of Greg Cook when he was with the University of Cincinnati, right there. We paid no attention. He got drafted, and it was, "Greg Cook. Who the hell is he?" University of Cincinnati. "You're kidding. Didn't know anything about him."

Quarterback Greg Cook wasted no time in taking command of the young team. He won the starting position in preseason, the Bengals closing the five-game practice schedule with three consecutive victories. But nothing changed when the audition ended and the games were for real. The regular season began with three consecutive games at Nippert, against Miami, San Diego, and Kansas City. An optimistic Bengals fan would have been hard-pressed to anticipate anything more than one victory, if that, over the Dolphins. After all, the '68 club had closed out with 10 losses in 11 games with touchdowns hard to come by.

With Cook performing like a swashbuckler, Cincinnati shocked all of pro football by winning all three of those games. He threw two touchdown passes in a 27–21 victory over Miami, then three more when San Diego fell 34–20. And then it was Kansas City, cochamp of the West in 1968, that fell, 24–19.

AL HEIM: Greg came from a town not too far from Cincinnati called Chillicothe, Ohio. He set all kinds of records at the University of Cincinnati. I'm sure he came around to watch our games when he was a senior. I know we were watching him. Paul would go watch him all the time. He was about six four, could throw the ball from one end of the field to the other. Had that air of confidence about him. He looked good on the field. He took over as the starting quarterback right away. We figured, "Boy, we've got somebody to get the fans going."

BILL WALSH: I was working with Greg personally on the field in the early spring; then it started to get tight because Canada had come up with a big offer. Paul Brown didn't believe that Canada could make a run at a player like Greg Cook, and they did. Paul was obligated to improve on it, and we signed Greg.

D. L. STEWART: He had flair, personality, [was] a good-looking young blond guy. Hometown boy. The first exhibition game, playing at Bowling Green, he launched a pass, must have been 75 yards in the air, on a line. He had an arm that was unbelievable.

AL HEIM: We were getting calls from all the national media. They wanted to see this guy Cook. They wanted to see how Paul Brown was doing this. And Nippert Stadium had a press box that wasn't as big as some living rooms.

But Greg Cook also fell in that game, crushed by the Chiefs' fearsome pass rush. It's doubtful that many among the crowd of 27,812 that squeezed into Nippert realized they had witnessed this golden age of Bengals football nipped near its bud.

BRUCE COSLET: The last quarter of the win over Kansas City was when he blew his rotator cuff out. He was rolling out and got hit. He threw the ball and got tackled and came down on his arm.

BILL WALSH: Bobby Bell hit Greg on a pass play that I called that I'll never feel good about. The pass protection wasn't strong enough. I feel terrible about it.

SAM WYCHE: After seven games, midway through the schedule in those days, the leading passer in the AFL was Sam Wyche. Right behind were names like Namath and Lamonica and Dawson. I've still got the little newspaper clip. And they benched me to put in this young kid who finished the season as one of the overall leaders.

Cook returned from his injury after sitting out only four games, all of which Cincinnati lost. He appeared to pick up in early November where he left off in late September. He threw two touchdown passes as the Bengals shocked Oakland and four more the following week to help salvage a 31–31 tie against Houston. But the injury was still there, more patched than fixed. The Bengals, the talk of pro football at 3–0, lost their last five games to finish 4–9–1. Greg Cook threw only three touchdown passes in those final five games, giving him 15 for the 14-game schedule. Finishing with the league's top quarterback rating, he became the Bengals' second consecutive Rookie of the Year as voted by United Press International.

BOB TRUMPY: The last game of the season when we played in Denver, he threw for 300 yards. Back then, throwing for 300 yards was a hell of an accomplishment. Cook appeared to be healthy. Then, in the off-season, he was playing basketball, went up for a rebound, somebody grabbed his shoulder, and that pretty much did him in.

BRUCE COSLET: They thought the injury was just a mild shoulder separation. They couldn't even diagnose rotator cuffs in those days. They had no arthroscopic surgery. They couldn't go in and look. They didn't have MRIs. Today, he would have been back the next year.

SAM WYCHE: With the exception of one or two games, he played that rookie year seriously injured with his right shoulder, a pretty key part of his body. As I remember, Paul kind of pushed him to fight though the pain.

D. L. STEWART: I said it then, and I'll say it to this day. There was no question he was going to be a superstar. I think he would have eclipsed Joe Namath. He certainly was every bit as good a quarterback, maybe better.

BILL WALSH: Greg's numbers were astronomical compared to today's quarterbacks. I think he averaged like 14.8 yards per attempt. Today, if you have 8 yards per attempt, you're hitting the ceiling. We had three receivers that averaged over 20 yards per catch, including Bob Trumpy at tight end. Greg could very well have been the greatest talent that the quarterback position had seen.

24

Heidi, Ho

There was no shortage of news coming out of the New York Jets during the off-season that preceded the 1968 campaign. Foremost was the bloodless coup that took place in May, when Sonny Werblin was suddenly bought out by his fellow owners. Don Lillis assumed the club presidency but died two months later. Phil Iselin then took control of the franchise.

On the field, Weeb Ewbank decided Joe Namath would benefit from a veteran quarterback presence on the roster. The Jets sent Mike Taliaferro to Boston for Babe Parilli, who had helped keep the Patriots in annual contention in the East.

The Jets showed flashes of brilliance early in the season but were wildly inconsistent—Namath included. He guided a masterful ball-control offense late in the opener at Kansas City to lead New York to a 20–19 victory over the Chiefs. And in a virtual homecoming game for Joe Willie when the Patriots moved their home game against New York to Birmingham, Alabama, the Jets scored a wild 47–31 victory. But they were embarrassed in Buffalo, 37–35, by a Bills team that wouldn't win another game all season. Namath threw five interceptions, three returned for touchdowns. And a 21–13 loss at home to the Broncos left New York with an ordinary 3–2 record and fears among Jets fans that the '68 campaign would again bring nothing better than mediocrity.

JOHN DOCKERY: At Buffalo, we told Joe, "Hey, we're the guys in the white uniforms! . . . Hey, Joe, c'mon, will ya?" It was a horrendous day. He had some great days and some bad days. Joe would throw a bunch of touchdowns, but he might throw a bunch of interceptions.

CURLEY JOHNSON: One of those Goddamn interceptions was meant for me, down on the goal line. I'd run a short square out. Butch Byrd jumped in front of me and went 90-something yards for a touchdown. After that game,

Coach Michaels was mad 'cause the defense had played a hell of a game. He was just about ready to accuse Joe of throwing the game.

Joe Namath: I never went through any major periods of frustration. One time warming up at Shea, I couldn't get a tight spiral and I was frustrated. I would throw the ball and turn around and cuss: "Damn, I can't get a good flight!" And Weeb said, "As long as it's getting there, don't worry." I played in a preseason game at Buffalo; I think I threw 10 passes and didn't complete one. And I believe the 11th pass was a touchdown.

Tony Veteri: I was a head linesman in the AFL starting in 1960. Joe Namath was a hell of a guy. He never moaned when he got hit. Never moaned about anything. He was always inquisitive when penalties were called against the Jets. He'd say, "What'd he do?" We'd answer him, and he'd turn around and tell the guys. Or, sometimes, when we had a guy who was bad, I used him as a policeman: "Joe, number 42 is really breaking my chops. Get on his back. Tell him to smarten up." And he would do that. Sometimes, the guy would come over and apologize.

Bob Talamini: We played Denver and were behind, got the ball and were driving. Weeb called me out of the play and said, "I want you to take five." "What do you mean?" He said, "We've got to get this clock stopped, and we don't have that many timeouts. I want you to fake an injury." I went back in and thought, "How am I going to do this?" I figured I'd go down on every play and then see if the pass was completed. If it didn't go out of bounds, then I'd have to stop the clock. Maynard caught a pass over the middle, and I started screaming and moaning. Well, they didn't tell the trainer. He came running out, thought I was injured, and said, "What's the matter?" I said, "What's supposed to be the matter? Weeb asked me to fake it." He said, "OK. We'll make it your knee." So they got me up and took me off. We didn't win, so I got up off the bench and walked to the dressing room. A reporter said, "What's the matter with your knee?" I said, "Oh, it's OK. I'm a fast healer."

The Jets didn't face any serious competition in the East that season, only token resistance from Houston. A four-game winning streak bookended by victories over the Oilers gave the Jets a comfortable cushion going into a November 17 date at Oakland that many considered a possible preview of the AFL Championship Game.

But no one could have anticipated the events of that day at the Oakland Coliseum or how they would be viewed—or not viewed—across the country.

For the Jets, the game at Oakland began their annual two-game pilgrimage to the West Coast to play the Raiders and the Chargers. The players made the gravity of their two-week mission clear by voting before making the trip to increase the fine for breaking curfew from $50 to $5,000. The team hotel in Oakland was located near the Raiders' headquarters, and when Weeb Ewbank wandered over to Raiders-land during one free spell he discovered that a place of honor in the club's offices was occupied by a blown-up photo of Raiders defensive end Ben Davidson and a helmetless Joe Namath.

The game was the late national telecast on NBC's schedule, filling the time slot from 4:00 to 7:00 P.M. eastern time. It would be followed on NBC by the children's movie *Heidi*.

DICK CLINE: I was a broadcast operations supervisor at NBC, which entailed being the supervisor on duty to make sure the network rolled smoothly and operated properly with whatever the schedule of the day was. I was assigned to do sports on the weekends, so that was sort of a subspecialty for me. I made sure that the right switches were thrown, that we were going to the right place at the right time. That if there were any outages of any sort, we got them fixed right away and wrote reports if something went wrong. I was there only for the events of the afternoon, so I probably would have come in around 11:00 A.M. or 12:00 noon, and I would have certainly normally been through around 7:00 P.M.

Each week that there was a sporting event, the very nature being that you never know when it's going to end, I would sit down during the week with the sales department and find out if anything was special that week. That week, it was the special movie *Heidi*. They told me it had to start on time because the Timex people—in those days, a single sponsor bought the time— bought from 7:00 to 9:00 P.M. It didn't raise any eyebrows because no football game had ever come close to going beyond three hours. But I wrote up those conditions during the week and sent them out companywide. And nobody called and said, "What do you mean? You can't do this!" On Sunday, I was there to see the network and the sports department did what was dictated in the set of conditions.

The start of the game lived up to the anticipation. New York took an early 6–0 lead on two field goals by Jim Turner. The Raiders countered with two touchdowns for a 14–6 lead. The Jets rallied with a touchdown late in the half. But when holder Babe Parilli tried to throw for two points and failed, New York headed to the locker room trailing, 14–12.

DICK CLINE: By halftime, it was clear the game was running long. I got a call from the executive producer, Scotty Connell. He was at his home and said, "We [NBC executives] just had a little chat. The game seems to be running a little long. If it gets serious, we'll talk again."

The Jets scored first in the third quarter to grab a 19–14 lead. Oakland came back downfield, inside the New York 20-yard line. Facing third down on the Jets' 13, fullback Hewritt Dixon was stopped short of a first down at the 11.

JIM HUDSON: I tackled Hewritt Dixon and felt something hit me in the helmet. It was a penalty flag. The official called me for a face mask. "Face mask!? I didn't come within 10 miles of his face mask!" We got into a big argument, and I got kicked out.

The double penalty on Hudson gave Oakland first-and-goal to go. Charlie Smith carried into the end zone on the next play and, with the point after, the Raiders moved back ahead, 22–19. The advantage, though, was short-lived. Namath heaved a 50-yard touchdown pass to Don Maynard, and Turner added another field goal to put New York ahead 29–22 midway through the fourth quarter. Yet the counterpunching continued. The Raiders fought back with a touchdown, and the Jets answered with another field goal. With a little more than a minute to play, the Jets were hanging onto a 32–29 lead. If they won, they would claim the franchise's first division championship. And because of the alternation of host cities for the AFL Championship Game, they would earn the right to host Kansas City, San Diego, or the same Oakland team for the right to play in Super Bowl III in Miami.

DARYLE LAMONICA: I threw a long touchdown pass to Charlie Smith, and it was called back. Johnny Sample came up and patted me on the butt and said, "Nice pass, Lamonica. Better luck next year." Well, that fired my Irish-Italian temper up a little bit. And I just said, "The game's not over yet."

DICK CLINE: In the fourth quarter, we were clearly running into trouble. Connell called me again, maybe at 6:30 or so. He said, "I'm going to call the company brass and see about getting permission to extend the time and stay with the game." I said, "Fine. I'll wait to hear that that has, in fact, happened." So I waited, and I waited. It got to be 10 minutes to 7:00, and I hadn't heard anything. So I called him. He had two separate phone lines at home. The one line was busy, so I called the other one, and that one was also busy. I was between a rock and a hard place. I had communication with the mobile unit in Oakland, which was a normal occurrence. But that was my only contact. Well, of course, they said, "We want to stay on the air." You heard that all the time and ignored it. Certainly, under those circumstances. So it got to be time, and I hadn't heard anything. So I pulled them off.

And NBC viewers in New York and up and down the East Coast spent the last 1:05 of the game watching *Heidi.* The more resourceful of Jets fans in the New York area quickly resorted to their radios to join WABC announcer Merle Harmon:

> Fifty seconds remaining. Lamonica goes back to throw. Lamonica looking. Lamonica throwing. He's got Charlie Smith on the 20! Down to the 15! The 10! Five! Touchdown! . . .
>
> Mike Eischeid to kick off, and downfield comes the football. He boots it on the ground. It's gonna be fielded by Christy at the 10. He's out to the 12. Christy . . . is . . . shaken. Fumbled the ball! It is recovered . . . by . . . Oakland for a touchdown! The ball bounced into the end zone and was recovered! It was recovered by Preston Ridlehuber for a touchdown! . . .
>
> Thirty-three seconds left. And Oakland has scored two touchdowns in nine seconds. . . . Blanda for the extra point. It's good. Thirty-three seconds left, the score, Oakland 43, New York 32.

CURT GOWDY: Mrs. Ewbank called the Oakland Coliseum, and the operator put her through to the dressing room. Somebody yelled, "Weeb! Your wife wants you on the phone!" He got on. She said, "Honey, congratulations! What a great win!" He said, "Win!? We lost!" And he slammed the phone down.

JIM HUDSON: One of the Oakland touchdowns came over my replacement. It was always tough to win in Oakland. The same officials were always there. Every game. Every game! You know that man [Al Davis] was the head of the AFL, and he hired all those officials.

JOHN FREE: The exit door to our locker room was within 75 feet of the game officials' locker room. Walt Michaels and our team doctor, James Nicholas, were trying to kick the door in. Weeb said, "John, go get those two and bring 'em in here!" I'm five foot ten, only 160 pounds. I finally got them to come back in, through some kind of threat.

WALT MICHAELS: Jim Hudson got thrown out for absolutely nothing. It was a kind of a game where the officials got carried away. Jim Fassel of the New York Giants once said, "I don't have enough money to talk about officials." Well, I didn't have enough money then to make a living, let alone talk about officials. I went down and talked to the officials. We had a great conversation. And I got fined by the league. I was very fortunate that Phil Iselin, one of our owners, had some extra money and they didn't take one-third of my contract. I wouldn't have been able to live.

DICK CLINE: All this time, I heard no phones at all. I got no input from anyone. During the station break before *Heidi* came on, the phone rang. First and only time. It was the president of the company. Not the president of the sports department, the president of the company, Julian Goodman. All he said was, "Go back to the game. . . . This is Julian Goodman. . . . Go back to the game." I said to him, "I'll try." And I did try. But there wasn't any way on Earth I could reverse that. The switch was made by some fellow working overtime on a Sunday out in the cornfields of Iowa listening for a cue. Then he got up, and he went home. It would have taken days to find the guy and get him back out there to that switching station.

I found out afterward why there were no phones ringing. From roughly about quarter to 7:00 on, people started calling in: "Is *Heidi* going to be on?" As we got to 7:00, people called in and said, "Are you going to stay with the game?" Then, after 7:00, people said, "Why isn't the football game still on?" The phone lines just blew. They couldn't handle the crunch. Nobody could talk to me, and I could talk to nobody. The only reason that Julian Goodman could call in was because he had a separate, private line. They put 26 fuses in the switchboard in the first hour trying to make it function. Each time they put one in, it would blow.

I finally got a hold of my boss after about an hour and warned him what had happened. He said, "Well, at least let's get a flashcaster up of the final score." I did that as quickly as I could. Of course, that just compounded it because I did it just as Heidi was trying to get out of the wheelchair or something and it covered her.

CURT GOWDY: I packed up my things to leave and started up the stairs. Suddenly, I heard, "Gowdy! Gowdy! Get back here! They want you down in the truck!" I came back and picked up the little phone to the remote truck. They said, "Uhhhhhhhhh. I hate to tell you, but they cut the game off." I said, "Jesus, how could they do that? What do you want me to do about it?" They said, "We want you to re-create the two touchdowns." I said, "You can't re-create that excitement!" "Well, give it your best shot. We're going to put some crowd noise in behind it. They want to play it on the news tonight and on the *Today* show tomorrow." So they racked the tape up, and I re-created the pass and the kickoff and the recovery.

FRANK RAMOS: Other than the television people, there wasn't anybody associated with the game that knew anything about what happened with *Heidi* until the game was over. We had no idea how big a story it was until we went down to Long Beach to practice for a week before playing at San Diego the next week. It was the lead story on the NBC affiliate that night on the 11:00 news in Los Angeles.

DICK CLINE: I was scheduled to have Monday and Tuesday off because I worked the weekend. I certainly didn't have Monday off that week. My boss wanted to see me at 8:00 in the morning. For that set of conditions, there was really no way that they could fire me, even though they might have wanted to. There were a lot of very impressive names on the distribution list, not the least of which were the people who were asking me. I hate to use that old "following orders" routine. But they informed me that if, based on what they found out and read in the conditions, I had decided on my own to stay with the game, I definitely would have been fired. For my health and well-being, it was the right thing to do. But not anyone else's. Quietly, NBC was thrilled. It indicated the number of people who apparently had an interest in the AFL. The following week, they used Heidi as promotional material. They had Joe Namath with *Heidi* sitting on his shoulder in the print ads.

The Jets easily won their first division title, clinching while at home enjoying Thanksgiving while the second-place Oilers were losing and dropping from contention. The West, though, painted a much different picture. Kansas City and Oakland tied for first place, each finishing 12–2 (a game better than New York) to set up a special division playoff game in Oakland. But what was expected to be a memorable dogfight turned into a decisive Raiders statement by a 41–6 score. The Raiders, minus Heidi, were coming to New York.

And Al Davis was working on the Jets' psyche even before the kickoff on a cold and blustery day at Shea.

HARRY SCHUH: My dad was a builder in New Jersey. Al asked me if I had my dad's phone number at home. I said, "Yeah." He said, "I just want to talk to him. Are they coming to the game?" I said, "Oh, yeah. Mom wouldn't miss this one."

A few hours before the beginning of the AFL Championship Game, there was Harry Schuh's father, building a shelter for the Raiders along the visitors' sideline.

HARRY SCHUH: But they made him tear 'em down because the home team didn't have any.

New York built a 10-point lead in the first quarter and continued to stay ahead, 20–13, going into the fourth quarter. George Blanda's third field goal of the game pulled Oakland within four points, and a five-yard touchdown by barreling Pete Banaczak with only a few minutes to play gave the Raiders their first lead of the game and quieted the large crowd. The Jets countered with a go-ahead drive, Namath hitting Don Maynard on his third touchdown pass of the game. But the Jets defense faced a stern test late after an interception by George Atkinson gave Oakland possession deep in New York territory.

DARYLE LAMONICA: I had 'em on the move, and there was no doubt in my mind that I was going to score. I actually took a play to get over on the left hash mark 'cause I wanted the wide side of the field on my right. We were down on the 30-yard line. It was just perfect. Charlie Smith was the receiver. I dropped back to throw, and Charlie released inside. He had to take a shallower release than he wanted. And I ended up throwing a lateral.

Most players, fans, vendors, anyone at Shea Stadium simply thought Lamonica's little drop-off was an incomplete pass. But New York linebacker Ralph

Baker at least suspected that the ball was lateraled, meaning it was passed backward and therefore was a live ball. Smith must not have. Baker scooped it up and raced for the opposite end zone. A recovered lateral can't be advanced, but just taking possession at that point of the game was a lifesaver for the Jets. New York had staved off mighty Oakland and won its first AFL championship.

Daryle Lamonica: I've had to live with that for a lot of years. I'd call the same play again. I was getting a lot of heat and pressure, and I tried to do something that I shouldn't have done. I should have just thrown the ball away.

25

Guaranteed

The 27–23 victory propelled the Jets to Miami and a Super Bowl III date with the Baltimore Colts. The Colts had set an NFL record for fewest points allowed in a season in compiling a 13–1 record. On offense, quarterback Johnny Unitas hurt his passing arm in the preseason and played sparingly. Journeyman Earl Morrall took over and earned NFL Player of the Year honors. In the NFL Championship Game, they faced the only team that had beaten them during the season, the Cleveland Browns. Even playing in Cleveland, the championship game wasn't even competitive—Baltimore 34, Cleveland 0. Little wonder that Las Vegas established the Colts as bigger Super Bowl favorites than either of the Green Bay teams, at 19 points.

Jets coach Weeb Ewbank arranged for his team to arrive in Miami 10 days before kickoff. He allowed the players to bring their wives and families and didn't put in a curfew until the Tuesday before kickoff. For game preparation, Ewbank's strategy fell into two main camps. One, he was constantly comparing members of this seemingly unbeatable Colts team with AFL players whom the Jets had handled. Two, he often noted that many players on the Baltimore roster were those whom he had coached back in the late '50s and early '60s. Combined, these factors began to help erase any doubts that Jets players might have had that they could compete with the mighty Colts.

JOHN FREE: We were flying from New York to Fort Lauderdale, and Joe was showing this pin to a player. He had bought it for his mother for Christmas, but because of our schedule, he couldn't go back to Beaver Falls. He was going to give it to her after the Super Bowl and was talking about checking it in at the front desk when we got to the Galt Ocean Mile because he was afraid of losing it. I was walking up the aisle when he was flashing it, and I said, "Joe, let me see that." It had a background of green emeralds, white diamonds intermingling. I counted the white diamonds, and there were 12. And we were playing the Super Bowl on the 12th and Joe's number was 12. I said to him, "No way we can lose."

The Galt Ocean Mile was where the Packers stayed the year before. It had two penthouses. Namath was in one, and Weeb was in the other. Wherever we stayed, the players were furnished a room and given a meal allowance. No matter where we went, most hotels have several suites. Joe always got a suite, and he paid the difference, which was payroll deducted.

JIM HUDSON: The first part in Miami, I never got in before daylight. We had a good time. They had to reschedule picture day on the Monday before the game. Namath and Snell and Boozer overslept. Can you imagine if somebody like Namath did that today?

DON MAYNARD: Everybody got to bring their wives. So everybody's going to different things or just eating out. Shoot, some of 'em got the kids, like Bob Talamini. He's got three kids down there. And he's telling his wife, "Here, buy them kids some ice cream. Gee whiz. Just get 'em away from me." He's trying to lie over there in the sun and relax. The next week, Weeb puts in the curfew, and that was it. Nobody really wanted to be out, anyway.

JOHN DOCKERY: George Sauer was my roommate. He's an interesting fellow. He's a perfectionist, ran patterns to perfection. I like George. He had other things on his mind. Football was kind of a love and hate relationship, reconciling the image of football and its brutality that a sensitive and intelligent guy like George would think about. I'd say, "Don't talk to me. You're an All-Pro. I'm just trying to get down on the kickoff and make a tackle so I'm here next week." Our room was a relatively cerebral place, but George was far more intellectual and deep thinking and searching than I was.

GEORGE SAUER JR.: I've never been that nervous in my life. It just wouldn't go away. I was seeing things in the game films and thinking, "This team has won 13 out of 14 games. Doesn't the other team see what they're doing?" I was watching the Browns' Paul Warfield run patterns against Lenny Lyles. I wanted to see if he was looking at the quarterback or the receiver, or why he let Warfield go a certain way. How can you have confidence against a team that won the NFL Championship Game 34–0? But we saw things. I remember bursting out in films: "Throw the ball!" 'cause the Browns' quarterback was just standing there when Warfield was five yards open. While everybody expected us to lose, we knew we had a good chance. That made me nervous.

CURT GOWDY: I called Weeb Ewbank when I got to Miami and asked him if I could come over and watch 'em work out. And he turned me down. I was very surprised. I had done eight of their games that year, and he was always very nice to me. He just said, "Curt, I'm not letting anybody in." So I begged him and said, "I don't want secrets or anything. I'd just like to check on the players. I won't bother anything." Finally, he said, "All right. Come on out. I've got guards on the gates, so you'll have to knock on the door." He let me in the gate. It was the weirdest practice I'd ever seen. There wasn't a word spoken. They'd hold up these big cards with the number of the play. All you could hear was the thud of the foot kicking the ball, the ball slapping in the receivers' hands, or the thud of body on body. These were the maddest guys, the most insulted guys, I'd ever seen. They'd been reading the papers. Twenty-point underdogs. What a joke.

Then I went over to watch the Colts work out. And Don Shula was great. He greeted me. We walked up and down the field. He was pointing out things to me. He said, "I know you want to know more about the players. Why don't you come over and have dinner with me?" I got on the bus and rode over with 'em. They were singing and laughing. I was sitting next to Shula, and he said, "Geez, listen to these guys. I'm really worried about this game. Football is all mental. Any time one team's more ready to play than the other, they can beat you." He went upstairs to change his clothes, and I was standing down at the bar having a beer. I saw Tom Matte, whom I'd known when I had broadcast college games when he was at Ohio State. We got to talking, and I said, "What are you going to do after the season?" He said, "Well, we get $15,000 for winning. I'm going to build a playroom on my home." He called over Dick Vogel, a great lineman, and I visited with him. I asked him what he was going to do. He said, "We get $15,000 for winning. I'm going on an African safari." I talked to four or five of them. They already had their money spent.

BABE PARILLI: I remember Lombardi said the Colts had the best defense in the NFL. They did so much blitzing that they beat all the NFL teams, and no one knew how to attack their blitzing situations. We had an automatic read on blitzes, didn't even audible. The quarterback and receiver read the blitz, and the receiver breaks his pattern. That was automatic.

JIM HUDSON: Weeb pulled one of the great things of all time. I can remember us laughing about it. He, of course, was the coach of the Colts when they beat the New York Giants in the '58 championship game. He showed us the films of that game. And a lot of guys were still playing. Now, it's amazing, but football players get about twice as good about every 10 years. We laughed at how bad they looked. And here we were, playing them again. Weeb was pretty clever.

WALT MICHAELS: Earl Morrall and I had played in a Pro Bowl game together. There were things that he would kind of telegraph on his throw. If you had some decent, quick backs, you could pick off a few. But the biggest thing about playing the Colts was convincing our players: "We went to the same colleges as those guys. We played in the same conferences."

PAUL ROCHESTER: Earl Morrall was at Michigan State, a little ahead of me. He could never throw long in college. I told Weeb, "He's a tremendous ball handler, a magic guy, but take the short stuff away."

PETE LAMMONS: We had been in Miami since the Thursday before. We hit the streets running. We didn't miss many parties. We had only seen Baltimore on TV, where they beat Cleveland in the championship game 34–0 and they beat Minnesota in a playoff game. We finally broke down into position groups and were watching films. Clive and Joe and Sauer and I and Bake, all the backs. Weeb was there. We were watching these films of how other teams offensively attacked Baltimore's defense. We got to looking and saying, "Run it back." Joe Kapp at Minnesota couldn't throw the ball from here over to that wall. And Cleveland didn't have much passing. We had the type of offense that could score on anybody. Finally, I said, "Damn, Clive. If we keep watching these films, we'll get overconfident." I didn't think anything about it at the time. That might be the smartest thing I ever said.

But there were no pad-toting newspapermen, no TV cameramen to splash Lammons's confident statement from coast to coast. It seemed like those opportunities were reserved for Joe Namath. It didn't take long for the Jets' brash star to make headlines in Miami, even when he wasn't trying.

JIM HUDSON: Joe and I were in Fazio's in Fort Lauderdale with two guys from Baltimore, Lou Michaels and Dan Sullivan. We had all been drinking, and they got into an argument about Catholicism—both Joe and Lou were Catholic.

JOE NAMATH: Lou and I had met before 'cause he and my brother, Frank, were buddies who went to Kentucky. We were standing at the bar, hadn't gone to our tables yet. Lou said, "We're gonna kick your butt." We started talking like that. Lou was kicking extra points and field goals and playing only in short-yardage situations, so I said, "Hey, Lou. What are you talking about, man? You're just a Goddamn kicker!" Whooooooaaaaa! His jaw came out, and he glared at me.

JIM HUDSON: I said, "Joe, I don't know about you. But I don't think you can whip Lou there, and I can't whip that big one's ass."

JOE NAMATH: And at least three guys in tuxedos suddenly said, "All right! Table's ready!" That's all there was to it. No big deal. It was guys busting chops. Lou and Dan Sullivan and Jim Hudson and I had dinner that night.

JIM HUDSON: We ended up giving them a ride back 'cause they didn't have a car.

WALT MICHAELS: The first place I heard about this was in the paper because Lou and I didn't talk the two weeks previous to the game. We talked very little during the season. In Miami, I didn't go over to his hotel. In fact, LeRoy Neiman went over to the Colts and painted and sketched Lou and came over to our practice and sketched me, and he said, "Your brother said hello."

There was one more Namath drama to play out before kickoff. It came on the Thursday night before the game, when Namath spoke before the Miami Touchdown Club. From the time that the Jets boarded the plane for Florida, Weeb Ewbank had encouraged his staff and players to begrudgingly accept the role of huge underdog. That cover was blown when someone at the banquet declared his skepticism for Joe and the Jets. Namath responded with his memorable guarantee: "We're going to win Sunday, I'll guarantee you."

FRANK RAMOS: The son of Townsend Martin, one of our owners, had planned a barbecue for Thursday night and invited all the players, the coaches, the whole staff. Joe really felt he should go with his teammates. But I encouraged Joe to go to the Miami Touchdown Club banquet that night for several reasons. One was that he was one of the featured recipients, the first AFL player to ever be named Professional Football Player of the Year.

JOE NAMATH: A fella in the back of the room came up with the same stuff we'd been hearing for 10 days: "You guys don't have a chance." Well, when you have a group of guys work together and try hard and have success, when someone comes in and tells them they can't do something, there's a level of anger that gets going. That's all it was. I was angry to hear that B.S. again. It wasn't planned.

DAVE ANDERSON: I was with Joe when he went down to make the speech because I was working on a book about the Jets that would be published if they won. He said what he said, and nobody thought it was a big deal. He had been saying things like that. Then it was a big headline the next day in the *Miami Herald.* Then, everybody started talking about it. To me, it was just another Namath conversation.

FRANK RAMOS: I wasn't aware of what Joe said until I picked up the *Miami Herald* the next day. The headline of Luther Evans's story all the way across the page, the lead story. I had to drive Weeb to the Doral Hotel where he was to do the Friday press conference. When he got in the car, I said, "Here. You'd better look at this before we go." He said, "Why did you do it, dad gum it!? We had 'em right where we wanted 'em!"

JOE NAMATH: I never thought about it being anything. I swear I didn't even think about it until we got to practice the next day. Coach Ewbank kind of talked to me. We were out in the middle of the field at the Orange Bowl with Clive Rush, our offensive coordinator, the three of us. And Coach Ewbank said, "What have you done? Look what . . . Joe, how could you do this? That team was so overconfident! Now you've given them something to get fired up about." I was sincerely apologetic. But I told them, "If they need clippings to get fired up, they're in trouble." My offensive linemen wanted to beat me up. They kept saying, "You're not playing against Bubba Smith! . . . You're not playing against Billy Ray Smith!" A lot of it was in jest, but some of it was serious.

MATT SNELL: Wednesday was the offensive day. Thursday was the defensive day. Friday, we worked on special teams, and Saturday was like a walkthrough. When we got the game plan from Clive Rush, who was a great coordinator, we saw we were going to establish the running game. He said, "We're only going to throw in special circumstances."

Boozer and I were going through the Friday paper, and they came out with a comparison position by position. They ranked Joe Namath and Earl Morrall as equals. All the other positions, we were rated inferior. I told him, "This is crazy. I went to school with Tom Matte. He's a great athlete, but he's not a better halfback than you. And Jerry Hill can't be better than me." We went through the whole thing, and he and I made a pact. "We know what the game plan is. We know we'll emphasize the run. If we get started and your play is working, I'm going to break my butt to make your plays go. And if my plays are working, I want the same commitment from you." And he said, "You got it."

JOHN FREE: Here's what I think of Joe Namath. When he came to camp that year, I convinced him that he ought to stop chewing tobacco. He's competitive, so I told him, "I'll bet you a hundred dollars you cannot abstain from tobacco to the end of the season and postgames included." To the best of my knowledge, he never touched tobacco. We were in Fort Lauderdale about five days before the Super Bowl. His mother wanted to come to the game and was reluctant to fly. Joe said, "Would you help my mother get a ticket from Pittsburgh to Miami?" It took me about a day to get her a ticket, I took it out of his check and told him the following day out in the locker room at Fort Lauderdale Stadium. Joe noticed a grounds crew man had some Red Man and told him, "Gimme some of that tobacco. I haven't had any for a long time." I was startled: "You've only got four more days!" He took a pinch, put it in the side of his mouth, grabbed his helmet, walked out. I said, "I can't believe you!" Ten or 15 minutes later, I walked through the tunnel up into the dugout. I saw all the damn tobacco lying 20 feet from where you come out of the dugout. He only did it so that I wouldn't owe him the hundred bucks. That tells you something about Joe Namath.

While Joe Willie was the natural focus of media attention, two of Joe's less loquacious teammates were involved in situations that played vital roles in the game's outcome. Dave Herman, who moved from right guard to right tackle to block Ike Lassiter in the AFL Championship Game, was called upon to play out of position again in the Super Bowl. He would be lined up opposite Bubba Smith, who was fast becoming the game's dominant defensive end. And Don Maynard, the record-setting receiver, faced the prospect of not being able to play because of the leg that he had injured against Cincinnati late in the season.

DAVE HERMAN: I hadn't even gotten off the plane in Miami before Weeb came running over to me: "What a great job, Dave. . . . Would you do it again?" I said, "You've got to be kidding." He said, "Do it again. I know you can do it." You thought I was nervous the game before? This *really* made me nervous. This time it was Bubba Smith—six foot eight, 320 pounds. Not only was he big, he was strong and quick. He was like a 1990s player back in 1969. Joe Spencer, the line coach, said the same thing. We're going to get into him and make him go through me, make him go over the top.

DON MAYNARD: I'd hurt my leg a little bit in the next-to-last game. So in the last game against Miami I didn't even play. But I played in the championship game. The leg didn't bother me. Then I got down to Miami, and one day I was out running. And it was warm. Good weather. I love the heat. It can't get too hot for me. I did a sharp turn or something and I felt like somebody stuck me with an ice pick. I went in and saw Doc Nicholas. That was Thursday. So Friday, I just warmed up and ran through stuff lightly. Then Saturday I got a cortisone shot. Shoot, I was lying on the table, got my leg up, and the doc, he was trying to find that tender spot. They give me a shot. I liked to have walked off the table. I hate needles, anyway. He assured me that I didn't tear nothing. He said, "The only thing, you've got a little sharp pain with scar tissue 'cause of a muscle tear, because scar tissue will build up where it's hurt." I kept a heating pad on it the night before the game.

CURT GOWDY: I was walking through the lobby where we were staying at the Americana Hotel out at the beach the morning of the game, and I heard, "Cowboy! Cowboy!" It was Howard Cosell. That's what he called me 'cause I am from Wyoming. "Cowboy! This is going to be a slaughter!" I said, "What do you mean? The Jets'll give 'em a good game." He said, "Cowboy, I never thought you'd sell out to the commissioner. The Colts'll kill 'em. I like Joe Willie Namath, but he may get a leg broken today." I said, "You watch. It's going to be a good game." He said, "Cowboy, you're pitiful." I got in the car with [Al] DeRogatis, and he said, "Ah, screw him. You know, the Jets are going to win this game. Just got a hunch. Their defense is a lot better than everybody thinks. And they've got a hell of a passing game. If they get some breaks, they can win."

DON WEISS: I thought we had perhaps a team in the Colts that was even stronger than what the Packers had been the first two years. And a lot of NFL people felt that way. They demolished a very good Cleveland team in the championship game, shut 'em out. Lost only one game, and that was to Cleveland early. One of the things we were concerned about as the third game approached, the first two games had been—except for the first half of the first game—pretty well one-sided. The idea of another one-sided game concerned the networks. Maybe the AFL *wasn't* competitive enough to do this.

JOHN FREE: There was a police escort to the game, a caravan of buses with the Jets followed by the Colts. We had three buses, two for the players and one for the players' wives. Some of the wives were driving cars and were between the Jets buses and the Colts buses. I was standing in the stairwell of the first bus. Just as we were approaching a drawbridge, it opened. Weeb said, "John, get that damn bridge closed!" Here were these boats, these yachts that had been waiting maybe 20 minutes. I said, "They have the right of way." He said, "Go over and do it!" I told the attendant, "Do you know who's on these buses? These are the New York Jets' team buses. There won't be a game unless we get through." It was a young fellow, and he fell for it. He said, "How many are there?" I said, "There are three buses and a couple of automobiles, but you've got to let the first two buses through right now." We were the only two that got through. That didn't set anything off right.

CURT GOWDY: Just before kickoff, I turned to Al DeRogatis and said, "How do you see this game?" He said, "If the Jets gain a hundred yards on the ground, they'll win." It's one of the best calls in the history of sports television.

After forcing the Jets to finish their first possession with a punt, the Colts drove to New York's 19-yard line. But they had to call upon Lou Michaels for a 27-yard field-goal attempt that slid right of the goal posts.

DON MAYNARD: About the third series, Joe and I found a coverage situation. He said, "I'm gonna check off and go for it." I said, "All right. I'll be there." Sure enough, he checked off and I was gone. I was about five yards behind the zone. And the ball was just too long. I just couldn't get to it. I think we only missed about two passes, long passes, in our whole career. And that may have been the only one that I actually kind of dived or really stretched out for where I lost my running balance. I went into a roll almost. That was in the first quarter. Then in the third quarter, we did the same thing. I caught one out of the end zone. But the rest of the game, it scared 'em enough that, from then on, they doubled and tripled me. Joe, he went to Sauer nine times and Lammons five and Boozer three and Mathis a couple. Shoot, I got the day off.

GEORGE SAUER JR.: Some writer later said that was the most important incomplete pass in Super Bowl history, which it was. It set the tone. "Gosh, we can't let Maynard run free." They spent the rest of the game worrying about Don, not knowing that he wasn't at all 100 percent. That was a pretty courageous performance by Maynard, very underappreciated.

The next threat came from Baltimore, driving inside the Jets' 10-yard line as the second period began following a fumble by Sauer. On third-and-four at the 6, Morrall's pass to Tom Mitchell in the end zone deflected off the reserve tight end's shoulder pads and into the waiting arms of New York cornerback Randy Beverly for a touchback.

GEORGE SAUER JR.: We were down on our 13-yard line, and Joe threw me a little turnout. I turned, and Lenny Lyles just knocked the heck out of me.

The ball went dribbling away. That set them up, and they moved in. Morrall threw a pass to Tom Mitchell, and Al Atkinson, our middle linebacker, tipped it with about three molecules at the end of his finger, just enough to send it off course. It went floating up high in the end zone, and Randy Beverly made a tremendous acrobatic interception. He did like a 360 in the end zone and turned back to where the ball was. Those two extraordinarily talented plays got me off the hook.

The Jets then coolly moved downfield primarily on the combination of Snell running over the left side of the offensive line and Namath completing short passes. With a second down and goal to go at Baltimore's 4-yard line, Namath again called what had been working.

MATT SNELL: It was the same play that we had called for the whole series, up and down the field. Weeb called it "19 straight," which meant I had the option to break the play any way I saw it. I would look at Boozer's block through Winston Hill. If Winston blocked his man out, Boozer would lead through on the inside on the linebacker. If Winston hooked his man, Boozer would lead outside. George Sauer ran Lyles off. By the time Mike Curtis got over there, I was in the end zone. I pulled a hamstring going into the end zone, but it wasn't bad. I taped it and continued to play.

JOE NAMATH: Remember I mentioned Lou Michaels playing on short yardage? I peeked out and saw him coming on the field, so I knew what defense they were going to be in. And knowing that, we ran a play to run on my first sound. Matt walked in pretty good.

JACK READER: I was the back judge, one of the officials from the AFL, one of the original AFL officials from 1960. I could see it unfold in front of me. They were sending Maynard and Sauer down on every play and Lammons over the middle. Then they'd run the damn swing passes in the vacated areas right behind the line of scrimmage. The Colts would lay off those wide receivers, and Namath would hit Sauer. Then they started moving back, and they opened up the running game. Then Baltimore was getting tight.

The balance of the half consisted of offensive misplays and frustration. Michaels fanned on another field-goal attempt, from 46 yards. New York's Jim Turner likewise failed from 41 yards. Tom Matte's 58-yard run put the Colts inside the Jets' 20 for the third time, only to have Johnny Sample—a retooled relic from Ewbank's Baltimore championship clubs of the late '50s—snatch the ball out of the air and take a seat at the 2-yard line. The Jets were pinned in the shadow of their own goal post, and Curley Johnson punted away just short of midfield with less than a minute before halftime.

With the Colts at the New York 42-yard line, there was time for only one more play. Morrall handed off to Matte, who appeared to be sweeping around right end. But he abruptly stopped and passed the ball back to Morrall. While this was going on in the backfield, wide receiver Jimmy Orr was racing down the left sideline alone because Jets cornerback Randy Beverly had pulled off his coverage. Morrall, standing at the bottom of the midfield logo, didn't appear to look in Orr's direction. He instead threw for Jerry Hill, who was running from the right side of the field toward the middle around the 10-yard line. Jets safety Jim Hudson cut in front of him, made the interception around the 12-yard line, and was tackled a few seconds later to end the half.

CURT GOWDY: I saw Jimmy Orr in the end zone. There was nobody near him. He was waving his arms and yelling, and there wasn't anybody within 20 or 30 yards of him.

JIM HUDSON: We knew they had the play and could see it all developing. In the man-to-man defense we were in, I immediately dropped off the tight end and onto the running back, Jerry Hill. He had always been one of the primary receivers on the play. The free safety, Billy Baird, picked up the tight end and hollered at me that it was coming. Believe it or not, when you're concentrating, you can really hear your teammates hollering at you over the crowd. When Morrall looked up, I was down on one knee. I was asking for the pass. When he threw it down the middle of the field, everybody came running.

CURT GOWDY: And that was the end of the half. I don't know how Morrall never saw Jimmy Orr. Shula always defended Morrall, saying that the Baltimore Colts band got out of the stands, was going behind the end zone, and their colors blended in.

WALT MICHAELS: People say Jimmy Orr was wide open. I'll take you into plays in every professional football game where a defender will slough off his coverage and a receiver will be wide open. That's fine. Let the quarterback see him every time. This became obvious because the cameras were on the play. There were about five ifs: if Earl was smart enough. If he would have seen it. If he had that much time. Nobody wants to give my cornerback, Randy Beverly, credit for the fact he could run a 4.3 and probably would have been back in time.

CURT GOWDY: Al and I went back to have a cup of coffee in the booth while the bands were all down on the field. I said, "We may have something here." He said, "I told you. The Jets are going to win."

DAVE ANDERSON: I had picked the Jets before the game, when Brent Musburger was taping predictions for his radio show in Chicago. I was writing the lead game story for the *Times*. At halftime, I was back in this room behind the press box. Arthur Daley from the *Times* was there. He was a longtime NFL guy and said this was "unbelievable" or "amazing." And I said, "Not to me."

BUBBA SMITH: They ran at me about three times. At halftime, I said, "Let me go over the center. I can stop Snell from running over there." Shula said, "Just play your fucking position."

JACK READER: At halftime, we went in and said, "This is a hell of a football game. We've got to stay on top of this." The NFL guys said, "Boy, these guys are really, really playing football."

MATT SNELL: We started the second half saying, "We've got to keep scoring, and let's hope they don't put Johnny Unitas in the game." We didn't know how bad his arm was or his shoulder. And Morrall was having a horrible game.

Baltimore wasted little time in falling back into its funk. On the first play from scrimmage following Curley Johnson's kickoff, Matte fumbled at the Colts' 33-yard line following an 8-yard gain. New York was marching toward the end zone until Bubba Smith finally solved the puzzle of Dave Herman and recorded his only sack. The Jets settled for a 32-yard field goal from Turner and a 10-point lead.

The following Baltimore possession epitomized Morrall's frustrations. His first-down pass from the Colts' 26-yard line was thrown over the head of tight end John Mackey. He then connected with Hill, but Larry Grantham stopped the play for no gain. On third down, backup linebacker Carl McAdams chased Morrall into a loss of two yards.

Another conservative Jets drive—conservative, for a quarterback who had thrown for a pro-record 4,007 yards only a season earlier—resulted in another field goal. Turner hit on a 30-yarder. With less than four minutes remaining in the third quarter, America's underdogs led, 13–0.

And Earl Morrall was introduced to the bench. Shula resorted to a sore-armed Johnny Unitas.

JOHN FREE: I was standing on the sideline when Unitas came into the game. Back when I was with Baltimore, we had a favorite expression: "Take us in, John." With his passes to Raymond Berry or Lenny Moore. He was so banged up, and I started reflecting back to all those years and said to myself, "Oh, don't bring him in. All they're going to remember is the last five minutes of his career." Matt Snell was standing about six feet from me and said, "You think if the case would be reversed, he would be saying that about us?" I didn't answer because that's the way you start something.

MATT SNELL: When they decided to go to Johnny Unitas, it just brought you chills. This man had performed miracles. But when he started throwing the ball, we could see he had nothing on it.

Even with Johnny U. trotting his high-tops under center, it was only more of the same as the third quarter gave way to the fourth. Baltimore went three and out; New York followed with a field goal from all of nine yards out for a 16–0 lead. And when Unitas tried to find Orr deep on the next series, Beverly snagged his second interception and the fourth for the New York secondary.

JOE NAMATH: We had a 16–0 lead, and we were conservative. We did not throw one pass in the fourth quarter. I never asked God to help us win a game, never prayed against anybody. But when there was 6:11 on that clock, I started praying: "Try and hurry that clock up a little bit."

The Colts finally put together the kind of march that most fans probably figured they would replicate all day long, though they figured it would have been with NFL Player of the Year Morrall at the helm. An 80-yard drive culminated in Hill's 1-yard touchdown run over left tackle. With darkness having fallen over the Orange Bowl, the clock behind the south end zone coldly reminded the Colts of their daunting task: Make up a 16–7 deficit with only 3:14 to play.

GEORGE SAUER JR.: Unitas scares you enough. I can't say enough about that man. So he drove 'em down there, and they got a score. Then they had an onside kick. I was on the onside-kick-receiving team, the hands team. Lou Michaels hit that thing, clipped it, and it was bouncing toward me like a ground ball on a sandlot. Just as I went down, it bounced up over my shoulders. They got the ball and marched down there, but they didn't score again. I was nervous the whole game.

CURT GOWDY: With a couple minutes to play, they told me in my ear from the truck that there were no commercials, to go ahead. And I said, "Ladies and gentlemen, you're sitting in on one of the most amazing upsets in the history of sports. This game may also change the future of football. If the AFL wins, the fans probably will accept them, embrace them, and there will be a lot of things changed in pro football."

DON WEISS: I've never seen any man look so desolate and defeated as Carroll Rosenbloom looked. He wanted to sit in the press box and sat right among the writers. I wasn't that far away from him, no more than 25 feet away. He was just devastated.

CURT GOWDY: I got heavily criticized for making that statement, but I really was honest about it. When I was a young announcer in Wyoming, I was taught to report the game and don't root. And I always did. They said I was gloating. I wasn't gloating. I was just reporting the facts.

Merle Harmon simply reported the facts as he called out Super Bowl III's final seconds to his WABC radio audience back in New York: "Unitas back to pass. Two seconds. One second. Unitas throwing to Richardson. He has the ball on the 49, brought down by Sample. The clock has run out, and the ball game is over. There is the gun, and the Jets are champions of the football world."

Namath jogged off the field to the locker room, pumping his right index finger high in the air, a scene captured and seemingly replayed in slow motion every January since. He completed 17 of 28 passes for 206 yards, hardly the stuff of statistical lore. Maynard didn't make a single catch. Snell was the offensive workhorse, shouldering a load of 30 carries for 121 yards and New York's only touchdown. Yet to no one's surprise, Namath was voted the game's Most Valuable Player.

MATT SNELL: You knew as long as the press decided who the MVP was, it was going to be Joe. That didn't bother me.

JOE NAMATH: They talk about Matt Snell, who was an MVP in that game. Dave Herman could have been the MVP. Bubba Smith had one sack, and that was because I thought we were running a quick post and George Sauer changed it. If Jim Turner didn't miss two field goals, he'd have been the MVP. And then there was Winston Hill. We did most of our running on his side.

DAVE HERMAN: At six foot eight, when Bubba would get down in his three-point stance, there was a sizable gap between his front foot and his back foot. So I would make contact with him while he was moving that back foot forward to get it in the ground. Basically, I was hitting him when he was on one foot, to take some of that power away from him. We had one play where he got close to Joe, may not have even touched him. I had no clue what the score was. All I thought about was that big number 78 over there.

PETE LAMMONS: Pete Rozelle hated to come down in that dressing room. When he presented the trophy, somebody said, "Welcome to the AFL!" He would rather have taken a beating than do that.

DAVE HERMAN: I put so much effort into that game that, when it was over, I just walked right off the field directly to the locker room. I was so, so, so, so tired. I was mentally and physically totally exhausted. There was Pete Rozelle with the trophy, and I said, "Put it down and get the hell out of here. That's ours."

LAMAR HUNT: Pete Rozelle leaned over to me and whispered, more just to catch my attention: "This is the best thing that could have happened to pro football."

FRANK RAMOS: It took me a long time to talk Joe into talking to the media. He didn't want to talk to what he called the NFL media. He would talk to the Jets writers that he knew and some AFL writers that he knew. Jerry Green from the *Detroit News* was trying to explain: "We're not NFL writers. We're writers from NFL cities." I finally got Joe to talk to all of the media. He talked for 45 minutes to an hour before he even took his uniform off.

JOE NAMATH: The one lasting thing is the feeling, the physical feeling. Emotional, mental, and physical. My body was alive, tickly for God knows how long, that we had won this thing.

GEORGE SAUER JR.: Having been so nervous during the week and during the game, just the sense of relief was my primary emotion. I didn't feel any great sense of elation. When we got back to the hotel, I talked Earl Christy into jumping into the pool with me. I don't think I relaxed until then.

BILL CURRY: It was a nightmare, a funeral. We were all so competitive, Coach Shula most of all. Great football coaches don't handle those things well. Vow to come back. That's about all you can do.

DON MAYNARD: From my standpoint, that was a dream. I wanted to beat the NFL. I never did agree to the merger, still don't today. I always wanted it to be the AFL against the NFL. We won, and then in the locker room, guys were standing around commenting like Talamini, saying, "Now, when you talk football, you can say the AFL in the same breath as you do the NFL." We beat 'em. We did it.

BOBBY BELL: I'll bet you 200-something players from the AFL came in the locker room. I was there. We were like family, man. We all stuck together.

JOHN FREE: I kept saying to Weeb during the week, "After every victory, there's a party." He said, "No! We're not even going to talk party." As soon as that gun went off, he said, "You can go make that party now." I had told the manager of the hotel to be at the phone for my call if we should be so lucky. I told him, "Our owners have more money than they know what to do with. You just keep everything coming, plenty of food, plenty of beer. And try to limit who gets in. I'll be coming with the buses, so there may be people there ahead of time, but don't let 'em in." And we did have a party.

JOHN HADL: I went down to the locker room briefly. Joe told me he wanted to go out with me, hang around a little bit. He finally got out, and we took off. We went out to Sonny Werblin's house and spent the whole night. We had a great time.

JOE NAMATH: We didn't need any party. Winning that game felt so good, you didn't need anything else.

BILL CURRY: We went over to Mr. Rosenbloom's house at Golden Beach. Burt Lancaster was there. Mr. Rosenbloom might have been the most crestfallen of all. We just said, "We'll be back and get this job done for you." And we did that, but it was not to be that day."

BUBBA SMITH: I don't like losing. Some people can lose and say, "We lost the game. Let's go party." I'm not that way. I happened to go over to what was supposed to be a victory party at Rosenbloom's, and people were having a good time. I was asking them, "How the hell can y'all get up and dance when we lost the biggest game of our lives?" That didn't make any sense to me. They asked me to leave. My mother was there. She was trying to explain that I don't drink, that I'd sipped some champagne. I caught a cab back to the hotel 'cause I didn't want my mother to have to leave. The cabbie asked me, "Are you Bubba Smith?" I said, "Yes." He said, "Man, don't be upset. All the smart money was on the Jets."

JOHN ELLIOTT: Most of the team left on Monday morning. I was going to Jacksonville for the AFL All-Star Game. The team had left, and I was in the lobby. Well, there was a big commotion around the front desk. The team had gone and forgotten the Super Bowl trophy. I got it and took it to the airport for the team to take back. That was the only time I touched it. Had my picture taken with it outside the hotel.

DON MAYNARD: It took a while to sink in. We stayed down there and enjoyed things for another day. Then we drove up to Jacksonville and went to the All-Star Game. It was neat. Even our opponents in the other dressing room of the other division—you would have thought they won the game, too.

Guys would come over to you, like Buck Buchanan. I'm just a receiver. He came over and said, "Aw, man." Hugged me. Gee, I barely knew the guy. They were so proud.

WALT MICHAELS: Lou and I didn't see each other again until we were back home. Of course, he was upset. He was a competitor. Anybody on that Baltimore team would probably feel the way that Lou did. I tried not to say a darn word. I don't care if it's my brother or Joe Blow. I don't rub in a victory. The worst thing for a while was Lou seeing the Super Bowl ring. Should have been theirs, he said. I said, "If pigs could fly, they'd crap all over us."

BUBBA SMITH: This might sound a little crazy, but I don't think the game was kosher. In order for the merger to go through, they had to win. If you read the terms of the merger, if they didn't establish credibility by the end of three years, the terms of the merger were null and void. You're talking the difference of millions and billions of dollars. The line opened at 18 and went down to 15 or something like that because a big bet had been placed on the game. And I know where the bet came from. It came from Baltimore, from someone on the team from what I understand.

Hell, we were inside the 20 three times in the first half and came away with no points. A Colts team? Those were interceptions. Even the flea flicker—nobody was within 30 yards of Jimmy Orr. He was the primary receiver, and the quarterback never looked that way. It hadn't happened all year. Then we got in the big game, then it happened. I called out some teammates, in the locker room and at the party. I almost got in a fight. With who? I'll leave that out.

Earl Morrall addressed what he considered the burning questions from Super Bowl III in a book that he coauthored, published later that year. That included the ever popular: why didn't you see Jimmy Orr in the end zone on the final play of the first half? His response: "I should have seen him. Countless people have told me he was wide open. But I had to turn to the right in order to take the pass from Matte, and when I looked up, Jimmy wasn't in my line of vision. Jerry Hill was, and I went to him."

DON WEISS: I don't recall any talk of a fix. I mean, there were a lot of people who lost a lot of bets. And there were a lot of people who were terribly surprised. I don't think any of us were aware of even rumors to that extent.

BILL CURRY: I want to be clear. The Jets definitely deserved to win that game, that I'm not denigrating their ability. They took Matt Snell and those great receivers and a good game plan, they controlled the football and knocked us off the ball. They forced errors on the other side, and we missed some field goals. They deserved to win. I've said that since I came to my senses a few days after.

26

From Super Bowl III to Bachelors III

Ah, to be young and a Jet. After subduing the mighty Colts, steps must have come lighter, the air fresher, each sunrise brighter—especially for those just getting in at sunrise.

Hey, wasn't that "the Four Jets" on with Carson? And what about Joe's latest commercial? Everywhere that New York turned, it seemed to bump into a smiling Jet.

BAKE TURNER: I think it was one of the Jets lawyers that put that group together, the Singing Jets. It was me, Maynard, Matt Snell, and Jim Turner. I can't remember what came first, the commercials or the Johnny Carson show. I sang "Four Strong Winds" and "I Like the Women," a Roger Miller song. Next thing, we started filming that commercial, the Four Jets for Score hair cream. It slowly died out because nobody sang but me.

But behind the guest shots and Noxema ads, America's favorite Fu Manchu mustache was hiding a frown. There was something going on with Joe Namath, beginning only days after the Super Bowl triumph, that threatened his very identity as quarterback of the Jets. It involved his Bachelors III restaurant in Manhattan.

MIKE BITE: After Super Bowl III, Joe was playing in the All-Star Game in Jacksonville, Florida. He called me and said, "These people are here, and they want to talk to you." I went to Pete Rozelle's room, and he gave me photographs of "undesirable" people who are fraternizing the Bachelors III restaurant. I said, "Joe, you know anything?" He said, "I don't know any of these people." The league wanted Joe to sell his interest, cease to be involved. I said,

"That's unconstitutional. I just came from Alabama, where all you people up North are criticizing me and saying, 'Oh, you don't let blacks come in.' What's the difference here? How can Joe say that guy's undesirable?" Joe was really an off-premises owner, anyway.

JOE NAMATH: It was frustrating, like when you were a little kid and you got called to the principal's office. I didn't do anything! They had policies on undesirable people. Who are undesirable people in a restaurant? I don't know.

BILL HAMPTON: I was driving Weeb to pick up Joe. These photographers' cars were chasing me down the street like cop cars. Weeb said, "Turn here! Turn there!" I said, "Holy Jesus! I don't know why I got this job!" I had to dodge press guys, camera guys. Both ways. Picked him up and took him down to the commissioner's office.

JOE NAMATH: I was at the stage that, "It's not right. It's not fair. I'm not gonna do that. I'm not gonna go with that. I'm gonna quit. I'm gonna retire."

PETE LAMMONS: Rozelle thought he had the upper hand in this deal. And he found out: "Oops. It ain't quite as strong as I thought." He misread Joe. Hell, there weren't any more mobsters in that place than there were next door at the shoe shop. We were going in there and having fun.

MIKE BITE: I was coming to Bachelors III one night. Before I got there, Joe and some friends went to Long Island. Some football player was opening up a restaurant. Then I heard on the street in front of Bachelors III before Joe got back that Joe had resigned from football. Now, I was staying with him. I sat there; then, all of a sudden, he told me he had resigned. He was sort of emotional by this point. I know when to shut my mouth; sometimes. I did shut my mouth, say my little prayers, and hope he was doing the right thing. The next morning, he had called a press conference at Bachelors III. As we were going out the door, the phone rang. I answered the phone and heard, "Hello. I wanna speak to Joe. This is Paul Bryant." "Yes, sir." I told Joe, "It's the man." Well, that ain't but one person. Joe came back in and took the call. And Joe told him he was going to do it. Joe did resign.

In a tearful news conference, Namath announced that he had been presented with an ultimatum by Pete Rozelle—sell the interest in what the NFL considered a haven for undesirables or be barred from playing in the league. Namath said he'd rather fight and quit, saying the NFL had no business in his business.

GEORGE SAUER JR.: I had heard about the press conference the night before and was tipsy when I heard about it. I get a little overemotional when I get sloshed, so I guess I started crying. I went to the press conference with a hangover and was talking to Howard Cosell. Cameras were all around, and I said, "Joe looks pretty serious about this. This is not really fair, what Rozelle's doing to him." I had no idea if it was fair or not. So Pete Lammons and Jim Hudson and myself said we weren't going to play, either. Talk about an empty gesture. By the time camp started, we were all there.

PETE LAMMONS: I was trying to negotiate my contract, too. I knew if we didn't have Joe playing, we didn't have anyone else to throw the ball. So I left camp. Throughout all those days, I'd go down to Bachelors III and Hudson would show up. The scope of everything was a little beyond me. If it worked out, fine. If it didn't, fine. A lot of other players probably felt the same way, but they couldn't afford to leave because they were married.

PAT SUMMERALL: Going to Bachelors III and being part of the group waiting to interview Joe I considered a deep insult because I was part of the NFL. But the New York press had adopted him as Broadway Joe. I stood in line to interview him. Wound up being friends. Used to play poker at his house every Thursday night.

MIKE BITE: We were out in Los Angeles where Joe was doing a movie with Kim Darby. When we got back, we understood we had to meet with the Jets and get this thing resolved. Joe, [agent] Jimmy Walsh, and myself got a cab, and the driver said, "Hey, Joe Namath! Tell Pete Rozelle to go to hell!" Two thousand cabs in New York City, and we had to get him?

PETE LAMMONS: Here's the biggest thing in sports, and everybody involved saw these dollar signs going down the drain. Neither one of them wanted to be the one who bowed down. They decided to negotiate behind the scenes.

FRANK RAMOS: I was kept abreast by the NFL. And Joe and I talked on a regular basis, and I was talking with Weeb. I was aware of the comings and goings, like when Joe would meet with the commissioner at his apartment. I was walking a fine line because I certainly wanted Joe to get back in it, and the league was putting their foot down while they were going through their investigation.

JOHN FREE: Camp had started at Hofstra, and Joe wasn't coming to practice. On a Monday, the players' day off, John Sample came over and said to Weeb, "Joe's over at the Meadowbrook Lounge. He'd like to have his ring, and he asked me to pick it up for him." Weeb said, "You tell Joe I'll have somebody bring it to him." He walked down the hallway and said to me, "I want you to take Joe's ring over to him." I said, "Take it over there, to the Meadowbrook?" It was a cocktail lounge. All the players went out there. It was just bulging with people during training camp. So I thought, "I'm going to do this just right." I got the box and took it over. It was dusk, still light out. As I walked toward the door, somebody must have looked out the window and said, "Here comes John Free." 'Cause when I opened the door, you could have heard a pin drop. As I walked the length of that cocktail lounge, which was about 130 feet, the crowd just parted, like Moses did with the Red Sea. I walked up to Joe and said, "I'm sorry I have to give you this ring here. I just wish you had been with us to celebrate everyone getting their rings." Nobody spoke a word. We shook hands, and he just said, "Thanks so much for the ring." What else was he going to say? Of all the guys, he should have been up on a pedestal getting it.

JOE NAMATH: I was sitting in Central Park while the team was out in training camp, watching the world go by. And I thought, "All these people walking around Fifth Avenue, all these people walking around the park—they couldn't care less whether Joe Namath plays football. I'm the only one that cares. And why am I not playing? Because something's not right? Sometimes it's not fair, and you still have to deal with it." But I knew in my heart I was missing it, terribly. So I went back to play. And Mr. Rozelle and I made the deal. I got out of the New York restaurant. That's the only one they were concerned with. We were opening in Boston, Florida, Tuscaloosa, and Birmingham—they couldn't care less. But New York was something they felt I needed to get away from, and I don't blame 'em. I just wanted to play football. I knew I was clean, but I wanted to play football.

PAT SUMMERALL: I thought he'd be back on the field. I don't think anybody thought his retirement was really going to happen.

With the Bachelors III adventure behind them, the Jets set out to prove that their championship performance was no fluke. But they stumbled and nearly lost their first time out as world champions, against—gulp—the College All-Stars before escaping with a 26–24 victory. And they faced the peculiar challenge that possibly the most important game of the season would be a contest in August that wouldn't count in the standings. On August 17, at the Yale Bowl in New Haven, Connecticut, the Jets met the New York Giants for the first time.

FRANK RAMOS: I'm not sure why we couldn't get together the first two years of interleague exhibition play. I know a lot of teams had their games scheduled far in advance. And we never played a home preseason game ever at Shea Stadium because of the baseball season, so I'm sure that complicated things.

WELLINGTON MARA: I don't remember. But for some reason, schedules were made several years in advance.

JOHN DOCKERY: That game was as serious as the Super Bowl. I couldn't believe it. Being from New York, I heard all this, "The Super Bowl was a fluke. The Giants are gonna beat the Jets." Still no respect. There was the NFL, the old establishment, the old guard, money. Joe Willie represented the younger generation—the white shoes and the llama skin rug. The Jets had this beat going on that was in tune with the younger generation. Everyone wanted to do the Giants in.

MATT SNELL: When you went in the bars on the East Side where everyone hung out, everybody said, "Wait'll the Giants get you guys. You think you guys are the world champions? You're nothin' 'til you beat the Giants. And we don't think you can beat the Giants." We heard that all off-season.

JIM HUDSON: We knew most of those guys. You ran into them. They went to the same places, and that made it a more interesting game. We knew they wanted to beat our ass, and we wanted to beat theirs.

DAVE HERMAN: They had policemen with dogs to get us out of the buses at the Yale Bowl. The stadium was Giants-oriented all the way. I played against a rookie, might have been from Princeton. One of the worst football players I'd ever run into. And I thought, "This is the Jets against the Giants? Give me a break."

JOE NAMATH: The Giants certainly deserved the following they had 'cause they had won championships before. We were still the AFL. Weeb took it seriously, and we took it seriously. But we also knew we were a better team. There might have been 80,000 in the Yale Bowl, and 60,000 of 'em had to be Giants fans.

PAUL LEVY: I'm from Hamden, Connecticut, a suburb of New Haven. The game came after my freshman year at Syracuse. I worked games as a rope guard, guarded a rope that separated the lesser seats from the more expensive seats. But I was an AFL fan. The guys I liked were Cookie Gilchrist and the Buffalo Bills and Jim Nance of the Patriots. And Floyd Little, who was from New Haven. A lot of the guys that I had met my freshman year in the dorm were from Long Island and were Jets fans, so I made arrangements that they could work that game, too. The New Haven area had always been for the Giants in football and the Yankees in baseball. People rooted for the Giants and stayed Giants fans. If somebody said, "Gee, the Jets have this guy George Sauer who's really great," people would immediately say, "Yeah, well, Frank Gifford was better." Matt Snell. "Well, Alex Webster was better." The Jets weren't even considered.

Namath had a terrific game as the Jets moved on top early and never looked back. And the star of the day was a Jets rookie, a punt returner from USC named Mike Battle who hurdled Giants punter Dave Lewis en route to an 86-yard touchdown. For the Jets, even basking in the glow of a world championship, they had finally slain the last giant, 37–14.

PAUL LEVY: I had a transistor radio with me. In the fourth quarter, Marty Glickman, the Giants' announcer then, said something like, "If I have to tell you the score, where the hell have you been?"

FRANK RAMOS: Joe was absolutely incredible. The whole team was. I think he was 14 out of 16, and I think one was dropped. And he threw three touchdown passes. And Mike Battle was a rookie who became a cult hero that day. He was a 12th-round draft choice from USC. I made a bet with Paul Zimmerman the day we drafted Battle that he would make the team, and it was satisfying to collect . . . a dollar.

Lou Duva: Mike Battle was one of about six football players that we wanted to bring in, see if they could fight, if they could punch and take a punch. This was when Muhammad Ali was out of boxing. The guy behind it was Rocky Marciano. The whole plan fell apart when Rocky died. I think it would have been a good thing. It would be a good thing today. I'd like to get involved in it.

Joe Namath: Mike was really a piece of work. All of us change a little bit, I guess, when we get a little firewater in us. Mike was just as sweet and straight as can be 'til maybe he started drinking a little bit. Don't dare him to do anything; he would. He started eating glasses and putting holes in the wall with his head. But the team loved him. He did everything on the field. Tried his butt off. Always came to work.

Frank Ramos: The crowd turned quickly. The crowd turned quiet. The most noise was the Giants fans serenading Allie Sherman, the Giants' coach, with "Good-Bye, Allie." And then just a couple of weeks later, Allie Sherman was fired.

Joe Namath: It was fun, yeah, 'cause we won.

27

A Changed Man

The Jets' monumental victory had a direct immediate effect on one other AFL team. A few weeks after Super Bowl III, the Patriots announced that Mike Holovak's term as coach, which included an AFL Championship Game loss in 1963, was over. Boston's search for a successor came down to a pair of assistant coaches who were on the different sides of the field at the Orange Bowl for the Super Bowl—Jets offensive coordinator Clive Rush and Colts assistant coach Chuck Noll. As simplistic as it might sound, New York's victory over Baltimore played a large role in determining the Pats' selection. Surely, there was potential embarrassment in choosing a member of the Colts' staff over a member of the Jets' staff. On January 30, 1969, Boston introduced Clive Rush as the team's new vice president and head coach. And George Sauer Sr. was also brought in from the new world champions, as general manager.

WILL MCDONOUGH: They were waiting to see what happened at the Super Bowl, and then they were going to talk to the two coordinators. The guy they really wanted was Chuck Noll, from Baltimore. The Colts were going to win the Super Bowl. That's who they had their eye on, but Pittsburgh did as well. I think they even interviewed Noll. All of a sudden, the Jets won. Like the wind, they moved right over to Clive Rush, though Joe Namath called every play in Super Bowl III.

You could write a book just on what happened in the year and a half that Clive Rush was in Boston. It was the most bizarre episode ever in the history of pro football. He was almost electrocuted at the press conference when he was introduced.

TOM YEWCIC: They did a press conference out at the airport, got him hooked up. He touched some kinds of wires, and he almost got electrocuted. Unbelievable.

WILL McDONOUGH: I went up to that first training camp at UMass, Amherst. I was clued in by some people: "Hey, this guy's a *really* strange guy." I was taking a walk with Bill Bates, the trainer, at 8:00 or 9:00 at night because there was no air-conditioning in the dorm. Batesie said, "Wait'll you get a load of this guy." I said, "Yeah, I heard he's a little different." "Different? He's a nut!" I said, "What are you talking about?" He said, "You just wait. Just wait and see." The next day, Gerry Moore, the P.R. guy, told me I could go meet with Rush one-on-one at 1:00. I went over and knocked on his door in the dorm. "Come in." I opened the door. Well, you'd have thought you were at the South Pole. Nobody else had air-conditioning in the dorm. He had two big air-conditioning units in there. There were almost Goddamn icicles hanging off. He was sitting behind a table. Got nothing on. Got a towel around his neck. "Hey, Coach. How ya doing?" "Tell you what," he said, "I can't seem to shake this cold." He had a jug on the table. He said, "Hey, wanna taste?" It was like that every day for a year and a half.

LARRY EISENHAUER: The first meeting he had with the players, we had one of those laughing bags. He was trying to talk to us about what he was expecting, and we kept on popping that bag. We kept passing it around the room. He never could find out who had it. He was running up and down the aisles. That exemplified what his whole first year of coaching with the Patriots was about.

Rush's task was to turn around a club that, after threatening to reach the Super Bowl during the 1966 season, had flopped to consecutive 10-loss campaigns. Less than two months after taking over, he made a flurry of trades. One of those trades in particular turned heads around the AFL. In making a trade with Miami, the Patriots acquired quarterback Kim Hammond, linebacker John "Beau" Bramlett, and the Dolphins' fifth-round pick in the 1970 draft. For this, the Patriots relinquished five-time AFL All-Star Nick Buoniconti.

WILL McDONOUGH: The previous year, Nick was a great player, a very outspoken player. The players considered him like the captain of the team. And he often beefed to the coaching staff. So the story went around that when Clive came in, he talked to some of the coaches who coached with the Patriots the year before and one of them said, "If you're smart, you'll get rid of

Buoniconti. He has too much to say on this team. He'll confront you all the time." And Clive didn't like to be confronted by anybody. So, out of the blue, they traded Nick.

Like two days after it happened, I was at Tommy Addison's house helping some players do a brochure for their football camp, part of which Nick owned. He came in and said, "I'm not going to Miami. They stink. That's it. I'm finished. I'm finishing up law school." And all the other players said, "Go down there! You're too young to quit." Eventually, he changed his mind, but he was dead serious.

EDWIN POPE: The new Patriots regime thought Nick was a clubhouse lawyer. Well, he *was* a lawyer. When he first came to Miami, he was pretty morose about the whole thing. Billy Neighbors, a starting guard who came to the Dolphins from the Patriots in the expansion draft, introduced me to Nick in the training room in Boca Raton. Nick looked at me, and I thought, "I don't think I've ever met anybody who wanted to be here any less than this guy."

Clive Rush immediately put his name in the Boston record book . . . at the wrong end. His first Patriots team limped out of the gate with a club-record seven-game losing streak swallowing the first half of the schedule. Brought to Beantown with a reputation as an offensive whiz, Rush watched as his Pats managed more than two touchdowns only once. The only solace was the fact that Boston still had both games against Miami, which reached midseason in barely better shape at 1–5–1, plus a game against the second-year Cincinnati Bengals.

GINO CAPPELLETTI: Finally, we beat Houston. Then we lost to Miami. It's kind of a blank memory, the fact that the team was just so horrendous. We weren't winning. I was still kicking, but my best years were behind me, and things were starting to change in terms of the team and the structure. A lot of the guys that I had played with were gone. You lose a little bit of the camaraderie that you had.

WILL MCDONOUGH: Clive used to say, "Paul Brown's the greatest coach that ever lived. I admire Paul Brown. Paul Brown was All-Ohio—Massillon, Ohio State, Cleveland Browns, Cincinnati." All week, he was talking about Paul

Brown, matching up with Paul Brown. This is what he was telling the players all week long. So, we were at Nippert Stadium. Two hours before a game, Clive liked to go out and walk around, wave. He loved it. His team would be in the locker room and he was sitting on the bench, all by himself. Gino Cappelletti was coming around with the special teams. Clive said, "Gino, c'mon over here. I want to talk to you a minute." Gino ran over: "What's up, Coach?" He said, "Here's what we're going to do today. I don't want to tell the other guys. It's a big surprise. The first time we get in close, we're going to kick a field goal on third down." Gino said, "Wait a minute, Coach. Why are we going to do that?" He said, "Because we're going to destroy Paul Brown's mind. He's a machine. He does everything by the book. And he's going to say what you said: 'Why are they doing that?' I'm going to distract him. I'm going to take him out of his game plan. That's my game plan, to take him out of his game plan." Thank God they never got to do it.

We had a guy named Charley Frazier. Nice kid. Clive used him to send the plays in. So they're standing there, first series, and Clive said to Charley, "OK, Charley, go in there." "Well, what's the play?" "There's no play." "What do you mean, there's no play?" "Charley, do what I tell you! Just run in the huddle, stand there, run back out." Mike Taliaferro was the quarterback. He said, "Where ya going, Charley?" "See you later. I'm going back to the bench." He did this three or four times. Finally, Charley said, "Coach, why am I doing this?" And Clive told him, "That's what Paul Brown's saying. 'Why are they doing this?'" And in the middle of the game, he was telling Taliaferro, "Send Carl Garrett in motion." Mike said, "We don't do that." "Send him in motion!" And we won the game!

BOB GLADIEUX: I was coming in that year from Notre Dame. The organization wasn't real solid. As time went on, it became evident Clive had personal problems. I went down to the final cut. It was the Thursday before the first game of the season. The turk hadn't tapped me on the shoulder, so I thought I made the team. After practice, I went home, called my family, friends. I was elated. Then I saw on the 6:00 news, "Bob Gladieux, final Patriot cut." I said, "What the hell is this?" That literally floored me and broke my heart. The next day, I went in, and there was Clive. He said, "Jeez, Bob. I'm sorry I didn't get to talk to you personally about this. It was a tough decision. I had to make a move. I want you on the taxi squad. I'm sure I'm going to get you right back up on the active roster. But if you don't want to, I've got a guy . . ." he pointed to the phone, and it was blinking. "I've got a guy on hold here from New York who'll take the job if you don't want it." I said, "Coach, I want to play. I'll do whatever you need." I had a $2,000 incentive bonus. He cut me for a week, saved that damn two grand, then brought me back up for the rest of the year and just broke my heart. I played the rest of the year on the kicking game.

DARYL JOHNSON: People accuse Clive of being on the outskirts of sanity. I liked him. The man was a straight shooter. He might have done some things you might consider strange. Like, in Houston, he didn't want to go around the block to get back to the hotel, so he made the bus driver turn the wrong way down a one-way street to get to the hotel. We were playing in San Diego, and he got upset and took us off the field. But, hey, what about Bobby Knight? Clive never threw chairs or helmets. I thought the majority of players played hard for Clive. People were upset that Clive would call this play or that play. It doesn't matter what you call; it matters whether you execute. If you don't block, it's not going to work. We were losing, and Clive always stayed upbeat.

HOUSTON ANTWINE: We knew that he drank a lot, but he was a good coach. He had winning on his mind, and that was what I was all about, so he worked out good for me. I don't know what other kinds of things were going on with him, but he was all about winning.

TOM YEWCIC: That was such a crazy situation when he was in Boston for two years. But I'll tell you this: Clive Rush had a great football mind. Clive was respected as a football coach. He wasn't respected as far as his personal problems were concerned. Once the players got a hold of something like that, they don't come back. They're gone.

WILL McDONOUGH: Clive was unstable. He was mentally ill. He really was. He should have never ever come into Boston to be the head coach. At the end of the first year, they put him in Mass. General. They told him, "Oh, we're gonna send you in for a physical." They were afraid to confront him. They tried to keep him in there for 30 days. Imagine, a physical for 30 days?

28

Changing of the Guard—and Many Other Positions—in Buffalo

For a club coming off pro football's worst showing the previous season, the Buffalo Bills attracted considerable attention going into the 1969 season. Buffalo had become the unlikely coaching oasis for John Rauch, who only a year earlier basked in the glory of a Super Bowl ride in his second season as head coach in Oakland. And the Bills placed themselves in a unique category by becoming the first pro team to draft a black quarterback with the intent of allowing him to play quarterback, James Harris from Grambling State in the eighth round.

But, with apologies to John Rauch and James Harris and most of the other things that were new about the '69 Bills, the show worth watching was the arrival of one Orenthal James Simpson. Buffalo's reward for turnovers and penalties and injuries that left it with a wide receiver starting at quarterback and "buzzard's luck," as Booker Edgerson called it, and everything else that went with a 1–12–1 embarrassment was the opportunity to move to the front of the line in the college draft, where one of the most heralded prospects to come out of college football was waiting. In winning the 1968 Heisman Trophy, O. J. Simpson set the record for the largest margin of victory in the voting in leading Southern Cal to the number four ranking in the country. He nearly took home the statue as a junior and would have become the first player to win it twice. Coming to USC following two years at San Francisco City College, he placed second to quarterback Gary Beban of crosstown rival UCLA despite leading the Trojans to a 21–20 victory over the top-ranked Bruins in one of the more memorable college football showdowns ever en route to winning the national championship.

Simpson was difficult to bring down in the open field and almost as tough to negotiate with in the open market, even in the climate of a common draft.

He and his agent, Chuck Barnes, opened the bidding with a package that included a $500,000 loan from the Bills to be paid back over four or five years. The head butting had officially commenced. Before it was over, there was a demand for $1 million over 10 years, a threat to sit out the entire season, a seemingly serious offer to sign with the Indianapolis Capitols of the Continental Football League, and—after missing camp and the first two exhibition games—an agreement to sign a four-year contract worth $250,000 in salary plus a $150,000 loan to be paid off in four years. Barnes actually indicated to Simpson that, while the deal wasn't what they wanted, a prolonged holdout could damage O.J.'s other nonfootball deals that could be added to a list that already included Chevrolet, Royal Crown Cola, ABC, and a role in an episode of CBS's *Medical Center* playing Bru Wylie—a pro football star in danger of forfeiting a huge bonus because of a mysterious disease. The deal was signed August 9, and two days later Buffalo mayor Frank Sedita met O.J. at the airport and presented him with the key to the city.

RALPH WILSON: O.J. wasn't happy about coming to Buffalo anymore than Jack Kemp was. When his agent mentioned the $500,000 loan, I said, "What do you want that for?" He said, "Well, so O.J. can buy stocks." And I said, "Well, we're not a bank here. Let him go down to the bank and borrow the $500,000."

JOHN RAUCH: There was a kid that was a halfback, Gary McDermott, who wore the jersey 32, O.J.'s number in college. Our P.R. man was the first to approach me: "O.J. has gotta wear 32. We've got to tell this guy . . ." I said, "I'm not doing that. I don't work that way."

RON McDOLE: He didn't come in acting like he was God. Everybody thought O.J. was going to demand to have his number. He said, "No, I'll take any number." So they gave him 36. But it didn't take them long to get rid of Gary McDermott.

ED ABRAMOSKI: O.J. had a big head—really. They used to call him Big Head or Water Head. That was only his close friends who could do that. We had to get his helmet from USC 'cause we couldn't get one in fast enough from Riddell.

Jack Kemp: He was treated like everybody else, except by the fans. He was a rock star. He wasn't garish. He was modest. A really good guy. Everybody liked him.

Billy Shaw: I looked at O.J. the same way I looked at Cookie and Jack when they came. He was an excellent, excellent player who could get us out of the hole, get us started again. In training camp, he took the regular rookie abuse from mature veterans. He was an excellent teammate.

Mike Stratton: It moved along really better than I expected. He kept a low enough profile that I think things started out very well. He was cognizant enough to what was going on to not be the be-all and end-all and the say-all of the team.

Booker Edgerson: We roomed together that year and ran the streets and did a lot of things together. He didn't like my attitude to the game, which he wrote in his rookie book—which we didn't know anything about at the time. My attitude was, you play the game the best you can while you're doing it and you go back home 'cause you can't play forever. He later said he didn't know what I was thinking then. He thought my attitude was bad because I had no expectations to do other things, that I would go back home to Rock Island and teach school or whatever.

Simpson missed the Bills' first two exhibition games before trotting out in the number 36 jersey for a game at Tiger Stadium in Detroit. His pro debut featured four carries for 19 yards in a 24–12 loss to the Lions. Three more exhibition defeats followed, including a homecoming at the L.A. Coliseum in which the Bills lost to the Rams 50–20 and O.J. collected 20 yards on five carries.

The yards behind the Buffalo offensive front didn't initially come as easily to O.J. as they had when he was behind the escort of John McKay's Student Body Right with the Trojans. In his regular-season debut against the new world champions, the Jets, O.J. carried 10 times for a modest 35 yards in a 33–19 New York victory. The year proved to be something of a moral victory for the Bills—improving from 1–12–1 to 4–10—yet a frustration for football's new royalty. He broke the 100-yard mark only once, collected 697 rushing yards and one concussion that forced him to sit out a game, and was never anointed the offensive workhorse in John Rauch's offense.

RON MCDOLE: The first thing O.J. ever did that I didn't like was when he got hurt, tore his knee up, he went home. We never had anybody go home in the middle of the season. A lot of players didn't like that. I think O.J.'s biggest problem when he came in was we didn't have the greatest offensive line. When you play in college, you probably play against three or four great players a year, if that. You don't play the same grade of competition that you run into in pro football every week. He was used to having holes blown out. He never really learned to set up blocks, get a defensive lineman to think he's going into that hole, commit on that side so the block would be easier and veer over into the other hole. So he didn't have much success, and that drove him crazy.

JOHN RAUCH: O.J. wanted to strictly be a running back. I failed to convince him that in pro football you've got to block for the quarterback, for the other back, get out of the backfield and catch a pass every once in a while. In Oakland I had Clemon Daniels, Charlie Smith, Pete Banaczak—they all did those things, and I expected him to do it. So he and I didn't get along—because of that, not because of a personality thing.

BUTCH BYRD: Nothing that John could do with O.J. could make that work. I could never figure that out. You've got this talent, maybe the best back since Jim Brown. John came out to practice one day and decided he was going to move O.J. to wide receiver. I said, "We are in deep shit. If that's the answer, we are in deep trouble."

The transition into the Rauch regime was an awkward, fractious process with many of the familiar faces from the glory days of 1964–65 moving on. Elbert Dubenion and Tom Sestak retired. Tom Janik was traded to Boston. And the preseason releases and camp cuts included Ed Rutkowski, the 1968 team MVP who bailed out the club by moving to quarterback, and Tom Day, the popular defensive end from North Carolina A&T whose grit and determination to play pro ball despite the assumptions of others could be found in the fact that he was assigned four uniform numbers during his eight-year stay in Buffalo. And even Rauch's mere presence in Buffalo, walking away from Oakland after producing two first-place teams, created questions.

JOHN RAUCH: I'm a football man, and I thought the basics of what Al Davis offered were good. I have a great appreciation for Davis's recommending me for the head-coaching job with the Raiders. But I got the feeling that he was trying to hold me back, and certain things happened that, when I found out about them, aggravated the heck out of me. So I made up my mind that I was going to leave as soon as I could. There were three jobs that came open—the Boston Patriots, Buffalo Bills, and Pittsburgh Steelers. Dan Rooney called me from Pittsburgh and said that he was interested. When I told him that I had another year to go on my contract, he kind of backed off. Ralph Wilson asked if I would be interested, and I said I would. I never got around to talking to anybody with Boston. My preference was Buffalo because I felt that I knew more about their personnel. I went in to Al and told him that I was leaving. He said, "Well, you know you've got another year to go on your contract." I said, "Yeah, I know that. But this thing is not working out for you or for me, and I think it's best that I move on." He said, "The only way I'll let you go is wherever you go, they pay a restitution for you. After all, you're taking a lot of knowledge from here." I said, "Al, if you stand in my way, I'll tell the news media everything I know about you." He said, "Say no more." And that was it.

The Bills had won championships a couple of years before. Players were getting old. I was letting some of them go. They were unhappy. I knew we had age and some guys were not performing as they had before. I was doing what I thought was the proper thing to do. When I played pro football, I got waived myself, and I thought the coach was a bad guy.

RON McDOLE: We had kind of a pipeline into Oakland and heard John was kind of difficult to work with. But we figured, here's a guy who's winning, and maybe he didn't like Al Davis. John came in, and he didn't trust anybody. You always got the feeling that he thought everybody was against him, all behind his back trying to plot this little scheme. And it got worse and worse and worse. We were just miserable getting through the first year.

MIKE STRATTON: He'd say, "We did it this way" when he was at Oakland. Well, I didn't like that worth a shit. And I didn't like it when he told one of our linemen, "You need to do something like this. This is the way Keating does it." He had a system, and he was going to make sure that the players fit into that. He was not going to develop any kind of system around the players. If you didn't do it the way his system said to do it, you were worthless to him.

Butch Byrd: O.J. came in in 1969, and Al Cowlings came in from USC in '70, both first-round draft choices. At that time, I still had a big mouth. John Rauch's style was to give quizzes on game plans. Then pages were graded, and John would come in and talk about the marks. One day John came in and was beside himself. He said something like, "I want to talk to you about these exams. The lowest mark on the exam was . . ." whatever the number was ". . . and it was O.J. And the lowest number on the defensive exam . . ." whatever it was ". . . was Al Cowlings'." They were sitting one row ahead of me, and I said, "Well, it was a damn good thing you guys played football at USC 'cause it's very clear you didn't go to class." So O.J. turned around and said, "What did you say?" The whole room got quiet. I could feel the blood rising. And I said it again. And O.J. said, "I'll see you after this meeting." I said, "Fine." The meeting took two hours. I didn't hear a word of it. I was thinking, "How did I get myself into this?" People don't realize O.J. was six two, 215. I was that big, and I wasn't sure I could whip him. Even if I did, it was going to be more of a tie, so I'm going to get hit. The defense got out first. Then the offense got out, and O.J. had his books. He was a good 50 yards away. Someone said, "There's Butch." He handed his books to whoever he was talking to. Instead of taking this path to the parking lot, he came across the grass directly toward me. I thought, "Son of a bitch, you're in it now." He came over and said, "Butch, I just want to apologize. I'll do better on the exam next time." And he turned around and walked away. I got in my car and said, "Thank you, Jesus!"

It wasn't like he was up here and the rest of the team was down there. Nice guy. We had the team over for Thanksgiving dinner. He came, nonassuming. I've never, ever seen anyone that good. He practiced with such ease, just ran around. Everyone else would be sweating. I have nothing bad to say about O.J.

James Harris's celebrated rookie season was short and far from sweet. He started the opener against New York but left early with a groin pull. From that point, he was unable to reclaim the position from Jack Kemp. And, in the horrendous 50–21 loss at Oakland in the sixth game, Harris's season ended with a knee injury soon after tossing his first touchdown pass as a pro. He threw passes in only four games, completing 15 of 36 passes for 270 yards. Some, ironically, went to Marlin Briscoe, who had made headlines as a black quarterback in Denver the previous year but was traded to Buffalo and made into a receiver.

MARLIN BRISCOE: James was extremely intelligent and gifted. I told him exactly what was going to happen to him. It was kind of hard for him to listen to what I had to say, but he was going to face a different type of racism. You see, James quarterbacked at an all-black college. I had a different mindset at an all-white college. It wasn't culture shock to me. He was real quiet. They thought he didn't have that outwardly cocky attitude that a quarterback should have.

JAMES HARRIS: I followed Marlin's career and what happened. When you saw a guy play well, then you hear that he's not going to be that team's quarterback of the future, you knew there were still some reservations. Once I got to camp, the NFL game was a learning process. I think I started as the sixth quarterback. I was confident in my ability, and I moved up the depth chart. It was exciting because it was something that hadn't been done before.

BILLY SHAW: If there was talent there, we didn't care if you were red, white, blue, or green. That wasn't an issue. He had a lot of talent. He could throw the ball for a mile.

JAMES HARRIS: Then came the Oakland game. I got hit by two guys, Ben Davidson and Ike Lassiter. It was pretty conclusive. I was out for the season.

MARLIN BRISCOE: In those days, they were categorizing us. I was the first black quarterback to start a game. He was the first to start a season. Instead of saying we were quarterbacks, there was always some kind of asterisk behind it.

29

A Fitting Finale

The AFL's final season appeared to come down to the same teams that dominated the '68 campaign—New York, Oakland, and Kansas City. And a new playoff format that would allow the top two teams in each division to advance—it gave the AFL two weeks of playoffs to match the NFL, which had advanced four division winners starting in 1967—seemingly paved the way for the Jets, Raiders, and Chiefs to reach the postseason.

For Kansas City, embarrassingly turned away from the 1968 AFL Championship Game through the 41–6 Western playoff loss at Oakland, the schedule presented an additional challenge. The Chiefs opened with four road games, though the opener at San Diego was followed by dates at lightly-regarded Boston, Cincinnati, and Denver. Nothing was taken for granted, despite a typical Stram preseason during which Kansas City reeled off a 6–0 record, when disaster appeared to have struck at B.C. Alumni Stadium.

HANK STRAM: We were playing in Boston, and we beat 'em. Lenny Dawson went into the game with a bad thumb from preseason. At the end of the game, he went in to hold for a field goal and hurt a knee. I didn't even know about it until we got on the plane. I didn't think it was that serious. Well, the next morning, the team doctor called and said, "I've got some bad news. We've got to operate on Lenny Dawson right now. He's got a ligament problem." I said, "Well, what other doctors can we send him to, to make sure of what the problem is?" We sent Lenny to a doctor in Oklahoma, who said, "If I think he needs an operation, I'll operate on him right then and there." I said, "Nope. You look at him carefully and then you call me." There was a Dr. Reynolds in St. Louis that I asked to come through Kansas City on his way home from a convention and meet me in my office and take a look at Lenny. I had a conference table in my office. Lenny was sitting on the table, eye to eye with the doc. Doc Reynolds said, "Leonard, you don't need an operation.

You just do what I tell you to do, and in six weeks you'll be able to play again."
So that's what we did.

Well, there were a few kinks that befell Stram's plan. His interim replacement
for Dawson was veteran Jacky Lee. That setup lasted less than a full game
because Lee broke a leg the next week in a loss to the second-year Bengals.
Having to resort to second-year player Mike Livingston, Stram hastily bolstered his stock at the position by signing veterans Tom Flores and John
Huarte. Livingston, though, played admirably as Kansas City stabilized and
stayed within striking distance of first-place Oakland. At midseason, Dawson was back in uniform and at the ready as Livingston took the Chiefs to a
6–1 record, one-half game behind the 6–0–1 Raiders.

Jacky Lee: After Mike Livingston took over, we had a very limited offense.
Our defense all of a sudden came alive. We had three great linebackers—
Willie Lanier, Bobby Bell, and Jim Lynch. On the line, we had Jerry Mays,
Buck Buchanan, Curley Culp, Aaron Brown. Aaron had not done anything
in pro ball until that last half of 1969. Defensive backs, we had Jim Marsalis,
Willie Mitchell and Emmitt Thomas and Jim Kearney and Johnny Robinson.
It doesn't get any better than that.

The second half of the Chiefs' season began at Buffalo, and Stram elected to
insert Dawson late in the game's opening half with the Bills owning a surprising 7–3 lead. The veteran rallied his teammates to a 29–7 victory that,
when coupled with Cincinnati's upset of Oakland, put the Chiefs in first place
in the division. Victories the next two weeks at home against the Chargers and
in a highly touted matchup of division leaders at Shea Stadium in New York
allowed Kansas City to clinch a playoff berth by mid-November. One negative through the seven-game winning streak was the death of Dawson's father
two days before the game in New York. Even in the face of family tragedy,
Dawson decided to go ahead and play. The final four weeks would determine
whether the Raiders, still clinging a half game behind, could catch the Chiefs.
The rivals were scheduled to meet in the next game, at Kansas City, and in
the season finale in Oakland.

Chiefs-Raiders act I was a nightmare for Dawson. He threw five interceptions, yet Kansas City held its own for most of the game. A last-minute field

goal by George Blanda gave Oakland a 27–24 victory and first place in the West. Each team won the following week, K.C. defeating Denver in a Thanksgiving Day game at Municipal Stadium in which Dawson aggravated the knee injury. Stram held his starter out of the next game, a 22–19 squeaker over Buffalo in which Jan Stenerud kicked the last of his five field goals with 1:59 to play.

That left the K.C.–Oakland rematch out on the coast. The winner would take the division and a home playoff date against Houston, standing 5–6–2 going into its final game. The loser would get reservations for New York to play the defending Super Bowl champs. Stram, proud to call himself one of pro football's top innovators, came up with one of his most unusual and controversial game plans.

HANK STRAM: I decided to go primarily with a ground game, passing only a minimum. I didn't want to take a chance at losing Lenny. Win or lose, we were still in the playoffs.

LEN DAWSON: I threw the ball only six times. We tried to win, but they were halfway protecting me by not throwing too many passes.

TOM KEATING: They ran out of this "four I." They had Lenny, a tight end, a fullback, and a tailback. They were just banging me in the middle all day and giving the ball to Mike Garrett. We won, but I took a hell of a beating.

That afternoon at the Oakland–Alameda County Coliseum, the Chiefs ran the ball 48 times to go with the aerial assault of six passes for 29 yards. That conservative approach succeeded in keeping Dawson in one piece and nearly won the game. Oakland grabbed a 10-point advantage and held on for a 10–6 decision to win the division with an impressive 12–1–1 record. The Chiefs, at 11–3, would presumably have to win at New York and Oakland to claim another AFL title and a second shot at a Super Bowl ring.

Shea Stadium's design—circular but open beyond the outfield end of the structure—made it a merciless place in which to try to pass or kick a football amid the winds coming off Flushing Bay in late December. The result was often politely called a defensive battle, as was the case when the Chiefs went into the fourth quarter of their playoff game with the Jets leading 6–3.

But a Shea crowd that was even larger than the gathering that witnessed the Jets win the '68 league title had every reason to stand and cheer in anticipation of another trip to the AFL Championship Game. First-and-goal at the Kansas City 1-yard line will do that. Would the K.C. season end with yet another 10–6 defeat?

MATT SNELL: We had four downs to get the ball in, but they knew we couldn't run the ball. Randy Rasmussen had twisted a knee. We didn't have Bob Talamini anymore. Back in the preseason, his wife had a car accident and he went to Weeb to ask for $10,000 to maintain a home in Houston with someone looking after his wife. Weeb refused, and Bob retired. So, with Randy hurt, Weeb had to send in Pete Perrault, who had bad knees. On third down, they had Joe roll out to the right, toward Bobby Bell, with the option of running or throwing a little dunk pass.

JOE NAMATH: Bobby Bell was not supposed to be there. You look at the films, he reacts a certain way. We faked the pitch, faked the handoff inside. Usually, he'd come back inside, but he didn't. He stayed out there.

BOBBY BELL: It looked like the same play, but Joe kept the ball. He kept the ball! I was looking at him going, "Hey, Joe!" He went, "Bell! What are you doing here?"

MATT SNELL: Now, if you were Bobby Bell, great athlete that he was, and Joe was rolling toward you, what would you do? You would take away the pass and make Joe run. You can always come up and tackle Joe 'cause he couldn't run. So Bobby played the ball heads up, strung it out.

New York had to settle for a seven-yard field goal from Jim Turner to tie the score at 6–6. The score wasn't tied for long.

LEN DAWSON: While that was happening, Otis Taylor came to me and, in the dirt, was diagramming a pattern that he thought he could run when we were in a particular formation. "This free safety has to guard me man-to-man. I can run a crossing pattern or a post pattern on him." We were running on the field, and Otis said, "You going to call that play?" I said, "Not 'til we get in the huddle. I want the rest of the guys to hear." I'll be damned, he was right. He went deep. I released the ball. I thought I'd overshot him by 10 yards. He had different gears than most people. He caught up with it, took it inside the 20. The next play, we scored a touchdown.

The Jets had two remaining opportunities to reclaim the lead. Namath threw 20 passes total, the drives resulting in one loss on downs and an interception by Marsalis. The New York Jets would not be the next Green Bay Packers. Their Super Bowl winning streak ended at one.

JIM TRECKER: The locker room was the quietest one I've ever been in. Dead still. A lot of shock because we should have won that game. You know, shoulda, coulda. Didn't. You just couldn't believe it was all over. We had gone 10 and 4, had a heck of a good season, and just came up short.

JOE NAMATH: I had said years earlier to Mr. Werblin: "You have race horses. If it's a muddy track and your horses don't run well in the mud, you don't run 'em, right? We've got the best passing attack in the league and the worst stadium to do it. Why don't we close that end of the stadium?" He smiled and looked at me and said, "It would cost more money to close that end than it did to build this stadium." It was a four-way wind, basically. Now and then, you'd catch a decent day. The Raiders game where we won the championship, the Kansas City playoff game—both those games were played in 20-degree temperatures with 40-mile-per-hour winds. It was a bitch.

MATT SNELL: For us, the end started back in preseason when Weeb wouldn't give Bob Talamini $10,000.

The following day, the other half of the AFL championship matchup was settled when the Raiders dominated the Oilers 56–7. Daryle Lamonica threw for six touchdown passes through the first three periods, while Oiler Pete Beathard's only scoring toss was a 57-yard interception return by Oakland defensive back George Atkinson. A Houston team that relied primarily on its defense to fashion a .500 record—good enough for second place in the weak Eastern Division—was left in shambles. The Oilers' only hope was to lock the Raiders in a defensive struggle, a hope that was long gone before the teams changed ends after the first period.

The Chiefs were headed back to Oakland, where they had last won in their Super Bowl season of 1966. There would be no saving Dawson for a future date. The last championship game in AFL history saw Kansas City try to become the league's only three-time champ, counting its triumph as the Dallas Texans in 1962, and the Raiders playing for the title for the third consecutive season despite changing coaches from John Rauch to John Madden. The winner would earn a trip to the first Super Bowl game to be played in New Orleans, coming the next Sunday instead of following a week's break.

TOM KEATING: John [Madden] had been the linebacker coach the year before. We had players older than him—Blanda, Cannon. Everything else was the same—the rest of the coaches, the players. But John was good. John was fun. The thing about him was, the rules weren't the same for everybody. He would allow for people's little foibles. You never had any rules about where you sat on the plane, what you had to wear, or anything else. He just wanted to make sure that everybody played. Show up for games. Be on time for meetings. Don't get arrested. He was not only a good coach but also a bright guy. John sometimes gives the impression that he's the guy who's been hanging around the bar. He was a psychology major in college, a very good student. No fool.

MICKEY HERSKOWITZ: Al Davis called me up and said, "I want you to do something for me. I want you to write a column about my coach," who happened to be John Madden. "He's the best coach in pro football, and nobody knows him." I said, "Al, nobody's *going* to know him as long as you're there. Everybody thinks you're pulling all the strings." I did plan to do a column on John, but Madden couldn't care less, and I don't think I ever got him on the phone.

BEN DAVIDSON: Rauch didn't appreciate the little goings-on other than football, but Madden loved that kind of stuff. One day in the Coliseum, they were switching over between baseball and football, and they had these movable metal bleachers. There was a big chunk of metal that they hadn't bolted on way up on the top of the stairs on the aisle, and there was a long rope there. So I went up before practice and tied a rope onto this chunk of metal then ran the rope down. It was pretty heavy, so I needed someone to help me. So Tom Keating and I . . . Well, practice went on, and we went over and got the rope and said, "Let's do it." We grabbed the rope and started dragging this piece of metal down the stairs. It was just so noisy: *clang, clang, clang, clang.* All the way down. We probably should have stopped halfway, but we pulled it all the way down. Some poor workers had to carry it back up. Anyway, Madden thought that was just great, all this noise: "Look at 'em! They're nuts! They're ready to play!"

Hank Stram thought his team might be more ready to play than he had even anticipated when the club left for California, thanks to an anonymous phone call that he received at the Mark Hopkins Hotel in San Francisco.

HANK STRAM: I got a call in my suite: "Hey, Coach. I've been a great fan of the Chiefs. My wife and I went to a tavern last night. Adjacent to my booth were two guys talking about the upcoming game. They were talking about game plans. I walked away from where we sat so I could look in the booth and see who they were. Coach, it was Daryle Lamonica! He was drawing plays. Then they got up and left, and he took all that stuff he was writing down and threw it in the garbage can as he was walking out the door. So I waited 'til the right time, and I grabbed that stuff. I thought it might be good for you to have." I said, "Oh, no. That's not necessary. Just come by and get some tickets." He said, "As long as I'm coming by, I'll drop this stuff off for you." I told a friend to pick up the stuff from the guy: "Open the door. Give him the tickets." He came by, and the stuff looked legitimate.

DARYLE LAMONICA: It just isn't true, but it makes for a good story.

Oakland struck first on a 3-yard touchdown run by Charlie Smith following a 24-yard pass from Lamonica to Warren Wells late in the first period. Kansas City answered late in the half when Wendell Hayes bulled over from the 1. The Raiders had opportunities to pull away in the third quarter yet came away empty each time. Oakland's initial possession of the second half reached the K.C. 31-yard line, but Blanda misfired on a 39-yard field-goal attempt. The Raiders quickly returned to offense when Keating recovered a fumble by Mike Garrett at the Chiefs' 33 on second down following the kickoff. The drive deflated after Johnny Robinson broke up a pass, injuring his ribs in the process, and after Lamonica had to briefly leave the game when he hurt his passing hand on the helmet of Kansas City's Aaron Brown. Again, Blanda came in for a field goal try; again, he missed, this time wide right from 40 yards. And Oakland's last venture deep into Kansas City territory ended when Emmitt Thomas intercepted a pass in the end zone. He gamely eschewed the idea of downing the ball for a touchback that would give the Chiefs possession at the 20 but made it out only to the 6.

An incompletion and a four-yard loss left the Chiefs on their 2 facing third-and-14. While not as desperate as having the Jets on their 1 as in the previous game, the Chiefs were staring down the possibility of the season imploding. Then Dawson eluded the rush and found Otis Taylor at the 35-yard line to continue a drive that ended with fullback Robert "the Tank" Holmes scoring on a five-yard run for an improbable 14–7 Kansas City lead with only a few minutes remaining in the third period.

LEN DAWSON: NFL Films called that one of the best throws and catches. They had us backed up. We hadn't been able to move at all. It was third-and-long. I was throwing out of the end zone. If we had to punt, they were going to have great field position. Otis Taylor made a phenomenal catch on our sideline that I think Al Davis to this day thinks he might have stepped out of bounds. That was *the* big play.

Lamonica returned, and the Kansas City defense was called upon to make numerous stops for the balance of the game, in part because of Chiefs turnovers. Jim Kearney intercepted Lamonica in K.C. territory, but Holmes gave the ball right back with a fumble. Jim Marsalis answered with an interception, but Holmes fumbled again. The secondary responded yet again, Thomas intercepting at the Kansas City 20 and racing all the way to the Oakland 18. Jan Sterenud's 22-yard field goal with 4:40 remaining in the fourth quarter forced the Raiders into a situation in which they would have to score twice to negate the Chiefs' 17–7 advantage. Kansas City actually gave up the ball one more time on a fumble, but Oakland failed to muster another scoring drive. Four lost fumbles for the Chiefs, four interceptions of Lamonica, and Kansas City was headed back to the Super Bowl.

LEN DAWSON: Our guys kept intercepting, and we kept fumbling. Johnny Robinson came off the field one time and said, "Damn it. If you guys fail us this time, don't bother to come out the next time we take over. We'll handle it."

BOBBY BELL: After we beat the Jets, we looked at each other—the defense, the offense: "Hey, there's no way we're going to be denied the championship."

Everybody was healthy. Everybody was strong. We went out there and just ran the ball on 'em. Coach Stram just said, "There's no way these guys can move the ball on you. We're just going to take five yards, four yards, three yards at a time and wear 'em down." And that's what we did.

DARYLE LAMONICA: About the start of the third quarter, I was throwing to the left side, and on the follow through I caught Aaron Brown on the helmet and dislocated my right thumb. I tried to ice it down and go with it, but I really couldn't. I shouldn't have been in. I couldn't even grip a football, and I was trying to palm it. You bust your butt and you work hard for all your league games to make it to the big game and get an injury. That's devastating.

JIM OTTO: I felt we were betrayed by the officials. One time, I think it was Otis Taylor who ran out of bounds and came back in to catch the ball. Another time, Kent McCloughan was called for interference and it really wasn't interference.

TOM KEATING: The first series, they ran a reverse and I tackled a guy in the backfield. The second series, I recovered a fumble. The third series, I got hit in the nuts on the sidelines and my mother thought I tore up my knee again. On defense, we seemed to be doing very well. We always figured you hold 'em under 20, you win the game. But our offense just couldn't do anything. It was a shock. I was ready to go to the Super Bowl again.

BILL GRIGSBY: The Raiders players were so sure they were going to win, that they were going to leave for New Orleans after the game, they had all their bags at the stadium. We were sitting on the bus after the game waiting to go to the airport. Here came all the Oakland players out of the stadium with their bags, heading home.

As if scripted as the closing act in a 10-year morality play, the team owned by the AFL's founder would represent the league for the fourth and last time in the interleague Super Bowl. Lamar Hunt's Kansas City Chiefs were double-digit underdogs, similar to the victorious Jets of a year earlier, when they faced the Minnesota Vikings at New Orleans' Tulane Stadium on January 11, 1970. Adding to Kansas City's burden was a report on NBC's *Huntley-Brinkley Report* on the Tuesday before the game that the Chiefs' star quarterback, Len Dawson, was linked to a Midwest mobster named Dawson. The report had actually been delayed for a couple of days and quickly became the talk of New Orleans, especially since the game was thought to be a runaway for a Minnesota team led by its "Purple People Eaters" pass rush.

HANK STRAM: When I got off the plane in Oakland for the game with the Raiders, Mark Duncan from the league office came over and said, "You can't ride the bus. You've got to ride with me to the hotel." I said, "What's up?" He said, "Terrible news. There's a big story coming out of Detroit that Len Dawson was involved in a betting scandal with another guy by the name of Dawson. We've got to talk. This story's going to break." I said, "Well, I don't believe it. I'll talk to Lenny and get the information as to what his relationship was with that guy." Lenny told me, "I met him when I was in Pittsburgh with Bobby Layne, met him one time. Then, during this season, he called me when I hurt my knee to see how I was. And he called me again when my dad died and offered condolences." So I told Duncan about it. He went off, made some calls, came back, and said, "I've got some great news. The deal is, they're not going to release the story."

There was no week off between the AFL Championship Game and the Super Bowl. We went back to Kansas City for a day, then left for the game on Tuesday. When we got off the bus from the airport in New Orleans, the story about Lenny had broken. Mark Duncan said, "The press is going to ask you all kinds of questions, but don't let them ask about anything other than the Super Bowl." I said, "Mark, if he doesn't talk about it, people are going to think he's guilty. I'm going to have a press release all set tonight, and we're going to have all the media in there." I talked with some of my good friends in the media—Joe McGuff from Kansas City, Bob Roesler in New Orleans, four or five guys whom I had confidence in. I asked them what they thought. They said, "That's a great idea." Mark Duncan passed along that Pete Rozelle said, "Tell Hank that if he's going to do that, that's his responsibility. We're not involved with it. It's the wrong thing."

LEN DAWSON: We stayed at the Fontainebleau Hotel and practiced at some school park. Early in the week, Hank Stram informed me that somebody was going to make some sort of a statement about me on NBC news that evening. In those days at the Super Bowl, hell, the reporters were knocking on my door wanting a statement. I said, "Hold on here a second." I went to Hank's room.

The team was trying to determine how to handle the media, brought in some people in the media. I said, "Why don't we tell them the truth? I do know the guy, hadn't seen him in years. He did call me when my father passed away during the season when I was hurt to offer his condolences. That's all I know about the guy." Bookie? Hell, I had no idea whether he was a bookie.

That was the top story all week. It was fortunate that the Super Bowl game that year was the week right after the championship game. There would have been *two* weeks of that stuff. That would have been really murder. It was tougher on my family. I was isolated at the hotel plus practicing. But my family had to go through it when they went to the grocery store, when the kids went to school.

HANK STRAM: Lenny came down to talk to the press on that Tuesday night, and we had his speech all set up for him. Our P.R. guy and I wrote the thing for him. The players had already gone to bed. The next morning, we had a team breakfast, and I wanted to get a reaction from them. I said, "We had a meeting last night. Lenny gave his story. It's in the paper. Does anybody have any questions?" E. J. Holub, our loudmouthed guy, said, "Yeah, I've got some questions, Coach. What time are we gonna eat, and when do we get our game tickets?" They all laughed like hell.

BOBBY BELL: Players got up and said, "Hey, Lenny. We understand what you just said. We've got to put that behind us. We're going out there and playing ball. We discussed it. We're not going to talk about it anymore."

Betting and wagering eventually took a backseat to blocking and tackling in the pregame coverage. The most pressing news on the injury front was whether Johnny Robinson—a Louisiana native and a team mainstay since the old Dallas Texans played before friends, relatives, and barbers with discount coupons—would heal quickly enough to play.

JOHNNY ROBINSON: I never practiced for the Super Bowl. I tore my ribs loose in the championship game against Oakland. I went up to knock down a pass, had my arms up. The referee hit me on a dead run down the sideline as I was coming down, butted me right in the ribs. With no extra week before the Super Bowl, I went to see the orthopedic people with the New Orleans Saints. They said, "You can't play." They then took me to a thoracic surgeon, and I told the guy, "If you can deaden this pain, I can play. No one else has played safety in 10 years for this team, and here's the biggest game. What can we do?" He injected me from the ribs all the way to my spine with this Novocain. He used a whole bottle. On that Saturday, it was the first time I had been in a locker room all week, first time I'd even talked about playing.

LEN DAWSON: Johnny Robinson was my roommate on the road. The day before the game, he said, "OK, I've heard the coaches. I've watched the film. I've read the newspapers. What about the Purple People Eaters? Can you guys score any points?" I said, "I think the game plan that Hank put together is as good as it could be. Yeah, we're gonna put some points on the board." Then I said, "What about our defense? Can you handle their offense?" He, without being cocky, said, "I've looked at the film all week. We're liable to shut these guys out."

JAN STENERUD: I remember teammates saying, "Heck, Oakland, the Jets have good offenses, and they only scored six and seven points against us." When Lenny was out, we relied a lot on our defense and not turning the ball over. And, offensively, we had the potential. Hank could come up with all kinds of stuff.

BOBBY BELL: We were, what, 17- or 18-point underdogs? There's no way those guys were that good. They were saying Minnesota was going to man-handle us all over the field. As a defense, we figured they might get two or three field goals. We said, "Hey, y'all get us about nine points and we can beat these guys."

E. J. HOLUB: We talked among ourselves to really think about what we were doing. Be emotional but not *too* emotional. In our first Super Bowl against Green Bay, we were blithering idiots. We respected the Vikings, but we had confidence because of Hank and his innovations and that rollout pocket. And, of course, with our kicking game—Jan Stenerud and Jerrel Wilson.

BILL GRIGSBY: One night before the game, there was a big dinner at Antoine's. Joe McGuff, who was sports editor in Kansas City, myself, several other people in this very staid, conservative, and beautiful place. Lamar was telling us about Minnesota, how they had double-crossed the AFL at the last minute and switched to the NFL. He was still upset over that. In the middle of the conversation, he started pounding on the table and screaming, "Kill! Kill! Kill!" Everybody in the place jumped about three feet and was looking at this Clark Kent–type guy.

LAMAR HUNT: There's a sequel to that, maybe one of the clearest images that I have of that week. My wife and I were staying at the Royal Sonesta Hotel. We went to get an elevator to go down to the lobby, only a floor or two. And the only two people on the elevator were Max Winter of the Vikings and his wife. When we got on, their faces looked like the image of fear. For a few precious seconds, we were the only people on the elevator. I don't think any words were spoken. I was very comfortable and confident that we were going to win. I didn't know what the big deal was. We had played the Vikings in the preseason the season before and beat them 13–10. Preseason games then were much more serious. And you've got to realize we were actually an older team than the Vikings, by one year. They had accomplished a lot, but it wasn't like you were playing the Green Bay Packers.

HANK STRAM: The night before the game, I got a call in our suite from Ed Sabol of NFL Films. Ed and I were great friends. He said, "I've got to talk to you." "Well, talk!" "No. No. I've got to come over to your room and talk." "Ed, I've got family and friends, too many people. I've got no time for you now." He said, "Goddamn it, I'm coming over to see you." And he hung up the phone. I was in the bedroom relaxing, and he walked right in like he bought the franchise. He said, "I want to wire you for sound tomorrow." I said, "Are you crazy? For the Super Bowl?" "Yeah, that's right. It'll be the greatest thing in the world. Nobody's ever seen a real live picture of what happens in a big game. You're the only guy who can do it." I said, "I've got a great idea. Go over and see Bud Grant." He said, "Bud never says nothing. We've got to have you." So I said, "Nobody will know about this, right? Nobody on the team. Lamar. Nobody." "No. We'll wire you two hours before the game in the locker room. Nobody will know. You won't even know you're wired for sound." I told him, "And if I don't like the film, *kaputski*." "That's a deal." Once the game started, I never gave it a second thought.

JOHNNY ROBINSON: Lenny and I went down to the French Quarter the night before the game to eat some oysters. A friend of mine, Jimmy Morab, had a restaurant down there. And he had an apartment with a big sauna and steam bath and a rubdown table. Lenny got a rubdown, took a steam bath.

I went out on the field in a warm-up for about 30 minutes before the game. The surgeon met me at the game and deadened it again. I looked like a pincushion. And that's how I made the Super Bowl. Hank got that surgeon a sideline pass, and he sat right on the end of the bench. I went and sat right next to him every time I came off the field in case my ribs came loose and punctured my lungs.

DON WEISS: We did not have our control booth situated so that the stadium PA announcer was in there with us. I had a phone hookup to him. The weather bureau people called and told him there was a tornado in the area of the stadium. He announced that without any kind of discussion with us. That's not exactly what you want a few minutes before kickoff.

JACKY LEE: Before the game started, they had these hot-air balloons take off from the stadium. It didn't work right, and one didn't get out of the stadium. I'm a pilot, and I was watching this thing thinking, "This thing is going to crash into the crowd."

DON WEISS: We were very fortunate the guys flying the balloons were professionals. The one guy got the flame expired before it went into this group of young ladies who were seated in this one section waiting to perform in the halftime show as Southern belles. One of them suffered a broken leg, but that was the most severe injury.

Tulane's tarp wasn't big enough to cover the field entirely. It hardly covered any part of the sidelines and was in poor condition. We didn't own one in those days, though we soon bought our own and our own equipment to suck up water. Several of the key floats went off the plywood tracks, went into the mud, stalled, and threw the timing off completely. We needed a tractor to pull 'em free. All these things happened in succession, starting with the tornado alert, then the balloons, then the floats.

JAN STENERUD: It was a windy, blustery day. Pretty cool. I was awful in pregame warm-up, but I still felt OK. They had so many camerapeople on the field shooting pictures and film, there was hardly enough room to kick. The opening kickoff was important. My first kickoff sailed out of the end zone pretty good.

The Vikings' offense was surprisingly docile in the first half. Minnesota's deepest penetration of the half was on the game's opening possession, and after facing fourth-and-10 at the Kansas City 39, Vikings coach Bud Grant elected to punt instead of trying a long field goal. If the intent was to pin the Chiefs deep in their territory, it didn't work. Bob Lee's punt went only 22 yards, downed at the 17.

Stenerud staked Kansas City to a 9–0 lead early in the second quarter with field goals of 48, 32, and 25 yards on the Chiefs' first four drives. The 48-yarder was the longest to date in the Super Bowl's young history. The drive leading to the second field goal was kept alive by a third-down pass interference penalty against Ed Sharockman. And the only touchdown of the half, a five-yard run by Mike Garrett on a power trap, was made possible when Minnesota's Charlie West fumbled the kickoff after Kansas City had taken its 9–0 lead. Minnesota's output at halftime: 102 total yards, two turnovers, and a missed field goal from 56 yards from Fred Cox in the half's closing minutes. The Chiefs led at the half 16–0, the same lead that the Jets owned over the Colts going into the fourth quarter a year earlier.

HANK STRAM: When I sent Jan in for the first field goal from 48 yards, guys on the Minnesota bench were punching themselves. "Look at that. The guy's crazy!" Jan kicked the ball like it had helium in it.

JAN STENERUD: I knew the wind wasn't a problem at all. I just hit it so-so, didn't make great contact. It cleared very easily.

HANK STRAM: On the 65 toss power trap, that was the only time we ran that play all year long. Minnesota's Alan Page was a great player. Quick. Sharp. Alert. In a short-yardage situation, they would put him in the gap between the center and the left guard. If the backs were split, it looked like there might be an outside play to Page's right. Then he'd have to get in the gap between the guard and the tackle. If he saw the tackle pull, he was going to run like hell. It worked just like you draw it up on paper. The other thing we did was run a lot of reverses with Frank Pitts. That was because Jim Marshall and Carl

Eller were so damn fast that we wanted to make sure we had them going the other way.

JAN STENERUD: Halftime took forever. We were leading against a team that was heavily favored. We had 30 minutes to hang on to win the world championship. And it seemed like with all the entertainment and all the other stuff, it took us forever to get back on the field.

LEN DAWSON: We got really conservative after the first half. When we got ahead, the way our defense was playing, it was no contest. Our defense was so dominant. They had Mick Tinglehoff at center, 225 pounds. He either had Buck Buchanan or Curley Culp over his nose on every snap. That didn't happen in the NFL in those days because they didn't play odd alignments. His job wasn't to block a big guy on his nose on a running play. I think that had to be a big factor in disrupting their running game. And they were like us; the running game set up the passing game. They really couldn't get anything done.

BOBBY BELL: Coach Stram told Lenny, "They don't want to give you the deep stuff? Take the short stuff to Otis. He can run."

The Vikings looked like they might make a game of it after all by marching in for a touchdown on their first possession of the second half. In gaining 69 yards on the 10-play drive, they resorted to only one third down and came about 30 yards short of matching their first-half yardage. There was still about 20 minutes to play with the Chiefs' advantage cut to 16–7.

But the momentum shift was short-lived. Kansas City countered with a touchdown of its own that was foreshadowed by Stram's comment about throwing short to Taylor and allowing him to use his speed to develop a big play. Taylor caught a sideline pass five yards from the line of scrimmage, broke away from cornerback Earsell Mackbee, and raced 41 more yards down the right side—eluding one more tackler, safety Karl Kassulke, at the 15-yard line, for the score that crushed Minnesota's spirit. The Vikings managed only five first downs the rest of the way, each of their three remaining drives ending in an interception. The final score: Chiefs 23, Vikings 7.

HANK STRAM: In all fairness, with no two-week time frame, we had the advantage because we did a lot of multiplicity in the American Football League. Theirs was a typical NFL team. They lined up and bang, bang,

bang. We thought it was important for us to throw in front of the defensive backs, which we did very successfully. The last touchdown was that kind of play for Otis Taylor.

OTIS TAYLOR: The point that people don't realize—and I will be the first one to say—we were first of all a running team. We passed at the most opportune time to loosen up things. If we had been more of an attack-pass team with the type of receivers we had, there's no telling what we would have done.

BOBBY BELL: We played one of the best defensive games we ever played. We had Buck, Aaron Brown, Jerry Mays, Curley Culp, Lanier, Lynch, Jimmy Marsalis, Emmitt Thomas, Johnny Robinson. Then there were the special teams—oh, man. On offense, we had so much speed. They never played against anybody like that. Their ends, Carl Eller and Jim Marshall, were supposed to kill Lenny. They cut 'em down.

JAN STENERUD: I felt so great about winning. Then I looked around the locker room and saw Lenny, who had played in the NFL when some people didn't think he was good enough to play. Jerry Mays was another team leader. And Buck Buchanan. They could have played in any league. And Johnny Robinson and Jim Tyrer and Ed Budde. I thought, "It must be great for these guys." And for Lamar and Hank and all those people who had really been around.

LAMAR HUNT: I don't remember even being there for the trophy presentation. It may have happened 'cause I don't believe in leaving the stands to go down on the field. I have never seen a video of the trophy ceremony. I don't remember the locker room being anything like in Miami when the Jets won, where anybody with any reasonable tie was in there.

TOM FLORES: Lamar was such a low-key guy. He just said all the right things. And very professional, very classy. No gloating at all. I was happy for him.

BOBBY BELL: The NFL was saying the AFL wouldn't last four years. It wouldn't last five years. Six years. Next thing you know, we were playing them. Next thing you know, Lamar ended up with the Super Bowl trophy. That was one of the highlights.

SAM BLAIR: Lamar still had enough little boy in him to show excitement. In the locker room at old Tulane Stadium, the whole media wanted to talk to him. I congratulated Lamar, and he shook my hand. He had a frozen expression on his face, like a little boy on Christmas morning who had gotten everything he wanted. Some people had written off the Jets beating the Colts the year before as a one-time-only fluke. It had become obvious that a lot of those teams in the AFL had really grown up. The player rosters were definitely on par with the best teams in the NFL. The Chiefs physically and strategically dominated the Vikings. In any matchup, the Chiefs were better.

HANK STRAM: We went into Brennan's after the game. The guys with us wanted to get a drink. Some little guy sitting at a table said, "Hey, Coach! Geez, boy, your team played a great game! What a team!" He reached in his coat pocket and pulled out a beautiful gold watch. He said, "I've watched your team during the course of the year. You're a great coach. This is a great team. For all the joy and entertainment I had watching your team play, I want you to have this." And he was from Minnesota!

LAMAR HUNT: We had the gall to plan a victory celebration at the Royal Sonesta Hotel. We didn't have any invitations. It was right there in the hotel for anybody who wandered by. We had a party there for a couple of hours. At that time, the game was blacked out in New Orleans and shown on tape at midnight. So we went upstairs then and rented a suite with a television set. With a bunch of friends, we sat around and watched the replay 'til about 3:00 in the morning.

JOHNNY ROBINSON: When I saw an AFL guy after the game, he said, "Man, we were right there with you." And the NFL guys that you saw, it was almost derogatory, like, "God, you beat me." Jimmy Morab had a party for me after the game. We had about 20 people there. And Paul Hornung, the former Packers star, was there. He was a friend of Jimmy's, too. And another NFL player that Jimmy knew well was there. They were cordial, but I could tell it was like all these players had been in the game.

LAMAR HUNT: It was, in a lot of ways, a dream come true. It was wonderful poetic justice to win that last game. It was the last game that was pure

AFL. It tied the Super Bowl series at 2–2, which was really a decisive factor in how the league was realigned.

In the *Minneapolis Star* the morning after the game, Dick Cullum wrote: "The Vikings may have used up more emotion while beating the Los Angeles Rams and Cleveland Browns to get to the Super Bowl than the Chiefs used in beating the New York Jets and Oakland Raiders. Football is a game of emotion."

The Chiefs still had some emotion after the game. Otis Taylor cried for 15 minutes.

Otis Taylor: It wasn't just a great day for us as a football team and for Mr. Hunt. It was a big day for Kansas City itself as a city. People in Kansas City are still talking about that game. There's not hardly a day in my life that people don't ask me about that game. Kansas City grew up as a town behind that championship.

The final appearance of AFL football came on January 17, 1970, at Houston's Astrodome. In the ninth and final league All-Star Game, the West defeated the East 26–3 before a crowd of 30,170. Jan Stenerud scored the last point in league history.

And with the release of the Super Bowl IV highlight film, Hank Stram's sideline performance in New Orleans—particularly the play call that resulted in Mike Garrett's touchdown run in the waning minutes of the first half—provided a glimpse of big-game coaching never previously captured.

Hank Stram: And people still come up to me in airports and say, "Hey, Coach. What about that 65 toss power trap play!"

30

After the AFL

The day before Joe Namath and the Jets shocked the Colts and the nation, Pete Rozelle announced that the NFL was studying two plans for realignment in 1970. One would leave the current league structures relatively unchanged but would likely move some NFL clubs to join the current AFL for balance. The second plan would start from scratch with no regard to league genealogy. Those who considered the NFL superior could surmise that this possibility would increase the chance of AFL teams being shut out of future Super Bowls, at least in the short term.

DAVE ANDERSON: I was told the original plan was to mix up all the AFL and NFL teams in the realignment. But after the Jets won, Phil Iselin, who took over after Sonny Werblin was bought out before the '68 season, told the NFL, "Our guys are staying together."

DON WEISS: That original merger committee started talking realignment in 1968. They compiled a report that, in effect, proposed that when realignment took place, the 16 NFL teams would stay in the National Football League with the same logo, and the American Football League would stay in its same 10-team alignment. They were talking about a linking schedule. Then, in the long-range plan of the merger, whatever new teams we added would be added to the AFL.

LAMAR HUNT: I favored that. But there were contractual things regarding Cincinnati. Paul Brown strongly said they bought an NFL franchise.

The only people satisfied with the realignment process might have been the clerks in the NFL's accounting office. The process dragged on into the first half of 1969. Frankly, no one from the NFL was enthusiastic about abandoning traditional and often financially lucrative rivalries to move in with the AFL underclass. Browns owner Art Modell identified his club as belonging to a select group of teams that must remain on the NFL side of the merger ledger. To subtract a member of that core, Modell said, would emasculate the league.

DON WEISS: You couldn't imagine how many different meetings we had. We met periodically in New York. We had a desperate meeting in New Orleans the day after Super Bowl IV, at which nothing really happened except that Rozelle had been through so many proposals that he said, "Could you at least give me a list of your nine best proposals?" There were other meetings that were scheduled immediately after that in January, long sessions where people slept on couches or the carpet. Rozelle didn't want 'em to leave the building. Some of them went as long as 36 hours.

There were three proposals in the wake of the AFL objection to the 16 and 10. One was to completely realign, without regard to NFL or AFL, a complete shuffling. The second one was taking intact certain divisions from each league and moving them around. The third one was moving three NFL teams to the AFL. There was long discussion but no agreement on the first two. The third was the one that they adopted unanimously.

With financial incentives attached, three teams agreed to take the plunge, and two of them were unlikely suspects—the Browns and the Baltimore Colts, only months removed from playing for the NFL championship. And there were the Pittsburgh Steelers, a franchise that had never won an NFL title and that might have been one of the few NFL casualties had the player war of the mid-1960s not resulted in a merger when it did. Rozelle credited Modell with volunteering his Browns in the name of keeping the rest of the NFL's Brahman core intact. Modell was not available to comment about the switch, having been hospitalized in New York with bleeding ulcers.

DON WEISS: It helped that there was a $3 million bounty for moving, but I think Modell volunteered regardless of being paid. The Steelers, particularly, had to be convinced to move. The one thing that convinced the Rooneys was they were assured that Cleveland was going and they would be able to maintain that rivalry. Then Carroll Rosenbloom was the last to go.

Although the "Sophie's Choice" portion of the decision had been reached, there was still the difficult matter of molding the new 13-team conferences into divisions. Each franchise sought a delicate balance, not easily satisfying every member, in its division placement. Ironically, it was only the expanded AFL, to be known as the American Conference of the NFL, which was able to come to a quick solution. The 13 remaining NFL franchises, the National Conference, hemmed and hawed and haggled and got nowhere. Five alignments remained under consideration when it became obvious that a group vote couldn't produce a winning format. Rozelle resorted to placing five slips of paper into a vase and having his secretary, Thelma Elkjer, pull one out. Sports history buffs should note that the format that began play in 1970 was officially "plan No. 3."

LIONEL TAYLOR: We could never have two original AFL teams play in the Super Bowl. I would love to see, like, the Raiders and Denver in the Super Bowl. I just can't believe that we accepted that. The NFL really rooked us.

Joe Namath and the Jets never returned to the Super Bowl, together or separately.

The merger brought only more injuries to Namath and frustration to a Jets franchise that was relegated to also-ran status when it entered the NFL. The long-awaited first regular-season meeting with the Giants was dutifully included immediately on the 1970 schedule, for Shea Stadium. But the Giants won easily, 22–10, and the Jets created little excitement in the years immediately following that. After the 1976 season—and seven years in the NFL that featured no better than a break-even record—Namath was granted a special waiver that allowed him to sign as a free agent with the Los Angeles Rams, reuniting with Chuck Knox, who, as a Jets assistant, had "recruited" him in the mid-1960s. The Rams won the NFC West with a 10–4 record, but Namath was simply a backup to starter Pat Haden and played in only six games.

Only twice have the Jets since reached within a game of returning to the Super Bowl. They advanced through the bizarre playoff tournament that followed the 1982 strike-interrupted and shortened campaign. But Don Shula gained a measure of revenge when his Dolphins blanked the Jets 14–0 on a mucky, muddy Orange Bowl field that Jets followers suspected was intentionally allowed to reach such a state to stymie New York's run-oriented attack. And in January 1999, Jets fans were practically packing for Miami and Super Bowl XXXIII when the Jets held a 10–0 lead over the Broncos in the third quarter of the AFC Championship Game. But New York couldn't handle such an opportunity, didn't score again, and finished with six turnovers. Denver's defending Super Bowl champions made off with a 23–10 victory.

Through all the years, the Jets have remained as pro football renters. They left Shea Stadium to become tenants of the rival Giants in the New Jersey Meadowlands beginning in 1984, hoping that they could return to New York before the end of the decade in their own facility. They're still waiting.

And in retirement, Broadway Joe eventually became a Hall of Famer and a family man. In 1984, he married a southern California actress named Deborah Lynn Mays who was taking voice lessons from the same teacher as Namath. They settled in South Florida and had two daughters, Jessica and Olivia. By the spring of 1999, Deborah Lynn was going by Tatiana and the 20-year difference between husband and wife had apparently taken its toll. She left for California, and he filed for divorce, subsequently falling into a state of depression that ended only when he was able to arrange for time together with his daughters.

And Joe still wouldn't talk to *Miami Herald* sports columnist Edwin Pope for what he considered a Super snub in 1969, until . . .

EDWIN POPE: In the year 2000, I was at a Dolphins-Jets game in Miami and found myself at the foot of an elevator with nobody there but Namath. After all those years of him ignoring me, I wasn't about to start glad-handing him. I didn't say anything, and he looked at me and said, "Edwin Pope. . . ." And I was waiting for what came next. ". . . Give me a big hug, man!" I was stunned. He gave me a big hug, then he turned me loose and said, "I never thought I would say that." I said, "I didn't, either." Thirty-one years it took him to say hello to me.

Another strange-but-true elevator tale:

DONNY ANDERSON: Something like 20-something years after Super Bowl I, I saw Fred Williamson in a celebrity golf tournament in Tahoe. The elevator closed, just he and I. And I said, "You don't know me, but I know you." He said, "Oh, I'm Freddie Williamson." I said, "I'm Donny Anderson." And he said, "Oh, man! That really didn't knock me out!"

And "the Hammer," who has made himself busy in the film industry since hanging up his white shoes, remains a member of Modesty Anonymous.

FRED WILLIAMSON: They used to invite me to the Chiefs and Raiders games. Lamar Hunt put an end to that. They'd invite the players to get up and talk at these banquets. I said, "The only reason I come is to see how ugly everybody was compared to the way I look, how out of shape all you guys are compared to how I look. You're all the same age as me, and you look like old men." So they didn't invite me back. OK.

Cookie Gilchrist was nearly a 1,000-yard rusher in each of his first four AFL seasons and was out of pro football less than two years later. Practically unstoppable on the field and sometimes uncontrollable off it, his career ended meekly with 10 carries for the Broncos in 1967.

Gilchrist settled in the Philadelphia area and apparently remains bitter about how he was treated during his pro football career. In 1983, he refused an invitation for induction into the Canadian Football Hall of Fame and quoted a Bible verse about hypocrisy when he delivered the news to CFL commissioner Jake Gaudaur. A trip to cookiegilchrist.com provides his views on economics, race relations, and many other issues.

Gilchrist rarely speaks with reporters, agreeing to an interview with a Canadian reporter following the Hall of Fame snub in part because he liked the reporter's astrological signs. When asked over the phone about an interview for this book, he replied, "You've seen my website, right? That'll tell you everything you want to know."

Paul Brown and the Cleveland Browns finally met on the football field in August 1970, in Cincinnati's new Riverfront Stadium. It seemed like a tricky optical illusion, the Bengals on one side of the field in their orange, black, and white uniforms, and the Browns on the other side wearing orange, brown, and white. A fourth-quarter touchdown pass from Sam Wyche to Chip Myers provided the margin of victory for Cincinnati, 31–24. Captain Bob Johnson presented the game ball to Paul Brown, and, as Bob Trumpy told the *Dayton Daily News* years later, "That's the only time I saw the old man shed a tear."

The Bengals' initial season in the NFL proved to be an eventful one. Cincinnati stumbled to a 1–6 start, then incredibly won its remaining seven games to finish 8–6 and win a division title in only its third season—by one game over second-place Cleveland. Paul Brown, eight years after being called into Art Modell's office and fired, was voted the NFL Coach of the Year. And the Bengals' efforts to retool following the loss of promising quarterback Greg Cook in 1969 planted the seed of an offensive revolution that current fans might not realize began in Cincinnati.

BILL WALSH: We had to replace Greg Cook. We signed Virgil Carter and reverted to a different style of offense, the origin of the so-called West Coast offense. Virgil took us to the division championship, which I think was an incredible job by Paul Brown, by Virgil, by all of us.

Sam Wyche strung out his pro football career with three clubs over nine years. Then he began to make his biggest mark on the sport, as a coach. He led his very own Bengals into the 1989 Super Bowl, where they were beaten in the closing minutes by Bill Walsh's San Francisco 49ers. He added five more seasons in charge of Tampa Bay before moving into broadcasting.

The same spirit that marked his overachieving playing career carried through his coaching days. He earned less national attention for reaching the Super Bowl than he did for his actions one chilly day in Cincinnati when he grabbed a microphone to admonish the hometown fans over the PA system when their rowdy behavior threatened to draw a penalty: "Will the next person that sees anybody throw anything onto this field point them out and get them out of here! You don't live in Cleveland! You live in Cincinnati!"

Wyche's voice became more familiar with fans when, after being dismissed by Tampa Bay, he became a network broadcaster. He was back on the sideline during the fall of 2002, as a volunteer assistant at Pickens High School in his home state of South Carolina. But it was with little of that familiar voice. During a biopsy of enlarged lymph nodes a few years earlier, doctors accidentally cut the nerve to his left vocal cord. It's a procedure that's irreversible. That immediately put an end to his TV career. On top of that, he later learned he suffered from a heart condition called cardiomyopathy that limits that amount of blood pumped throughout his body. He was ordered onto immediate medication facing the possibility of a heart transplant down the road.

The combination of throat and heart medications left Wyche listless until Andy Tweito, the football coach at Pickens, took the awkward step of asking the former Super Bowl coach if he would like to help out with his high school team's offense. Wyche accepted, as well as taking on a position as a substitute teacher. With the new sub supervising the offense—albeit with a voice that didn't rise above a conversational level—the Pickens Blue Flame finished the regular season 9–1 and reached the state playoffs.

Lou Saban, coach of three AFL teams during the 1960s, was only getting warmed up.

The stay in Denver, where he had hoped to lead the success-starved Broncos to glory starting in 1967, ended in 1971. He was back in Buffalo right after that—a period highlighted by O. J. Simpson's record-setting rushing campaign in '73—but he marched into Ralph Wilson's office two days before a game, owning a 2–3 record, and told his boss that he had lost the team and was quitting.

Saban's career path since has resembled an out-of-control car that has left the road and careened over hill and dale. He returned to college football for a third stint with brief stops at Miami and West Point, reported to his old assistant coach George Steinbrenner with the New York Yankees for a few years, even served as an assistant on a high school staff and a defensive coordinator in the Arena League (they play defense in that league?). In 2002, he finished his second season as head coach at little Chowan College in North Carolina.

And when visiting Saban before the '02 season (his 52nd as a coach) at his home near Myrtle Beach, South Carolina, it was fitting to notice that his front yard featured . . . a For Sale sign.

Sonny Werblin wasn't done changing the face of pro football when he was suddenly bought out by his Jets partners in the spring of 1968, only months before his $427,000 quarterback leveled the playing field of all pro football. In the early '70s, he helped New Jersey governor William Cahill pull off one of the most stunning coups in sports—getting the New York Giants, once Werblin's hated rivals, to abandon the nation's biggest and most glamorous city to go play 12 miles west of Manhattan in an area politely called the New Jersey Meadowlands. Moving into what would be called Giants Stadium beginning in 1976, the Giants managed to enjoy the best of both worlds. They played in a spacious new facility with acres of available parking in the Jersey suburbs yet still retained the name New York Giants . . . despite the presence of thousands of "Property of New Jersey Giants" T-shirts that appeared seemingly only days after the move was announced.

Werblin eventually moved his business address back across the Hudson River, to Madison Square Garden to work with New York's basketball Knicks and hockey Rangers in the late 1970s into the mid-1980s. He died of a heart attack in November 1991 at age 81.

Ben Davidson's Raiders career ended following the 1971 season; then he was reunited with Fred Williamson on the set of the hit movie *M*A*S*H*. But he was flagged for one more roughing penalty in retirement. In 2001, a San Diego Superior Court judge ordered Davidson, then 60 years old, to pay $10,720 to a 13-year-old after a jury determined that Big Ben assaulted the kid in the laundry room of the Harbor View Villas apartment complex that he owns. Ben—at six five, 230 pounds—got fed up with the boy—five four, 110 pounds—and a couple of his friends for interfering with another tenant who was trying to do her laundry. The mother of the boy accused Davidson of choking her son. Said Ben following the verdict: "Never again will I take matters into my own hands."

Jim Otto went on to become the embodiment of the Raiders, from being undrafted by the NFL to becoming the only first-team All-AFL center for 10 years, in a 15-year career that led to the Pro Football Hall of Fame. He was so proud of the one league championship team that he played on, the '67 Raiders, that he gave his AFL championship ring to his father-in-law in Miami for safekeeping. That ring was stolen during a 1979 burglary, and Otto assumed he would never see it again. At least until September 1984, when Otto received a call from an elementary school principal in West Linn, Oregon. It seemed that 9-year-old Chip Rapp went to the lavatory to wash his hands and spotted something shiny in the nearby shower.

Otto's fanatical dedication to playing the game, no matter his state of health, dominated his life after football. He has had more than three dozen surgeries, had both shoulders replaced, had both knees replaced a total of eight times, had his back fused twice, and had his right leg nearly amputated. He survived three brushes with death during the 1990s: a bacterial infection, a burst artery in a leg, and an ailment that left him in such a state that he had to go without a knee for six months before becoming healthy enough for a replacement surgery.

When the 1960s ended, the Miami Dolphins were far from the talk of pro football. They had won no more than five games in any of their four seasons in the AFL. Their average home crowd at the Orange Bowl had inched into the mid-30,000s—helped by unusually large gatherings to see the world champion Jets and Bills rookie O. J. Simpson—and they resorted to moving one of their 1969 home games to Tampa.

That was all about to change, dramatically, starting in the coach's office.

EDWIN POPE: When George Wilson finally got the ax, I was the guy who suggested Don Shula to Joe Robbie. I was sitting in his office in downtown Miami one day after the '69 season. Back then, Robbie and I were still good friends. He had already made up his mind to get rid of George, but he hadn't chosen anybody. He was fooling around with the idea of trying to get Bear Bryant from Alabama. They did a lot of talking, but Bear finally turned him down.

BILLY NEIGHBORS: Alabama people had been on Coach Bryant for going 6–5, and he knew Joe Robbie. Coach Bryant called me one morning in 1970 after I retired. He said, "I'm going to Miami. I want you to meet me in Birmingham, and I'm going to become the head coach down there. I want you to be a player and a coach." He told me what they were going to pay him, over $300,000 I recall, and some ownership of the damn franchise. He was going to try to get Lee Roy Jordan and Babe Parilli there. Hell, I thought it was a done deal. Then, about four or five hours later, he called me back and said, "Forget it. It's been called off. I've decided to stay here." Thank God he stayed at Alabama.

EDWIN POPE: I said to Robbie, "If you're going to fire George anyway, and I don't think you necessarily should, how 'bout Don Shula?" And he was captivated by that. He didn't say anything for a couple of minutes, which was extremely rare, almost unique. Then he said, "That's the man. How would I get a hold of him?" I said, "Well, our beat writer, Bill Brubaker, went to school with Don Shula at John Carroll in Cleveland. Brubaker could get a hold of him." Robbie called Brubaker and instigated the whole thing.

Shula took the parts that he inherited from George Wilson, and, with a couple more key additions such as Paul Warfield and Jake Scott, the Dolphins became the NFL's most successful team of the early 1970s. In their first four seasons under the former Baltimore coach, they reached the conference championship game, lost one Super Bowl, and won two others. That included the legendary 1972 team that went undefeated with, ironically, Earl Morrall subbing for an injured Bob Griese for much of the season as he had done for

Shula with Johnny Unitas in 1968. No other NFL team has achieved an undefeated season since, and the '72 Dolphins toast their legacy each year when the last perfect record has been erased from pro football's standings.

LARRY KING: Here's why I knew we'd win the Super Bowl after the undefeated season. We were underdogs. They made the Redskins a one-point favorite. I drove from Vegas to L.A. with Jimmy the Greek, and he was swearing to me the Redskins were a great bet because the NFC was so much tougher than the AFC. The Dolphins worked out in Long Beach. The morning of the Super Bowl, I went down to breakfast, must have been quarter to seven. There was no one in the coffee shop except Bob Griese, so I went over and sat down with him. He looked at me—this was the day he was going to play in the Super Bowl—and said, "Do you think the property values on Key Biscayne can keep going up?" And I thought, "Hey, if this guy's got this much locked in, he ain't gonna lose today."

Who would have thought that trying to stash an injured player on the waiver list over a weekend could nearly lead all the way to 1600 Pennsylvania Avenue? But in the AFL's twisted offshoot of "six degrees of separation," Jack Kemp injured a hand, was hidden on the waiver wire, was discovered and claimed by Buffalo, led the Bills to two league championships, settled in western New York, was elected to Congress, and gave up the play-calling role only when he agreed to serve on Bob Dole's presidential ticket in 1996.

As the 1970 season approached, Bob "Harpo" Gladieux wondered if he would be cut by Clive Rush and the Boston Patriots on the eve of the season again— even if he wouldn't hear the word a second time on the 6:00 news.

BOB GLADIEUX: It came down to the final cut again on the Thursday before the season. Nobody said a thing to me. I went back home. Then I got a look at the evening newspaper—Bob Gladieux, final Patriot cut. Two years in a row, they did that. I figured, "That's it." So I went downtown to rock and roll and hoot it up. I was downtown 'til Sunday morning. I never made it home. I met some friends, my girlfriend. We just partied—Thursday night, Friday night, Saturday night, Sunday. I woke up and said, "Ah, heck. I'm going to the game." I had a buddy, Jack, who was going. He picked me up. I had a tall pack of Schlitz. I got to the stadium and bought a program and bullshit my way in and we sat down. While Jack was getting me a hot dog, they said on the PA system: "Bob Gladieux, please report to the Patriots' dressing room." I said, "God, I don't believe what I'm hearing." Just then, they said it again. I turned and looked around. I saw Jerry Richardson, one of the assistant coaches, coming down the steps. I ducked. I was down on all fours on the concrete. "What the hell am I doing? Christ, I'm snockered!" The ol' G.E. lightbulb went off with a dollar sign in it. I thought, "Get down there for the money! They've been taking it from you for two years!" What happened was, John Charles from Purdue went out and warmed up. When he came back in, they tried to force him into signing a contract. They said, "You're going to sign this or we're going to cut you." He said, "Cut my ass!" They cut him, and then they had my uniform. That's the way they operated. They said, "Get dressed. You're activated." I thought, "Don't light any matches." I had about eight minutes to get dressed.

We lost the toss and were kicking off. I was straightening my pads out and thinking, "Protect yourself. Avoid all contact." I was running down, toward the wedge. My buddy came back with my beer and hot dog and said, "Hey, did anybody see the guy that was here? That damn 'Harpo.' You've got to watch him all the time." The wedge was coming at me, and I said, "I don't want any part of this." I went around the left side of the wedge and the darn ballplayer from Miami came around the right side. I met him head on. Smashed him. Made the tackle. Then, on the PA, they said, "Tackle made by number 24, Bob Gladieux." My buddy, there with a beer and a hot dog, said, "No way!" I played the whole game on special teams.

Bob Gladieux lasted longer on the '70 Patriots than Clive Rush did. Boston won its opener, 27–14, over Miami in Don Shula's debut as Dolphins coach. The Pats then dropped six straight, which gave Rush custody of the franchise's two longest losing streaks in only a season and a half. And that was long enough for Patriots ownership. His record as Boston coach was only 5–16, and there was the continuing series of bizarre incidents on and off the field. He died in August 1980 at the age of 49.

DARYL JOHNSON: In 1970, the Wichita State plane went down. He knew a coach at Wichita, and to honor his friend, Clive decided to have this thing called the "black power defense" because, in those days, you didn't see 11 black guys on defense. And we didn't *have* 11 black guys to play defense, so we had to draft a white guy to play safety, Tom Janik. We didn't know we were going to institute this during a real game. We went to Cincinnati for the last game. I guess Clive and Paul Brown had some kind of relationship. Clive decided we were going to use the defense in that game, and we could make *Ebony* magazine, all of the sports highlights. The guys were kind of half for it. He put us in the game when it was third-and-35, figured, how bad could it be? Touchdown! That was the first and the last "black power defense." We still laugh about it. It was a statement that Clive was trying to make, and he was way ahead of his time. Now you look at defenses in the National Football League, it's hard to find a white guy.

Those who considered George Blanda too old to play football in the mid-1960s must have been absolutely flabbergasted to watch him in the next decade. It appeared in 1970 that his days as even a backup quarterback were through and his lone remaining value to the Raiders would be as a placekicker for a year or two. But at age 43, he put together a magical 1970 season by coming off the bench as an emergency quarterback and also providing late-game heroics as a kicker to help the Raiders win their fourth consecutive Western Division title in the AFL and AFC. He was directly responsible for late-game heroics each week during a stretch of four wins and a tie, this from a man nine years older than his coach, even two years older than Al Davis.

Blanda finally retired following the 1975 season having claimed NFL records for years played (26) and points scored (2,002). He was inducted into the Pro Football Hall of Fame in 1981 and continues to work for the Raiders in a special assistant capacity.

When contacted by phone for this book, he wasted little time in expressing his opinion of the project: "I usually don't like to talk to people like you."

Long after George Blanda had played his last pro football game, Wahoo McDaniel was still wrestling. Every couple of months throughout the mid-1970s, he was losing his NWA Mid-Atlantic title to Ric Flair, then winning it back, then losing it again. It was pretty easy to tell whose turn it was to win.

And so it went into 1980s and even the '90s. Wahoo was once attacked by Rowdy Roddy Piper's bounty hunter, Abdullah the Butcher, whose use of a foreign object bloodied him so much that several TV stations carrying the show received complaints from viewers.

His top salary as an AFL player was $42,500. He said that, in his best-paying season amid the turnbuckles, he brought in more than $600,000. And Wahoo had virtually disappeared from the sports consciousness—finally retired to Charlotte, North Carolina—until it was learned in the late '90s that he desperately needed a kidney transplant. He refused to go on dialysis, seeing how it ravaged his father in his final days only a few years earlier.

Wahoo died in April 2002 in Houston at the age of 63 of complications brought on by renal failure and diabetes, while on a waiting list to receive a transplant. A memorial service was held in his boyhood home of Midland, Texas, and his ashes were scattered on the waters of his favorite fishing lake, near Del Rio, Texas.

RIC FLAIR: From golf to fishing to hunting to wrestling, football. You name it. Wahoo just wanted to be the best at everything. He was a scratch golfer playing on two hours' sleep, probably two quarts of Crown Royal the night before. Wahoo would get up at 5:00 in Dallas, go tee off at 6:00 with Lee Trevino, Mickey Mantle, and Charley Pride. He'd lose $2,000, go wrestle that night in Fort Worth, get up the next morning, and go play golf again and win back $1,500. We had a lot of fun, more fun than two guys should ever have had together.

Those dental school classes that Billy Cannon took while playing pro football led to a successful orthodontist practice well after he retired from football in 1970. It was estimated that his practice in Baton Rouge, Louisiana, where he had been anointed as royalty since starring for LSU in the late '50s, was worth $300,000 annually. That's why it shocked the populous there in 1983 when Cannon and five other local men were charged with participating in a counterfeiting scheme. The 1959 Heisman Trophy winner, his financial portfolio apparently ravaged by poor investments and gambling debts, led a ring that printed about $6 million in $100 bills. When local Secret Service agents learned who was in charge of the operation, they were embarrassed and almost reluctant to tell the U.S. attorney investigating the case. Cannon was found guilty, sentenced to five years in federal prison, and fined $10,000. He sold his practice and surrendered his license. He served two and a half years in Texarkana, Texas, and was then moved to a Salvation Army halfway house back in Baton Rouge. His orthodontist license was reinstated following a 40-hour refresher course.

Numerous attempts over a two-year period to interview him for this book went without response. "He just doesn't see the need to do interviews anymore, to go back over all that business again," said Thomas Moran, a longtime friend of Cannon and owner of the Baton Rouge restaurant where Cannon's Heisman Trophy is displayed. "The few times that he has, he feels he's gotten burned."

Alex Karras has reached Long Beach, Indiana.

Pete Rozelle's Super Bowl finally reached the Rose Bowl in Pasadena, where he had wanted it played since its inception, in January 1977. And when it did, Rozelle found himself faced with the prospect of doing something that was unthinkable a little more than a decade earlier. He had to present the NFL's championship trophy to a man who wanted to bring the league to its knees. Amid the revelry of the victorious Oakland Raiders locker room following their Super Bowl XI triumph over Minnesota—the irony of the Raiders winning their first world championship over the city whose snubbing of an AFL franchise made it possible for Oakland to enter pro football wasn't lost on longtime AFL loyalists—Pete Rozelle presented the Vince Lombardi Trophy to Al Davis. To Rozelle's credit, he actually had congratulated Davis before the televised presentation, up in the Rose Bowl press box before the public trophy ceremony.

They were thrown together for years afterward, like oil and water. There was another postgame Super Bowl ceremony for Rozelle when Davis's Raiders won again in January 1981 over Philadelphia. Then came the prolonged legal battles, through which Davis moved his club from Oakland to Los Angeles without standard league approval in 1982 (adding a third Super Bowl win as the L.A. Raiders in January 1984) and then, incredibly, back to Oakland again in 1995. He was inducted into the Pro Football Hall of Fame in 1992.

Along the way, Davis has limited his availability for commenting on his legacy in pro football. He allowed a rare glimpse of the deep feeling that he has for his pro roots before Super Bowl XXXVII in San Diego. He was part of a ceremony to unveil a statue of former *San Diego Union* sports editor and columnist Jack Murphy, whose efforts were largely responsible for the Chargers moving south from Los Angeles in 1961 as well as the establishment of major league baseball there late in the '60s. At the ceremony, Davis said, "Someday, I'd like to see a stadium with a million people in it. All the people from the American Football League, marching like they do at the Olympics."

When approached in person about setting up an interview for this book, he laughed and said, "Well, you can try to call me." Not one of the messages left for him over a period of almost two years was returned.

Of the eight original AFL coaches in 1960, Hank Stram was the last one standing. The first game that he coached as a member of the NFL was the one that every coach yearned to coach in at one time—the College All-Star Game, against pro football's world champions. What he did not win again was another playoff game. He took only one more Chiefs team to the postseason and was beaten by Miami in the only game longer than the 1962 Dallas-Houston AFL title game—a record three hours, 22 minutes, and 40 seconds. Kansas City went 5–9 in 1974, marking Stram's third losing season. Lamar Hunt ended the 15-year relationship by flying to San Francisco and handing the only coach that he had ever hired a memo stating that he was fired. Stram returned to the sidelines a year later for the New Orleans Saints but for only two dismal seasons. He finished with 131 regular-season wins over 17 seasons and retired across Lake Pontchartrain in Covington, Louisiana. He was elected to the Pro Football Hall of Fame in 2003.

O.J. did get the running business down, all right. He ran for 250 yards, an NFL single-game record. He ran for 2,003 yards, an NFL single-season record. And after his football career was over, he ran through airports and eventually ran from the law in a white Bronco.

His attorney, Yale Galanter, agreed at one point to make the Hall of Famer available for an interview for this book. Despite dozens of follow-up contacts, the interview never took place.

AL BEMILLER: After I retired, I used to do security on the field. And O.J. used to come up to me and talk to me for five, six, seven minutes an hour before the game. I know a lot of other dudes who wouldn't waste their time with me. O.J. was a welcome sight.

BUTCH BYRD: After football, I think O.J. separated from the group, from an economic standpoint and maybe a celebrity standpoint. Hertz and the other endorsements and the movies and such took him to a new level. On occasion, Buffalo has something every year, some sort of get-together, he would come back. But it was different. On one occasion, he had bodyguards. Something changed.

Following the knee injury that sidelined him for most of the 1969 season, James Harris was never again a factor in the Bills' quarterback situation. A new heir apparent to Jack Kemp was found the following year when Dennis

Shaw was drafted out of San Diego State in the second round. Harris was waived in September 1972, soon after Lou Saban's return to Buffalo.

He returned to the NFL in 1973 in Los Angeles, as the backup to the Rams' John Hadl. Harris took over the following year when Hadl was traded to Green Bay, and he led the Rams to division titles in 1974 and '75, the latter resulting in a berth in the NFC Championship Game. But despite such success, Harris was the odd man out in 1976 when Los Angeles brought in Pat Haden, a local favorite from USC who had played previously for the Southern California Sun in the short-lived World Football League. Harris's career finished down the coast in San Diego, where his only starts in three seasons with the Chargers came during a contract holdout by Dan Fouts.

Harris eventually enjoyed a pro football championship in a front-office capacity, as part of the 2000 Ravens. In 2003, he became vice president of player personnel for the Jacksonville Jaguars.

BUTCH BYRD: He was probably the most talented quarterback that I played with. The problem that James Harris had, when he was with the black ballplayers, he was a tower of power. When he was with O.J. and Marlin Briscoe and Haven Moses and the like, he was the equal to everybody. Unfortunately, as I recall it, he had a problem with white ballplayers. James came out of the South, from a predominantly black school. And to sit there and command a white ballplayer to do something, in my opinion, initially wasn't in his makeup. The success that he had four or five years later—I think the reason why it took him that long was that he had to get used to telling white ballplayers what to do and how to do it.

Nine seasons after James Harris threw his last pass, Washington's Doug Williams became the first black quarterback to lead a team to a Super Bowl victory.

Three of the original eight AFL owners are still running those clubs—Lamar Hunt with the Chiefs, Ralph Wilson with the Bills, and Bud Adams, his Oilers now known as the Tennessee Titans.

Lamar Hunt spread his sports influence far and wide while continuing to operate the Chiefs as an NFL club. In the early 1970s, he spearheaded a successful men's tennis tour called World Championship Tennis. He continued a role that he began in the late '60s as a proponent for big-league pro soccer both in the former North American Soccer League and the current Major

League Soccer, where his franchise in Columbus, Ohio, plays in the nation's only soccer-specific pro facility. He was inducted into the Pro Football Hall of Fame in 1972. And he still commutes to Chiefs games from Dallas.

Ralph Wilson's Bills became an awkward symbol of both NFL success and failure in the early '90s by becoming the first team to reach four consecutive Super Bowls—and lose them all. The stadium that he built in suburban Orchard Park, New York, in the early 1970s now bears his name. And he still commutes from Detroit.

RALPH WILSON: Buffalo hasn't changed much. It's the most passionate city in the country for pro football. The old families went to the game at the "Rockpile" and took their little boys. Now those boys are grown up, and they have kids, and they come to the games. It's sort of the fabric of the community. You can't go in a grocery store or a restaurant anywhere and not see people in Bills caps and Bills jerseys. You don't see that in Detroit. The town has been declining in population and economically for years. It's gone from the 14th TV market to the 47th in 40 years, but the fan interest isn't declining.

The volatile municipal marriage of Bud Adams and Houston came to a bitter end in the mid-1990s, the Oilers being the only one of the 10 AFL franchises not to reach the Super Bowl at that time. Adams insisted that the once-fabled Astrodome was no longer an acceptable NFL venue and moved the team to Nashville, Tennessee. In the NFL's version of the Residence Inn, the team spent a year in Memphis, Tennessee, and a year at Vanderbilt Stadium in Nashville—known each of those seasons by the ill-fitting name Tennessee Oilers—before the club's current plush home was ready for occupancy. In 1999, Adams finally got to the Super Bowl, his renamed Titans falling one yard short of beating the St. Louis Rams. And he commutes from Houston.

And he finally bought those champion Oilers rings, some 20 years later.

The three years of AFL-NFL exhibition play in the late 1960s resulted in 43 NFL wins, 28 AFL wins, and 1 tie. The Super Bowl scorecard following the 2003 game in San Diego listed 21 victories for NFL-NFC clubs and 16 for the AFL-AFC. And it must be noted that 6 of the 16 American triumphs have been by the three transplanted teams—the Colts, Steelers, and Browns (winning as the Ravens). Two franchises that came into the NFL in 1970 from the AFL have yet to win a Super Bowl in their histories—Cincinnati and the Houston-Tennessee club. And the two teams that brought the AFL Super

Bowl glory, the teams that might have kept the merger plans moving forward by winning—the Jets and Chiefs—haven't been back as members of the NFL.

And, frankly, the AFC-NFC rivalry really isn't much of one anymore. It began to fade even before the teams had come together in 1970.

JOHNNY ROBINSON: The kids coming in through the common draft in the late '60s had no idea of the rivalry with the NFL. Jimmy Marsalis came in, the Chiefs' number one draft choice at cornerback in 1969, started right away. I kind of took Jimmy under my wing. Man, he didn't have any idea about the competition between the AFL and the NFL. Didn't mean a thing to him. Not one iota. I can't express how quickly it disappeared among the players. It was like you were talking about something in space.

TOM FLORES: There weren't too many of us that were there from the start through its entire existence. I was sorry to see us lose our identity. I would have preferred that we stayed the American Football League and the National Football League, but it didn't work out.

BEN DAVIDSON: I wish it was still the AFL instead of the AFC. Make that *C* back into an *L*. Make it official.

Yes, it was one "L" of a league. From vertical striped socks in Denver to Orange Crush and John Elway's back-to-back Super wins. From the Patriots' telling players not to turn down the covers to Adam Vinatieri's last-second field goal to win Super Bowl XXXVI. From Oakland's Señors to Al Davis and "Just win, baby."

So the next time you're watching the Super Bowl's halftime extravaganza, peppered with those multimillion-dollar 30-second commercials, take a moment and thank Bambi and Cookie and Wahoo—and Broadway Joe, of course—and a guy named Ralph Pittman. Today's game wouldn't be the same without them.

APPENDIX

A RECORD OF THE AFL

All-Time W-L-T Regular Season and Postseason in AFL

1960–1969 Seasons

Team	W	L	T	Pct.	AFL Titles
L.A./San Diego	87	52	6	.621	1
Dallas/Kansas City	84	55	5	.601	3
Oakland	80	60	5	.569	1
Houston	78	62	4	.555	2
New York	70	67	6	.510	1
Buffalo	67	71	6	.486	2
Boston	64	69	9	.482	0
Denver	39	97	4	.293	0
Miami	15	39	2	.286	0
Cincinnati	7	20	1	.268	0

All-Time W-L-T Regular Season and Postseason for the 10 AFL Teams Against Each Other

1960–2002 Seasons

Team	W	L	T	Pct.	AFL/AFC Titles (Seasons)
Oakland/L.A./Oakland	264	184	10	.587	5 ('67, '76, '80, '83, '02)
Miami	200	157	4	.560	5 ('71, '72, '73, '82, '84)
Dallas/Kansas City	231	206	9	.559	3 ('62, '66, '69)
Houston/Tennessee	180	175	5	.507	3 ('60, '61, '99)
L.A./San Diego	206	221	10	.483	2 ('63, '94)
New York	200	217	8	.480	1 ('68)
Buffalo	208	231	7	.474	6 ('64, '65, '90, '91, '92, '93)
Denver	198	222	7	.472	6 ('77, '86, '87, '89, '97, '98)
Boston/New England	196	221	9	.471	3 ('85, '96, '01)
Cincinnati	91	141	1	.392	2 ('81, '88)

Annual AFL Standings, Postseason Results, Award Winners

1960

West	W	L	T	Points	Opponents	Attendance
Los Angeles	10	4	0	373	336	15,665
Dallas	8	6	0	362	253	24,500
Oakland	6	8	0	319	388	12,469
Denver	4	9	1	309	393	13,049

East						
Houston	10	4	0	379	285	20,019
New York	7	7	0	382	399	16,375
Buffalo	5	8	1	296	303	15,980
Boston	5	9	0	286	349	16,894

Championship Game: Houston 24, Los Angeles 16 (January 1, 1961; Houston; 32,183)
All-Star Game: none
Most Valuable Player: Abner Haynes, Dallas (UPI)
Coach of the Year: Lou Rymkus, Houston (UPI)
Rookie of the Year: Abner Haynes, Dallas (UPI)

1961

West	W	L	T	Points	Opponents	Attendance
San Diego	12	2	0	396	219	27,859
Dallas	6	8	0	334	343	17,571
Denver	3	11	0	251	432	10,644
Oakland	2	12	0	237	458	7,655

East						
Houston	10	3	1	513	242	27,861
Boston	9	4	1	413	313	16,516
New York	7	7	0	301	390	15,231
Buffalo	6	8	0	294	342	19,058

Championship Game: Houston 10, San Diego 3 (December 24, 1961; San Diego; 29,556)
All-Star Game: West 47, East 27 (January 7, 1962; San Diego; 20,973)
Most Valuable Player: George Blanda, Houston (AP, UPI)
Coach of the Year: Wally Lemm, Houston (AP, UPI)
Rookie of the Year: Earl Faison, San Diego (AP, UPI)

1962

West	W	L	T	Points	Opponents	Attendance
Dallas	11	3	0	389	233	22,201
Denver	7	7	0	353	334	25,498
San Diego	4	10	0	314	392	21,987
Oakland	1	13	0	213	370	10,985

East	W	L	T	Points	Opponents	Attendance
Houston	11	3	0	387	270	28,612
Boston	9	4	1	346	295	21,518
Buffalo	7	6	1	309	272	27,922
New York	5	9	0	278	423	5,165

Championship Game: Dallas 20, Houston 17, 2 OTs (December 23, 1962; Houston; 37,981)
All-Star Game: West 21, East 14 (January 13, 1963; San Diego; 27,641)
Most Valuable Player: Cookie Gilchrist, Buffalo (AP, UPI)
Coach of the Year: Jack Faulkner, Denver (AP, UPI)
Rookie of the Year: Curtis McClinton, Dallas (AP, UPI)

1963

West	W	L	T	Points	Opponents	Attendance
San Diego	11	3	0	399	256	27,356
Oakland	10	4	0	363	288	17,435
Kansas City	5	7	2	347	263	21,510
Denver	2	11	1	301	473	18,888

East	W	L	T	Points	Opponents	Attendance
Boston	7	6	1	317	257	24,267
Buffalo	7	6	1	304	291	19,674
Houston	6	8	0	302	372	23,339
New York	5	8	1	249	399	14,792

Eastern Division Playoff: Boston 26, Buffalo 8 (December 28, 1963; Buffalo; 33,044)
Championship Game: San Diego 51, Boston 10 (January 5, 1964; San Diego; 30,127)
All-Star Game: West 27, East 24 (January 19, 1964; San Diego; 20,016)
Most Valuable Player: Tobin Rote, San Diego (AP), Lance Alworth, San Diego (UPI)
Coach of the Year: Al Davis, Oakland (AP, UPI)
Rookie of the Year: Billy Joe, Denver (AP, UPI)

1964

West	W	L	T	Points	Opponents	Attendance
San Diego	8	5	1	341	300	24,237
Kansas City	7	7	0	366	306	18,126
Oakland	5	7	2	303	350	18,196
Denver	2	11	1	240	438	16,894

East						
Buffalo	12	2	0	400	242	36,762
Boston	10	3	1	365	297	28,522
New York	5	8	1	278	315	42,710
Houston	4	10	0	310	355	20,254

Championship Game: Buffalo 20, San Diego 7 (December 26, 1964; Buffalo; 40,242)
All-Star Game: West 38, East 14 (January 16, 1965; Houston; 15,446)
Most Valuable Player: Gino Cappelletti, Boston (AP, UPI)
Coach of the Year: Mike Holovak, Boston (AP), Lou Saban, Buffalo (UPI)
Rookie of the Year: Matt Snell, New York (AP, UPI)

1965

West	W	L	T	Points	Opponents	Attendance
San Diego	9	2	3	340	227	28,915
Oakland	8	5	1	298	239	21,012
Kansas City	7	5	2	322	285	21,493
Denver	4	10	0	303	392	38,427

East						
Buffalo	10	3	1	313	226	43,811
New York	5	8	1	285	303	54,877
Boston	4	8	2	244	302	20,443
Houston	4	10	0	298	429	34,408

Championship Game: Buffalo 23, San Diego 0 (December 26, 1965; San Diego; 30,361)
All-Star Game: All-Stars 30, Buffalo 19 (January 15, 1966; Houston; 35,572)
Most Valuable Player: Jack Kemp, Buffalo (AP), Paul Lowe, San Diego (UPI)
Coach of the Year: Lou Saban, Buffalo (AP, UPI)
Rookie of the Year: Joe Namath, New York (AP, UPI)

1966

West	W	L	T	Points	Opponents	Attendance
Kansas City	11	2	1	448	276	37,010
Oakland	8	5	1	315	288	36,215
San Diego	7	6	1	335	284	26,531
Denver	4	10	0	196	381	27,457

East	W	L	T	Points	Opponents	Attendance
Buffalo	9	4	1	358	255	42,732
Boston	8	4	2	315	283	27,163
New York	6	6	2	322	312	59,395
Houston	3	11	0	335	396	25,414
Miami	3	11	0	213	362	26,276

Championship Game: Kansas City 31, Buffalo 7 (January 1, 1967; Buffalo; 42,080)
All-Star Game: East 30, West 23 (January 21, 1967; Oakland; 18,876)
Most Valuable Player: Jim Nance, Boston (AP, UPI)
Coach of the Year: Hank Stram, Kansas City (AP), Mike Holovak, Boston (UPI)
Rookie of the Year: Bobby Burnett, Buffalo (AP, UPI)

1967

West	W	L	T	Points	Opponents	Attendance
Oakland	13	1	0	468	233	39,450
Kansas City	9	5	0	408	254	45,072
San Diego	8	5	1	360	352	39,616
Denver	3	11	0	256	409	33,114

East	W	L	T	Points	Opponents	Attendance
Houston	9	4	1	258	199	26,447
New York	8	5	1	371	329	62,433
Buffalo	4	10	0	237	285	40,066
Miami	4	10	0	219	407	28,982
Boston	3	10	1	280	389	23,144

Championship Game: Oakland 40, Houston 7 (December 31, 1967; Oakland; 53,330)
All-Star Game: East 25, West 24 (January 21, 1968; Jacksonville; 40,103)
Most Valuable Player: Daryle Lamonica, Oakland (AP, UPI)
Coach of the Year: John Rauch, Oakland (AP, UPI)
Rookie of the Year: Dickie Post, San Diego (AP offense), George Webster, Houston (AP defense, UPI)

1968

West	W	L	T	Points	Opponents	Attendance
Oakland	12	2	0	453	233	46,958
Kansas City	12	2	0	371	170	48,416
San Diego	9	5	0	382	310	43,313
Denver	5	9	0	255	404	40,192
Cincinnati	3	11	0	215	329	25,763

East	W	L	T	Points	Opponents	Attendance
New York	11	3	0	419	280	61,965
Houston	7	7	0	303	248	40,483
Miami	5	8	1	276	355	30,962
Boston	4	10	0	229	406	22,351
Buffalo	1	12	1	199	367	35,971

Western Division Playoff: Oakland 41, Kansas City 6 (December 22, 1968; Oakland; 53,605)
Championship Game: New York 27, Oakland 23 (December 29, 1968; New York; 62,627)
All-Star Game: West 38, East 25 (January 19, 1969; Jacksonville; 41,058)
Most Valuable Player: Joe Namath, New York (AP, UPI)
Coach of the Year: Hank Stram, Kansas City (AP, UPI)
Rookie of the Year: Paul Robinson, Cincinnati (AP offense, UPI), Dick Anderson, Miami (AP codefense), George Atkinson, Oakland (AP codefense)

1969

West	W	L	T	Points	Opponents	Attendance
Oakland	12	1	1	377	242	53,102
Kansas City	11	3	0	359	177	49,360
San Diego	8	6	0	288	276	46,311
Denver	5	8	1	297	344	46,693
Cincinnati	4	9	1	280	367	27,299

East	W	L	T	Points	Opponents	Attendance
New York	10	4	0	353	269	62,917
Houston	6	6	2	278	279	44,203
Buffalo	4	10	0	230	359	40,923
Boston	4	10	0	266	316	21,345
Miami	3	10	1	233	332	34,687

Interdivision Playoff Game: Kansas City 13, New York 6 (December 20, 1969; New York; 62,977)
Interdivision Playoff Game: Oakland 56, Houston 7 (December 21, 1969; Oakland; 53,539)

Championship Game: Kansas City 17, Oakland 7 (January 4, 1970; Oakland; 54,544)
All-Star Game: West 26, East 3 (January 17, 1970; Houston; 30,170)
Most Valuable Player: Daryle Lamonica, Oakland (AP, UPI)
Coach of the Year: Paul Brown, Cincinnati (AP, UPI)
Rookie of the Year: Greg Cook, Cincinnati (AP offense, UPI), Bill Bergey, Cincinnati (AP defense)

AFL-NFL Super Bowls

Super Bowl	Score	Date	Location	Attendance
I	Green Bay 35, Kansas City 10	January 15, 1967	Los Angeles	61,946
II	Green Bay 33, Oakland 14	January 14, 1968	Miami	75,546
III	N.Y. Jets 16, Baltimore 7	January 12, 1969	Miami	75,377
IV	Kansas City 23, Minnesota 7	January 11, 1970	New Orleans	80,562

All-Time AFL Team

Chosen by 1969 AFL Hall of Fame Selection Committee Members

Offense	Position	Team(s), Years
Lance Alworth	flanker	San Diego 1962–69
Don Maynard	end	New York 1960–69
Fred Arbanas	tight end	Dallas/Kansas City 1962–69
Ron Mix	tackle	Los Angeles/San Diego 1960–69
Jim Tyrer	tackle	Dallas/Kansas City 1961–69
Ed Budde	guard	Kansas City 1963–69
Billy Shaw	guard	Buffalo 1962–69
Jim Otto	center	Oakland 1960–69
Joe Namath	quarterback	New York 1965–69
Clem Daniels	running back	Dallas 1960; Oakland 1961–67
Paul Lowe	running back	L.A./San Diego 1960–68; Kansas City 1968–69

Defense

Jerry Mays	end	Dallas/Kansas City 1961–69
Gerry Philbin	end	New York 1964–69
Houston Antwine	tackle	Boston 1961–69
Tom Sestak	tackle	Buffalo 1962–68
Bobby Bell	linebacker	Kansas City 1963–69
George Webster	linebacker	Houston 1967–69
Nick Buoniconti	linebacker	Boston 1962–68; Miami 1969
Willie Brown	cornerback	Denver 1963–66; Oakland 1967–69
Dave Grayson	cornerback	Dallas/Kansas City 1961–64; Oakland 1965–69
Johnny Robinson	safety	Dallas/Kansas City 1960–69
George Saimes	safety	Buffalo 1963–69

Special Teams

George Blanda	kicker	Houston 1960–66; Oakland 1967–69
Jerrel Wilson	punter	Kansas City 1963–69

BIBLIOGRAPHY

Books

Acho, Jim. *The Foolish Club*. New York: Gridiron Press, 1997.

Anderson, Dave. *Countdown to Super Bowl*. New York: Random House, 1969.

Brodie, John, and James D. Houston. *Open Field*. Boston: Houghton Mifflin, 1974.

Brown, Paul, with Jack Clary. *PB: The Paul Brown Story*. New York: Atheneum, 1979.

Carroll, Bob. *When the Grass Was Real: Unitas, Brown, Lombardi, Sayers, Butkus, Namath and All the Rest: The Ten Best Years of Pro Football*. New York: Simon & Schuster, 1993.

Carroll, Kevin. *Houston Oilers: The Early Years*. Austin, Tex.: Eakin Press, 2001.

Curran, Bob. *The $400,000 Quarterback or the League That Came in from the Cold*. New York: Macmillan, 1965.

Didinger, Ray; Herskowitz, Mickey; Lamb, Kevin; McGrane, Bill; Musick, Phil; and Strother, Shelby. *The Super Bowl: Celebrating a Quarter-Century of America's Greatest Game*. New York: Simon & Schuster, 1990.

Fowler, Ed. *Loser Takes All: Bud Adams, Bad Football and Big Business*. Atlanta: Longstreet Press, 1997.

Fox, Larry. *Broadway Joe and His Super Jets*. New York: Coward-McCann, 1969.

Fox, Larry. *The New England Patriots*. New York: Atheneum, 1979.

Hanks, Stephen. *The Game That Changed Pro Football*. New York: Birch Lane Press, 1989.

Hartman, Sid, with Patrick Reusse. *Sid!* Stillwater, Minn.: Voyageur Press, 1997.

Horrigan, Jack, and Mike Rathet. *The Other League: The Fabulous Story of the American Football League*. Chicago: Follett Publishing, 1970.

Izenberg, Jerry. *The Rivals*. New York: Holt, Rinehart and Winston, 1968.

Kramer, Jerry, with Dick Schaap. *Distant Replay*. New York: G. P. Putnam's Sons, 1985.

Maher, Tod, and Bob Gill, eds. *The Pro Football Encyclopedia*. New York: Macmillan, 1997.

Maiorana, Sal. *Relentless: The Hard-Hitting History of Buffalo Bills Football*. Vols. I and II. Lexana, Kans., and Coal Valley, Ill.: Quality Sports Publications, 1995 and 2000.

Marvez, Alex. *Wild Ride! The Illustrated History of the Denver Broncos*. Dallas: Taylor Publishing, 1998.

McGuff, Joe. *Winning It All: The Chiefs of the AFL*. Garden City, N.Y.: Doubleday, 1970.

Morrall, Earl, and George Sullivan. *In the Pocket: My Life as a Quarterback*. New York: Grosset & Dunlap, 1969.

Namath, Joe Willie, with Dick Schaap. *I Can't Wait 'Til Tomorrow . . . 'Cause I Get Better Looking Every Day*. New York: Random House, 1969.

Neft, David S., Richard M. Cohen, and Rick Korch. *The Sports Encyclopedia: Pro Football, The Modern Era 1960–1995*. 14th ed. New York: St. Martin's Griffin, 1996.

Otto, Jim, with Dave Newhouse. *Jim Otto: The Pain of Glory*. Chicago: Sports Publishing, 1999.

Ribowsky, Mark. *Slick: The Silver & Black Life of Al Davis.* New York: Macmillan, 1991.

Sahadi, Lou. *Len Dawson: Pressure Quarterback.* New York: Cowles Book Company, 1970.

Simpson, O. J., with Pete Axthelm. *O.J.: The Education of a Rich Rookie.* New York: Macmillan, 1970.

Smith, Robert L. *The Buffalo Bills: A View Through the Lens of Robert L. Smith.* Elma, N.Y.: RLS Publishing, 1996.

Staubach, Roger, with Sam Blair and Bob St. John. *First Down, Lifetime to Go.* Waco, Tex.: Key-Word Publishing, 1974.

Stram, Hank, with Lou Sahadi. *They're Playing My Game.* New York: William Morrow & Co., 1986.

Sullivan, George. *Touchdown! The Picture History of the American Football League.* New York: Putnam, 1967.

Twombly, Wells. *Blanda: Alive and Kicking.* Los Angeles: Nash Publishing, 1972.

Weiss, Don, with Chuck Day. *The Making of the Super Bowl: The Inside Story of the World's Greatest Sporting Event.* Chicago: Contemporary Books, 2003.

Wismer, Harry. *The Public Calls It Sport.* Englewood Cliffs, N.J.: Prentice-Hall, 1965.

Periodicals

Associated Press
Atlanta Journal-Constitution
Baltimore Sun
Bergen (N.J.) Record
Boston Globe
Boston Herald
Buffalo News
Charleston (S.C.) Post and Courier
Charlotte Observer
Cincinnati Enquirer
Colorado Springs Gazette
Daily News of Los Angeles
Dallas Morning News
Dayton Daily News
Denver Post
Fort Worth Star-Telegram
Fresno Bee
Houston Chronicle
Houston Post
Houston Press
Indianapolis Star
Journal News of Westchester County, N.Y.
Kansas City Star

Lewiston Morning Tribune
Los Angeles Times
Miami Herald
Milwaukee Journal Sentinel
New Orleans Times-Picayune
New York Daily News
New York Observer
New York Post
New York Times
Newsday (Long Island)
Orange County Register
Orlando Sentinel
Palm Beach Post
Quincy Patriot Ledger
Rocky Mountain News (Denver)
San Diego Union-Tribune
San Francisco Chronicle
The Sporting News
Sports Illustrated
St. Louis Post-Dispatch
St. Petersburg Times
Star Tribune of Minneapolis–St. Paul
Sun-Sentinel of South Florida (Fort Lauderdale)
Tampa Tribune
Toledo Blade
Toronto Star
USA Today
Washington Post
Washington Times
Worcester Telegram & Gazette

Website

ESPN.com

INDEX